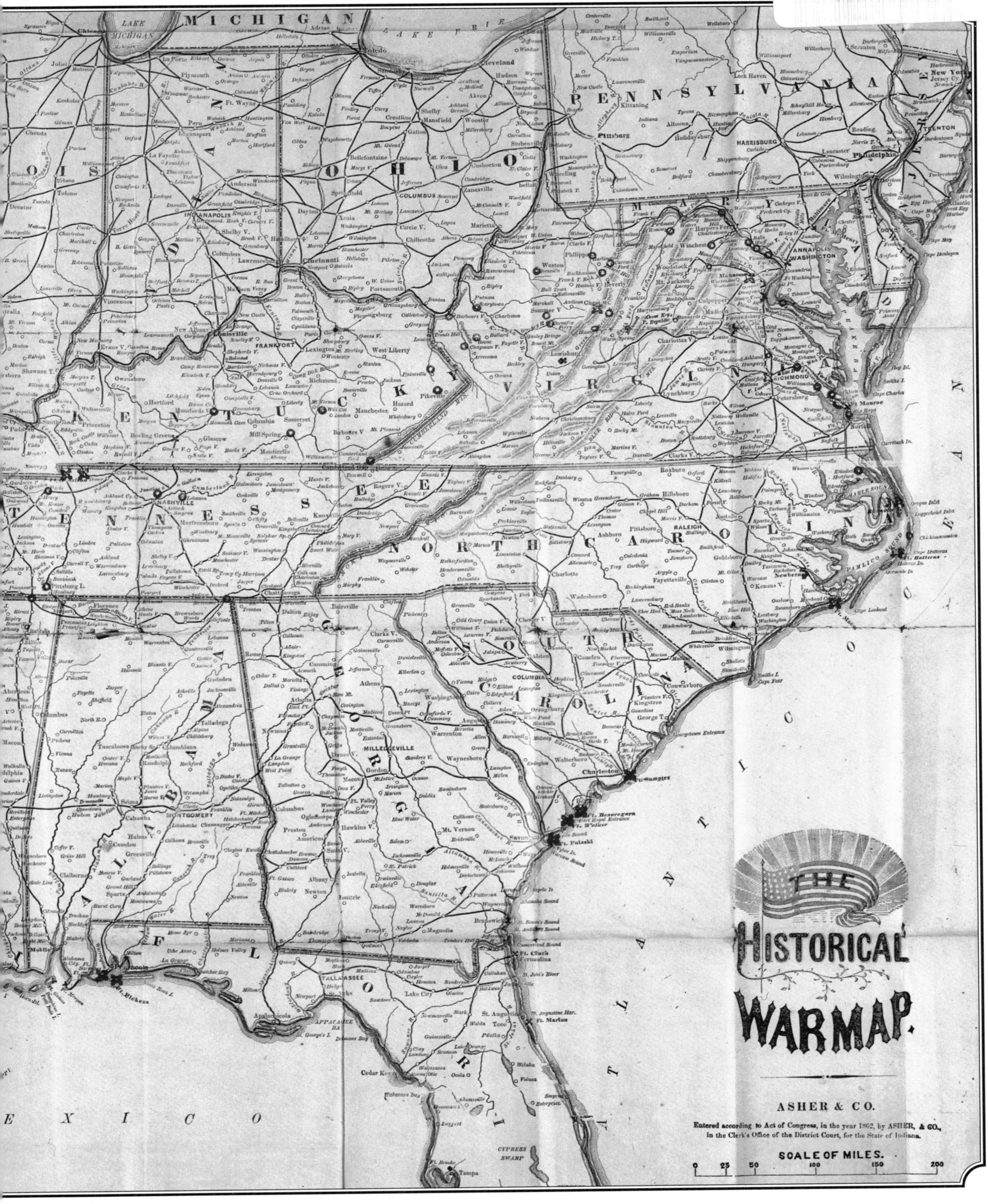

THE
HISTORICAL
WARMAP.
ASHER & CO.
Entered according to Act of Congress, in the year 1862, by ASHER, & CO., in the Clerk's Office of the District Court, for the State of Indiana.
SCALE OF MILES.
0 25 50 100 150 200
MICHIGAN
LAKE MICHIGAN
LAKE ERIE
PENNSYLVANIA
OHIO
KENTUCKY
VIRGINIA
TENNESSEE
NORTH CAROLINA
SOUTH CAROLINA
GEORGIA
ALABAMA
FLORIDA
ATLANTIC OCEAN
MEXICO
CYPRESS SWAMP

REBELS & YANKEES

THE FIGHTING MEN OF THE CIVIL WAR

REBELS & YANKEES

THE FIGHTING MEN OF THE CIVIL WAR

The experience of America's epic conflict through the lives of the men who fought it
Featuring a unique photographic record of personal memorabilia and weaponry

WILLIAM C. DAVIS

TECHNICAL ADVISOR: RUSS A. PRITCHARD

A Salamander Book

This edition published in 1989 by
SMITHMARK Publishers, a division of
U.S. Media Holdings, Inc., 16 East 32nd Street,
New York, N.Y. 10016

9 8 7 6

SMITHMARK books are available for bulk purchase for sales promotion and premium use. For details write or telephone the manager of special sales, SMITHMARK Publishers, 16 East 32nd Street, New York, N.Y. 10016. (212)532-6600

ISBN 0-7651-9838-X

All correspondence concerning the content of this volume should be addressed to Salamander Books Ltd, 129–137 York Way, London N7 9LG, England

Credits

Project Manager: Ray Bonds
Editor: Tony Hall
Designer: Mark Holt
Indexer: David Linton
Color artwork: Jeff Burn © Salamander Books Ltd
Line artwork: Kevin Jones Associates
© Salamander Books Ltd
Color photography: Don Eiler, Richmond, Virginia
© Salamander Books Ltd
Filmset: SX Composing Ltd, England
Color reproduction: Kentscan Ltd, England
Printed in Italy

Acknowledgments

In the preparation of this book we received the generous assistance and advice from militaria collectors and museum directors and staff in the United States. Without the help of the individuals and organizations listed below, this record of Civil War militaria could not have been assembled. We would also like to extend a very special thanks to Russ A. Pritchard, whose work and support have been invaluable to the success of this project.

INSTITUTIONAL COLLECTIONS

The Museum of The Confederacy, Richmond, Virginia
David C. Hahn, former Curator of Collections
Malinda S. Wyatt, Registrar
Guy R. Swanson, Curator of Manuscripts and Archives
Corrine P. Hudgins, Photographic Assistant
Rebecca Ansell Rose, Curatorial Assistant

Virginia Historical Society, Richmond, Virginia
Linda Leazer, Assistant Curator of Special Collections

The Civil War Library and Museum, Philadelphia, Pennsylvania
Russ A. Pritchard, Director

PRIVATE COLLECTIONS

J. Craig Nannos, Ardmore, Pennsylvania
Benjamin P. Michel, Millburn, New Jersey
Don Troiani, Southbury, Connecticut
Russ A. Pritchard, Wayne, Pennsylvania
George Lomas, Hatboro, Pennsylvania
Michael J. McAfee, West Point, New York
CDR James C. Reuhrmund, USN (Ret), F.R.N.S., Richmond, Virginia

CONTENTS

INTRODUCTION 7

CHAPTER ONE
OFF TO WAR 9

CHAPTER TWO
DRILL, DRILL & MORE DRILL 31

CHAPTER THREE
LOAD & FIRE 49

CHAPTER FOUR
JOIN THE CAVALRY 67

CHAPTER FIVE
ROLLING THUNDER 95

CHAPTER SIX
LIFE AT SEA 113

CHAPTER SEVEN
TENTING TONIGHT 131

CHAPTER EIGHT
WILLING SPIRITS & WEAK FLESH 153

CHAPTER NINE
IRON BARS A PRISON MAKE 169

CHAPTER TEN
THE DEADLIEST ENEMY 185

CHAPTER ELEVEN
ON THE MARCH 199

CHAPTER TWELVE
THE FACE OF BATTLE 217

CHAPTER THIRTEEN
VICTORY & DEFEAT 237

APPENDIX 249

INDEX 253

BIBLIOGRAPHY 256

INTRODUCTION

It is a century and a quarter now since the fields and meadows of America erupted in internecine warfare. The scars of that conflict have long since disappeared both from the land and from the descendants of those people who fought one another. What remains is chiefly pride, amazement, and a certain sense of nostalgia for what on the surface seems to be a simpler time, with easier choices and more clear-cut definitions of right and wrong. But it is a deceptive view that many engage in, and people of today need only look under the veneer of heroism and glory and carefully examine the story of the men who actually fought that war, to discover that we are more like them than we realize.

The American Civil War remains its nation's central national epic. Americans cannot hope to understand themselves without coming to some understanding of the war that changed the "Union" into the "United States". To fathom that war, we must inevitably look into the minds and hearts of the men in the ranks who first to last bore the brunt of it. It is they, not their officers, nor the statesmen behind the lines, who stood the fire, who kept up their determination in the face of hardship and defeat, who had the will to make any sacrifice along the road to victory.

Individually their names are all but forgotten except by their descendants. A very few are remembered for some special act of heroism, or because they left behind some particularly revealing memoir of their army days. Most are recalled only collectively, for no one will ever forget the celebrated exploits of the Army of the Potomac, the Army of Northern Virginia, or the Army of Tennessee. But we must never forget that the common soldiers in blue and gray *were* those armies, and what those forces achieved, they achieved only because of their men in the ranks. All the generals and field officers of the war could have accomplished nothing without those troublesome, grumbling, insubordinate, and indomitable, private soldiers, corporals and sergeants. Likewise, the captains and admirals on their ships could not have steamed a gallant inch without the seamen who manned them.

It is the story of these fighting men of the Civil War that is told here. Unfortunately, it is a story not often told, as attention is more often directed toward the glamorous generals and stirring battles of the contest. From time to time, historians have turned their eyes to the simple soldier and his life in camp and field, most notably the late Bell I. Wiley, whose magnificent books *The Life of Johnny Reb* and *The Life of Billy Yank* remain classics after the passing of a generation. Any new work attempting to look into the lives of the enlisted men must owe an enormous debt to this pioneer who wrote with such originality and feeling for the simpler people of the war. Certainly this new work owes much to the ground-breaking done by this inspiring mentor, and beloved friend.

Yet there is some ground which Wiley did not cover, and new material which has come to light in the decades since he wrote. Furthermore, no one has previously attempted to present the story of the Civil War soldier in the sort of 'multi-media' approach presented here. Mingled with the text are scores of period photographs and drawings which lend illustration to the words. Scores of full-color images depict in vivid detail the *things* which were so much a part of the soldier's life, and so precious to him – weapons, uniforms, personal items, even souvenirs. And specially prepared artwork depicts the men actually in uniform, together with major items of equipment from cartridges to warships. The effect of it all, it is hoped, is to present not just an impersonal intellectual understanding of these men, but a *feeling* for them by *seeing* them as closely as one can without the benefit of time travel.

Much of what is written is said in their own words, from both letters and diaries. Consequently, the reader must bestow upon them a measure of charity. Like most people of their time they enjoyed only a rudimentary education. For every college-educated soldier there were ten thousand whose reading and writing ranged from barely passable to non-existent. Even educated men of the day were somewhat casual about their spelling. The common soldiery, however, were almost blissfully unconcerned. Where quoted in this work, they are allowed to speak for themselves, misspellings, bad grammar, and all; it was a part of them. Yet somehow despite this their *meaning* is rarely if ever cloudy. They wrote as they thought and acted, directly. They rarely apologized for themselves, and no one need do so now.

These are the faces of young men off for the adventure of their lives and the experience of a generation. But it would be a costly enterprise. Two in every ten would never see home again.

UPHOLSTERY

CHAPTER ONE

OFF TO WAR

After decades of debate, threats, counter-threats, compromise and concessions, the sectional controversy between North and South over slavery and Southern nationalism finally boiled over in 1860. When the Democratic Party, for generations the upholder of Southern rights, split into two factions and presented two nominees for the Presidency, its self-destruction was assured. When the new Republican Party nominated Abraham Lincoln, an avowed opponent of slavery, and it was evident that the Democratic split would result in his election, Southern extremists declared that they could no longer live within the old Union. Lincoln's election in November came without a single Southern vote, but still he won the Presidency. Almost immediately South Carolina took the lead, and on December 20, a state convention announced that "the union . . . is hereby dissolved." Following South Carolina's secession, ten other states eventually attempted to leave the Union. On February 8, 1861, at Montgomery, Alabama, representatives of those states adopted a constitution for the new Confederate States of America. The next day they chose Senator Jefferson Davis of Mississippi as their President.

Davis had been in office only two weeks when Lincoln was inaugurated. Confrontation between the two sections was inevitable, for Lincoln was pledged to retain possession and authority over all Federal property and installations in the South, while Davis's government was resolved to occupy them, by force if necessary. Several Federal arsenals fell to the Confederates without incident, but finally, at Charleston, South Carolina, where secession began, Davis came up against a Federal garrison which would not leave. After months of negotiations and threats, on April 12 Confederate shore batteries opened fire on Fort Sumter, forcing its capitulation the following day. There would be war, and north and south of Mason and Dixon's line thousands rushed to enlist before the fun was over.

"BY GARD, if I had known then as much as I do now I would [have] had a hart."[1] The lament of Private Jim Slattery of the 13th Massachusetts spoke volumes about all the trials endured and lessons learned by the three million men who marched to war during 1861-5. Barely one of them knew what to expect. They were a new people in a new era, facing a very new sort of conflict. These men of North and South, innocently answering the call of flag and country, had never mustered in legions in crowded encampments, or been away from home for months and years at a time, living out under the open heavens, marching in unison step, and slavishly following the orders of more privileged officers they often regarded as fools. Army food was as yet an unrevealed mystery to them, as were the horrors of military medicine awaiting the sick and wounded, or the prison hells ready to swallow up the captured. The routine of army life for the common soldier would be an awakening for them all, relieved only by those inerasable traits ingrained in the nature of all America's lowly; their folk-humor, rowdiness, the love of sport and frolic, and fear of their god.

And out of their four years of war, these Johnny Rebs and Billy Yanks would forge a legacy uniquely their own. They fought and died as Americans do; the examples of sacrifice and daring they set in campaign and battle would never be surpassed. But they rarely became soldiers. They remained always simple civilians, temporarily "reassigned". Reb and and Yank alike carped incessantly at the army and everything in it, and became masters at looking out for themselves.

Most of all, they knew who they were. These simple soldiers were not the planters and politicians who made the war. Yet while they grumbled about its being "a rich man's war and a poor man's fight", they did not shirk that fight. Though

Bright, enthusiastic, hopeful young men like members of this militia unit posing on New York's Broadway on July 4, 1860, were the first to rush to the colors when the call came a year later.

at the same time, they had a sense that what they did and suffered might never be recognized. Barely had the war come to an end before one proud Confederate lamented that amid all the outpouring of boastful memoirs and florid accounts of battles and leaders, few "would hardly stop to tell how the hungry private fried his bacon, baked his biscuit, smoked his pipe".[2] They accepted it as part of the lot of the common soldier, a price they paid toward a greater end. Yank and Reb alike could agree with Sergeant Ed English of New Jersey when he wrote in 1862 that, "A man who would not fight for his Country is a scoundral! I cannot get tired of soldiering while the war lasts", he confessed. He had to be there, for all his unsung trials. "Though humble my position is", he wrote, "gold could not buy me out of the Army".[3]

As the war dragged onward year after year, a time would come when gold was about all that would buy a man *into* the army. The first volunteer enlistments were for terms usually of 90 days – a year at most – when everyone expected the war to end before the summer of 1861 was out. When it did not, many regiments simply ceased to exist, while many more re-enlisted, first for a year, and later on for three years or the term of the war, both North and South. But in the first great rush of enthusiasm and patriotism that followed secession and the firing on Fort Sumter, the fever to volunteer for the fight fed virtually upon itself. Thousands of young men on both sides of Mason and Dixon's line sensed intuitively what the editor in Richmond, Virginia, John M. Daniel expressed in his newspaper: "The great event in all our lives has at last come to pass. A war of gigantic proportions, infinite consequences, and indefinite duration is on us, and will affect the interests and happiness of every man, woman, or child, lofty or humble, in this country. We cannot shun it," he said. "we cannot alleviate

Below: Rustics as well as towns-folk came forward. In what would one day become West Virginia, ill-clad recruits in Morgantown line up to fight for the Stars and Stripes. They made great fighters, but not soldiers.

Top: In the first rush of enthusiasm, militia units like these Kentucky State Guardsmen, parading in Louisville, enlisted in the Confederate cause wholesale, taking with them everything from uniforms to weapons.

Above: Spurred on by exhortations from stump and pulpit, regiments in the North responded to the call. Men like these unidentified zouaves in Rochester, New York, prepared to defend the Union.

it, we cannot stop it. We have nothing left now but to fight".[4]

When the English journalist William Howard Russell passed through North Carolina after Fort Sumter, he saw "flushed faces, wild eyes, screaming mouths", and heard men and women shouting so boisterously that nearby bands playing "Dixie" could not be heard.[5] North Carolina was ready to fight, though it was still in the Union. So was Indiana, where Governor Oliver Morton responded to President Lincoln's call for six regiments with the boast that he could furnish fifty times their number. And when a New Yorker asked a recently arrived volunteer from Massachusetts how many other Bay Staters would follow in his wake, he boasted, "How *many*? We're *all* a-coming!"[6]

Spurring them on from every press and pulpit were the fiery exhortations of the zealots who helped bring the conflict in the first place. "I hear Old John Brown knocking on the lid of his coffin and shouting, 'Let me out! Let me out!'", cried the abolitionist Henry B. Stanton. "The doom of slavery is at hand. It is to be wiped out in blood. Amen!"[7] And far to the south in New Orleans, a plantation overseer offered up a prayer that, "every Black Republican in the Hole combined whorl Either man woman or chile that is opposed to negro slavery . . . shal be trubled with pestilents & calamitys of all Kinds & Dragout the Balance of there existence in misray & Degradation".[8]

Aroused by such invective, the young manhood of the nation could hardly fail to respond. North or South, the words of the Boston *Herald* thundered just as loud: "In order to preserve this glorious heritage, vouchsafed to us by the fathers of the Republic, it is essential that every man should perform his whole duty in a crisis like the present".[9] To encourage and profit by the spirited wave sweeping over the continent, every public square and courthouse lawn sprouted mass meetings with stirring martial music, posturing politicians, swaggering young recruiting officers, and an excess of swooning damsels. Aging veterans of bygone days tottered to the stand to remind one and all of their proud traditions. At least one woman in the audience would arise and shout that she would "go in a minute if she were a man", while at a rally in Skowhegan, Maine, a company of ladies manned the village cannon and fired thirty-four rounds.[10]

Then it was time to enlist. "Who will come up and sign the roll?" shouted the recruiting officers, and forward they came, a rushing wall of young men with all the zeal of repenting sinners at a backwoods revival. The whole event played out to the tune of the most shamelessly unself-

Corporal, 7th New York National Guard

The 7th New York State Militia (also called National Guard), was an old pre-war organization that dated back to 1806, its membership composed of the cream of New York City society. Called the "old graybacks" thanks to their uniforms, members of the 7th served for seven years, drilled every month and paid for their own uniforms and equipment. For any young man, membership in the regiment was distinctly a social plus. In the crisis after Fort Sumter, the 7th quickly volunteered to go to the relief of Washington, being one of the first units to arrive in April 1861. They remained there until late May, when the immediate crisis abated and they returned to New York. They were not called "graybacks" for nothing, their short shell jackets and kepis were light gray with black trim, while their other equipment was either black oilcloth or canvas. They also carried with them a distinctive red blanket and were armed with a Model 1855 rifle-musket.

conscious display of patriotism yet seen. Even some of those in the press who did their best to encourage the feeling had to admit that at times it seemed a bit overdone. "The Star-Spangled Banner rages most furiously", wrote a Detroit editor. "The old inspiring national anthem is played by the bands, whistled by the juveniles, sung in the theatres." Indeed, he heard the anthem, "hammered on tin pans by small boys, and we had almost said barked by the dogs."[11]

They stepped forward for all manner of reasons. For some, in their enthusiasm, enlisting just seemed the right thing to do. Standing back would let down friends and community, even family, risk missing all the fun and glory and, worse, hazard the chance of being branded a coward. The pressures on a young man's pride and sense of honor were profound. Enlisting friends urged their comrades to follow them. Fathers gazed toward the rifle on the wall and lamented that they were too old to go. Worst of all were the sweethearts. "If a fellow wants to go with a girl now he had better enlist", wrote an Indiana boy.[12] The song on the young belles' lips was: "I am Bound to be a Soldier's Wife or Die an Old Maid". When an Alabama youth showed reluctance to rally to the colors, his sweetheart, angry at his behavior, broke off their engagement and sent him a skirt and petticoat with the note: "Wear these or enlist".[13]

More than this appeal to pride and shame, thousands of young men enlisted simply to see a change. The army was something different from struggling behind a plow or scrivening at a desk. War was adventure, the great adventure of their generation. There would be glory, excitement, new places to see. Many of these boys had never been outside their own home counties. The wild life of the army promised enticements that few of them had ever known. And even to men who had seen battle before, the allurement of adventure was the same. Texan Walter P. Lane was forty-five years old and already a veteran of the Texas Revolution and the Mexican War when he enlisted in 1861 as a private in a company of

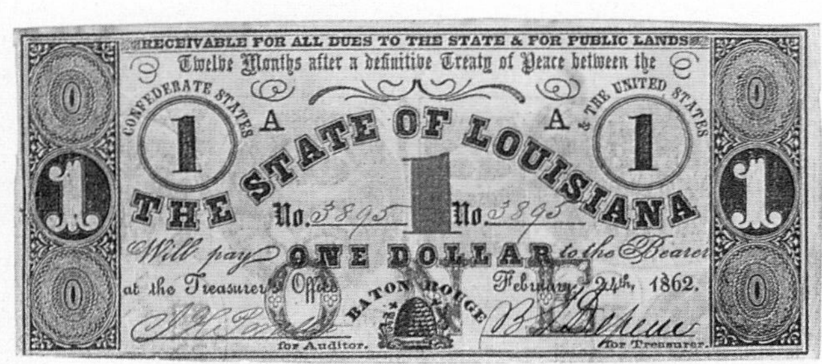

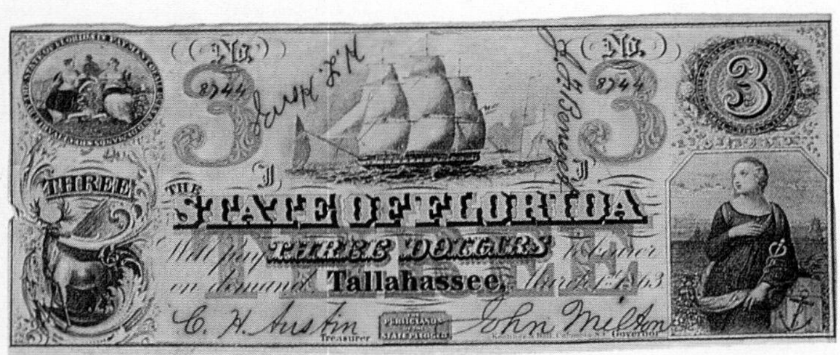

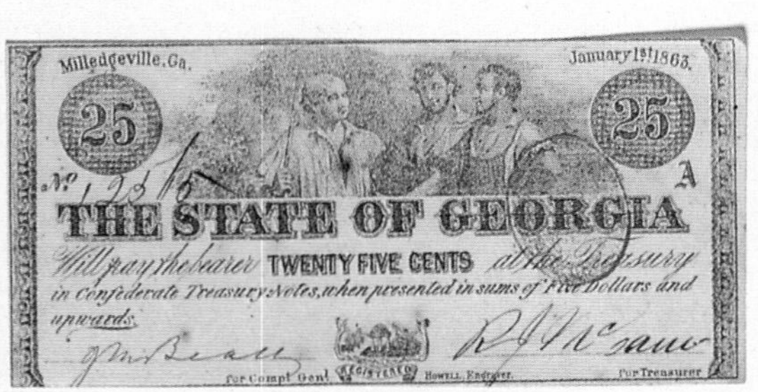

Southern Banknotes

The banking system had been chaotic before the war, and improved little during it. Every state, even many towns had their own currency.

1 State of Alabama five dollar bill 1864
2 State of Georgia fifty dollar bill, 1862
3 State of Arkansas ten dollar bill, 1862
4 State of Louisiana one dollar bill, 1862
5 State of Florida three dollar bill, 1863
6 State of Louisiana five dollar bill, 1863
7 State of Georgia twenty-five cent note, 1863
8 State of Louisiana twenty dollar bill
9 State of Mississippi two dollar and fifty cent bill, 1862
10 State of North Carolina twenty dollar bill, 1862
11 State of Mississippi ten dollar bill, 1862
12 State of Missouri three dollar bill, 1862
13 State of North Carolina ten cent note, 1862
14 Bank of the State of South Carolina ten cent note, 1862
15 Bank of the State of South Carolina fifty cent note, 1862
16 State of North Carolina seventy-five cent note, 1863
17 Bank of Tennessee five dollar note, 1861

Artifacts courtesy of: The Museum of The Confederacy, Richmond, Va

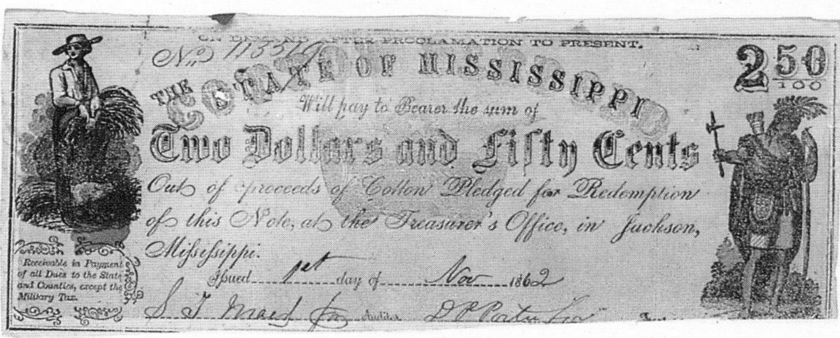

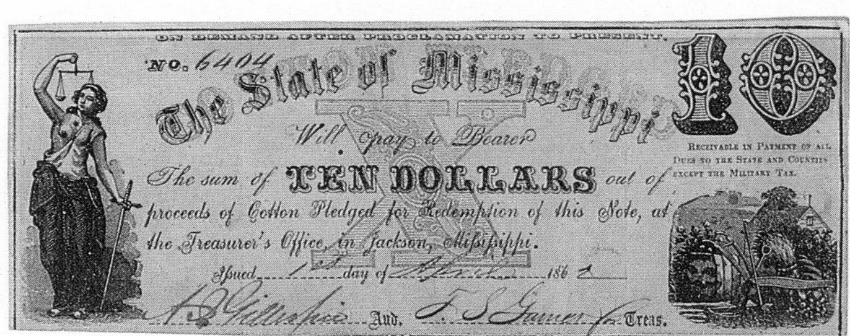

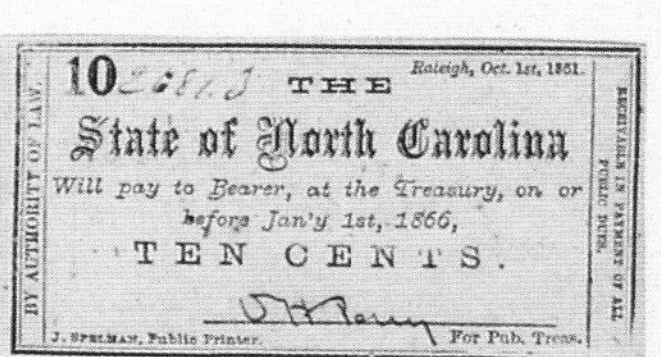

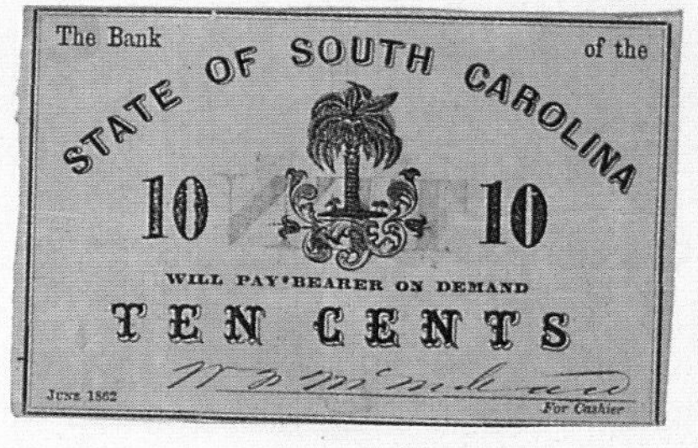

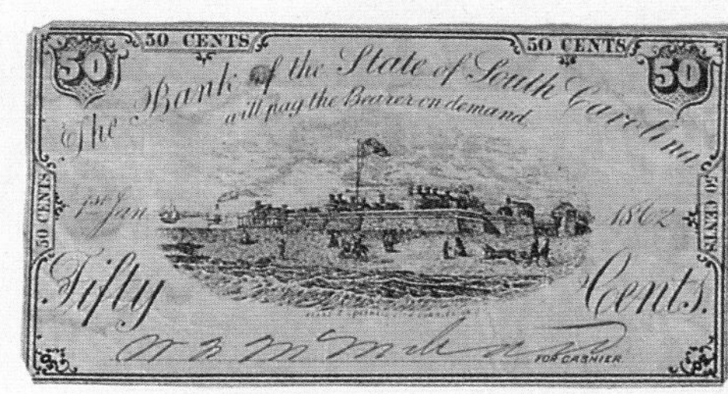

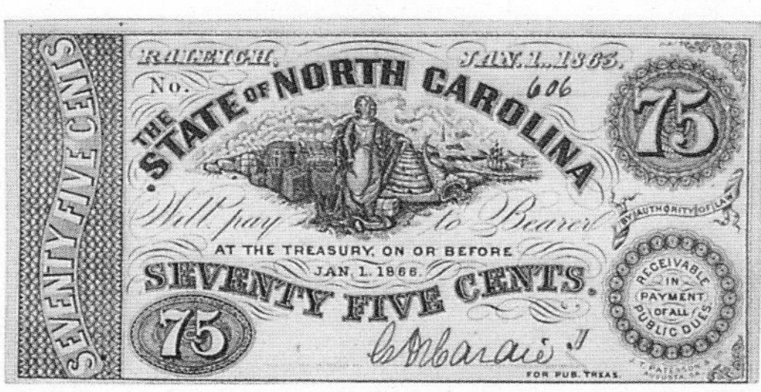

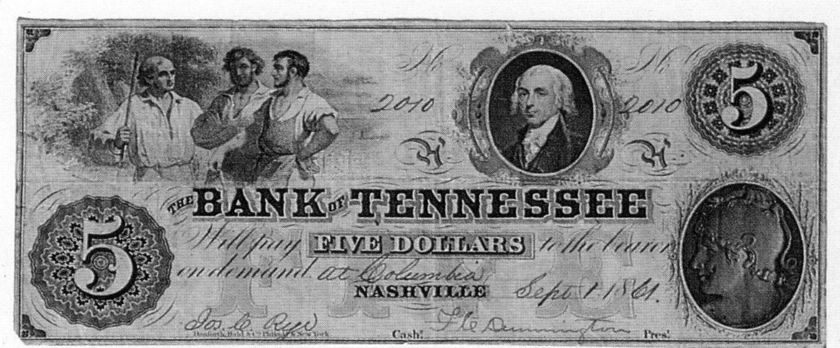

cavalry, "wishing", as he said, "to have a finger in that pie".[14]

Even economics played a part in luring men into the ranks. To be sure, the pay of a Union private was not particularly generous, just $13 a month, while for a Confederate it would be $2 less. Yet North and South alike were suffering from widespread unemployment and recession, and army pay was enough to live on – and it was supposedly steady. Better yet, many states were paying enlistment bounties or bonuses to those who joined – and later those who re-enlisted – often amounting to several hundred dollars. "It is no use for you to fret or cry about me", explained Enoch Baker of Pennsylvania to his wife, "for you know if I could have got work I wood not have left you and the children."[15] It remained for the years ahead to teach Baker and others that pay would not always be as regular as they supposed. In the South some men would go a year at a time without being paid, only to find their currency so inflated that it bought next to nothing anyway.

Certainly there were loftier motives on both sides. "I tell the boys right to their face I am in the war for the freedom of the slave", declared Chauncey Cooke of Wisconsin.[16] For Cooke and many Northerners like him, the war became in time a crusade to end slavery. "Slavery must die", wrote a Green Mountain corporal, "and if the South insists on being buried in the same grave I shall see in it nothing but the retributive hand of God."[17] Some would even look upon the early years of Yankee failure on the battlefield as a punishment for acquiescing on the issue for so long. Yet their sentiments were much in the minority. Among the two million men who would wear the blue of the Union, less than one in ten felt any real interest in emancipation. And for every Federal who voiced his sympathy for the plight of the slaves, there were a legion of others who disagreed. "If some of the niger lovers want to know what most of the Solgers think of them", wrote Private Charles Babbott of Ohio, "they think about as much as they do a reble. they think they are Shit asses."[18]

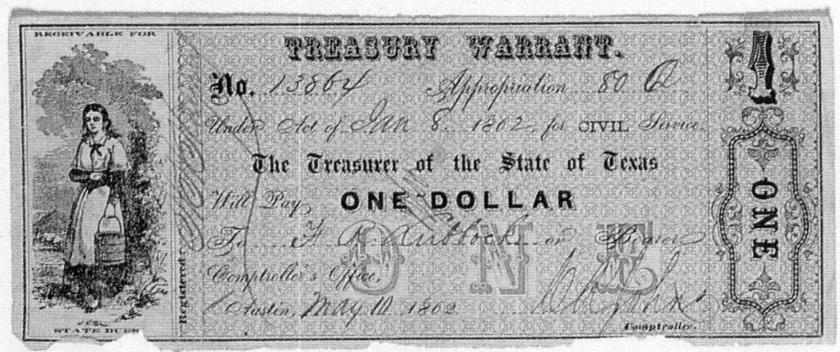

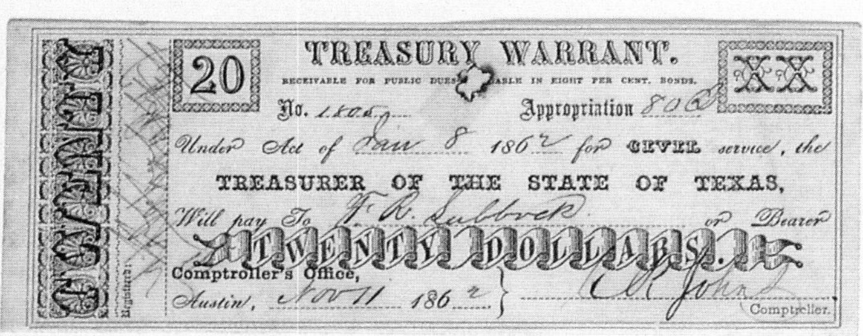

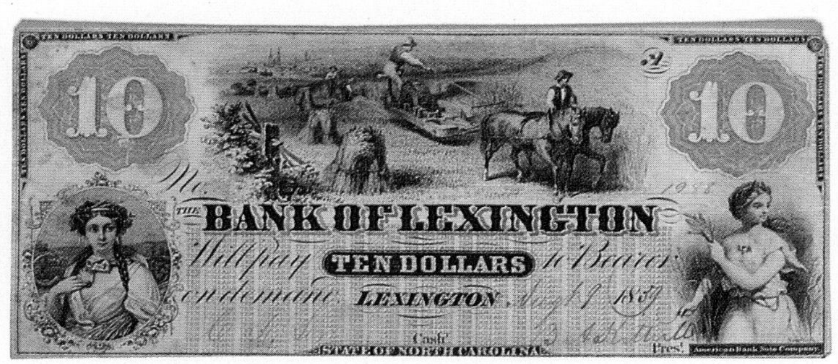

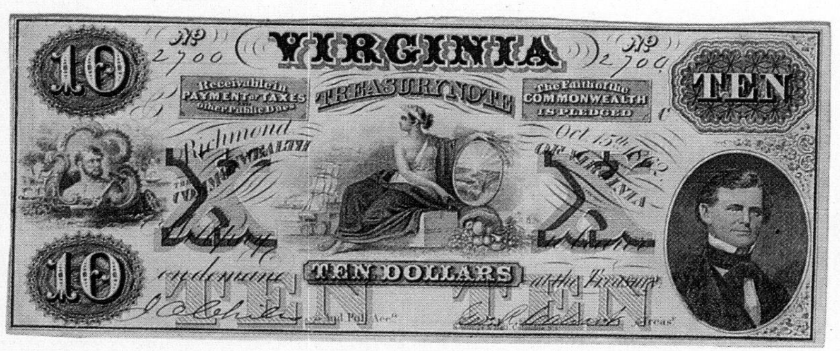

Southern Banknotes

1 State of Texas one dollar bill, 1862
2 Confederate Treasury ten dollar bill, 1863
3 State of Texas twenty dollar bill, 1862
4 Confederate Treasury ten dollar bill, 1863 (reverse)
5 Commonwealth of Virginia five dollar bill, 1862
6 Bank of Lexington, North Carolina five dollar bill, 1859
7 Commonwealth of Virginia ten dollar bill, 1862
8 Florida one dollar bill, 1864 (overprint)
9 C. H. Nobles and Co., Sutler's fifty cent note, 1862
10 Augusta Insurance and Banking fifty cent note, 1862
11 Charles Page, Sutler's twenty-five cent note, 1862
12 The Manufacturer's Bank of Macon five dollar bill, 1862
13 Butte County, Georgia ten cent note, 1862
14 Ocoee Bank of Cleveland, Tennessee one dollar bill, 1862
15 Parish of Iberville, Louisiana twenty-five cent note, 1862
16 Keatinge and Ball, Columbia two dollar bill, 1864
17 Arkadelphia Exchange two dollar bill, 1862

Artifacts courtesy of: The Museum of The Confederacy, Richmond, Va

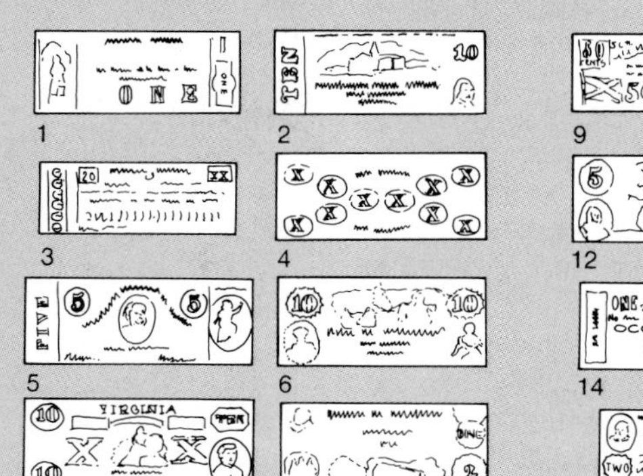

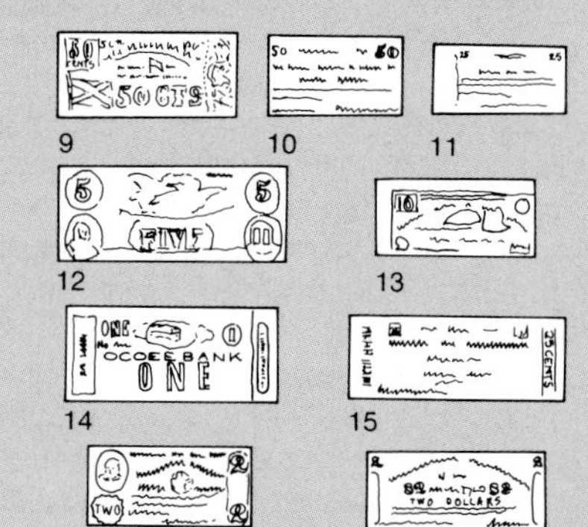

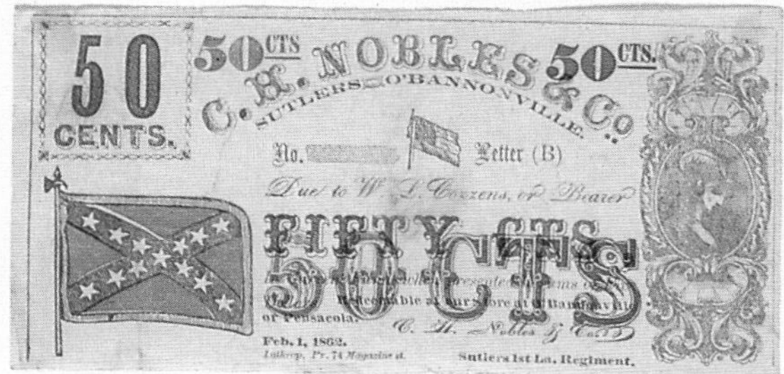

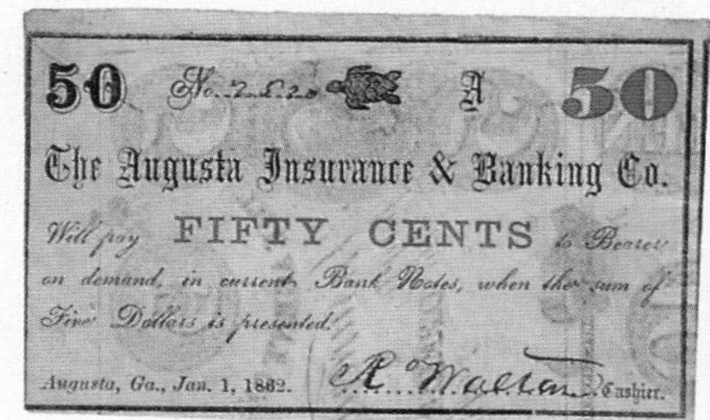

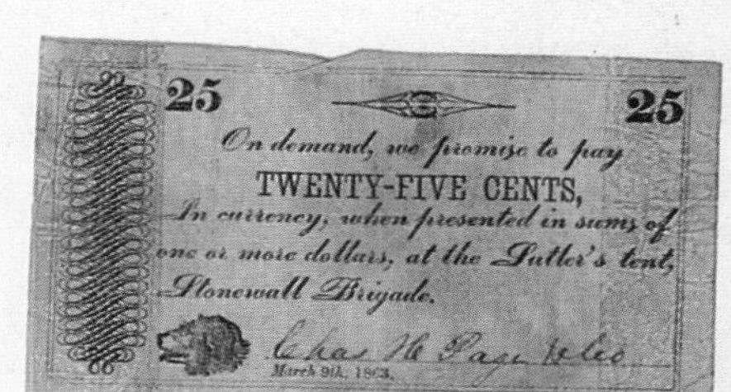

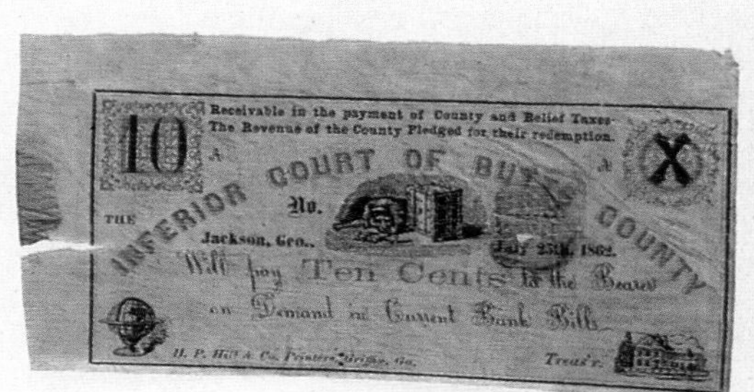

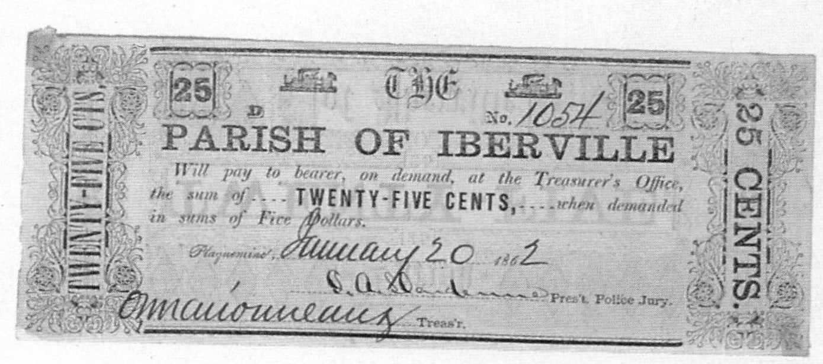

Far more pervasive was the sense of duty to cause and country. In the South that meant the defense of its lands and institutions. In Virginia immediately after secession, Benjamin W. Jones found that, "the determination to resist invasion – the first and most sacred duty of a free people – became general, if not universal".[19] That determination sent him into the army, and thousands more with them.

Bred for generations to view Northerners as hypocritical fanatics bent on destroying the Constitution, most Southerners were thoroughly convinced of the righteousness of their cause. Further, theirs was a militant society, and they looked upon themselves as by nature better soldiers and fighters than Yankee shop keepers. Defense of the South, to them, was as holy a task as the American Revolution, and the enlistees vowed to bear hardships as great as Washington's before they would fail. "I & every Southern Soldier should be like the rebbil blume which plumed more & shinned briter the more it was trampled on & I believe we will have to fight like Washington did", wrote Sergeant John Hagan of Georgia, "but I hope our people will never be reduced to destress & poverty as the people of that day was, but if nothing elce will give us our liberties I am willing for the time to come."[20]

While military inclinations did not dwell in the North in the same degree as they did below the Potomac, still they abided much in the western frontier, where Lincoln's call for volunteers met with a more enthusiastic reception. Yet, as in the new Confederacy, militarism stood well behind a sense of duty and purpose in impelling those young men to rush forward and sign the muster rolls. "I did not come for money and good living", Private Samuel Croft of Pennsylvania wrote in 1861. Looking at the glistening bayonets of his regiment, "Knowing that the bayonets are in loyal hands that will plunge them deep in the hearts of those who have disgraced", he said, "that flag

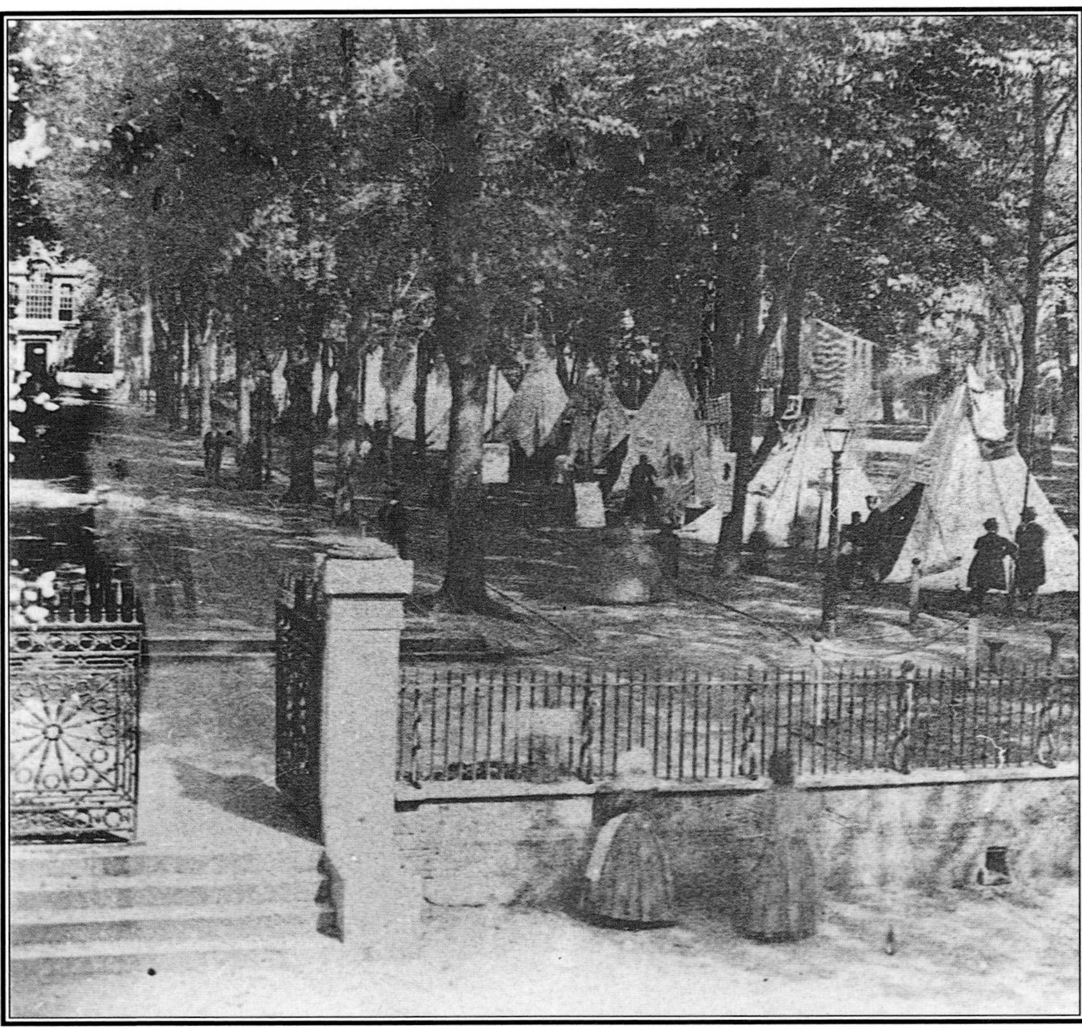

Above: In 1861 at Independence Square in Philadelphia, tents sprang up as the green was used to bivouac new recruits. The scene of the Declaration of Independence now saw the fight to preserve it.

Below: Confederates, like Federals, often enlisted in groups, even families. Often two, three, four, even five brothers took their oaths together, fighting and dying in the same regiment, like these Rebs.

which has protected them and us, their freedom and ours, I say again I am proud and sanguine of success."[21] Sergeant English of New Jersey, himself the son of Irish immigrants, spoke for all, native or foreign-born: "The blind acts of unqualified generals and Statesmen have had no lasting impression on the motives which first prompted me to take up arms or chilled my patriotism in the least", he wrote in 1863. "As long as God spares my health and strength to wield a weapon in Freedom's defense, I will do it."[22]

For all the differences that brought about the war, and those that impelled the men on either side to enlist, the Northerners and Southerners who rushed to take up arms were more alike than not. They came overwhelmingly from the farms of rural America; and not just in ones or twos. Whole companies and regiments were raised in the same locality, bringing with them their own local values and customs.

Fully one half of the men who donned the blue had been farmers, and almost two-thirds of the new Confederates were trading the plow for the gun. Carpenters, clerks, laborers, and students made up much of the remainder, but in fact over 300 different occupations were represented in the Union Army, and over 100 in the Confederate. In the North, it would be rare for any trade not to have at least one member in a brigade, which afforded the new regiments a remarkable self-sufficiency in the field. When a weapon or piece of equipment fell in need of repair, there was usually someone near at hand with the experience and knowledge to set it aright. The South would suffer somewhat thanks to a lesser degree of diversity, and no one ever knew quite what to do with those soldiers who listed as their pre-war occupation that of "gentlemen".

Just as the majority on both sides were white, native-born, Protestant, and unmarried, so were they all primarily young men. Four out of five in both armies were between eighteen and twenty-nine. Many sixteen and seventeen year olds wrote the numeral "18" on slips of paper and put them in their shoes. When asked by a recruiting officer how old they were, they could say that they were "over eighteen". The youngest Confederate soldier was probably Charles C. Hay of Alabama. He was just eleven when he enlisted in 1861. He was not alone in his youth, for many other children served in the Southern armies. Indeed, after the brief fight at Farmington, Mississippi on May 9, 1862, General P.G.T. Beauregard called the "especial attention of the Army to the behavior of Private John Mather Sloan of the 9th Texas, a lad of only 13 years of age." The boy lost a leg in the fighting, but could only exclaim that "I have but one regret I shall not soon be able to get at the enemy".[23] The youngest soldier of the war, however, Private Edward Black, joined the 21st Indiana as a musician, aged nine.

While the youth of the soldiers enlivened camp life and infused an enthusiasm in battle that enhanced morale, the armies took some stability from the maturity of soldiers at the other end of the allotted three score and ten. Not all of the drummers in uniform were the children of folklore. David Scantlon of the 4th Virginia was fully fifty-two years old. A member of Virginia's Richmond Howitzers recalled knowing personally, "six men over sixty years who volunteered, and served in the ranks, throughout the war".[24] In North Carolina, in July 1862, E. Pollard joined the 5th Infantry and gave his age as sixty-two, though he was probably above seventy and had to be discharged soon after for being "incapable of performing the duties of a soldier on account of rheumatism and old age".[25] Yet once more it was

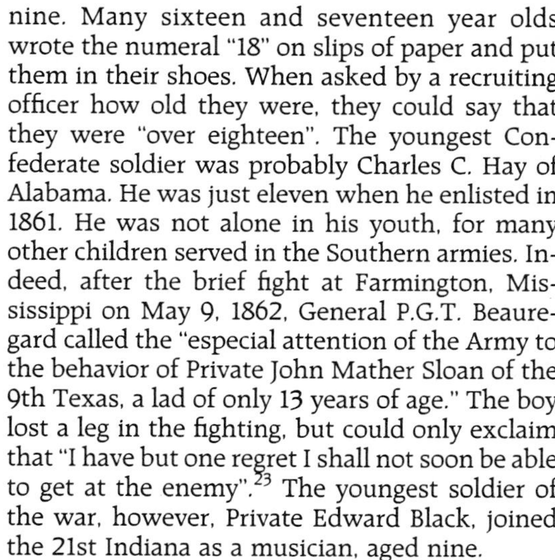

Above: For the most part Reb and Yank were young men, and many not even men at that. This little boy is barely big enough to hold his pistol and support his buttons, yet thousands like him managed to enlist.

Below: Like some of these boy musicians in the 93rd New York Infantry, the 10 and 12 year olds often found their places in the army in the supposedly non-combatant roles of fifers and drummers.

Below: Tall or short, young or old, they all brought with them the exuberance and innocence of youth. Many an uncomfortable looking lad would grow into his uniform by hardship and experience in camp and battle.

left to the Yankees to reach the greatest extreme. Curtis King was the oldest soldier of the war when he enlisted in the 37th Iowa in November 1862, aged eighty.

Whatever their age, they were healthy men, inured by the hard life of the fields or the factories. The ruggedness of military life posed few challenges to their hardened constitutions. "I am well, and I think this kind of life agrees with me", a Virginia cavalryman wrote to his family in the autumn of 1861. "I weigh the same as I did when I left home – one hundred and twenty-five pounds – but all there is of me is bone and muscle, very tough and very active."[26] The men tended to be lean when they enlisted, and to stay that way. No one grew fat on army grub and marching.

Neither were they overly tall. The average ran between five feet five inches and five feet nine. The shortest Federal had to hustle some to keep up with his comrades in the 192nd Ohio. He was just three feet four inches from boot to sole to kepi, and it would have taken two of him, end to end, to approach the tallest Yankee. Captain David Van Buskirk of the 27th Indiana stood just an inch short of seven feet, the loftiest pinnacle in a 100-man company that boasted eighty men above six feet. The 380-pound Van Buskirk was described as "a 'whale', but some of the others are whales, too, but a trifle smaller". When he was captured in 1862 and sent to a Richmond prison, Van Buskirk became such a curiosity that a Rebel entrepreneur put him on exhibit as a freak, labeled "the biggest Yankee in the world". Even President Jefferson Davis came to see him, to be astounded when the impish Van Buskirk claimed that, "Back home in Bloomington, Indiana I have six sisters". They told him goodbye when his company marched off to war, he said. "As I was standing with my company, they all walked up, leaned down and kissed me on top of my head."[27]

But undoubtedly the loftiest man of the entire war was Private Henry C. Thruston of Texas. He enlisted in a Morgan County company with his four brothers, the shortest of whom stood six feet six inches! Incredibly, this ample target served through the war taking only two wounds, one of them a slight grazing on the top of his head, a rare occasion when firing "too high" was

Above: Taken just a few days after the April 1861 bombardment, with Confederates posing in triumph, this image of the gorge of Fort Sumter offers only an impression of the damage done by the Rebel batteries.

Below: This rare view of the casements from the interior of Fort Sumter shows not only the unfinished condition of the fort, but also the tomb-like cavities from which the Yankees and their guns fought.

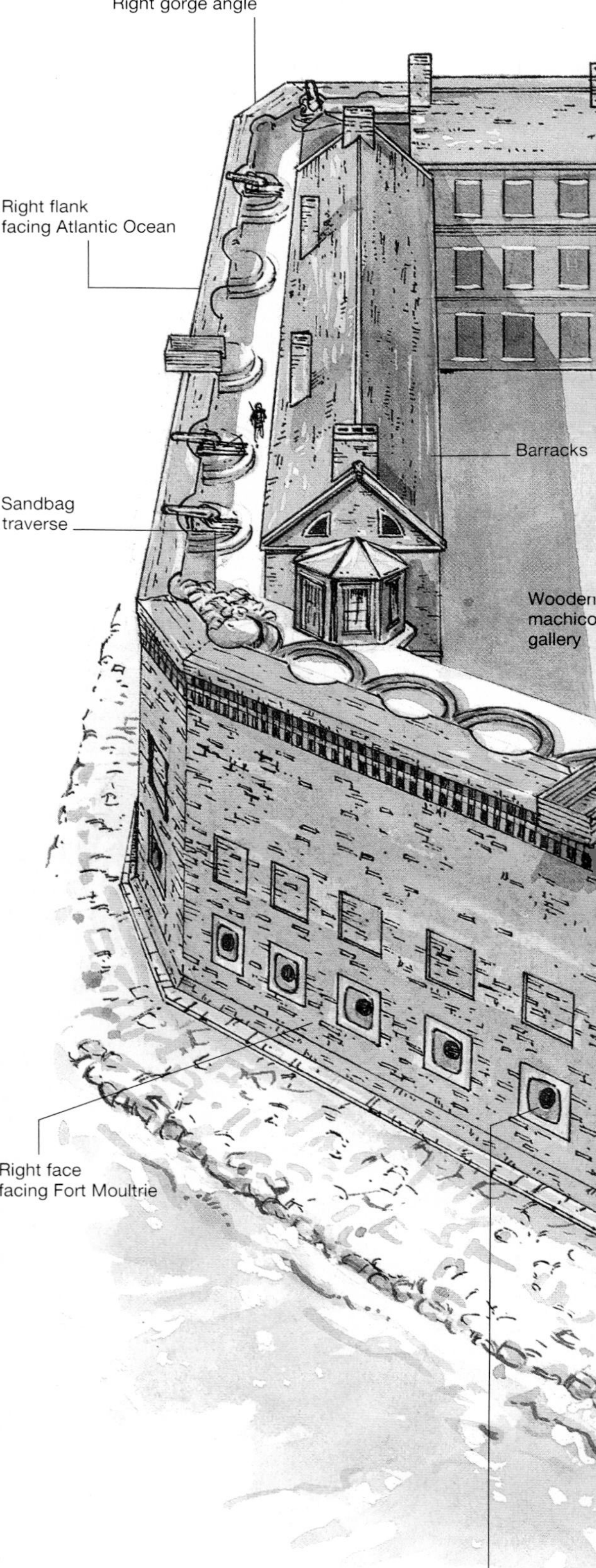

no problem for the enemy. When not wearing his top hat, Henry Thruston stood seven feet, seven and one-half inches, a genuine Texas tall tale.[28]

Whatever made them different or the same, most of the men North and South who answered the call were native-born Americans. Yet stepping forward with them, to lend their own special talents and accent to Civil War soldiering, were tens of thousands of foreigners of every caste and nationality. Company H of the 8th Michigan numbered among its men, 47 New Yorkers, 37 Michiganders, 26 other native Americans, 7 Canadians, 5 Englishmen, 4 Germans, 2 Irishmen, 1 Scotsman, 1 Dutchman, and one mysterious fellow who simply listed his nationality as "the ocean".[29]

It was hardly an unusual national mix in the Union army. Some camps were a virtual babel. In one Yankee regiment hosting fifteen different national origins, the colonel had to give orders in seven separate languages. Many of the immigrants spoke English indifferently at best, making communication often a nightmare. In Major General Franz Sigel's command in 1864, his orders given in German had to go through three successive translations from German to Hungarian to English, and back to German, before they filtered through his international staff to his German-born men in the ranks. He was never a great general, but given the party game nature of his chain of communications, it was a miracle that all of his men even marched in the same direction.

Fort Sumter, Charleston Harbor, SC

When the Confederate shore and water batteries opened fire on it, Fort Sumter was still unfinished. It was an example of the masonry seacoast fortifications built by the United States in the first half of the 19th century to protect rivers and major harbors. Designed to hold 146 heavy cannon, only 15 were mounted when secession came in December 1860. Defending Sumter posed some special problems. To begin with its garrison had to deal with the fact that it had not been designed to fire at "home territory" in Charleston. Its guns and embrasures almost all faced out to sea. In the end, only 21 guns on the lower casement tier, and several others on the exposed upper parapet were usable in the barrage which began at 4.30 am, April 12. Despite a spirited defense they were not enough to forestall the inevitable surrender which came on April 13. Only one Federal was killed in the siege, and that was during the final evacuation.

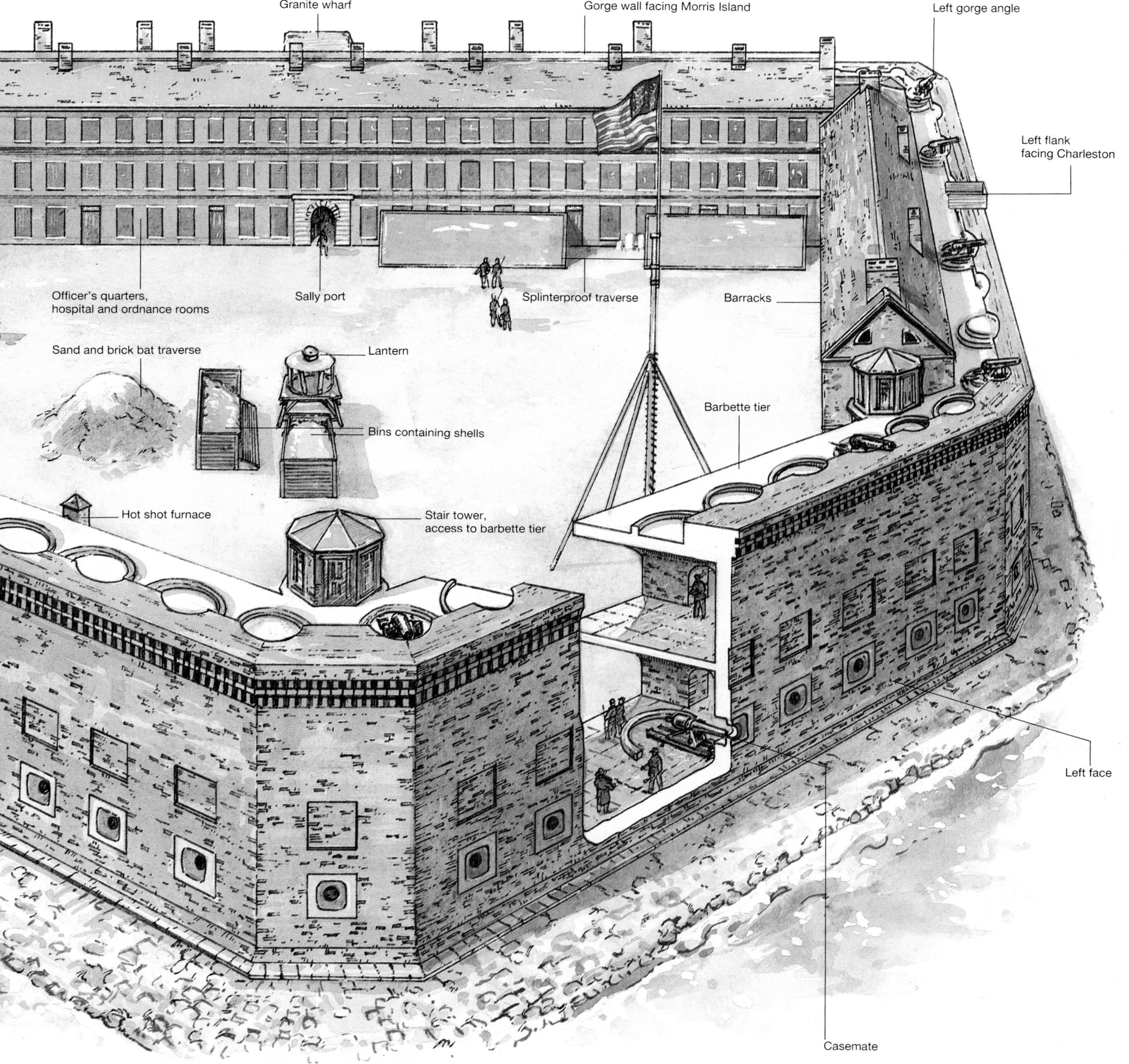

These immigrants had come rushing to America, refugees from the European upheavals of the 1850s and the Irish potato famines. Available land and work attracted the majority of them to the North so that by 1860, nearly a third of the North's male population were foreign born. The fact that Lincoln gave general's commissions to popular men like Sigel, Carl Schurz, Thomas Meagher, and others, was a powerful inducement for their fellow immigrants to enlist under their banners.

Over 200,000 Germans served in the Northern armies, with several regiments composed entirely of them. The 9th Wisconsin did not number a single non-German in its ranks. New York furnished ten regiments that were predominantly composed of Germans, and Ohio did the same. "I fights mit Sigel", many of them sang as they marched off to war, only to learn that they were often despised by native-born soldiers, and that their beloved Sigel was an incompetent who got a good many of them killed. Fellow Yankees regarded them as "dumb Dutchmen". Worse, because they were often ill-led, as with the Union XI Corps, they suffered more than their share of defeats and panics. But the "Dutchmen" were technically skilled and suited by culture to military discipline, which, added to their impeccable devotion to the Union cause, made them valuable allies. Philip Smith of the 8th Missouri, a German immigrant, wrote in his diary on the day after the defeat at Bull Run that he had: "grasped the weapon of death for the purpose of doing my part in defending and upholding the integrity, laws and the preservation of my adopted country from a band of contemptible traitors who would if they can accomplish their hellish designs, destroy the best and noblest government on earth."[30]

Much the same sentiment would be heard from the Irishmen wearing the blue. But they were a different sort of soldier entirely. While many joined to save the Union, it has to be said that quite a few of the 150,000 who served the North were in it purely out of the Celtic love of a fight. "There is an elasticity in the Irish temperament which enables its possessor to boldly stare Fate in the face, and laugh at all the reverses of fortune", wrote Felix Brannigan of the 79th New York.[31] In the fight at Winchester, Virginia, in September 1864, an officer reported seeing one "wild looking Irishman" who was loading and firing his weapon as fast as he could, mumbling an occasional prayer, and shouting as he fired, "Now Jeff Davis, you son of a bitch, take that",

Above: One of the more colorful Yankee units was the 79th New York Infantry, commonly known as the "Highlanders". Made up chiefly of Scots immigrants, they wore kilts and Glengarry caps early in the war.

Above: Perhaps the most famous of all largely immigrant units was the 69th New York, the "Fighting 69th". Many of its men were captured at First Manassas and pose here in their prison at Castle Pinckney.

Below: The size and number of immigrant regiments often led to their organization into larger units. This is the headquarters of the Irish Brigade at New Creek, West Virginia, during the winter of 1862.

giving his head a twist at the same time and his eyes looking wildly in front.[32]

At least twenty regiments, most notably Meagher's Irish Brigade of the 9th, 63rd, and 88th New York, were composed almost entirely of men from Ireland. These Irish soldiers were rowdy and insubordinate, but they were also fierce fighters, especially on the offensive. As one of their generals said, "I would prefer Irish soldiers to any other". They had more dash, more élan, were more cheerful, and more enduring than other soldiers. "They make the finest soldiers that ever shouldered a musket."[33] And they never lost their good humor. At the Battle of Ocean Pond, Florida, in 1864, Brigadier General Joseph Finnegan, himself an Irishman, yelled to his son and aide, "Go to the rear, Finnegan, me b'ye, go to the rear! Ye know ye are yer mither's darlin'!"

Over 60,000 Englishmen and Canadians served the Union, as well as a varied selection of Frenchmen, Scandinavians, Hungarians, and even a very few Orientals. The 79th New York was made up mostly of Scotsmen who wore kilts early in the war, until the derisive laughter of fellow soldiers every time they climbed over a fence drove them to adopt trousers.[34]

In 1864 Colonel Theodore Lyman, of General George G. Meade's headquarters, sneered: "By the Lord! I wish these gentlemen who would overwhelm us with Germans, negroes, and the offscourings of great cities, could only see – only *see* – a Rebel regiment, in all their rags and squalor. If they had eyes they would know that these men are like wolf-hounds, and not to be beaten by turnspits."[35] Foreign-born soldiers were never popular with their native-born counterparts.

Yet some of those Rebel "wolf-hounds" were themselves immigrants, though in far smaller numbers. There was one brigade of Irishmen, several German regiments, as well as a Polish "legion". A European brigade of mixed nationalities came from Louisiana, and was commanded by the resplendent French Count Camille Armand Jules Marie, Prince de Polignac. His men abbreviated that considerably, and simply called him "Polecat". A company of Georgia mountaineers listened in utter marvel as the Prince gave his orders in French. "That-thur furriner he calls out er lot er gibberish", drawled one, "an thum-thur Dagoes jes maneuvers-up like Hell-beatin'-tanbark! Jes like he was talking sense!"[36]

Often overlooked in both armies were the much smaller numbers of native minorities who wore blue and gray. Perhaps as many as 12,000 Indians served the Confederacy, most of them members of the Five Civilized Tribes living out in the Indian Territory. In all, the Confederates would raise some eleven regiments and seven

Sergeant, 79th New York Infantry "Highlanders" 1860-61

Few Yankee regiments of the war were quite as distinctive – or as ridiculed – as the famed 79th New York Infantry, the "Highlanders". Modeling itself after the 79th Cameron Highlanders of the British Army, its initial core of four companies was formed in 1859 entirely of Scots immigrants. With the outbreak of the Civil War its strength was increased with enlistments of English and Irish, as well as other foreign-born men, but its dress would remain distinctly Scottish. In full-dress the men wore kilts, a doublet, sporran, hose, garters and silver-buckled shoes. In the field, however, they quickly changed to light blue trousers, which they are reported to have worn at First Manassas, or Cameron tartan pants; dark blue blouses, and a regulation kepi which replaced the Glengarry cap with its checkered border. Nevertheless despite the stares an intrepid few kept their kilts and trews.

battalions of Indian cavalry out there, not to mention a few hundred other red men scattered through some of the white Confederate regiments from North Carolina, Tennessee, and Kentucky. They did not exactly look the picture of the Rebel soldier. "Their faces were painted, and their long straight hair, tied in a queue, hung down behind", wrote a Missouri Confederate. "Their dress was chiefly in the Indian costume – buckskin hunting-shirts, dyed of almost every color, leggings, and moccasins of the same material, with little bells, rattles, ear-rings, and similar paraphernalia. Many of them were bareheaded and about half carried only bows and arrows, tomahawks, and war-clubs."[37]

Ill-treated and ignored even by their own superiors, the Indian soldiers had only half a heart in the cause, and much the same could be said of the 6,000 or more who wore the blue. All too often they were enlisted only to take advantage of old tribal hatreds, pitting Union Indian against Confederate Indian, and all too often they ignored army regulations and fought in the old ways. But they certainly lent color to the muster rolls of North and South. Spring Frog, John Bearmeat, Alex Scarce Water, Big Mush Dirt Eater, Warkiller Hogshooter, George Hogtoter, and Jumper Duck, were all soldiers of the Union, and these were simply anglicizations of Indian names probably impossible to pronounce.[38] In the Confederate First Kentucky Brigade there served a Mohawk sachem named Konshattountzchette, whose name was spelled in so many different ways that his official record could never agree with itself. His fellow soldiers simply preferred to call him Flying Cloud.[39]

Native born, too, were the few thousand Mexican-Americans who took up arms. The 1st New Mexico was known as Martinez' Militia during its Union service, and two Colorado regiments contained far more Sanchez' than Smiths.[40] On the other side sat the 33rd Texas, led in part by Refugio Benevides and manned mostly by Mexicans. They, like the Indians, would receive little attention from their government.

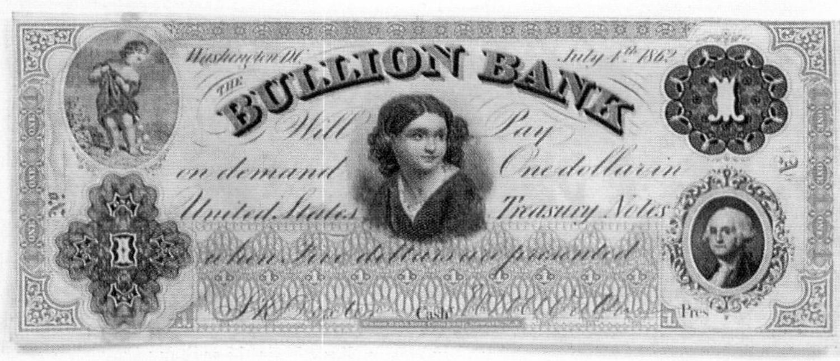

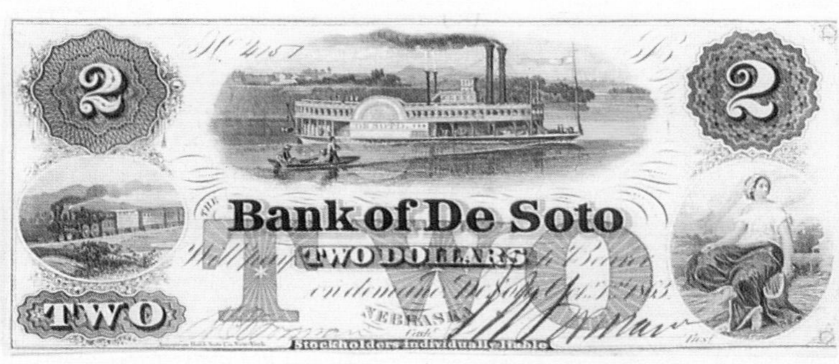

Union Banknotes

Many banks issued their own paper currency, as did some stores. This helped to keep local money spent locally, but did the soldiers little good.

1 US Treasury one dollar bill, 1862
2 US Treasury two dollar bill, 1862
3 US Treasury five dollar bill, 1862
4 US Treasury ten dollar bill
5 Bullion Bank of NJ one dollar bill
6 Bullion Bank of NJ three dollar bill
7 American Bank of Baltimore, one dollar bill
8 Bank of De Soto, Ne, two dollar bill, 1862
9 Egg Harbour Bank, NJ two dollar bill
10 Bank of Montgomery County, Pa, one dollar bill, 1865
11 Somerset and Worcester Savings Bank, Maryland, three dollar bill, 1862
12 The Sanford Bank, Maine, ten dollar bill, 1861
13 North Western Bank, Pa, five dollar bill, 1861
14 The Merchants' Bank, Trenton, NJ, two dollar bill
15 Bank of Crawford County, Meadville, Pa, five dollar bill, reverse 1863
16 North Western Bank, Pa, one dollar bill, 1861

Artifacts courtesy of: CDR James C. Ruehrmund, USN (Ret), F.R.N.S.

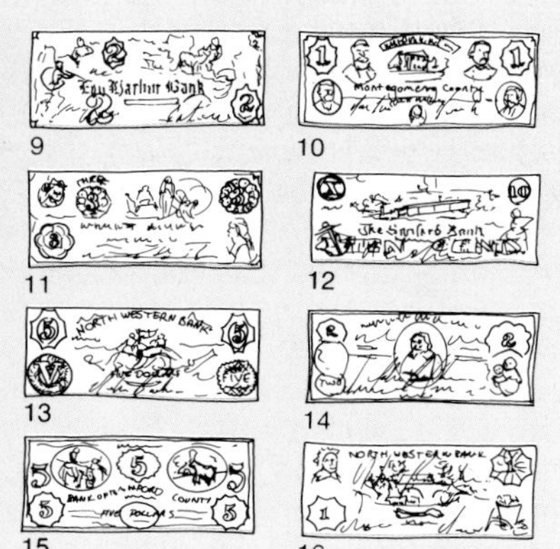

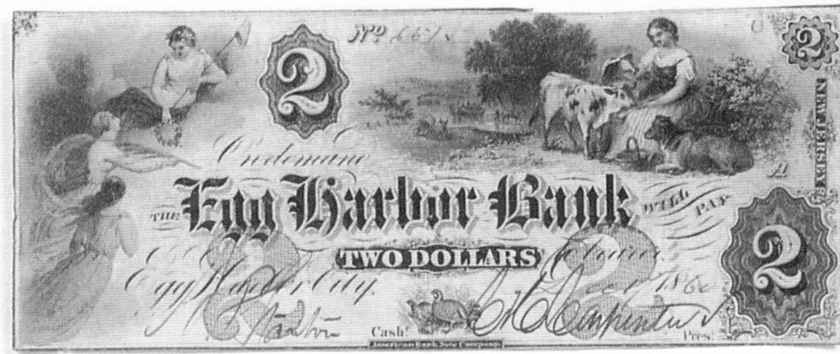

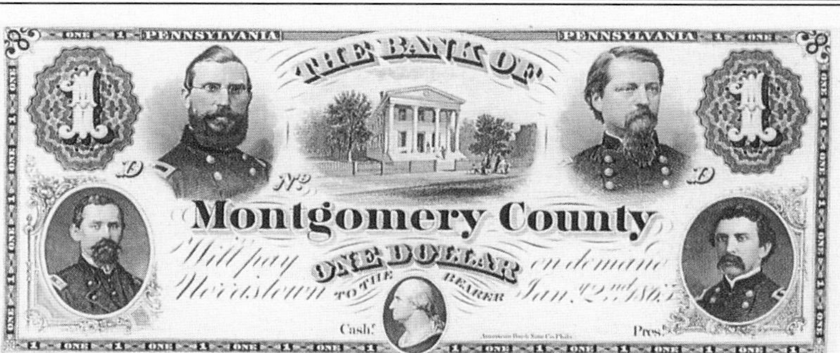

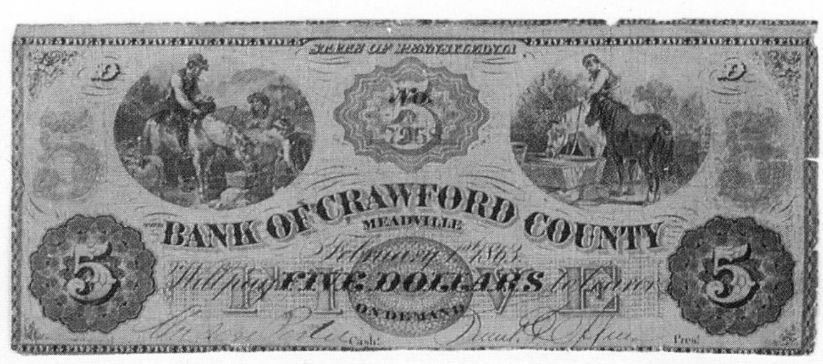

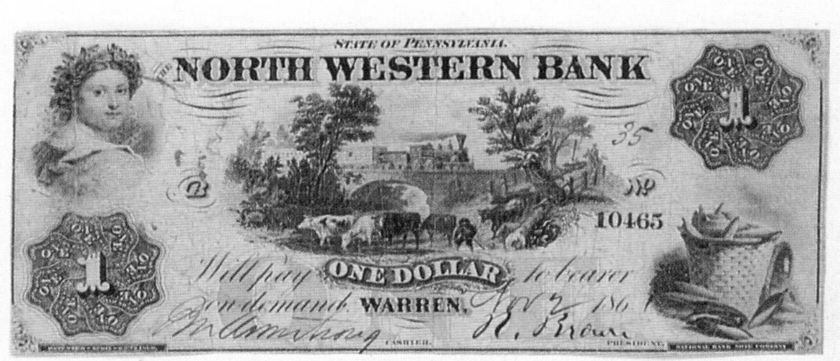

But not so the continent's largest minority. Out in Kansas in 1863, Major General James G. Blunt spoke of the non-white soldiers in his command, and declared emphatically that, "I would not exchange one regiment of negro troops for ten regiments of Indians."[41] Blacks, too, would step forward to the recruiter, though not without the trials and setback that ever accompanied their progress in America. Yet they would fight and prove themselves.

Many openly argued against enrolling blacks, both among civilians and white soldiers. "Thair is a great Controversy out hear about the niggar Question at present", wrote an enlisted man of the 110th Pennsylvania. "If they go to Sending them out hear to fight they will get Enough of it for it Will raise a rebelion in the army that all the abolisionist this Side of hell Could not Stop. the Southern peopel are rebels to the government but thay are White and God never intended a nigger to put white peopel down."[42] Besides fears that arming Negroes would degrade the army, and even risk rebellion among them, most asserted that it would be a threat to white rule. "They are good for such purposes as throwing up breastworks and digging canals", said an Illinois private, "but I cannot think they are a class that should be armed."[43]

By late 1861 abolitionists and poiliticians began to argue that the Union Army could use black numbers to bring a speedy conclusion to the war, and at the same time the army would teach them discipline and prepare them for their place in postwar society – whatever that place was to be. But the issue was politically explosive, especially in the still loyal slave states like Missouri and Kentucky, and Lincoln had to be wary. Not until September 1862, after a string of humiliating defeats, was Lincoln ready to risk his Emancipation Proclamation. The border states were at least secure to the Union now, and redirecting the war into a crusade for black freedom would strengthen the North with European powers wavering between Union and Confederacy. Lincoln declared the Proclamation as a military necessity

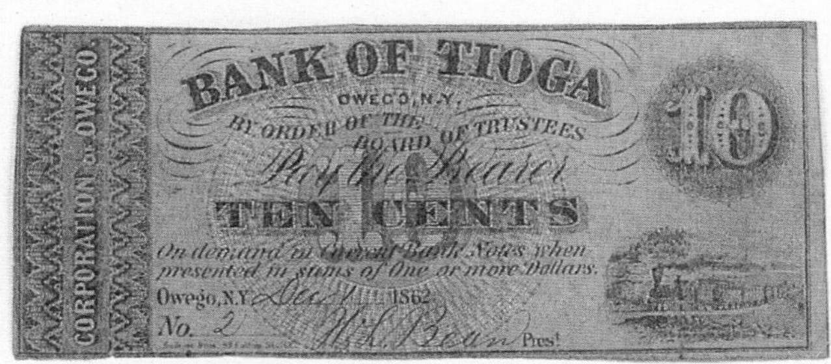

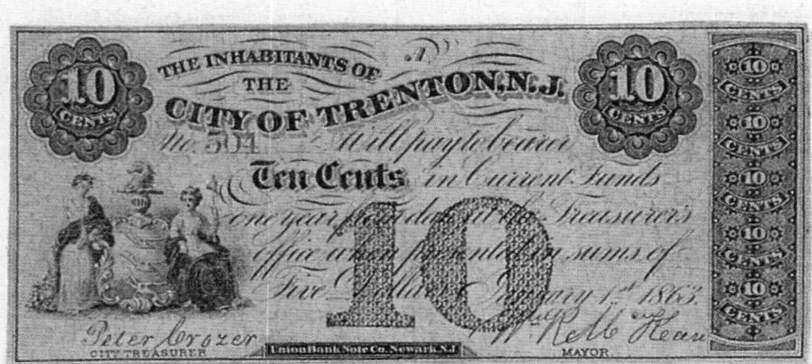

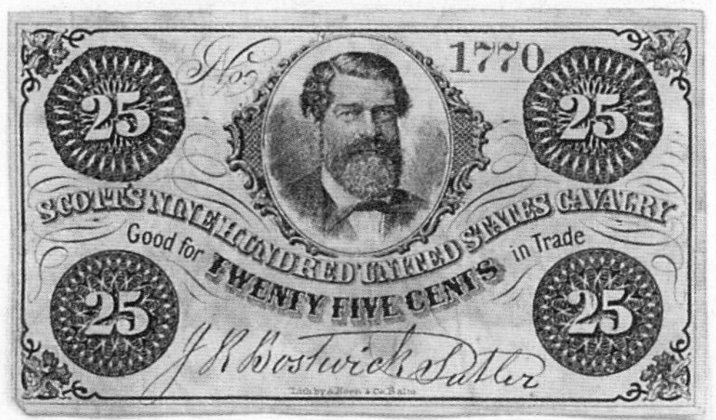

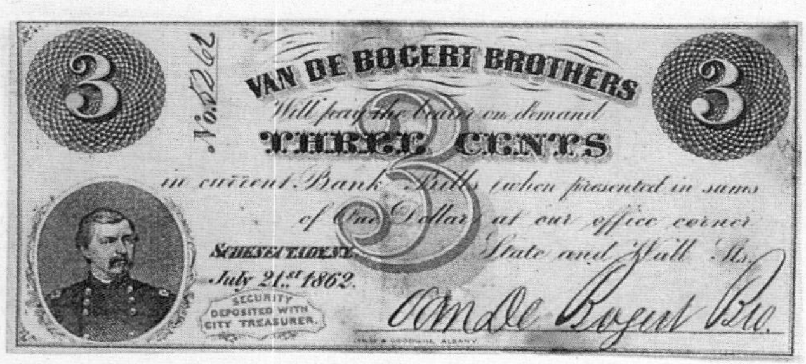

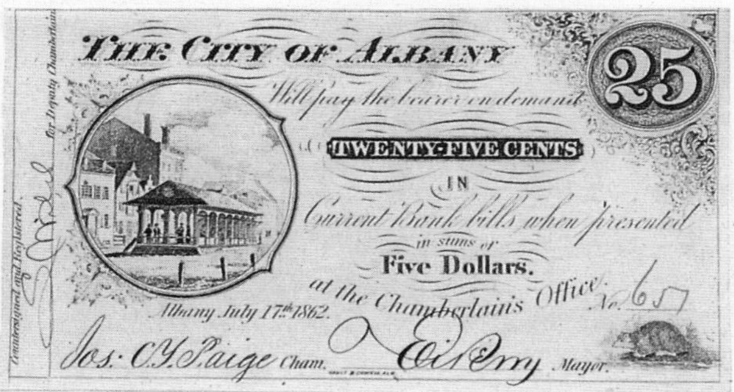

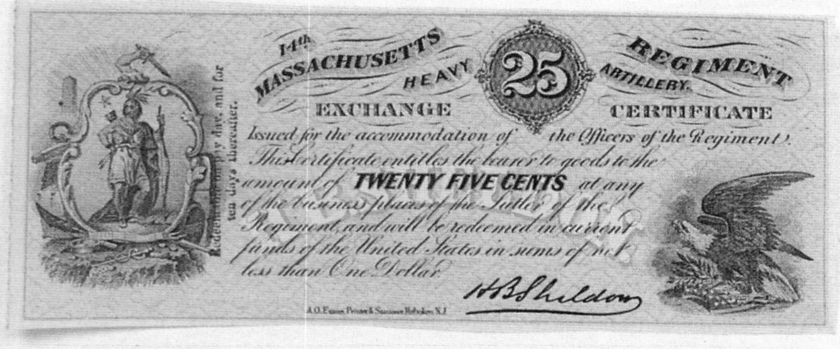

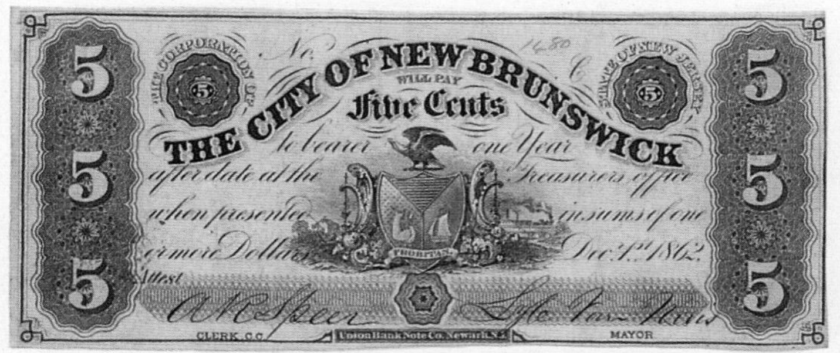

Union Banknotes and Coins

1 Bank of the Borough of Easton, Pa, ten cent note, 1862
2 City of Wilmington, five cent note, 1862
3 Farmers' and Merchants' Bank, NJ, ten cent note, 1862
4 Bank of Tioga, NY, ten cent note, 1862
5 Treasury of Trenton, NJ, ten cent note, 1862
6 Cavalry exchange note
7 Van de Bogent Brothers, NY, three cent note
8 City of Albany, twenty-five cent note, 1862
9 Regimental twenty-five cent certificate
10 City of New Brunswick, twenty-five cent note, 1862
11 Selection of small denomination coins
12-15 US Post Office notes for five, ten, twenty-five and fifty cents
16-19 US Treasury notes for five, ten, twenty-five, and fifty cents
20-22 US Treasury notes for three, five and twenty-five cents
23–24 Obverse and reverse of a US Treasury fifty cent note
25 Summit County Bank, Cuyahoga Falls, State of Ohio, five cent note, 1862
26 Treasury of the Village of Roundout five cent note, 1862
27 Farmers' Bank, NY, five cent note, 1862

Artifacts courtesy of: CDR James C. Ruehrmund, USN (Ret), F.R.N.S.

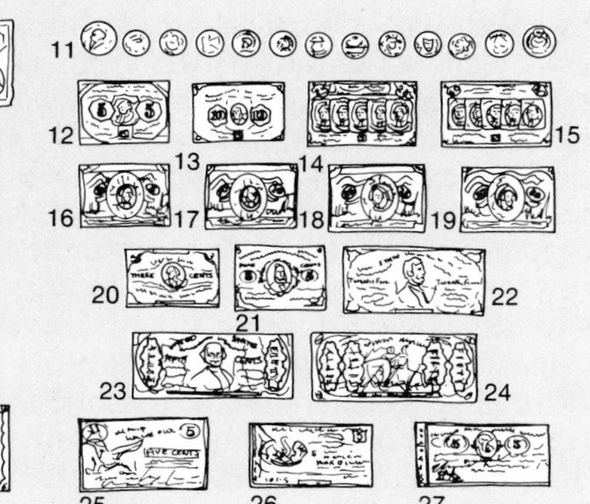

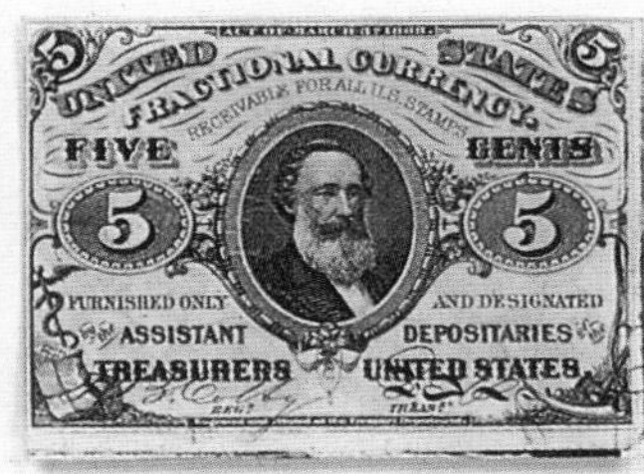

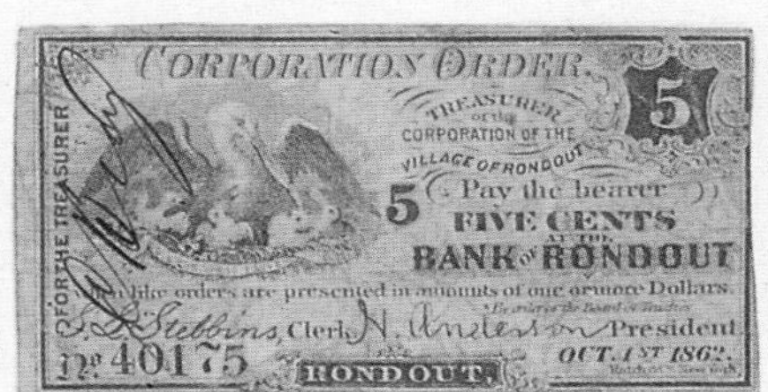

which craftily opened the way for him to authorize enlistment of black soldiers in January 1863.

Gradually most Northerners came around to the notion. As the sight of Negroes in uniform became more and more commonplace, they were slowly accepted, though not as equals. White soldiers welcomed them to do menial tasks like digging ditches and latrines, thus saving the whites those duties, while ambitious young officers saw opportunities for advancement by taking higher commissions in black regiments. Not until the war's end would there be a very few Negro officers in their own outfits, and not until 1864 would be the black soldier finally receive the same pay as his white comrade. There was open discrimination of every kind, but they endured.

The worst hostility came from white soldiers, some of whom believed that authorities favored the blacks. After a day of shoveling mud in December 1864, a New Hampshire soldier grumbled that, "Some of the Boys say that Army Moto is First the Negro, then the mule, then the white man."[44] Most thought blacks were lazy and insolent, and many resented the Negro as the primary reason that they were all fighting in the first place. "I have slept on the soft side of a board, in the mud, and every other place that was lousey and dirty", grumbled Private Richard Puffer of the 8th Illinois. "I have drank out of goose ponds, horse tracks, etc., for the last eighteen months, all for the poor nigger; and I have yet to see the first one that I think has been benifitted by it."[45]

Blacks and whites were often in fights when they met outside their encampments, and not a few Billy Yanks were just as ready to shoot a Negro as a Confederate. In the battle at Ocean Pond, or Olustee, in February 1864, a Virginia Rebel wrote that, "The negroes saw a hard time; those who stood were shot by our men, those who ran by the Yankees."[46]

In the end, some spirit of comradeship arose with a few white soldiers. What changed white soldiers' – and civilians' – minds the most was the black man's performance in battle.

General Blunt's declaration about the worth of a Negro regiment came from first-hand knowledge. During the last three years of the war, black Yankee regiments participated in 39 major battles and over 400 skirmishes, and Blunt himself led them in battle at Honey Springs, in the Indian Territory, on July 17, 1863. Opposing Confederates had brought slave shackles with them, expecting to take the blacks. Instead, Blunt's 1st Kansas Colored Volunteers routed them. While abolitionists constantly overrated black solders' qualities, and opponents underrated them, nevertheless much of their subsequent behavior on the battlefield was outstanding. Particularly at Port Hudson, Louisiana, in May 1863, and at Fort Wagner, South Carolina, two months later, Negro regiments distinguished themselves.

They did so at considerable extra risk not faced by whites, for the Confederate government never countenanced blacks as legitimate solders. Enraged Southern soldiers sometimes murdered those that fell into their hands, and later in the war a few "massacres" occurred. Even when the politically motivated rhetoric is sifted for exaggeration, still it is certain that most especially at Saltville, Virginia and Fort Pillow, Tennessee – both in 1864 – hundreds of defenseless blacks were murdered.

Nevertheless black troops did win acceptance and even a measure of respect. A total of 176,895 of them served the Union, and 68,100 – more

Above: When given a chance to step forward and fight for his brothers' freedom, the free negroes of the North came out in tens of thousands, serving proudly like these men of Company E, 4th US Colored Infantry.

Below: One of the many ironies of the war is that a conflict which came about because of the black man seemed at first to have no place for him. At first blacks could act only as servants and mean laborers.

Trooper, Sussex Light Dragoons, CSA

While cavalry uniforms in the Confederacy were more informal than in the other services, still the outfit of the Sussex Light Dragoons was particularly out of the ordinary. They wore a high-topped blue cloth kepi with yellow braid with a brass insignia carrying the letters "S.L.D." Enlisted men wore dark blue trousers and tucked into them a "plastron" panelled shirt front in buff or yellow. Carbine, revolver and saber completed their outfitting. The origins of the unit are historically obscure, but it probably originated as Company C of the 5th Virginia Cavalry, raised in Sussex County. Its men were later merged into other Virginia cavalry battalions which served in the Army of Northern Virginia under Lee. The unit itself saw little active service, being chiefly stationed in and around Norfolk before being redesignated in the spring of 1862. Their characteristic dress stayed with them throughout their period of war service.

than a third – died in uniform, mostly from disease. Yet nearly 3,000 of them fell in battle, and the Yankee government acknowledged their bravery by awarding at least twenty-one of them its newly created Medal of Honor. Just after the Battle of Nashville in December 1864, Major General George H. Thomas rode over the bloody field where blacks lay in death beside whites. "Gentlemen, the question is settled", he said to his staff. "Negroes will fight".[47]

It was a question, however, that would never be answered in the Confederacy, and was dangerous even to ask. With 3 million slaves and 135,000 free blacks in the South in 1861, Rebels had an enormous manpower reserve if they had chosen to mobilize it. Many of the slaves felt great loyalty to their masters. Several hundred asked to be allowed to take arms to defend a Southern homeland that was *theirs*, too, when war broke out. And many did go to war as cooks and servants, occasionally even performing picket duty.

In a few cases, blacks informally served Confederate soldiers. The 9th Virginia listed Jacob Jones as a musician, and another black known only as "Joe" served as a teamster with the 13th Virginia Cavalry. Occasionally in battle one of these blacks, caught up in it all, would grasp a fallen weapon and go into fight himself. But Confederates had a deep-felt conviction that giving Negroes any sort of chance for equality posed a mortal threat to Southern culture. "The day you make soldiers of them", said Georgia statesman Howell Cobb, "is the beginning of the end of the revolution. If slaves will make good soldiers, our whole theory of slavery is wrong."[48]

Above: In a hundred fights, regiment after regiment of blacks, like the 1st United States Colored Infantry, shown here on parade in November 1864, demonstrated that they could and would fight and suffer.

Only as the war was coming to a close, in March 1865, in response to foreign pressure, and by the slimmest of votes, did the Confederate Congress approve legislation authorizing black enlistments. One such unit did appear in Richmond, only days before the city fell. Whites standing by threw mud at them when they marched past.

White or black, red or brown, native or immigrant, once enrolled all of these Johnny Rebs and Billy Yanks were much the same – raw, untrained, unready new recruits, with no resemblance to real soldiers. Sometimes they banded together in informal companies before setting off for the camps of instruction. "There was nothing very martial in the appearance of the company", recalled a Virginian of Lee's Light Horse of Westmoreland County. "The officers and men were clad in their citizen's dress, and their horses caparisoned with saddles and bridles of every description used in the country. Their only arms were sabres and double-barrelled shotguns collected from the homes of the people."[49]

The mandatory physical examination they received on arrival at the rendezvous camp was barely cursory at best, often nothing more than a few questions. "You have pretty good health, don't you?", a surgeon asked Charles Barker of the 23rd Massachusetts. When Barker allowed that he did, the surgeon felt his collarbone, asked if he suffered from fits or piles, and promptly pronounced him fit for duty.[50] No small wonder then that as many as 400 women actually managed to pose as men, enlist, and serve in the ranks. One of them, Jennie Hodgers, enlisted in the 95th Illinois as Albert Cashier, served entirely through the war without discovery, and continued her pose until struck by an automobile in 1911. When that revealed her sex, one of her old messmates recalled of their enlistment that, "when we were examined we were not stripped. All that we showed were our hands and feet."[51]

Once past the surgeons, the men – and women – formally swore to "bear true allegiance" to their government and its flag and "to serve them honestly and faithfully against all their enemies or opposers whatsoever, and observe and obey the rules of the President", and so forth. It was their final act as civilians.

Below: These Louisiana Confederate zouaves photographed in New Orleans in 1861 are, like so many North and South, untrained and undisciplined. Yet when it comes time to fight, they will forge a record unexcelled.

Above: Even women would not be kept from the field, as witness Jennie Hodgers, seated at right in her guise as Private Albert Cashier. Her pose remained undetected throughout the war, even by close comrades.

Below: All across the varied landscape of America they spread their tents, made their encampments, lined up for inspections and made ready to take the war to the enemy, like these New Hampshire boys in 1862.

References

1 Arthur A. Kent, *Three Years with Company K* (Cranbury, N.J., 1976), pp.15-16.
2 Bell I. Wiley, *The Life of Johnny Reb* (Indianapolis, Ind., 1943), p.13.
3 Bell I. Wiley, 'A Time of Greatness', *Journal of Southern History,* XXII (February 1956), p.23.
4 Frederick S. Daniel, *The Richmond Examiner During the War* (New York, 1868), p.13.
5 William Howard Russell, *My Diary North and South* (Boston, 1863), p.92.
6 Allan Nevins, *The War for the Union* (New York, 1959-71), I, p.88.
7 James M. McPherson, *Ordeal by Fire* (New York, 1982), pp.149-50.
8 Wiley, *Johnny Reb*, pp.16-17.
9 Howard C. Perkins (ed.), *Northern Editorials on Secession* (New York, 1942), II, p.731.
10 Bell I. Wiley, *The Life of Billy Yank* (Indianapolis, Ind., 1951), p.18.
11 *Ibid.*, p.18.
12 *Ibid.*, p.21.
13 Bell I. Wiley, *Confederate Women* (Westport, Conn., 1975), p.142.
14 Walter P. Lane, *Adventures and Recollections of . . .* (Austin, Tex., 1970), p.83.
15 Wiley, *Billy Yank*, p.38.
16 *Ibid.*, pp.40-1.
17 *Ibid.*, p.42.
18 *Ibid.*, p.43.
19 B.W. Jones, *Under the Stars and Bars* (Richmond, 1909), p.1.
20 Wiley, "Time of Greatness", p.22.
21 *Ibid.*, p.23.
22 *Ibid.*, p.23.
23 Wiley, *Johnny Reb*, p.332.
24 William M. Dame, *From the Rapidan to Richmond and the Spotsylvania Campaign* (Baltimore, 1920), pp.2-3.
25 Weymouth T. Jordan (comp.), *North Carolina Troops, 1861-1865: A Roster* (Raleigh, N.C., 1966-), V, p.180.
26 Susan L. Blackford (comp.), *Letters from Lee's Army* (New York, 1947), pp.48-9.
27 Roger S. Durham, "The Biggest Yankee in the World", *Civil War Times Illustrated,* XIII (May 1974), pp.29, 31.
28 'The Tallest Confederate', *Civil War Times Illustrated,* XIII (November 1974), p.42
29 Wiley, *Billy Yank*, p.311
30 Bell, I. Wiley, *The Common Soldier of the Civil War* (New York, 1975), p.79.
31 *Ibid.*, p.102.
32 *Ibid.*, p.103.
33 *Ibid.*, p.106.
34 Bell I. Wiley, and Hirst D. Millhollen, *They Who Fought Here* (New York, 1959), pp.8-9.
35 Theodore Lyman, *Meade's Headquarters, 1863-1865* (Boston, 1922), p.208.
36 James C. Nisbet, *Four Years on the Firing Line* (Chattanooga, 1915), p.46.
37 Wiley, *Johnny Reb*, p.325.
38 Wiley, *Billy Yank*, pp.316-17.
39 William C. Davis, *The Orphan Brigade* (New York, 1980), p.102.
40 Wiley, *Billy Yank*, p.310.
41 *Ibid.*, p.319.
42 Bell I. Wiley, "Billy Yank and the Black Folk", *Journal of Negro History,* XXXVI (Spring 1951), p.48.
43 "War Diary of Thaddeus H. Capron, 1861-1865", *Journal of the Illinois State Historical Society,* XII (1919), p.358.
44 Wiley, *Billy Yank*, p.109.
45 Leo M. Kaiser, ed., "Letters from the Front", *Journal of the Illinois State Historical Society,* LVI (Summer, 1963), p.154
46 Robert U. Johnson and C.C. Buel (eds.), *Battles and Leaders of the Civil War* (New York, 1884-88), IV, p.418.
47 Dudley T. Cornish, *The Sable Arm* (New York, 1956), p.261.
48 U.S. War Department, *War of the Rebellion: Official Records of the Union and Confederate Armies* (Washington, 1880-1901), Series IV, Volume III, pp.1009-10.
49 R.L.T. Beale, *History of the Ninth Virginia Cavalry in the War Between the States* (Richmond, 1899), p.9.
50 Wiley, *Billy Yank*, p.23
51 *Ibid.*, pp.337-8.

CHAPTER TWO

Drill, Drill & More Drill

The great question after the first rush to the colors was where North and South would first meet in battle. Almost inevitably it had to come in Virginia, for the Confederates had moved their national capital to Richmond, just 100 miles south of Washington, ensuring that major efforts to protect both capitals would result in heavy troop concentrations in the area. The first skirmishes came at isolated places, and in civil riots in cities like Baltimore and St. Louis where citizens with Southern sympathies clashed with Federal troops. Seeing Rebel flags flying just across the Potomac from Washington at Arlington and Alexandria, Federal authorities occupied both towns in May, and took their first blooding. Soon the armed forces themselves were meeting each other in inconsequential skirmishes in western Virginia and on the Virginia peninsula at Big Bethel. There were small fights west of the Mississippi, too, at Boonville, Missouri, as both sides fought over control of that teetering state.

Yet all this was a prelude for what was to come in the summer. In western Virginia a Federal army under a new general, George McClellan, in two small battles seized control of much of that loyal part of Virginia, soon to become a new state. Out in Missouri, after suffering a setback at Carthage, Federal forces met the Rebels once again at Wilson's Creek on August 10 in the most important battle of the war in that state. The Confederate victory there opened up much of the state for Southern occupation and demoralized the beaten Union forces.

Towering over all, however, both in proportion and importance, was the battle of July 21, along the banks of Bull Run, near Manassas Junction, Virginia. Called by both the stream and the town's name, it was a decisive Confederate victory that sent the defeated Yankees streaming back to the safety of Washington and gave Southern morale a giant boost, and Union resolve a severe test. Both sides were soon to learn that it would not be such a short war after all. There was a long road of training ahead for men in blue and gray.

THE FIRST basic training the new recruits received frequently took place at the regimental rendezvous, well before the men marched away to join the armies. A little drill, some exposure to weapons, informal organization into companies, and perhaps the issuing of uniforms, was all they did. In many regiments, an additional ritual was the election of their officers.

These were volunteer outfits, and the custom in the old Union for decades had been for volunteers to select their own commanders. There were good reasons for such a seemingly unmilitary practice. For one thing, many regiments were raised by the personal magnetism and local reputation of one or two individuals, and men who enlisted because of their regard for the man who recruited them would naturally want him to command. Also, independent as always, the American citizen-soldier would resent having some outsider imposed upon him by the War Department. The policy inevitably led to all manner of excesses, with venal men bribing others to vote for them. The system, unfortunately, led to a host of inexperienced and incompetent men being put in command of regiments, where only time and attrition would weed them out.

In campgrounds from Maine to Texas, the task of turning raw recruits into soldiers took place on the drill field; as here in the camps of the 1st Connecticut Artillery near Washington, D.C.

Above: Early in the war as the young men rushed to the colors, like this gold-braided soldier of the 31st New York Infantry, they came in a dazzling array of ersatz uniforms, often sewn by wives or sweethearts.

Above: For these new soldiers the day of their leaving for war was a great occasion. Here the 1st Michigan Infantry receives its colors in Detroit on May 1, 1861, ready for their first taste of battle at Bull Run.

Below: As with these men of the 7th New York State Militia, who were among the first to answer the call, the new colors would be a source of endless pride, many sacrificing themselves in battle by carrying them.

Inevitably a delegation of ladies from hometowns came to the public square on departure day to bestow an ornate flag, frequently sewn from their wedding dresses, upon the regiment. Flowery fustian speeches invariably accompanied the proceeding. "This eve we were presented with a flag by the Ladies of this town", a Bay State officer wrote on July 22, 1861. "A very homely young lady (though she was the best looking one in town) made a speech which she learned (at least she thought so, but I did not for she went through with [it] about as smooth as one might come down a rocky hill in the dark)."[1] Then an officer accepted the proferred banner in glowing words of thanks and promised never to disgrace the cloth.

Sometimes the ceremony did not go too well. In Fayetteville, North Carolina, the ladies came up with the flag well enough, but all were too shy to attempt to make the obligatory speech. Instead, they asked a local orator of small repute to do it for them. Alas, he appeared on the stand apparently much the worse for drink, wavered on his feet and plunged through his speech by fits and starts, then proceeded to repeat most of it over a second time. That done, overcome, he sank into his chair and wept.[2]

Stirring as such festivities could be, and often were, the big moment in the recruit's life came when he and his regiment left for the field. It was a time of mixed feelings: elation at the glorious prospect ahead, and sadness in parting from family and friends. A reporter found a company of students from the University of Iowa "in first rate spirits" and "rightly impressed with the patriotic duty confided to their hearts and muskets". Yet many a soldier suffered last-minute second thoughts about leaving. "One of the men whilst bidding his wife good buy Whimpered a little and Showed Signs of backout", wrote William Shaw. "His Wife told him if he was agoing to Cry about it to pull off his Breeches and she would put them on and go in his place and he might go home and tend the Farm."[3]

Private, 9th New York Infantry Regiment "Hawkins' Zouaves"

In 1861 Rush C. Hawkins, a veteran of the Mexican War went to work finding men for a new regiment. Starting with members of the old pre-war Company of New York Zouaves, he enlisted enough men to muster his 9th New York Infantry on May 4, 1861. Thanks to their uniform, they were quickly dubbed "Hawkins' Zouaves". They fought at Big Bethel in June, 1861, then went on to campaign in North Carolina before returning to take part in the Battles of Antietam and Fredericksburg. They were mustered out in May 1863. The uniforms that gave them their name were typical of zouave outfits: skullcap, short jacket and baggy pants tucked into white leggings. Armed with 1861 Springfield's and bayonet, they lent color to their army. Though how colorful it was in 1863 is open to debate. Hard wear and a uniform that looked as if it were made for Rebel target practice may have toned it down.

It was a host of average and unusual units that said those farewells and marched or sailed or steamed off to war. Four out of five of them were infantry, the backbone of the army. Artillery comprised only six percent of both armies, and cavalry made up the rest. On either side, these units reflected the colorful diversity of Americans in culture, education, and taste. The Richmond Howitzers, the Washington Artillery of New Orleans, South Carolina's Hampton Legion, and the Oglethorpe Light Infantry of Savannah, boasted the affluent and educated flower of Confederate society. Lexington, Virginia's Washington College furnished seventy-three students for the Liberty Hall Volunteers – fully a quarter of them studying for the ministry. At the opposite extreme were companies of farmboys so raw and unschooled that over a quarter of the men in the 11th North Carolina's Company A, for example, could not sign their names, and exactly half of the recruits for another company could only make their mark on the muster roll when they enlisted.

They marched out of their hometowns garbed not only in righteousness, but also cloaked in nicknames calculated to terrify the enemy. Out of the woods and hills of the Confederacy came the "Tallapoosa Thrashers", the "Bartow Yankee Killers", the "Dixie Heroes", "Hornet's Nest Riflemen", "Clinch Mountain Boomers", "Franklin Fire Eaters", and the "Tyranny Unmasked Artillery". It would be hard to decide just who was to be intimidated, however, by the one East Tennessee company enigmatically known as "Bell's Babies".[4]

The North, too, had its share of unusual outfits. The 7th New York, composed of the fashionable elite of Grammarcy Park, went to war with 1,000 velvet-covered footstools among its equippage. "Birney's Zouaves", the 23rd Pennsylvania, averaged just nineteen years of age in the ranks, while the 37th Iowa was restricted to men over forty-five and, not surprisingly, was known as the "Graybeard Regiment". To enlist in "Ellsworth's Avengers", the 44th New York, a recruit had to be unmarried, thirty, at least five feet eight inches tall, and of demonstrably good moral character. The officers of the 48th New York were all ministers of the gospel, and in honor of their colonel called themselves "Perry's Saints". The 33rd Illinois contained so many college professors that it became known as the "Teacher's Regiment". Its officers were frequently accused of ignoring any order that was not framed in precisely the correct spelling and syntax. A vow to "touch not, taste not, handle not spiritous or malt liquor, wine or cider", led a band of Iowans to be dubbed the "Temperance Regiment".[5]

By the second half of the war, however, the men marching off to the regiments were not to be so high toned. The battlefield was a voracious consumer of men, and as the war dragged onward without conclusion, the first enthusiastic and patriotic rush of enlistments settled down to a trickle. The most motivated men had signed on early. What remained were the under- and over-age, the uninterested, the infirm and the cowardly. Inevitably the need to fill the vacancies in the ranks forced both the governments of Washington and Richmond to resort to conscription, the military draft. It was never popular with anyone, and unfortunately it tended to bring into service many of the least desirable, with the result that the overall quality of soldier in the regiments declined steadily after 1863.

Ironically, the threat of the draft actually inspired many men to join of their own volition. Better that than be branded as a conscript, and at least an enlistee usually got a cash bonus. "God knows that the country needs men and I regard it as the duty of every able bodied man who can possibly do so to enlist at once, the sooner the better", wrote W.H. Jackson of Vermont, adding "and it is better by far to enlist voluntarily than to be dragged into the army a conscript. Nothing to me would appear more degrading."[6]

Conscripts, substitutes – those whom wealthy men paid to go to war in their place – and naive youths flooded into the Northern and Southern armies after 1863. The lines drawn along wealth and class by the substitute system rankled the poor especially. "All they want is to get you pupt up and go to fight for their infurnal negroes", complained an Alabama hill farmer, "and after you do there fighting you may kiss there hine parts fur all they care."[7] The lament of it being a "rich man's war and a poor man's fight" was heard

Union Zouave Uniforms and Equipment

Numbers *1-5*. Uniform of Corporal Walter H. Mallorie, Co. B, 76th Pa. Vols. "Keystone Zouaves"

1 Zouave fez
2 Uniform pantaloons
3 Short jacket with insignia and badge
4 Jambiére, or outer legging of leather
5 Uniform gaiter
6 US brass belt plate
7 Uniform jacket of 72nd Pa. Vols worn by Private Edward A. Fulton when wounded at Antietam
8 Corps badge
9 Model 1845 French Infantry Bugle, carried by G.W. Freeman, Co. H, 62nd Pa. Vol Infantry
10 Wooden small arms ammunition box for 1000 rounds

Numbers *11-13*. Uniform of 114th Pa. Vols, "Collis' Zoauves", worn by Private Thaddeus Paxon, Co. F, who died of disease January 11, 1863

11 Embroidered uniform jacket
12 Pantaloons
13 Fez
14 Fez complete with regimental badge which belonged to Private Latham Avery Fish, Co. C, 9th NY Vol. Infantry, and worn at Antietam
15 Screwtop tin drum canteen

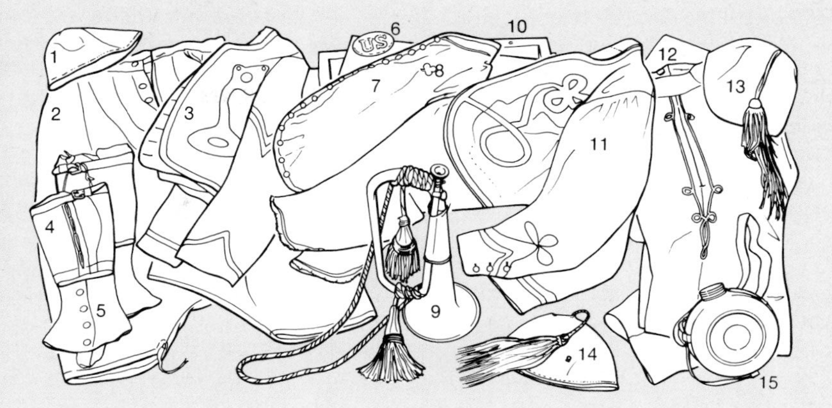

Artifacts courtesy of: Don Troiani, military artist

on both sides of Mason and Dixon's line.

Another problem with these later recruits was the condition they were in when they reached the camps. Doctors, themselves often not too competent, were shocked at what they saw. Some recruitment "brokers", who received a commission for every man they induced to enlist, actually persuaded inmates of a New York insane asylum to sign up as substitutes, leaving it to the army physicians to worry over what to do with them. A New York artillery unit had to eliminate more than a third of its new replacements in 1864, all for unsound health. Men commonly showed with missing or impaired limbs, failed eyesight and hearing, and often communicable diseases. As a result, the veterans in the ranks felt a natural skepticism toward the new recruits in later years, sometimes approaching loathing.

"They were moral lepers", complained one Yankee. "They were conscienceless, cowardly scoundrels, and the clean-minded American and Irish and German volunteers would not associate with them." They were, he protested, "the weak, the diseased, the feeble-minded, the scum of the slums of the great European and American cities." Many were blackguards, and others "the rakings of rural almshouses and the never-do-wells of villages." Such strong words about "the worthless character of the recruits who were supplied to the army" were commonplace, and few veterans would have offered a dissent.[8] Sergeant Charles Loehr of the 1st Virginia Cavalry looked at a number of replacements received late in 1864 and complained that "some of them looked like they had been resurrected from the grave, after laying therein for twenty years or more."[9] A New Englander was even more emphatic when he declared that "such another depraved, vice-hardened and desperate set of human beings never before disgraced an army."[10]

Undoubtedly much of this disdain stemmed from the widely known fact that a huge proportion of these later recruits would desert, many of them men who enlisted under false names to get a bounty, fully intending to run away at the first

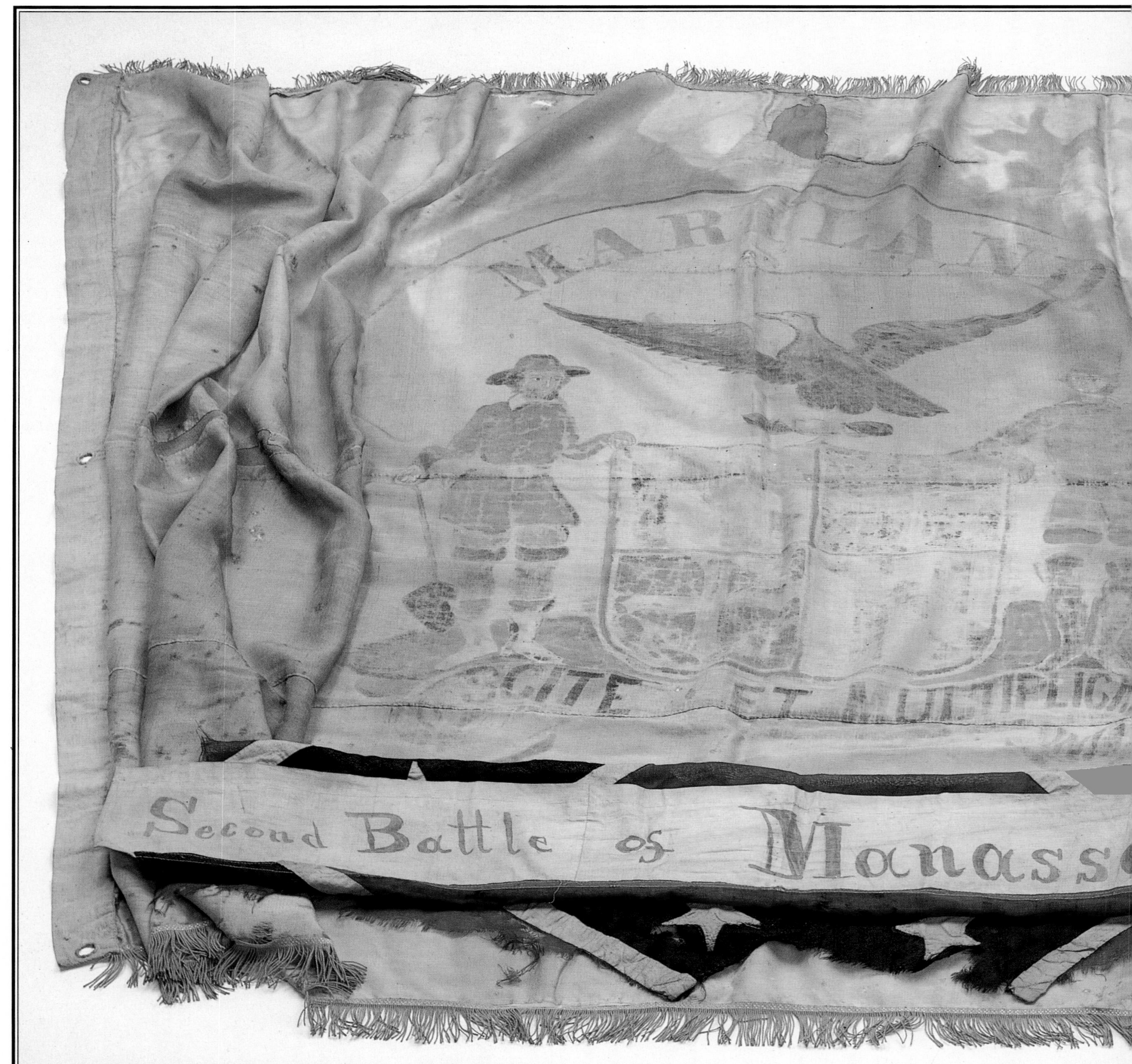

Confederate Unit Flags

When Johnny Reb marched off to war, he carried aloft the silks and cottons of his native state, proudly emblazoned with the patriotic sentiments of his spirit, the loving wishes of his homefolk and the defiance of his foe. "Victory or Death", some regimental banners proclaimed, echoing their Revolutionary forefathers. Some flags carried their units' nicknames, like the "Bartow Yankee Killers" and "Floyd Rangers". Sometimes the colors had been lovingly sewn out of the fabric of wedding dresses. Often they were adapted from the flags of local militia. Frequently they were simply sewn bits of color to act as symbolic banners until the national government furnished genuine regulation banners. Of course, complete military uniformity in flags, as with every other facet of army supply, always evaded the South. Material such as silk, cotton, wools; wedding dresses, even grain sacks all did service as battle colors.

1 Maryland State Seal flag
2 Confederate First National Flag carried by the "Dixie Rangers"
3 Army of Northern Virginia battleflag fragment
4 Battleflag of the 3rd Florida Infantry

Artifacts courtesy of: The Museum of The Confederacy, Richmond, Va

opportunity to enlist again and again under different names. The only salutary effect of the sorry business was that the men who stayed in the ranks were the better soldiers, and seasoned veterans. "If new men won't finish the job", said one man from Massachusetts, "old men must, and as long as Uncle Sam wants a man", he was ready and willing to stay in the service.[11] Thus it would be left chiefly to the real Johnny Rebs and Billy Yanks to finish off what they had begun. The original volunteers of 1861 and 1862 re-enlisted in vast numbers when their first hitches expired, evidence that though their enthusiasm might have been tempered, yet their conviction to the cause and sense of duty remained high.

Perhaps it was also in part due to the fact that the old veterans knew the life of the soldier intimately, and had grown accustomed to it, however much they might resent and resist its regimentation. Certainly they knew all too well the endless lot of the private soldier, and that was drill. The first taste they had seen of marching in time and step in their recruiting camps hardly prepared them for the incessant bondage to drum and bugle to follow. Private Oliver Norton of the 83rd Pennsylvania aptly captured the essence of the military's preoccupation with evolutions. "The first thing in the morning is drill", he wrote home, "then drill, then drill again. Then drill, drill, a little more drill. Then drill, and lastly drill. Between drills, we drill and sometimes stop to eat a little and have roll-call."[12]

Those first days in training camp were hectic and confused. At 5 a.m. the reveille calls of the bugles jarred sleep-fuddled men out of their blankets more rudely than the wakening calls of the mothers and wives they had left behind. For the farmboys, the early rising was little problem, but for the city-bred and the sons of wealthy planters and businessmen, being aroused before dawn took more than a little getting used to. Almost drunkenly they shambled out on to the company street or parade ground and stumbled to find their places in the line, pulling on what clothes they had remembered or were able to find in the dark. "Some wore one shoe, and others appeared shivering in their line", newspaperman George Townsend wrote. "They stood ludicrously in rank, and a succession of short, dry coughs ran up and down the line."[13]

Above: More typical of the haphazard array of clothing on Southerners, is Edwards' image of these drilling men of the 9th Mississippi. Shirts, hats, coats – nothing matches, except their determination.

Even at this early hour there could be some drilling in store for them before they were sent to their breakfast. Then came guard posting and sick call, followed by the host of chores necessary to keep the camp neat and – when possible – clean. Then came "dinner", the noonday meal, several hours of fatigue duty, and two or three more hours of regimental drill. Around 5 p.m., when they had already been actively engaged for a full twelve hours, the men returned to their tents with an hour to prepare themselves and their weapons and equipment for the 6 o'clock dress parade. That done, supper was waiting for them in the huge boiling cauldrons at the mess tents, and then, finally, they had a couple of precious hours to themselves before the 9 o'clock "lights out". It has been a packed day for the new men, and each day was just like the one before it, with only some respite on Sundays with church services and perhaps a few extra afternoon hours of free time.

Much of this unrelenting activity was designed to keep the soldiers too busy to get into trouble, as well as to accustom them to following orders automatically and without question. Neither goal was ever achieved entirely. "We had good organization, good men, but no cohesion", William T. Sherman lamented after the Federal defeat at First Manassas or Bull Run in July 1861; "no respect for authority, no real knowledge of war."[14] The soldier hated taking orders, and many officers shrank from giving them. Men obeyed those directives which seemed sensible and sound to them, but often only because they saw the use of such orders. If a man, a volunteer, doubted the wisdom of an order, he was very likely to question it at least, and refuse to obey at worst. Additionally the close personal familiarity between officers and men worked against discipline. Men in the ranks could find their brothers and childhood playmates put in positions of authority and it was hard to stand quietly and stoically take orders from someone they had grown up with. It was hard to salute and stand at attention before one whom the private saw not as his officer but as a neighboring farmer, the village

Below: Confederate photographer Jay D. Edwards captured this scene of raw recruits being drilled in Fort McRee, Pensacola, Florida, early in 1861. These men present a uniformity rarely seen in Rebel armies.

blacksmith, or perhaps his old school teacher.

It was to break down all these impediments to discipline that the war departments of North and South imposed a regimen of drill and training upon their soldiers. In fact, since both Union and Confederate armies were largely officered in the early days by men who had served in the pre-1861 military service, the "Old Army" as it was called, and since many had shared military education at the United States Military Academy at West Point, the manuals and methods they used to train the new regiments were virtually identical North and South.

There were a number of drill manuals available, including one penned by General Winfield Scott in 1835, a translation of a French work. By 1860, however, most of his work had been revised and updated by William J. Hardee, soon to become a Confederate lieutenant general. *Hardee's Tactics*, as it became known, was the most influential manual in the first two years of the war, especially since it included maneuvers designed to incorporate the influence of the rela-

Above: The training camps teemed with men trying to master the drill manuals. Here at Camp Butler, near Cairo, Illinois, the parade ground echoed in 1861 to the sounds of marching feet and swearing officers.

Below: Some of the formations they learnt dated back to the time of Napoleon and were rarely used, such as this square designed to break up cavalry charges, demonstrated by this Yankee outfit in Virginia.

Below: Learning to advance in skirmish order. This formation enabled scattered parties of men to move in advance of the main body, using their rifle fire to harass and disrupt the enemy before an assault.

tively new rifled musket upon the movement of men. Indeed, so versatile was *Hardee's* that it came out in several editions "tailored" for its users, including one for black troops, another for the fancy French-inspired zouave regiments, another for the use of militia, several Southern editions, and one Northern edition which omitted Hardee's name from the title page.

Hardee exerted a lot of influence on the Civil War battlefield. He prescribed that the line of battle move in two ranks, one behind the other. Skirmishers who moved in advance of the main lines were to operate in four-man squads, and the time-step at which men moved was updated to allow for a "double quick" speed of up to 180 steps a minute. With a rifled musket able to fire two or three rounds per minute in the hands of skilled infantrymen, soldiers had to move faster than ever before. Hardee decreed that markmanship had to be improved through target practice, and that some units should be designated to move at a rate of five miles per hour while still keeping some order. In the main, however, it was still a manual in the Napoleonic tradition, assuming that battles would be fought between armies standing upright in the open, and firing by volley.

Even Hardee was soon superseded, however, with the 1862 publication of Silas Casey's *Infantry Tactics.* Casey was a Union brigadier himself, and at fifty-five one of the oldest and most experienced officers in the service. He issued his work in three volumes covering individual and company drill, battalion drill, and evolutions for brigade and corps units. It was the first comprehensive manual adapted and designed for the kind of military organizations then in service, and it was quickly adopted by both sides. Unlike its predecessors, however, it benefited from its author's year and more of field experience on the battlefields of Virginia. Casey knew that raw American volunteers were easily baffled by all the obscure jargon of most manuals, much of it in French or German. He greatly simplified his descriptions of maneuvers, using everyday language that was clear and concise. Inexperienced

Southern State and Confederate Buckles and Plates

1 Oval Maryland State Seal Plate
2 Maryland State Seal sword belt plate
3 Oval Mississippi State Seal plate
4 Alabama State Seal sword belt plate
5 Oval Alabama State Seal plate
6 Louisiana State Seal plate
7 Oval South Carolina plate
8 Texas plate
9 Oval plate of the Alabama Volunteer Corps
10 Virginia State Seal sword belt plate
11 Oval Texas plate
12 Virginia State Seal sword belt plate
13 CSA plate, Eastern Theater
14 Oval CS plate with beaded border, Western Theater
15 CSA rectangular plate, silvered
16 CSA plate, Eastern Theater
17 CS sword belt plate
18 Oval CS plate, Eastern Theater
19 CS rectangular sword belt plate
20 Oval CSA plate
21 Pewter CSA plate, Western Theater
22 Oval CS plate, Western Theater
23 CSA plate, Western Theater
24 Oval CS plate

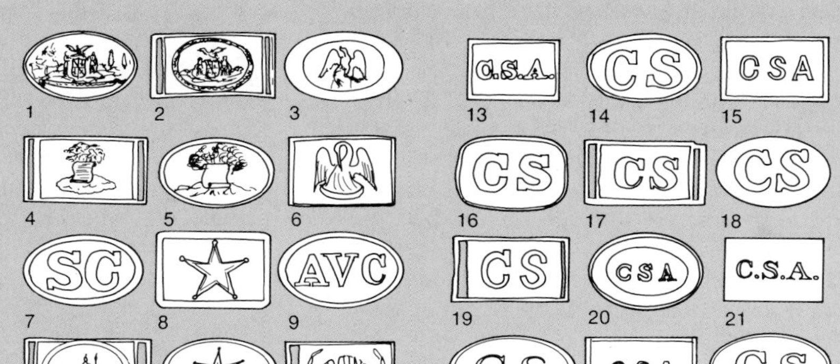

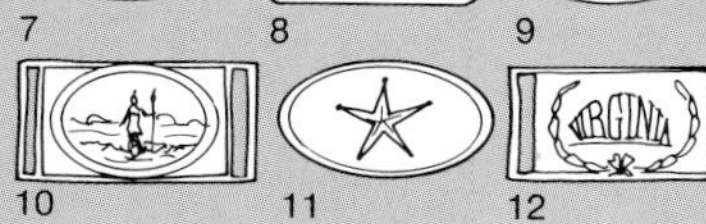

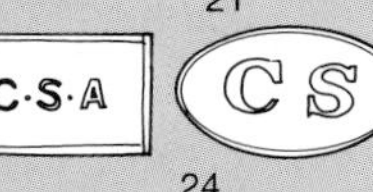

Artifacts courtesy of: Virginia Historical Society, Richmond, Va

officers could intelligibly work out where they were supposed to be in brigade drill, and simple country boys could understand what was expected of them. "If the system here set forth shall in any manner cause our armies to act with more efficiency on the field of battle", wrote Casey, "and thus subserve the cause of our beloved country in this her hour of trial, my most heartfelt wishes will have been attained."[15]

Whichever manual they were trained from, the daily exercises of the soldiers, North and South, were much the same. Most regiments, especially at the war's outset, plunged into their drilling with an enthusiasm which only waned as the days of practice seemed to go on interminably. "It is drill, drill, battalion drill, and dress parade", wrote one soldier of his daily regime.[16]

The officers were out to achieve two specific tactical goals with their drill. One was morale, *esprit de corps*. A regiment or brigade which looked smart at its evolutions took pride in itself, and unit pride was a powerful motivator once the men went into battle. The other goal was what they described as "tactical articulation" in the moments prior to combat. Simply put, it meant the speedy and precise movement of large numbers of men from one point to another. A commander needed to be armed with a whole set of commands to move men down a road in ranks of four, or to march them across country, over fences, through woods, across streams, to turn them left or right, or about face, with all manner of natural and manmade obstacles to impede their progress. Getting them from a column into a battleline several hundred yards wide in just a few moments would have taken forever if a commander simply told the men to break ranks and make a line. By having a succession of specific commands, however, he could tell a thousand men how to do so almost instantly, with no confusion. This was especially important when some generals had to move not just companies or regiments, but brigades of three thousand or more, and even divisions and corps which could number up to five times that number.

Confederate Infantry Equipment

What the Rebel soldier wore showed the deplorable state of Confederate supply. Scores of regiments equipped themselves locally before going off to war, but as clothing and equipment wore out it was often up to the private soldier to replace it himself. Even what the Richmond government did manage to distribute was often of wildly varying quality. Uniforms alone varied from gray so dark as to be almost blue, to butter-nuts and browns – all of it supposedly the official "cadet gray". As for the items prescribed as "regulation issue", only a few regiments raised early in the war ever got them all. In time, an issue of new socks would be a memorable day.

1 1st Sergeants frock coat
2 Forage cap
3 Linen havelock
4 Trousers for 1st Sergeant's frock coat
5 Uniform vest for 1st Sergeant's frock coat and trousers
6 Shirt
7 Cartridge box
8 Cap box
9 Fayetteville rifle
10 Brogans
11 Wooden canteen name of owner inscribed
12 Haversack
13 Model 1860 Colt Army revolver and holster
14 Side knives

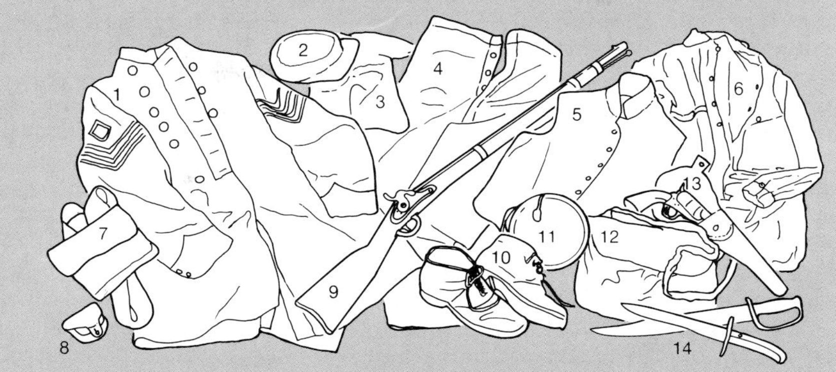

Artifacts courtesy of: The Museum of The Confederacy, Richmond, Va

Contrary to the impression they had at the time, Civil War soldiers probably suffered less drilling than did their counterparts in later wars. They exercised by squads, companies, and regiments, practised the manual of arms, and learned to perform the requisite turns and facings. They learned their formations in order of battle, how to stand at attention and rest, how to march both in common time – ninety steps per minute – and at the several faster paces. They learned these things individually, and by the company and regiment, and so forth. Those assigned as skirmishers – and it could be anyone, so everyone learned the routine – had to learn how to move in advance of the main line in any direction, how to withdraw, how to fire from the ground or prone position, and how to fire while moving.

Since all of the essential orders could not be heard from a single voice by hundreds or thousands of men on the parade ground, much less in the din of battle, the men had to learn a host of drum rolls and bugle calls which specifically transmitted certain orders. There were fifteen general drum and twenty-six bugle "calls" for the men in the ranks, and twenty-three more bugle and drum calls for skirmishers. In battalion drill, the men had to learn to open and close ranks, to shift from line of battle to a column and back again, changing front in battle formations to meet a cavalry attack, and so forth. In regimental and brigade drill, it was very much the same.

No wonder that, even with Casey's simplified tactics, many officers and men were bewildered by it all as they began their turns on the drilling field. Frequently, even the simplest exercises left green young officers at a loss. When Captain Daniel Candler of Georgia found that he was marching his company directly toward a fence, he was at a loss over what to do. At the last instant he ordered the men to halt. "Gentlemen", he then announced, "we will now take a recess of ten minutes. Break ranks! And when you fall in, will you please re-form on the other side of the fence."[17]

When ambitious leaders tried to impose the

Union Infantry Equipment

For the men in blue, equipment – while sometimes scarce – was usually plentiful and of standard quality. Even though Billy Yank had to cope with shoes that did not fit, wool uniforms that were too warm in summer and too soggy in the wet, only the more remote units had real trouble replacing essential pieces of equipment or uniform.

1 Hardee hat
2 Infantryman's overcoat
3 Neck stock
4 Forage cap
5 Soft knapsack
6 2nd Corps Headquarters flag
7 Model 1840 Non-commissioned Officer's sword and shoulder belt
8 Enlisted man's shoulder scales
9 .69 caliber cartridge box
10 Haversack
11 Model 1858 covered tin drum canteen
12 Brogans
13 Sack coat
14 Infantryman's uniform trousers
15 Model 1842 rifled and sighted musket
16 Infantry accoutrements: belt, cap box, bayonet and scabbard, cartridge box
17 Soft knapsack
18 Soft knapsack

Artifacts courtesy of: J. Craig Nannos Collection: 1-5, 7-14, 16-18; The Civil War Library and Museum, Philadelphia, Pa: 6, 12

more intricate drill practised by some of the zouave and other parade ground units on these raw new recruits, the result was all too predictable. Virginia artilleryman George Eggleston lamented that in some regiments "maneuvers of the most utterly impossible sort were taught to the men, every amateur officer had his own pet system of tactics", he went on, "and the effect of the incongruous teachings, when brought out in battalion drill, closely resembled that of the music at Mr. Bob Sawyer's party, where each guest sang the chorus to the tune he knew best."[18] Welcome, indeed, was the down-to-earth officer who could cut through jargon and simply make his point with the men. When Captain John Trice of the 4th Kentucky Infantry was asked what he would do to meet the Yankee foe, he answered, "Well, Major, I can"t answer that according to the books, but I would risk myself and the Trigg County boys, and go in on main strength and awkwardness." Another backwoods officer, quizzed on the orders he would give to move his unit obliquely to one side, responded that the proper jargon evaded him, but he would "move the reegiment *stauchendicilar* to the right".[19]

Even when they understood their officers and their drill, all too many men were unfamiliar with their new weapons. In the first few weeks of training, and in the months of drill that followed, accidents were inevitable. Cavalrymen drilling with sabers in their hands for the first time frequently drew blood from their horses and themselves as they tried to master the heavy and clumsy weapons. Artillerymen new to their posi-

Private, Washington Light Infantry

Composed of young men from the best Rebel families, the Washington Light Infantry of Charleston, South Carolina was typical of the more high-minded companies to volunteer for Confederate service at the war's outset. When the call finally came, some of Charleston's finest went off to war in 1861 accompanied by servants, picnic hampers and ornate tents. It was July 1863 after they had served in and around Charleston after Fort Sumter, that the WLI was merged into the 25th South Carolina Infantry. The regiment remained in its native state until early 1864, when it moved to Richmond and the seige of Petersburg. Most of the regiment was later captured at Fort Fisher, North Carolina. Early in the war the regiment was well kitted-out and wore a well-tailored gray blouse, with gray or natty white trousers and carried their initials in the "WLI" badge on their kepis. Armed with Mississippi Rifles, they fought for the confederacy from first till last.

Above: This cavalryman is apparently blowing 'draw sabers', as he has his own partly unsheathed. This Yank and his mount are the picture of the cavalryman – lean, lightly equipped for speed, and dashing.

tions could be even more dangerous. For practice one day, members of one Massachusetts battery took aim on a tree atop a hill some 1,000 yards distant. Yet they carelessly set the elevation screws on their guns for 1,600 yards instead, and then calmly lobbed their shells completely over the tree, and the hill, and into a village on the other side.

As for the infantrymen, they would spend most of their time with their rifles, but they also had to master the use of a terrible, much-feared weapon at its muzzle, the bayonet. Thanks to legends from earlier wars, and the initially accepted tactics of this one, nothing held more terror for a soldier than the thought of facing a bayonet charge. The sharpened triangular blade, eighteen inches or more in length, with deep grooves presumed to allow a victim's blood to drain effectively, had won battles in past conflicts thanks merely to the frightening aspect of a line of brightly polished blades advancing across the field. In this war, however, their role would prove to be less than minor. Only four out of every thousand wounds treated by Union surgeons would come from the bayonet and saber combined. Most men would use them as candlesticks and fire spits. In fact, they inflicted far more wounds on the practice field as recruits tried to wield them in the complex bayonet drill. When one Green Mountain boy watched his regiment at practice, he found that they looked like "a line of beings made up about equally of the frog, the sand-hill crane, the sentinel crab, and the grasshopper; all of them rapidly jumping, thrusting, swinging, striking, jerking every which way, and all gone stark mad."[20] Ironically, many of these weapons were turned to more peaceful use after the end of the war. Farmers in the impoverished South often converted them into scyths, sickles and hoes.

Below: Soldiers, like these well-equipped Yankees with their Harper's Ferry Rifles, sword-bayonets, full knapsacks with bedrolls, and well-leathered shoes were the ideal that North and South sent to war.

Above: Men of the 1st Ohio Heavy Artillery drilling with a Parrott rifle, probably near Knoxville, Tennessee. Often a danger to their own side, such gunners would learn to do great damage to the enemy.

Yet in time they all learned enough to get where they had to be, and do what they had to do. Despite a few outfits which became so proficient at their evolutions that they engaged in and won drill competitions, most regiments simply followed their orders out of habit. They became soldiers, of a sort; they never became drill-perfect performers.

References

1 Wiley, *Billy Yank*, p.30.
2 Wiley, *Johnny Reb*, pp.21-2.
3 Wiley and Milhollen, *They Who Fought Here*, p.28.
4 Wiley, *Johnny Reb*, p.20.
5 Lurton D. Ingersoll, *Iowa and the Rebellion* (Philadelphia, 1867), pp.501, 513.
6 Wiley, *Billy Yank*, p.38.
7 *Journal of Southern History*, XXIII (December 1957), p.525.
8 Wiley, *Billy Yank*, p.284.
9 Charles T. Loehr, *War History of the Old First Virginia Infantry Regiment* (Richmond, 1884), p.53.
10 McPherson, *Ordeal*, p.410.
11 John G.B. Adams, *Reminiscenses of the Nineteenth Massachusetts Regiment* (Boston, 1899), pp.79, 89.
12 Oliver W. Norton, *Army Letters, 1861-1865* (Chicago, 1903), p.28.
13 Wiley, *Billy Yank*, p.45.
14 William T. Sherman, *Memoirs* (New York, 1890), I, pp.209-10.
15 Silas Casey, *U.S. Infantry Tactics. . .* (Philadelphia, 1862), I, p.7.
16 Paddy Griffith, *Rally Once Again* (Ramsbury, U.K., 1987), p.105
17 Wiley and Milhollen, *They Who Fought Here*, pp.41-2.
18 George C. Eggleston, *A Rebel's Recollections* (New York, 1875), p.20.
19 Davis, *The Orphan Brigade*, p.50.
20 S. Millett Thompson, *Thirteenth Regiment of New Hampshire Volunteer Infantry* (Boston, 1888), p.221.

SIEGE OF

CHAPTER THREE

Load & Fire

Mercifully for both sides, the Union defeats at Bull Run and Wilson's Creek ended most active campaigning for the rest of 1861, as both North and South struggled to build the kind of armies needed for continental warfare. More Southern successes in Missouri came later in the year, but it was not to be until the early part of 1862 that the North would strike back. The blow came as a thunderbolt named Grant in the west, and a young Napoleon named McClellan in the east.

Envisioning a campaign to split the Confederacy in two by taking control of the Mississippi River, a new brigadier, Ulysses S. Grant, led a combined land and riverborne attack against Forts Henry and Donelson, guarding access to the Tennessee and Cumberland Rivers. If he could take them, he could use those rivers to isolate large portions of the western Confederacy, securing his own base on the upper Mississippi, and driving a wedge deep into the Confederate heartland. In February he took them both within ten days, then moved south along the Tennessee almost to the Mississippi border. There he became briefly careless, and was taken by surprise when General Albert Sidney Johnston's Confederate army caught him on April 6 and commenced the Battle of Shiloh. In the bitterest fighting ever seen west of the Alleghenies, Grant was pushed back and almost beaten, but he held his ground, and the next day pushed his foe back. For the first time a major Federal army had met and held its own against the enemy. A few weeks later New Orleans fell to Commodore David Farragut's fleet, thus securing the Union hold on both ends of the Mississippi.

Meanwhile in Virginia, McClellan, urged on by cries of "on to Richmond", had taken his Army of the Potomac by water to the peninsula between the James and York Rivers, attempting to take Richmond by the back door. But Rebel General Joseph E. Johnston held him in a siege at Yorktown for fully a month, buying Richmond precious time, and revealing McClellan's overcautious side. It was a busy spring, with the sound of thousands of guns everywhere and a voracious need for more and better weapons.

WHEN THE war commenced, boastful Confederates proclaimed that, "We can lick 'em with cornstalks". Four years later, the war and their Southern nation a memory, they had to add, "But, d--m 'em, they wouldn't fight us that way!"[1] Of course, neither side would fight that way. If they had, it would have made for a very peculiar, and mercifully bloodless sort of war. But cornstalks would have to wait for another time, for in 1861 the plowshares were beaten into swords, and North America became an armed continent.

Nothing could have been more fortuitous than the timing of the war's coming, at least so far as the makers of weapons were concerned. For the men who had to use and suffer by those arms, of course, it was a different story. Because only now was the nation technologically 'ready' for a civil war. Had the two sides come to blows thirty or even twenty years earlier, there would have been little contest. In 1840, with almost all small arms in the country still smoothbores, the sections simply could not have fought a war that was either very costly in human lives, or very effective on the battlefields. In 1861, however, the technological development of the country ensured that when brother fired upon brother, he could do so with terrible force, and with a steady supply of weapons to equip the millions of men of military age north and south of the Mason–Dixon line.

In a war that would see all manner of innovative weapons come and go, none would achieve the place earned by the Henry repeating rifle, here being carried by the 7th Illinois Infantry.

In the previous decade especially, there had come to fruition a manufacturing revolution called, for want of a better name, the American System. It was, in essence, the forerunner of modern mass production. Weapons and machinery of war which formerly had to be made slowly and largely by hand, were now made almost entirely by machine, by something approaching assembly line techniques. As well as these "advantages", advances in ballistics now gave the gun, through rifling, a major advance in range and accuracy. Thus, consciously, North and South had waited until they had the capability to wage a real and bloody war, before they actually began one.

A generation before the firing on Fort Sumter, American soldiers were still carrying old-style flintlock muskets, which were smoothbores with a limited range and, within that range, indifferent accuracy. A series of inventions, however, gradually put in motion a rapid technological evolution during the first half of the 19th century. Among these in particular was the development of the percussion lock.

No more did the soldier have to pour powder into a flash pan, and hope that the flint striking the frizzen would send sparks into the pan, ignite the powder, send a flame through a vent into the barrel, and finally discharge the piece – he hoped without putting out his eye with sparks or flint chips in the process. Now a copper percussion cap simply fitted over a nipple affixed to the weapon's breech. The hammer striking the cap sent a spark into the barrel. Barring a defective cap, a clogged nipple, or a weak hammer spring, the lock would fire every time, and in all weather, and with a faster rate of fire. Research into ballistics established marginally more accurate sights, and even more important strides were made in the general acceptance of rifling for improving accuracy and range. Probably most significant was the introduction of the cylindroconoidal Minié bullet, generally if inaptly called the "minnie ball". Where spherical bullets or balls had been used before, the new Minié was more stable in its flight, greatly improving accuracy, while its hollow base, which expanded into the barrel's grooves at firing, ensured that it took full advantage of the benefits of rifling.[2]

Below: Like this Rebel recruit with his shotgun and 'D' guard bowie knife, Johnny Reb often went to war armed with whatever he could find at home, since his government could often supply him with very little.

All of these improvements foresaw the change in attitude toward the infantryman which the Civil War would help bring about. Older and less effective weapons had constrained the foot-soldier's functions to those of massed fire by volley, the hope being that at least some of the ill-aimed balls would find a mark. But by 1860 technology had a weapon ready that did not need to rely upon numbers. In the hands of a sufficiently skilled marksman, the rifle-musket could be deadly at ranges up to 500 yards. The war would actually play a large role in the evolution of the infantryman, but when it began the old mass tactics were still the accepted military wisdom, with the odd result that in the first years of the conflict, many of the weapons carried into battle were superior to their users' abilities.

The weapon that almost all soldiers had to try to master was, of course, the shoulder arm. A hint of what such weapons could do was given in the war with Mexico several years before, when the Model 1841 United States Rifle was used with deadly effect by a Mississippi regiment commanded by then Colonel Jefferson Davis. Dubbed thereafter the Mississippi Rifle, it was the first officially designed and issued military percussion rifle in America, and fathered a succession of refined models which appeared prior to and during the Civil War itself.

Yet when war broke out in 1861, and the men mustered from Maine to Texas, they brought with them not only the Model 1841s left over from the Mexican War, but also a bewildering variety of other weapons, some dating from even earlier conflicts. As state and national governments struggled to equip their regiments, double-barrelled shotguns, hunting rifles and fowling pieces, flintlocks, caplocks, muzzle-loaders and new breechloaders, single-shot and repeaters, pop-guns barely big enough to kill a squirrel, and mammoth .69 and .75 caliber "smoke poles", all came into the camps in the hands of the new recruits.

Observers often wondered just who stood to suffer the greater damage from them. "I think it would be a master stroke of policy to allow the secessionists to steal them", wrote Yankee journalist Frank Wilkie after seeing one such shipment of arms. "They are the old-fashioned-brass-mounted-and-of-such-is-the-kingdom-of-Heaven kind that are infinitely more dangerous to friend than enemy." Thinking of the tender shoulders of the young soldiers, Wilkie added they "will kick further than they will shoot".[3] And when they did fire, they often proved dreadfully inaccurate. At one practice shoot with .69 muskets, only three out of 160 balls hit a barrel at 180 yards. General U.S. Grant later declared that a soldier armed with one of these antique "pumpkin slingers" might "fire at you all day without you ever finding it out".[4]

Despite their variety, almost all of the muzzle-loading weapons required precisely the same routine from the soldier, a routine which Casey in his *Tactics* reduced to a dozen commands and twenty specific motions. At the command, "Load", the soldier stood his rifle upright between his feet, the muzzle in his left hand and held eight

inches from his body, at the same time moving the right hand to his cartridge box on his belt. At "Handle Cartridge", the paper-wrapped powder and bullet were brought from the box and the powder end placed between the teeth. The next two commands brought the cartridge to the muzzle, poured the powder into it, and seated the Minié in the bore. "Draw rammer" elicited the appropriate action, and "Ram" send the bullet driving down the bore to sit on the powder charge. Another command replaced the rammer, then came "Prime". The soldier brought the weapon up and extending outward from his body with his left hand, while with his right he pulled back the hammer to the half-cock position and reached into his cap pouch, removed a cap, and placed it on the nipple. Now came the real business. "Shoulder"; he put the rifle to his right shoulder. "Ready"; he took the proper foot stance and returned the piece to a verticle position at his right side, his right hand on the lock, his thumb pulling the hammer back to full-cock. "Aim"; up went the rifle to his right shoulder, his head to the butt so that his eye could sight between the opened "V" notch at the rear and over the blade sight at the muzzle. His finger sat ready on the trigger. "Fire"; and he did.[5]

In the hands of a careful, practised marksman, these weapons, especially the rifles, were capable of substantial distance and accuracy, but, even with months of practice and new and improved weapons, the fact is that the marksmanship of the average Civil War soldier never proved to be exceptional. In the hands of Johnny Reb and Billy

Private, Maryland Guard Zouaves

In 1861, the fanciful uniform of the French-Algerian zouaves created a rage that swept through both North and South. Of Rebel zouave units one of the most prominent were the Maryland Guard Zouaves. Organized from some of the better families of that bitterly divided state, the Zouaves served well throughout most of the campaigns of the Army of Northern Virginia. They were easily identified by their dark blue baggy trousers with their red stripes, and their red shirts beneath short zouave jackets with red trimming. A solid red kepi with blue band completed the outfit on top, while white canvas leggings did the same at the other end. The potential for confusion is obvious, for they looked almost the same as Yankee zouaves. Indeed, with subtle variations, these colors and styles were prevalent among the majority of zouave units on both sides and were such that one zouave could hardly tell another as friend or foe.

Yank, these guns were more often than not just a lot of smoke and noise. Some officers actually declined to issue to their men live cartridges during skirmish drill, for fear of the mishaps that almost inevitably followed. A British observer viewing the training camps around Washington during the first months of the war wrote that: "the number of accidents from the carelessness of the men is astonishing".[6] Almost every day the Capital's press carried reports of men killed or wounded by the accidental discharge of weapons in the camps, even in the soldiers' tents. And when the men were allowed to practise with real charges, as well as in the actual heat of battle, they invariably aimed too high.

Having experienced this himself, Casey actually added to his "Fire" command a warning to instructors to "be careful to observe when the men fire, that they aim at some distant object, and that the barrel be so directed that the line of fire and the line of sight be in the same vertical plane".[7] He even suggested practice firing at objects both above or below them, so that the soldiers might overcome the natural tendency to shoot high. It did not work. No wonder that years after the war it was calculated that, on average, a Civil War soldier on either side burned 240 pounds of powder and hurled 900 pounds of lead bullets, for every single man actually hit.

At first, the governments North and South looked to arms purchased from Europe to fill their needs, for American armories needed time to gear up for war production. Most of them came from Austria and Belgium, and they almost uniformly won nothing but loathing from the soldiers. They usually either turned out to be so flimsy and ineffectual that soldiers dubbed them "European stovepipes", or else so heavy and clumsy that they were called "mules". When Dresden-made rifles were issued to a Wisconsin regiment, one private decried the "miserable old things" as liable to "do about as much execution to the shooter as the shootee."[8]

Rifles from Belgium and Austria came in .70 and .54 calibers. The Belgian guns were notorious

Imported Longarms

Starting the war with no arms industry, the Confederates quickly began to import weapons from abroad. Indeed, throughout the war, foreign gun makers, especially in Great Britain, would supply a heavy proportion of weapons. In fact, despite the blockade, the importation of arms remained so successful that at the war's end there were more than enough guns, just too few men to wield them.

Tens of thousands of Confederate longarms, both those that saw action, and those which did not, were sold as surplus after the war or else recast in foundries as such things as farming implements.

1 British Pattern 1853 Enfield rifle-musket
2 Belgian Pattern 1842 Short rifle
3 British Pattern 1853 Short rifle
4 Saber bayonet for the British 1853 Short rifle
5 Kerr's Patent Rifle, British
6 British Brunswick Rifle
7 Bayonet for Brunswick Rifle
8 British pattern water bottle (canteen)
9 Cartridge box for British Pattern 1853 Rifle-musket and Short rifle
10 British Whitworth Patent Rifle with telescopic sight

Artifacts courtesy of: Virginia Historical Society, Richmond, Va

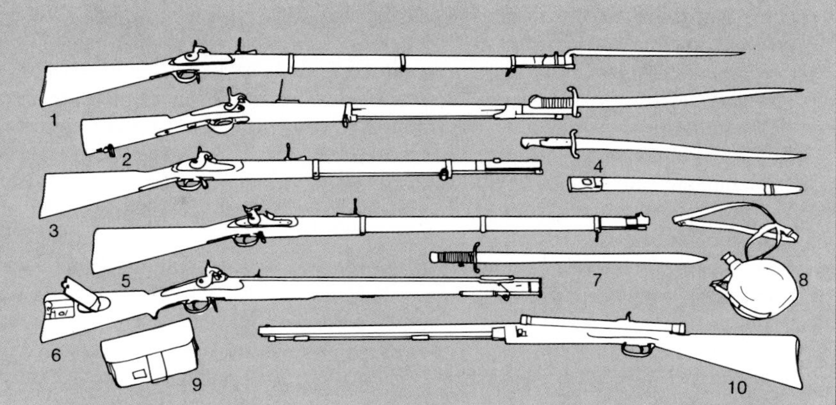

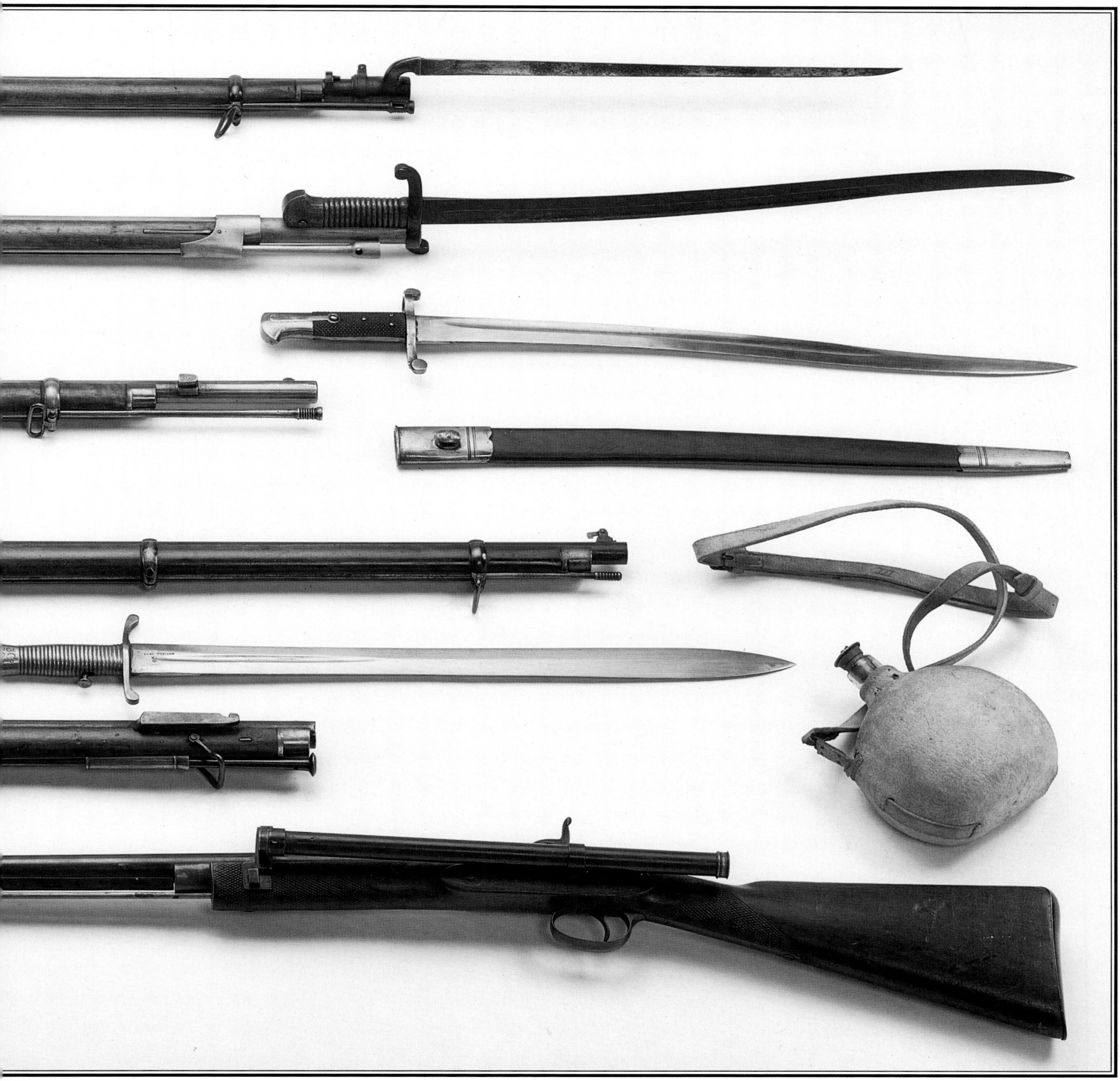

for their terrible kick, no doubt enhancing their "mule" sobriquet. Worse, they proved to be so shabbily made that some came with crooked barrels, and others simply fell apart after limited service. One Indiana boy declared his Belgian rifle to be the "poorest excuse of a gun I ever saw".[9]

The Austrian model was no better. Its mass and weight made it the terror of any soldier issued one. General Grant testified before a Congressional committee that the weapon so terrified his men that in battle they would simply hold on to it like grim death, "shut their eyes and brace themselves for the shock".[10] One Confederate who found himself burdened with a "mule" speculated that the Austrians for whom it was originally made, "must be hard, large-fisted fellows". The weapon "is certainly the most ungainly rifle mortal ever used, being furnished with a heavy oak stock, and trappings of iron and brass, sufficient to decorate a howitzer".[11] Nevertheless, until they were able to make or purchase better arms, both sides bought thousands of these "mules" and "pumpkin slingers" and "stovepipes". Estimates suggest that Union and Confederacy combined acquired more than half a million such execrable weapons.

Rather quickly, however, both governments settled down to two basic and favored shoulder arms, the U.S. Springfield Rifle – in one of several variants – and the British-made Enfield. The Springfield especially became the workhorse weapon of the Union Army, with 1,472,614 of them purchased on contract by the War Department in Washington, along with 428,292 Enfields. Together they tallied almost three times the combined numbers of all other shoulder arms purchased by Washington, ample evidence that the army recognized the truth of what one of its foes, a boy in the 16th Mississippi, declared when he wrote that: "Springfield and Enfield Rifles generally do best".[12]

The origins of the Springfield can be traced back to the old US Rifle Model 1841, which saw its first active service in the 1846-8 war with Mexico. A short, two-banded weapon just four

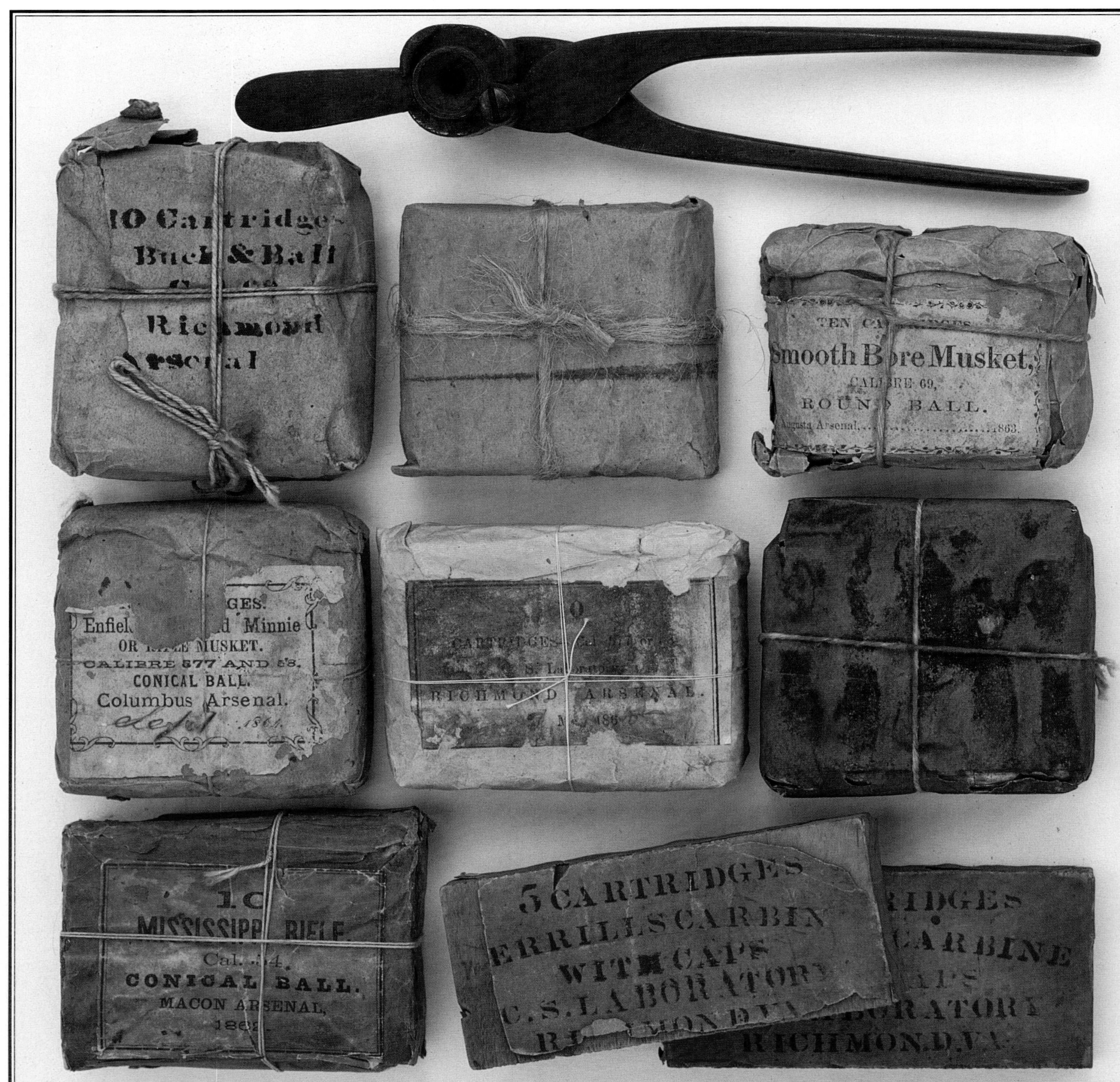

Confederate Small Arms Ammunition, Fuses and Bullet Molds

1 Bullet mold for a British made .557 caliber rifle
2 Richmond Arsenal .69 caliber buck and ball cartridges
3 .58 caliber cartridges
4 Augusta Arsenal .69 caliber round ball cartridges
5 Columbus Arsenal Enfield or Minié Rifle cartridges, .577 or .58 caliber
6 Richmond Arsenal .58 caliber cartridges
7 Lynchburg Arsenal .69 caliber cartridges
8 Macon Arsenal .54 caliber cartridges
9 and 10 Two packets of Merrill's Carbine cartridges
11 British .577 caliber Rifle-musket mold
12 .44 caliber pistol cartridges
13 and 14 Two packets of .36 caliber pistol cartridges
15 and 16 Cannon friction primers
17 Cannon quill primer
18 Friction fuse
19 Richmond Arsenal friction primers
20 and 21 Richmond Arsenal five second fuses
22 Individual three-second fuse
23 Selma Arsenal friction primers

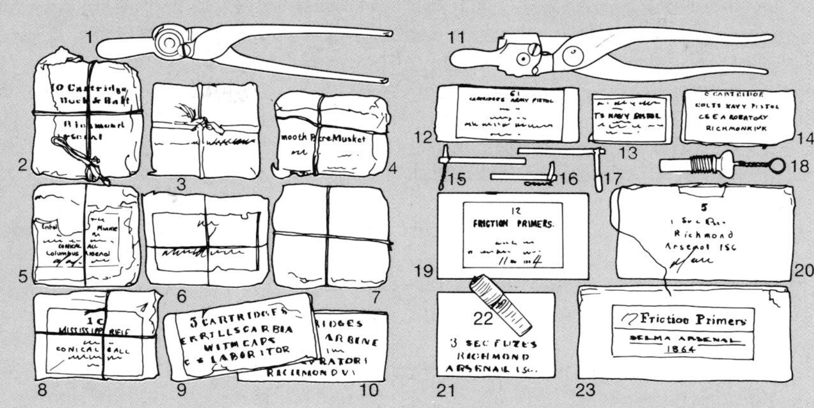

Artifacts courtesy of: Virginia Historical Society, Richmond: 1-5, 11-12
Ben Michel Collection: 6, 7, 8, 13: The Museum of The Confederacy, Richmond, Va: 9, 10

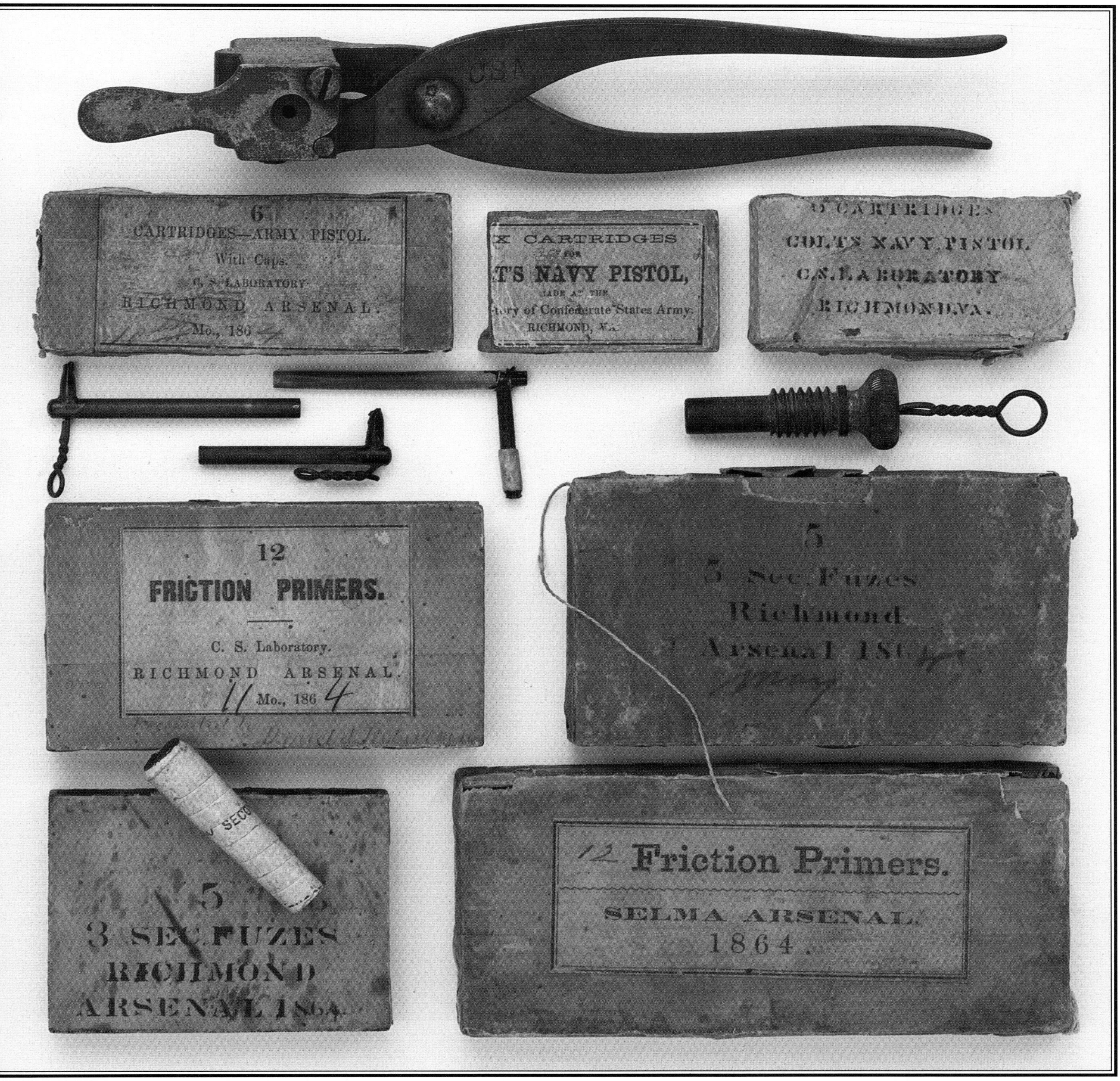

feet long and weighing a little over nine pounds, it combined the percussion system with the new Minié bullet in powerful .54 caliber. The 1841 model was adapted in a new version in 1855, and then, the bore enlarged to .58 caliber, it evolved into the Model 1861 rifle-musket which, with modifications, dominated the field of Union longarms for the duration of the war. The armory at Springfield, Massachusetts produced over 800,000 of them, hence its more popular designation as the Springfield Rifle. Springfield was unable to keep up with the demand, however, and the War Department was forced to manufacture another 900,000 of the weapons under contract with private firms.

The Springfield was, and remains, probably the simplest, sturdiest, most dependable and effective percussion military longarm ever designed. Its 40-inch bright steel barrel was held to a walnut stock by three bands spaced along the tube, making the gun four feet eight inches in length overall, and just over nine pounds in weight. Before being adopted officially in 1861, it had undergone extensive testing the year before. The results were everything the designers could have wished. A single man was able to load and fire the weapon ten times in five minutes, and in that test he put six of his bullets into a two-square-foot target 100 yards distant. Allowed to take his time, the same man put all ten bullets into a target less than one foot square at the same distance; at 300 yards he got them all inside two and a half square feet; and at 500 yards he put one into a target of four square feet.

At the same time, it demonstrated awesome penetrating power with that big bullet and sixty grains of black powder. It could punch through eleven inches of pine boards at 100 yards, and almost six inches at 500 yards. "The rifled musket, of the calibre of .58 of an inch is a decided and important improvement", concluded the examining board, "and considering the compactness, lightness, accuracy at long ranges and the use of the bayonet, the arm is in every respect well-adapted to the general service of Infantry."[13]

Union Ammunition and Accoutrements

Though the North created some kind of uniformity in its weaponry, still the variety of ammunition remained enormous.

1 Percussion cap box
2 and 3 Percussion caps as issued
4 Lawrence primers for the Sharps carbine
5 .58 caliber ball paper cartridge
6 Muzzle-loading .69 caliber ball paper cartridge
7 .50 caliber Smith cartridge
8 .52 caliber Sharps cartridge
9 .54 caliber metal cartridge for Burnside Carbine
10 .50 caliber metal cartridge for Maynard carbine
11 .52 caliber Sharps and Hankins metal cartridge
12 .44 caliber metal cartridge for Henry repeating rifle
13 Tin of British-made Eley brand percussion caps for Colt pistols
14 Pistol bullet mold
15 Pistol tool
16 Packet of .31 caliber paper cartridges for a Colt pocket pistol
17 Packet of .44 caliber paper cartridges for a Colt revolver
18 Open packet of paper cartridges for .44 caliber Colt

Artifacts courtesy of: The Civil War Library and Museum, Philadelphia, Pa.

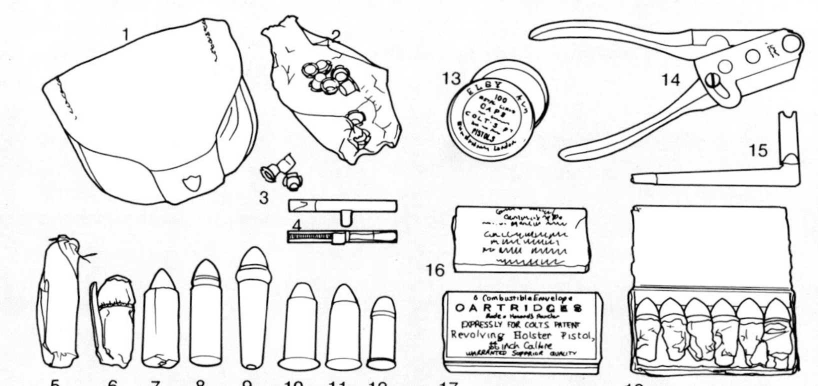

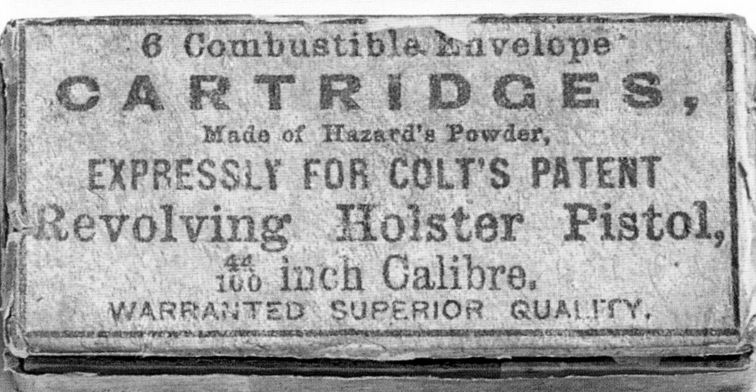

Indeed, in some tests, a trained man could load and fire up to six times per minute though, significantly, that allowed no time for taking steady aim. Tests that looked toward such rapidity revealed the still prevailing preoccupation with volume, rather than accuracy, of fire.

Two other models followed the 1861 Springfield. Both were introduced in 1863, but neither made much more than subtle, cosmetic changes to the 1861 design. Seeming to understand that it had created a classic, the War Department did not tamper with it. Indeed, it would be the very last muzzle-loading model ever adopted by the United States Army. The men who carried it regarded the sleek, graceful marriage of walnut and steel with general admiration. A New Hampshire private boasted that, "We have not got the enfield rifles but the spring field. They are just as good and a good deel lighter." When he and his comrades test fired them, they set up a target that rudely impersonated Jefferson Davis, and then blazed away at it until they had expended 600 rounds. "We put 360 balls into a mark the size of old Jeff," he boasted, adding with relief that "They do not carry so big a slug as our old [Belgian] rifles and are not as heavy by 6 lbs which is considerable on a long march."[14] Each Springfield cost the Treasury between $18 and $25 depending upon the manufacturer. When Lincoln sent his soldiers forth, armed with a Springfield, a bayonet, and forty rounds of ammunition, he sent them well-girded for war.

Below: Looking bemused in spite of his armament, this Reb carries two Colt Navy .36 caliber pistols and a US Model 1855 single-shot pistol with carbine shoulder stock; a weapon that was quickly superseded.

The Enfield was somewhat less favored by Billy Yank, even though it was two inches shorter, and overall nearly a pound lighter. One of its best features was that the British .577 caliber bore could accommodate the .58 bullet then in use for the Springfields and some other makes, thus making the ordnance officer's job a little bit easier. Some maintained that it enjoyed a slight edge in accuracy, but that was always a very subjective judgment, depending far more upon the marksman than the rifle. Still, it was an excellent weapon which thousands of Federals found more than satisfactory. "Our Co. and Co. A get beautiful Enfield rifle", a Billy Yank wrote in his diary in 1862. "We are all right now."[15] And across the lines in the Confederacy, the Enfield quickly became the predominant shoulder arm, so much so that in June 1862 the Richmond government made .577 the official caliber for all Confederate arms, thus patterning them after the bore size of the Enfield. The Rebels bought more than 120,000 of them during the war.

Lest the seeming uniformity of Springfield and Enfield give the impression that the Civil War soldiers' weaponry was rather one-dimensional, it needs to be pointed out that this was, in fact, an aberration. All the Springfields and Enfields combined amounted to no more than forty percent of all the shoulder arms used by the two governments. In fact, there was a virtual jumble of differing weapons in use throughout the war. In 1863 the Union Army officially recognized seventy-nine different models of shoulder arm, both rifles and muskets, another twenty-three models of carbines, and nineteen different pistols and revolvers. The Confederacy "recognized" any weapon it could get, but for both governments the proliferation of models meant that hard-pressed ordnance chiefs had to procure a bewildering variety of ammunition. In the Confederate Army of Tennessee in August 1863, just forty-five percent of the men carried Enfields or captured Springfields in compatible calibers. Another seven percent fought with older .54 Mississippi Rifles and other models. More than a third of the army, thirty-six percent, still lugged old Model 1817 and later .69 smoothbores. Nearly ten percent had .52 and .53 caliber Hall Rifles, and 900 men, three percent of the army, were still cursed with the massive .70 Belgian "mules".

Indeed, for the Confederates, arms procurement would always be a haphazard affair, and at one time or another almost every Johnny Reb took care of the matter for himself by picking up a lost or abandoned Yankee rifle from a battlefield. Indeed, this accounted for Lee's Army of Northern Virginia being the best equipped of all the Confederate armies, for the simple reason that in all its battles it faced – and for two years defeated – the best equipped of the Federal forces, the Army of the Potomac.

In June and July of 1862, Lee's men captured 35,000 stands of arms; in August another 20,000; 11,000 more in September; and yet another 9,000 in December. Late that same year the Army of Tennessee, by contrast, took only a total of 27,500 mixed muskets and rifles. Yet these were still a welcome relief to men, many of whom were actually carrying shotguns and old British Tower muskets left over from the War of 1812.

What the Rebels captured, however, hardly ended their armament woes, for the variety of what they took only increased the burden of supply they already felt. After the Battle of Fredericksburg, Virginia, in December 1862, the 9,000 weapons captured by Lee came in every size and description: 250 Springfields; 3,148 Model 1841 muskets in .69 caliber; 1,136 older muskets of varying dimensions; 772 of the .54 Austrian guns; another 78 of the .70 Belgian "mules"; 478 of the .54 Mississippi Rifles; and a scattering of other calibers, including even 13 flintlocks. This sort of rearmament by scavenging continued right up until the end of the war, and saw wide practice by both sides, for even some Union regiments were indifferently armed. The 14th Indiana went to war with most of its companies carrying smoothbores, and only a few sharpshooters equipped with real rifles. Finally, when the Confederates left the field after their defeat at Antietam in Maryland, in September 1862, the "Hoosiers" were able to scour the fields for abandoned rifles and get themselves uniformly armed.[16]

It could be a frustrating experience for a man in blue or gray to find himself in a regiment that was inadequately or incompletely equipped. As late as Fredericksburg there were still several dozen

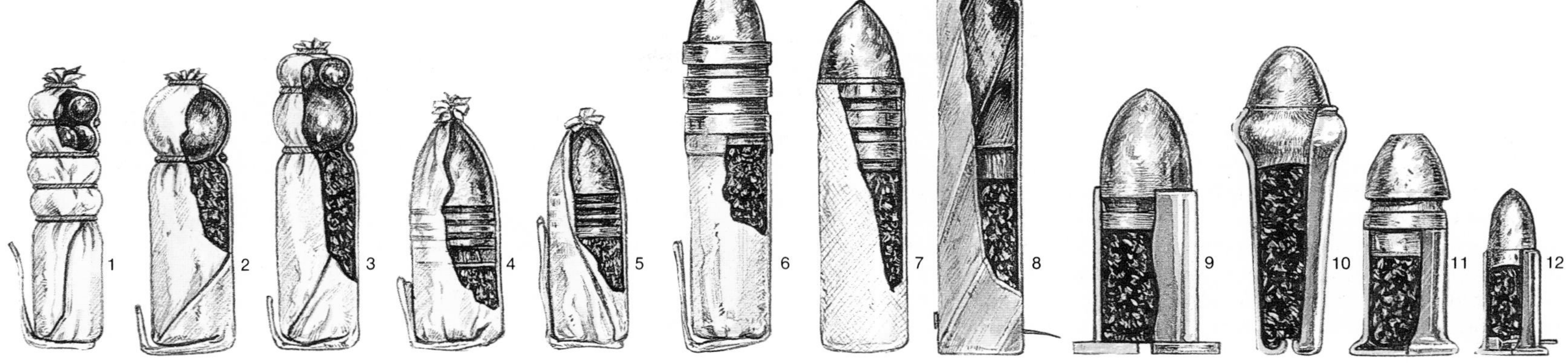

Muzzle-loading and Breechloading Cartridges

The war created the need for millions of cartridges for an enormous variety of different calibered weapons.

1 12-shot load of buckshot for a .58 rifle or musket
2 .69 caliber ball cartridge
3 .69 caliber buck and ball cartridge
4 .69 caliber Minié cartridge with wooden plug
5 .58 caliber Minié cartridge
6 Paper Sharps cartridge
7 Linen Sharps cartridge
8 A 6-sided cardboard Whitworth cartridge
9 Metal-cased Maynard cartridge
10 Metal-cased Burnside carbine cartridge
11 Metal-cased Henry repeating rifle cartridge
12 Pin-fire cartridge with pin in position

men in one Rebel Texas brigade with no guns at all. In most Confederate outfits, and not a few Yankee units as well, the process of rearming was a constant effort. Rebels especially often brought their own guns to war with them, some of them old muskets and shotguns even dating back to the previous century.

The smoothbores were wildly inaccurate at anything more than close range, and to counter this the Southerners often turned them into ersatz shotguns by firing a load they called "buck and ball", three smaller buckshot loaded behind the full-sized ball. As soon as they could trade with a dead or captured Yankee, they did. At Shiloh the 9th Kentucky Infantry dropped its old smoothbores for hundreds of captured Enfields. In the East, the 21st Virginia went into the Battle of Gaines' Mill with a hodge-podge of captured Springfields, Enfields, Mississippi Rifles, and smoothbores, but soon took enough from the enemy to uniformly equip the entire regiment. Well aware of the trouble their ordnance officers would have in providing ammunition for this jumble of calibers, the soldiers took special pains to capture as many cartridges as possible along with them. In time, if they could take or acquire bullet molds, they simply made their own cartridges. "We take a stick 4 or 5 inches long the Size of the Caliber of the Gun", wrote one Confederate, "and Wrap around a piece of paper which we have prepared. A little of the paper Sticks over the end of the Stick & is tied with String[.] the Stick is withdrawn the Bulit or Shot as the case may be [is] inserted than a wad & next the Charge of Powder Accurately measured then the paper is nicely twisted to Keep the powder from leaking out."[17] Some Missouri Rebels actually used sewing thimbles as molds when they poured their lead, poking a pointed stick into the still liquid metal as it cooled to give it a hollow base. "This gave the bullet the form of a minnie ball which just fitted our guns", wrote one of the Missouri boys, "and we could shoot through a boxcar three hundred yards away."[18]

With all this variety of weaponry even within a regiment, commanders had to be careful how they apportioned the guns they had. As a rule, the rifles – if there were any – went to two companies which in battle occupied the extreme left and right flanks. It was believed that this would help them act as a stabilizing influence over the less adequately armed line companies. It may also have been a way to combat the frustrating taunting that many Yankees threw across the lines at regiments they discovered to be equipped with smoothbores. A few well-placed shots from those flank companies could discourage an insulting enemy who purposely exposed himself in order to mock the inadequacy of his opponents' guns.

Even as late as 1863, more than a third of the regiments in the Union Army of the Potomac were armed with two or more differing shoulder arms requiring differing ammunition, and the 1st Minnesota had no less than four. Like their Southern counterparts, they did the best for themselves that they could when their own ordnance officers could not supply them adequately. A kind of hierarchy of preference took informal effect in both armies when it came to battlefield captures, and soldiers repeatedly "traded up" until they had what they wanted. The weapons preferred, of course, were the Springfield and Enfield. Next most admired was the still reliable Mississippi Rifle. "Our choice was the Mississippi Rifles", a North Carolinian wrote in 1861.[19] A sharpshooter tried to get a British Whitworth rifle if he could find one, for its unrivalled accuracy, and any private soldier who happened upon a pistol usually kept it to augment his private arsenal, even though regulations did not allow the infantryman a side arm.

The Civil War, however, did not just come along on a wave of technological advance in weaponry. At the same time, it fed the wave and pushed it forward, giving rise to a seemingly incalculable number of new innovations in weaponry, and the development of new weapons themselves. Consequently, the soldier who scoured the battlefield for something better than his current longarm might find himself choosing

Below: No better testimony can be found to the effect of Civil War weapons than in the many thousands who perished, like this Confederate killed at Gettysburg in July 1863 and photographed by Alexander Gardner.

from a variety of often exotic guns. Many were little more than copies. From the outset of the war, while Confederate agents sought to buy weapons overseas, Southern industry struggled to convert itself to the wartime production of its own ordnance, and to a surprising degree succeeded. Two major armories at Richmond and at Fayetteville, North Carolina, were established for the manufacture of rifles, most of them essentially imitations of the Springfield or Enfield. At the same time a number of private manufacturers converted their machinery to gunmaking, and under contracts from Richmond produced their own weapons, again chiefly copies. As time went on, however, the armorers, public and private, became more inventive. First they made conversions, such as turning shotguns into cavalry carbines, or adapting flintlocks to the percussion mechanism.

But then the wave of interest in breechloaders that was sweeping the North, crossed the lines and passed through the South. A breechloader offered several distinct advantages, assuming it worked efficiently. It was especially good for the cavalry service. Reloading a muzzle-loading carbine while astride a horse and in motion was a tiring challenge for even the best cavalryman, and simply too awkward for most to attempt in battle. A breechloader, however, did not require the time-consuming and clumsy ramrod operation and could be reloaded with the piece held close to the rider instead of at arms' length, which galloping could make impossible. It could also be accomplished much faster, whether riding or standing. That was part of the problem it faced with officialdom, for old line army officers, distrustful of the infantryman's marksmanship and profligacy with ammunition, feared that a man armed with a breechloader would simply squander away his ammunition that much faster without using it to effect.

Nevertheless, a host of breechloading designs came from Confederate manufacturers, though most were little more than experimental, and few saw even limited production thanks to insuffi-

American and Imported Pistols used by Confederate Forces

The handguns carried by Johnny Reb wre almost all in the hands of the cavalrymen. Most of these weapons were foreign imports, or else Southern-made copies of Samuel Colt's pistols.

1 Wesson and Leavitt Army revolver
2 British Kerr .44 caliber revolver
3 Belt and holster for Kerr revolver
4 British Webley double-action revolver, .44 caliber
5 Colt Model 1848 Army revolver, 3rd Model
6 French pin-fire revolver. A popular weapon in Europe, which used a French percussion system invented in the 1820s
7 British Beaumont-Adams revolver
8 Tin of British Eley percussion caps
9 Belt and holster for Beaumont-Adams revolver
10 British Tranter single-trigger revolver
11 British Tranter double-trigger Navy revolver. These weapons used a double-action lock which was cocked by the lower trigger and fired with the upper
12 Pistol bullet mold
13 British Tranter double-trigger Army revolver

Artifacts courtesy of: Virginia Historical Society, Richmond, Va

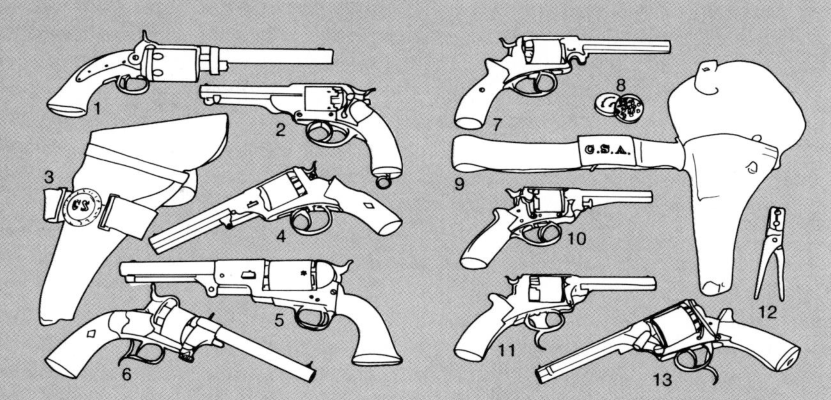

cient machinery and raw materials. J.H. Tarpley patented a breechloader in which the breech-block – the rear of the barrel, including the nipple – simply hinged upward, allowing the paper cartridge to be set in place before the block was closed again. The Perry carbine had a lever which, when lowered, tilted the block upward, exposing an opening into which the cartridge was inserted. Other lever-operated carbines had breeches which rose straight up or lowered downward, and George Morse of Greenville, South Carolina, even manufactured a few score breechloaders that accepted the relatively new self-contained metallic cartridges which held the bullet in a brass or copper casing along with the powder, and which was discharged by striking the base of the casing with the gun's hammer, the precursor to all modern cartridges. Confederates even made their own fairly successful copy of the most popular of all Yankee breechloaders, the Sharps Rifle, but as with all of these new weapons, quantities produced were few.

This was not so in the Union though. The proliferation of new varieties was dazzling, and thousands were produced. There came the Burnside carbine, actually the pre-war invention of Ambrose Burnside, by 1862 a Major General and commander of the Army of the Potomac. Other carbines – breechloaders – came off the assembly lines with names like Star, Maynard, Remington, Merrill, Terry, and Gibbs. The best of them all, however, was surely the one invented by Christian Sharps. It was a simple, yet invariably reliable weapon. A lever which also acted as trigger guard was pulled down, which also lowered a block at the breech, exposing the open barrel. The soldier simply inserted a linen-wrapped cartridge into the barrel, and the act of raising the lever and block once more clipped off the back of the linen, exposing the powder. A cap placed on the nipple readied it for firing. Sharps manufactured them in carbine and rifle models, and Washington purchased nearly 90,000 of them during the war, making it the most prevalent percussion breechloader of the war. Lincoln himself placed the first

Union Longarms and Equipment

Despite a frenzy of invention in the North, spurred on by the war and lucrative government contracts, only a few of the guns newly invented and patented ever saw as much service as the single-shot Springfield. Almost weekly, despite this, hopeful inventors came forward with everything from rapid-fire repeaters to exploding bullets, all of them to meet the skepticism of the War Department. A whole section of the ordnance branch was devoted to the evaluation of all new types of patented arms, using photography and systematic ballistics tests.

1 Rifleman's waist belt and saber bayonet, Model 1855
2 US Model 1841 Rifle
3 Waist belt for a US enlisted man
4 Cartridge box for a rifle-musket
5 Sharps "New Model" 1859 Rifle
6 Colt Model 1855 Rifle
7 Spencer Rifle: introduced in 1863 this eight-shot breechloader was one of the most successful repeating rifles used by Union forces
8 Henry Rifle
9 Greene Rifle

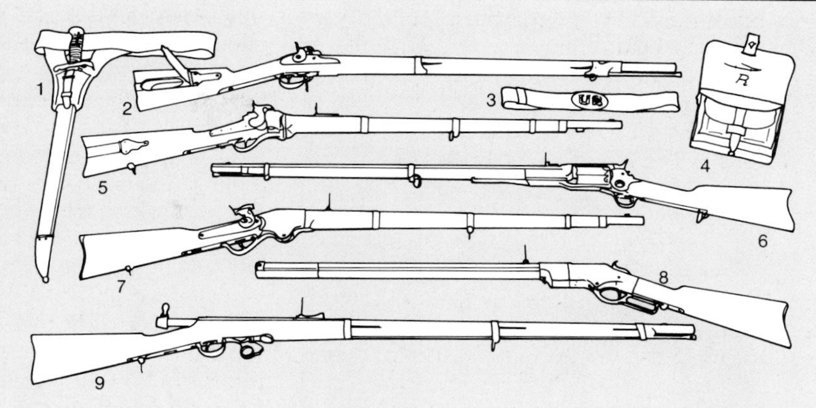

Artifacts courtesy of: The Civil War Library and Museum, Philadelphia, Pa: 2, 5, 6, 7, 8; J. Craig Nannos Collection, Philadelphia, Pa: 1, 3, 4

order after seeing a demonstration of the weapon's ease and accuracy.

Indeed, it was Lincoln's personal interest which put an even more inventive weapon in the hands of several thousand Billy Yanks. Ironically it was the invention of a man of peace, a Quaker named Christopher M. Spencer, yet his brainchild came to be regarded by many as the best single rifle of the war. He patented it just a year before the war began.

A tube that inserted into the butt of the gun held seven metallic self-contained cartridges. Pushing the trigger guard-lever down opened the breech, allowing the spring in the tube to shove a cartridge forward into the barrel. Pulling the lever back readied the gun for fire. All the operator had to do otherwise was cock the hammer before he lowered the lever. After firing, the lever also served to eject the spent casing. "Mr. Lincoln's gun", it was called after the President himself test fired it and took a hand in having it issued to some of his regiments. After some refinements as the war progressed, it could pump out fifteen shots in a minute, with both telling accuracy and a deadly punch.

In all, about 106,000 Spencer carbines and rifles were bought by the Lincoln government, and they saw service in nearly every theater of the war. Men armed with them felt almost invincible at Gettysburg, Chickamauga, Atlanta, Petersburg, and elsewhere. After fighting at Bermuda Hundred, Virginia, in 1864, one Connecticut Yankee declared that, "the Rebs made three charges on us but we stood up to the rack with our seven shooters. The Rebs hate our guns", he continued; "they call then the Yanks 7 Devils[;] they say the G.D. Yankeys stand up there with their G.D. coffy mills wind em up in the morning, run all day shoot a thousand times." Exaggeration aside, he and thousands of others agreed that, "well they are a good rifel".[20]

Spencer's was not the only repeater either. The Colt Patent Firearms Company adapted its popular Colt revolver pattern into a longarm with the Model 1855 Colt Revolving Rifle. The .58 caliber weapon was the first repeater ever adopted by the US Army, but its experience with it was such that it prejudiced attitudes toward repeaters until the Spencer came along. The Colt's revolving six-shot barrel had a problem with accidentally discharging several chambers at once which, for the

Berdan's 1st US Sharpshooters

A few US units won special notice for their rifle-skills, none more so than the 1st and 2nd Regiments of US Sharpshooters, commonly known as Berdan's Sharpshooters after the colonel of the 1st Regiment, Hiram Berdan. Seeing their role as skirmishers and special marksmen, Berdan selected experienced men and armed them with the best weapons available, the Sharps Rifle in .52 caliber. Many also carried telescopic sights. With a view towards camouflage, Berdan clothed his men in green kepis or hats and dark green uniform blouses. In keeping with the rest of the army, their trousers were light blue, but these too were later changed to green. They were held to the boots with canvas or leather leggings. By 1864, losses in Berdan's outfits were such that the Sharpshooters almost ceased to exist. At the end of that year they were consolidated into a single unit, and by early 1865 they were dispersed into other regiments.

soldier whose left hand was out in front of the barrel supporting the rifle, could be costly, even fatal. Though some saw continued use during the war, most were sold off by Washington for a mere 42 cents each to get rid of them.

Most revolutionary of all was the rifle that came from the New Haven Arms Company, the Model 1860 Henry Rifle. This was the military firearm of the future. A simple lever-action repeater that could fire sixteen .44 caliber bullets as fast as the operator could work the lever, it made a single soldier almost an entire company. Whole regiments such as the 7th Illinois were armed with it, and the enemy soon learned to fear and envy them. When a Reb of the 24th Virginia captured a Henry late in the war, he proclaimed himself "the best equipped man in the army".[21] Yanks felt the same way. An Indiana boy paid $35 – "all the money I had" – to buy one in 1864. "They are good shooters and I like to think I have so many shots in reserve." Certainly it disconcerted the enemy. "I think the Johnnies are getting rattled", he wrote some months later after using the Henry; "they are afraid of our repeating rifles. They say we are not fair, that we have guns that we load up on Sunday and shoot all the rest of the week. This I know, I feel a good deal more confidence in myself with a 16 shooter in my hands than I used to with a single shot rifle."[22]

It is altogether fitting that the repeaters, the weapons of the future, were not manufactured to be used with the weapon of the past. The Henry Rifle could not accommodate a bayonet, and it is just as well, for of the millions of other Civil War weapons which did allow the attachment of the bayonet to the end of the barrel, only the barest fraction ever drew blood. Like the sabers carried by cavalrymen, they came to be regarded largely as encumbrances left over from some earlier notion of warfare. In America in 1861 faced with a greater kind of firepower, they did not fit.

Beyond his rifle and his bayonet, Johnny Reb and Billy Yank had no other standard issue weapons to wage their war. A few carried pistols, though many threw them away when they found little use for them. Many, especially Confederates, brought large bowie knives with them, and these they kept, though again they did little damage to the foe. One Federal regiment even carried lances – which they soon abandoned – and early in the conflict the Confederacy intended to arm a few units with pikes. Thankfully it never happened, and first to last the footsoldier relied upon his rifle or musket. For all their clumsiness with them, their poor marksmanship, and their grumbling and complaining over certain models, the common enlisted men came in time to be comfortable with their weapons, to care for them and protect them, and even in time to use them well enough to kill and maim hundreds of thousands of their own kind.

No one "licked" anybody with cornstalks in this war, nor did another Confederate live up to his optimistic boast that, "we can whip the Yankees with popguns". It took rifles, millions of them, carried by men who came to learn soon enough in the face of combat, that in battle a man's weapon and his understanding of it was his strength, and sometimes his salvation.

Above: Marksmanship could even win you celebrity. Private Truman Head, nicknamed "California Joe", of Berdan's 1st United States Sharpshooters, became much lionized for his skill with the Sharps Rifle.

Below: Whatever their weapons, Rebel and Yank carried them with pride. Here Henry Kelly of the 1st Battalion, 1st Virginia Cavalry, poses with his Colt Revolving Carbine and Colt Navy .36 Revolver.

References

1 William A. Albaugh and Edward N. Simmons, *Confederate Arms* (Harrisburg, Pa., 1957), p.47.
2 Wiley, *Billy Yank*, pp.62-3.
3 Cyril B. Upsham, "Arms and Equipment for the Iowa Troops in the Civil War", *Iowa Journal of History and Politics*, XVI (1918), p.18.
4 "Diary of Colonel William Camm, 1861 to 1865", *Journal of the Illinois State Historical Society*, XVII (1926), pp.802, 813; U.S. Grant, *Personal Memoirs* (New York, 1885), I, p.95.
5 Casey *Infantry Tactics*, I, pp.42-8.
6 Russell, *My Diary*, p.396.
7 Casey, *Infantry Tactics*, I, p.48.
8 Fred A. Shannon, *The Organisation and Administration of the Union Army, 1861-1865* (Cleveland, 1928), I, p.139; Francis A. Lord, *They Fought for the Union* (Harrisburg, Pa., 1960), p.141.
9 Wiley and Milhollen, *They Who Fought Here*, p.112.
10 *Ibid.*, p.112.
11 Wiley, *Johnny Reb*, p.290.
12 Wiley and Milhollen, *They Who Fought Here*, p.106.
13 *Ibid.*, p.105.
14 Bell I. Wiley, "The Common Soldier of the Civil War", *Civil War Times Illustrated*, XII (July 1973), p.41.
15 Wiley and Milhollen, *They Who Fought Here*, p.107.
16 Wiley, *Johnny Reb*, p.289.
17 *Ibid.*, p.293.
18 *Ibid.*, p.293.
19 Wiley and Milhollen, *They Who Fought Here*, p.107.
20 Wiley, "Common Soldier", p.42.
21 Wiley, *Johnny Reb*, p.289.
22 Wiley, *Billy Yank*, p.63.
23 Wiley and Milhollen, *They Who Fought Here*, p.121.

CHAPTER FOUR

JOIN THE CAVALRY

The summer of 1862 was one of intense activity and Union setbacks almost everywhere. After finally taking Yorktown, McClellan pushed slowly on toward Richmond, only to be nearly defeated in battle at Fair Oaks in May. Then late in June both he and the new Confederate commander before him, Robert E. Lee, planned attacks. McClellan's began first, but half-heartedly, and Lee responded in a series of fights that would become known as the Seven Days' Battles. Time after time Lee gained an advantage, but miscarried orders or tardy subordinates denied him the crushing victories he might have had. Still, McClellan, already timid, and convinced that he was outnumbered despite his own 2:1 advantage over Lee, was slowly pushed back. McClellan did not immediately leave the Peninsula, but Richmond was saved from immediate threat.

What helped in that salvation was the brilliant campaign by Lee's eccentric lieutenant, General Thomas J. "Stonewall" Jackson. In a series of battles in the Shenandoah Valley, 100 miles northwest of Richmond, he met and successively routed three separate Yankee armies, creating such an uproar in Washington that large reserves were called away from McClellan to protect the Federal capital. In time, Washington created a new army, the Army of Virginia, under General John Pope, intending to send it south to crush Richmond between Pope and McClellan. Yet Lee foiled Pope when the armies met once again along Bull Run, and the second Battle of Manassas ended in a Union defeat as had the first.

Out in the west the only real achievement was the occupation of Corinth, Mississippi, an important rail center. But Farragut's attempts to take Vicksburg by water failed, as did a Yankee advance on Chattanooga, Tennessee.

Making matters worse, the Rebels were humiliating McClellan with their cavalry. On June 12-15, Lee's cavalry chief, General "Jeb" Stuart, led his horsemen in a ride completely around McClellan's army, over 150 miles, doing much damage with the loss to himself of but a single man.

OUT OF those tens of thousands of young men who flocked to the recruitment centers in the first days of the war, many went with a special branch of the service in mind. Lured by the romantic notions of gay cavaliers, bedecked with plumes and flashing sabers, riding merrily through the countryside, and cutting a dashing picture before the ladies, a host of enlistees chose the newly forming cavalry regiments for their service. Inevitably these and other preconceived notions about cavalry service would be proven false, as they would be in every aspect of the war. Indeed, in the spring of 1861, the role, if any, of the mounted arm in the coming fray was entirely uncertain. If any of those confused and faintly frightened young men could have looked ahead, however, they would have seen that the cavalry as it was at the war's outset, and as it would become by war's close, was destined to play an integral part in the national tragedy.

Nowhere could this be seen more clearly than in two events almost four years apart. On June 1,

What young man North or South could resist the temptation to don the dashing and colorful uniform of the *beau sabreur*? With sword in hand, astride his charger, the cavalryman *was* adventure.

1861, in a minor skirmish at Fairfax Courthouse, Virginia, the first Virginia Confederate to die in battle was a cavalryman. On April 9, 1865, when Robert E. Lee, general-in-chief of the Confederate armies, surrendered the Army of Northern Virginia at another courthouse town, Appomattox, it was because Federal cavalry had cut off his last avenue of escape and trapped him between it and Grant's legions.

As 1861 dawned, even with the nation in crisis, few seemed yet to appreciate the need that would be felt for substantial numbers of horsemen. Indeed, with the peacetime neglect that afflicted every branch of the service, the United States Army on December 31, 1860, counted just five regiments of mounted men: the 1st and 2nd Dragoons, the 1st and 2nd Cavalries, and the Regiment of Mounted Riflemen. Worse, these regiments lay scattered all across the western expanse beyond the Mississippi River, protecting frontier posts against hostile Indians. Not a single company of organized cavalry was within a thousand miles of Washington and the scene of impending action.

Of the five colonels commanding the regiments, four would go to the new Confederacy, including Lee and Albert Sidney Johnston. Many officers of lesser rank, men like William J. Hardee, James Ewell Brown Stuart, John Bell Hood, Richard Ewell, Earl Van Dorn, Joseph Wheeler, and more, would also resign to "go south", many of them to become Rebel cavalrymen. In the 2nd Cavalry alone, seventeen of its twenty-five officers resigned to don the gray.[1] Worst of all, almost none of the officers, regardless of their loyalties, had any real experience or understanding of the role of cavalry in major military operations. They had spent their careers engaged in small actions and outpost duty, confronting at best only modest parties of Indian irregulars.

In fact, in 1861, cavalry doctrine North and South, as preached at the military academies and in the tactical manuals widely circulated, showed little development since the days of Napoleon. The Army's standard text, *System of Cavalry Tactics*, was twenty years old, and was borrowed almost in its entirety from a French book. It still reflected the Napoleonic ideal of using cavalry in masses – up to 12,000 in some of the Emperor's battles – to thunder down upon, intimidate, and plunge through enemy infantry lines. The value of cavalry, read a West Point text, "resides in its shock".[3] Furthermore, despite some Napoleonic examples of horseman riding to battle, then fighting dismounted very effectively, the prevailing notion remained that, in the words of Captain George B. McClellan, "The strength of cavalry is in the spurs and sabre". And this is what he wrote in an all new cavalry manual published in 1861, just as war was commencing.

Above: For a war destined to be called "modern", this one would still have some age-old elements. This man of Company E, 6th Pennsylvania Cavalry, would go to war carrying a 9-foot long Norway fir lance.

Below: "Rush's Lancers" they called the 6th Pennsylvania, though they soon discarded their lances for carbines. Men of Company I pose in Virginia with their antiquated weapons, sometime prior to May 1863.

In other words, cavalrymen in this new war were expected to behave as in wars more than a century before – to ride to battle, then dash into the fray in the overwhelming mounted saber charge. Very few, though McClellan and General Winfield Scott were among them, seemed to suspect that the wooded ground and narrow roads of America might make inoperable the cavalry tactics used in Europe decades before, and that new ideas would be needed. Almost everyone who gave the branch of service any thought, continued to regard it first and foremost as the realm of dashing gallants in resplendent garb, the *beau sabreurs* of the military. No one had quite escaped the notion of one of Napoleon's marshals who said that cavalry, in the last analysis, served best to add a bit of class and style to battles which were, otherwise, just tawdry brawls.[3]

Lincoln and his administration blundered badly at first by entirely ignoring the mounted arm, probably because, like most, he failed to grasp its necessity in the war to come. Incredibly, only a few more immediately available companies of the existing regiments were called east in the days after Fort Sumter, and no plans went forward to raise new regiments. In his first call for

Trooper, 1st Virginia Cavalry Regiment, CSA, 1861-2

The 1st Virginia Cavalry began the war as a group of independent companies of horse from the Shenandoah Valley, organized into a regiment by J.E.B. Stuart, later of course to become a Major General. In the First Battle of Bull Run in July 1861, they achieved renown as the dreaded "Black Horse Cavalry", though the origin of the sobriquet is obscure. For the remainder of the war they performed outstanding service with the Cavalry Corps of the Army of Northern Virginia. Stuart's horsemen wore chiefly homespun clothing of plain gray or butternut, with black facings on their light-gray short jackets and trousers. They were well armed and carried Sharps carbines by leather shoulder belts, the standard model US cavalry saber of the time and Colt Navy .36 pistols. Many of their weapons were captured from the US Cavalry. Broad-brimmed black hats with plumes completed their attire.

volunteers, Lincoln said nothing about cavalry, and when Northern governors offered to send mounted units, the War Department issued orders to accept no cavalry.[4] Expecting a short summer's campaign before the rebellion was put down, Washington continued under the influence which had always kept the cavalry small – economy. Horses were expensive to maintain.

Then came the disaster at First Manassas or Bull Run. General Irvin McDowell, with an army numbering close to 37,000, marched into Virginia with just seven companies, fewer than 700 horsemen, riding along. As a result, he moved almost completely in the dark, with no useful reconnaissance, no scouting reports, and in the battle itself, no substantial mobile force to exploit a breakthrough or guard his flanks. Worst of all, he had nothing with which to neutralize the enemy cavalry, which itself consisted only of the 1st Virginia Cavalry commanded by Colonel 'Jeb' Stuart. Filled in advance with dread of the so-called "Black Horse Cavalry", Federal infantrymen panicked when Stuart rode out of some woods against them. Later, at the critical moment of the battle when McDowell's shaky flank was wavering, Stuart with infantry support put that flank into a flight which soon became a general rout.[5] McDowell's lack of cavalry, and Stuart's presence, did not alone account for the Yankee disaster, but they did reveal that cavalry could not be overlooked. Furthermore, as McDowell himself would point out after the fact, cavalry was most needed for gathering information while operating in an enemy's country, and for shielding from an enemy one's own movements. Already, from bitter experience, men were beginning to sense glimmers of change.

But learning remained slow, especially in the Union, and old habits of economy at the price of innovation died hard. It cost nearly a half million dollars to raise and fully equip a mounted regiment, and many professional soldiers doubted the point of it. Old General Scott, for instance, shared the disdain and suspicion of many infantrymen for their mounted compatriots.

Confederate Cavalry Artifacts

No soldier of the war caught more of the dash and the flair of the era than the cavalryman, and especially the Confederate trooper. His exploits celebrated in both song and legend, he became in the hearts of his people the *beau sabreur*, the knightly paladin riding through the smoke of battle in daring raids against hopeless odds, to defend his country, home, hearth and honor.

1 Battleflag
2 Slough hat with star insignia
3 Reins and bit
4 Model 1859 McClellan saddle
5 Girth
6 Model 1859 Sharps carbine
7 Haversack
8 Shell jacket
9 Canteen
10 Gauntlets
11 Carbine cartridge box
12 Model 1840 cavalry saber, complete with scabbard
13 Pair of field glasses
14 Saddlebags
15 Remington New Army revolver complete with holster and percussion caps
16 Pouch for percussion caps
17 Federal Officer's sword belt
18 Pair of spurs
19 A pair of leather high riding boots

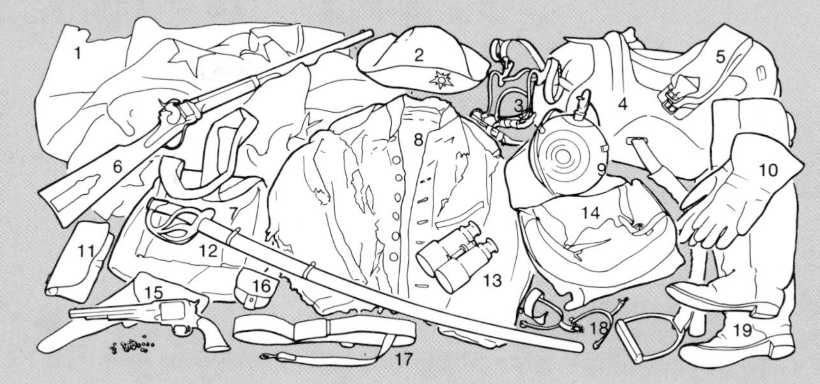

Artifacts courtesy of: The Museum of the Confederacy, Richmond, Va

It was also a question of time. Current military wisdom maintained that it took three full years to adequately train a cavalry officer, and nearly as long for the men in the ranks to be trained and disciplined. Since this would be a short war, there was little point in raising such outfits. The conflict would end before they could render any useful service. Besides – and here came the early expressions of a prejudice against volunteers that almost all professional soldiers repeated again and again – such work as the cavalry would be required to do was best left to the Regulars, and the five regiments in service would be enough. Small wonder, then, that in Lincoln's call for forty regiments for three years' service that spring, only one of these regiments was to be of cavalry.[6]

In the end, political pressure placed on Lincoln by his governors induced him, in turn, to move the War Department into accepting the first volunteer cavalry regiments. And after the disaster at Bull Run, Washington's attitude changed dramatically. Within six weeks of the defeat, there were thirty-one mounted volunteer regiments in service, and eighty-two by December 31, more than 90,000 cavalrymen.[7]

Across the lines, in the new Confederacy, the story was much different. It helped that President Jefferson Davis himself once served as a lieutenant in the 1st US Dragoons, and later as secretary of war for President Franklin Pierce he showed considerable interest in studying French cavalry technique. Even more important was the emotional attraction which the dashing mounted service had for the more high-spirited young men of the south. Accustomed since youth to riding, and inspired from childhood by stories of Revolutionary forebears like the "Swamp Fox" Francis Marion, "Light Horse" Harry Lee, and other cavalry heroes, sons of high-born and wealthy families were anxious to lead new regiments of heroes. Many a farmboy eagerly enlisted to serve them, especially after the exaggerated stories of Stuart's "Black Horse Cavalry" at Manassas assured them that all the real glory would be had in the saddle.

Union Cavalry Artifacts

1 Carbine cartridge box
2 Metal curry comb, used in horse grooming
3 Lance with pennant, (in total nine feet long), of the type used between 1861 and 1863 by the 6th Pennsylvania Cavalry, Rush's Lancers
4 Cavalryman's gauntlets
5 Cavalryman's, shell jacket
6 Forage cap
7 Double-breasted overcoat for mounted troops
8 Picket rope
9 Rubber blanket
10 Regulation US Army saddle, the Model 1859 McClellan saddle with blanket roll
11 Shoulder sling for a carbine
12 Rolled overcoat
13 Saber belt
14 Pair of field glasses and case
15 Bugler's shell jacket
16 Saddle bags
17 Model 1860 Spencer breechloading, repeating carbine
18 Model 1860 saber, with protective scabbard and tassel
19 Regulation curb bit and reins
20 Girth
21 Saddle blanket
22 Bugle
23 Farrier's pocket knife

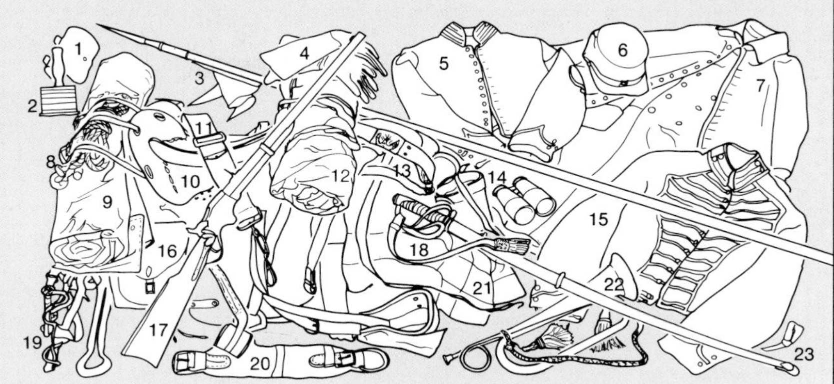

Artifacts courtesy of: J. Craig Nannos Collection: 5-10, 12-13, 15-16, 19-22; The Civil War Library and Museum, Philadelphia, Pa; 1-4, 11, 14, 17

Above: A typical Yankee cavalryman, especially those out in the western theater, looked lean and sparsely equipped, if he was experienced. Pistol in belt, saber at his side, he was ready for action.

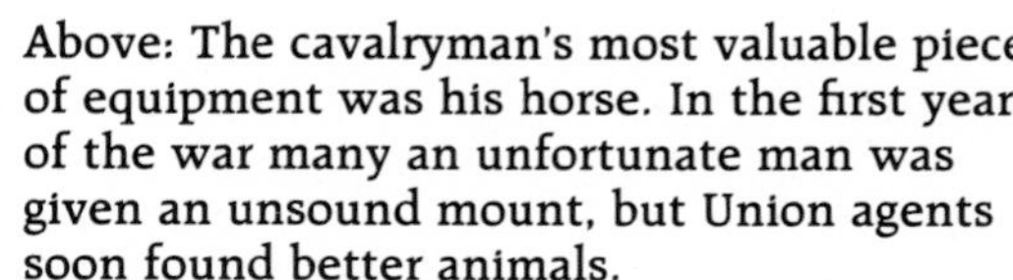

Above: The cavalryman's most valuable piece of equipment was his horse. In the first year of the war many an unfortunate man was given an unsound mount, but Union agents soon found better animals.

Below: Ohio cavalrymen such as these came to typify the look of the rugged western Yankees who filled the ranks of the Union cavalry. Young, lean, with few frills, they were tough business in the saddle.

North or South, the story of raising the volunteer regiments proved much the same. Once a governor authorized a new regiment, an appointment to its colonelcy went to the man who would raise it. He might be an officer from another branch of the service, a prominent politician whose popularity could lure 1,200 or so to enlist, someone to whom the governor owed a favor, or from whom he sought one. There were as many considerations for appointment as there were men to commission; presidents and secretaries of war also often got involved in designating new colonels. In short, it was American political democracy in action. However he got his appointment, once the colonel enlisted his men – later General Philip H. Sheridan would declare that the ideal cavalryman was between 18 and 22 years old, and about 130 pounds – he equipped them with whatever the governor, or the Capital, provided. Few regiments on either side went off to war with everything their army regulations required, but almost every trooper had the basics – revolver, saber, carbine, saddle, and horse. Beyond that, equipment depended upon good fortune, and the whim of the quartermasters.[8]

Not only did the Confederacy begin the war with the first victories – Fort Sumter, Big Bethel, and Bull Run – but from the first it enjoyed almost undisputed pre-eminence in the mounted arm. That came in part from having a head start in enlistments, and a more enlightened attitude towards cavalry. After all, Confederates knew the war would be fought on their own territory, and they knew best from riding all those fields and roads just how cavalry could use them. Moreover, it cannot be doubted that Southerners were by and large better horsemen thanks to having more experience in a predominantly rural society. The Southern policy of men providing their own horses meant that a cavalryman did not need weeks or months to get accustomed to his mount. North of the Potomac, where all horses were issued by the government, a mount and rider met for the very first time when they started training together. Additionally, a Rebel rider went to war knowing he had a sound, healthy horse. In the Union, already suffering the abuses of contract frauds and dishonest traders, tens of thousands of unsound animals were bought and, through faulty inspection procedure, allowed to get into the hands of green recruits.

It hardly afforded cause for wonder, then, that for two years after the commencement of the war, the Confederate cavalry reigned supreme in every theater of the war, and Southern mounted leaders quickly became national heroes. Even one of their foes, General William T. Sherman, would declare that Confederates were "splendid riders, first-rate shots, and utterly reckless". He frankly termed them "the best cavalry in the world".[9]

One of the first of them to achieve prominence was a 33 year old Virginia farmer named Turner

Above: Yankee horsemen like these shown at rest in Georgia in 1864, quickly learned how to take their comfort where they could. Pitched tents, a brush "shebang" for shade, and a fiddle were all they needed.

Ashby. Adjudged by many to be a born leader, and a horseman of unquestioned skill, young Ashby went from command of a company of horsemen at the war's start, to a leadership of all the cavalry in General Thomas J. "Stonewall" Jackson's army in the Shenandoah Valley in 1862. He used his men as Jackson's eyes, watching enemy movements, and masking Jackson's own movements, behind a screen of cavalry. He harassed enemy communications, gathered intelligence, and moved quickly wherever needed. It was the traditional role of the cavalryman, and only Ashby's death on June 6 kept him from rising even higher.

His role as premier cavalryman was quickly assumed, however, by Stuart. Manassas made him a hero overnight. Handsome, a born leader, daring to the point of rashness, and prone like many to get carried away with the sheer joy of being bold, Stuart would be *the* cavalryman east of the Alleghenies for the next two years. And in the spring of 1862, as commander of the cavalry corps of the Army of Northern Virginia, he would quickly show how horseman could best – and worst – be employed. Lee sent him on a bold expedition to find the enemy's exposed right flank and to hit his supply lines if they were vulnerable to attack. Stuart turned what was to have been a reconnaissance into a stunning ride completely around General George B. McClellan's army. They rode all day June 12, 1862, without stopping. The next day they pressed on, Yankee horsemen nipping at their heels. Skirmishing went on all day. "Friend and foe alike were soon enveloped in bellowing clouds of dust, through which pistol and carbine shots were seen darting to and fro like flashes of lightning", wrote a Rebel trooper.[10] Surprising and capturing enemy camps, the Confederates took what they could and destroyed the rest. In the end, Stuart took 165 prisoners and 260 horses and mules, and revealed what the mounted arm could do. He had spread consternation in the enemy rear, done considerable damage, gathered useful intelligence, and brought away much needed captures. Yet there had been no saber slashing charges, no grand and glorious battles. It was, rather, hit and run with pitched battle something to be avoided; the prototype of a host of raids to follow in this war, both for better and for worse.

Below: Helped considerably by his array of weapons, even this innocent-looking young man in blue quickly came to adopt a warlike posture. The lad here has saber in hand and a Model 1855 pistol carbine across his lap.

Stuart's ride also revealed something else about the cavalry service as it began its evolution. He went beyond his orders. The information Lee wanted could have been obtained with far less dash and risk. Because he was successful, few gainsaid Stuart's feat, even Lee calling it a "brilliant exploit". But by its very flamboyance, it also alerted McClellan to the danger of vulnerability which Lee was seeking. The Federal leader soon shifted his army, denying Lee the chance of a crushing blow. In short, Stuart's zeal may have ruined the very opportunity that he had discovered for Lee. That zeal, that enchantment with the romance and dash of the cavalry service, would plague both sides time and again, especially with the example of the gallant Stuart urging others to emulate his flair.

No one on either side could doubt, of course, that there was romance in the life of a cavalryman. To a generation raised on the novels of Sir Walter Scott, the mounted warrior of 1862 could seem remarkably similar to Ivanhoe. To a society, especially in the South, whose daily speech made commonplace use of terms like "gallant" and "chivalrous", a man such as Stuart easily took on the mantle of knighthood. For the men in the ranks, even, a little of that aura caught hold. Few could resist the romance of a scene witnessed by Heros Von Borke, of Stuart's command. "It was, indeed, a magnificent sight as the long column of many thousand horsemen stretched across this beautiful Potomac", he wrote. "The evening sun slanted upon its clear placid waters, and burnished them with gold, while the arms of the soldiers glittered and blazed in its radiance. There were few moments, perhaps, from the beginning to the close of the war, of excitement more intense, of exhilaration more delightful".[12]

Of course there was far more to it than that. North and South the life of the average mounted soldier was not markedly different, nor was it greatly varied from that of the other branches of the service. For all the glamor of youthful expectations, real soldiering turned out to be weeks of inactive camp life for every day of glorious battle. Drill, foraging for food, tending to animals and equipment, occupied an inordinate amount of time, and what time was left, the troopers took care of with gambling, prank-playing, and simply lolling about camp. Yet for the cavalryman there was, at least, an added dimension of mobility thanks to his horse. The need for frequent scouts and reconnaissance, even when the armies sat in winter quarters, allowed the troopers to break the monotony of camp life.

Better yet, from the point of view of the cavalryman, that mobility allowed him a far greater opportunity to scavenge and, occasionally, to plunder. This, and the natural inter-service rivalry that arises in all armies, rather quickly led to the mounted arm being the most resented of all, in and out of the military. A Federal officer in Arkansas in 1862 complained that, "Cavalry are plenty among us, and go in any direction you may for miles you will find their horses hitched near every dwelling". They scoured the country, he lamented, "and generally help themselves to anything they wish". Creating the most resentment of all was the almost universal experience of the weary and footsore infantryman asking at a house for something to eat, only to be told that, "the cavalry has been here and there is nothing left".[13]

Adding to the hostility was the fact that, with the evolution of cavalry doctrine slowly taking it away from participation in pitched battles,the big fights were almost exclusively the realm of infantry and artillery. As a result, men in those branches rarely saw horse soldiers actually engaged in combat. Inevitably this led to the taunt of "whoever saw a dead cavalryman." When a mounted unit passed a marching column, the foot soldiers invariably hurled insults, and one

Confederate and Imported Cavalry Carbines and Artillery Musketoons

1 Dickson, Nelson and Company carbine with ramrod displayed in stowed position
2 J.P. Murray carbine
3 Ramrod for use with J.P. Murray carbine depicted above
4 British Pattern 1853 Enfield musketoon with ramrod displayed in stowed position
5 British Terry's Pattern 1860 carbine with breech mechanism seen in open position for re-loading.
6 Ramrod for use with Terry's Pattern 1860 carbine depicted above
7 J.P. Murray musketoon complete with ramrod in stowed position
8 British design of gun tool
9 British Pattern 1853 Enfield carbine with ramrod shown in stowed position
10 Tallahasee carbine with ramrod shown in stowed position
11 Branding iron with CS motif
12 Fabric-covered tin drum type of water canteen complete with strap
13 Spurs manufactured by the Memphis Novelty Works, Tennessee
14 Tarpley carbine with hammer cocked
15 Le Mat carbine

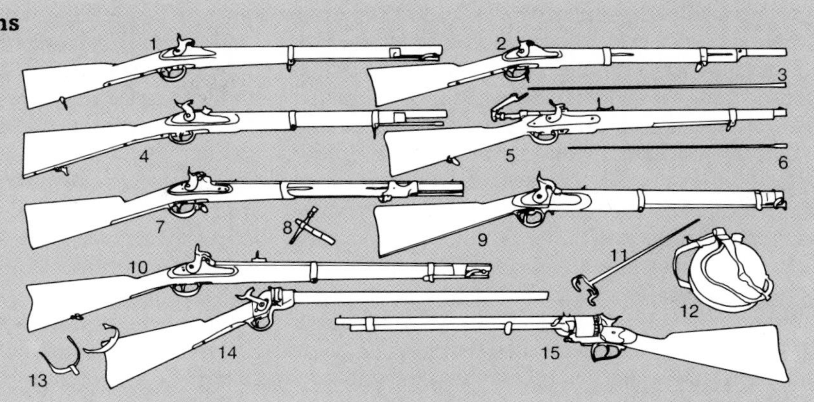

Artifacts courtesy of: Virginia Historical Society, Richmond, Va: 1-13, 15; Ben Michel Collection: 14

resentful soldier even declared that cavalrymen went so far out of their way to avoid danger that, instead of being a branch of the army, they should really be termed a life insurance company. The cavalry "will never fight", complained a Rebel soldier. "I think it is useless to have them in the army eating rations".[14] They were, in the words of an equally cynical Yankee, "mere vampyres hanging on the infantry – doing but little fighting but first in for the spoils".[15]

Such expressions proved neither fair nor entirely accurate, but it is a fact that all cavalrymen became accomplished plunderers to a degree. It was actually a necessity in the Confederacy, where the government never kept pace with the needs of its soldiery after 1861. Rebel horsemen rarely had full uniforms and equipment, or if they did when they first went to war, replacements for worn-out gear later on proved almost impossible.

Many a trooper carried a shotgun instead of a hard-to-get carbine. Hand guns came in all descriptions, from the multi-shot Le Mat revolver with shotgun barrel affixed that Stuart carried, to old Mexican War single-shot horse pistols. While all cavalrymen probably acquired a saber at the outset, many later gave it up in favor of a dirk or bowie knife, and many more Rebels carried no cutlery at all, which shows how quickly the notion of saber charges died away. In General John Hunt Morgan's Kentucky cavalry, by the middle of the war any man who carried a sword "would be forever after a laughing stock for the entire command", one of his scouts recalled.[16] And the partisan raider John Singleton Mosby, "Gray Ghost of the Confederacy", declared of sabers that "the only real use I ever heard of their being put to was to hold a piece of meat over the fire for frying".[17] Thus, for all the other pieces of equipment that a Rebel horsemen might try to acquire by hook or by crook, he rarely replaced his sword. Indeed, many intentionally "lost" the cumbersome weapons once they learned one of the basic lessons of this war, namely that the increased range and firepower of rifled weapons in the hands of infantrymen made the Napoleonic

Confederate Cavalry Carbines and Artillery Musketoons

1 S.C. Robinson Sharps carbine
2 Morse carbine with breech exposed for re-loading
3 C. Chapman musketoon complete with ramrod
4 Keen, Walker and Company carbine with breech mechanism in open position for re-loading
5 Carbine cartridge box complete with loops for attachment to waist belt
6 Bilharz, Hall and Company rising breech carbine with breech mechanism exposed for reloading
7 Alternative style of carbine cartridge box
8 Cook and Brother carbine
9 Bilharz, Hall and Company muzzle-loading carbine complete with ramrod
10 Militia carbine cartridge box with shoulder harness for carrying
11 Cap box as attached to waist belt
12 Cook and Brother musketoon, complete with ramrod
13 Richmond carbine with hammer cocked. Also including strap for carrying and ramrod for loading
14 Fabric-covered tin drum water canteen with stopper, and shoulder carrying strap attached

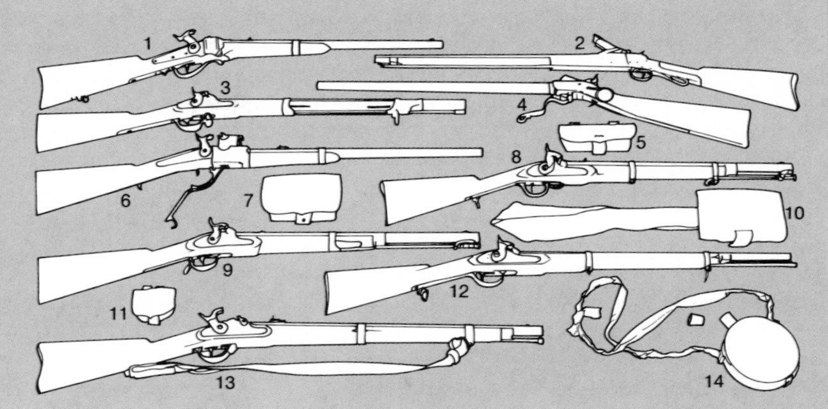

Artifacts courtesy of: Russ Pritchard Collection

cavalry saber charge not only obsolete, but suicidal. "Certainly the sabre is of no use against gunpowder", Mosby concluded, and given the latest infantry weapons, he was right.[18]

Ironically, it was in the Union Army, which seemed for so long to lag behind the Confederates in leadership, experience, and everything else except manpower and supply, that the ideal role of Civil War cavalry first evolved. Perhaps it came thanks to Northerners being less hidebound by a mounted tradition, less wedded to classical notions of cavalry doctrine. Whatever the case, Federal horsemen, though they started the war substantially behind their foes in experience and competence, gradually erased the difference. It was a hard road, for following the débâcle at Bull Run, Yankee cavalry in the East remained virtually inactive through the winter of 1861-2, trained and ready, and withering from boredom. And 1862 did not go any better for them. In the Peninsular Campaign, from March through July, the role of Union cavalry was dismal. McClellan brought too few regiments with him, misused the ones he had, and suffered the humiliation of Stuart's ride with barely a show of mounted resistance. At roughly the same period Turner Ashby so outrode, outfought, and outwitted the Yankee horsemen sent against him in the Shenandoah, that Union generals in Virginia that summer complained universally of the miserable quality of their own cavalry, "weak in numbers and spirit".[19]

Only better leadership, more efficient organization, and actual field experience would raise the Federal cavalry to the level of the Confederates, but it was slow in coming. That summer a significant change did come when General John Pope, taking command of the Army of Virginia, directed that all cavalry units within each army corps be consolidated, to serve under a corps chief of cavalry. At least after this the horsemen would not be inefficiently dispersed among infantry brigades, and it paved the way for a time not far off when, like the Confederate horse, they would all be consolidated into a single cavalry

Union Cavalry Carbines

1 Sharps 'New Model' 1859 breechloading carbine with back sight in raised position
2 Starr carbine
3 Maynard 1st Model carbine 'broken' for re-loading
4 Box used to contain cartridges for Union carbines. Loops at rear enabled it to be attached to waist belt
5 Alternative design of carbine cartridge box with waist belt loops
6 Gallager carbine
7 Merrill late model carbine with breech open for re-loading
8 Joslyn Model 1864 carbine
9 Gwyn and Campbell early model carbine with back sight in raised position
10 Carbine sling with attachment device
11 Smith carbine 'broken' to permit reloading
12 Burnside 4th Model carbine with breech mechanism partly exposed
13 Spencer carbine with breech mechanism partly exposed and back sight raised. Also showing spring-fed tubular magazine extended for reloading
14 Blakeslee cartridge box intended for use with Spencer carbine shown above

Artifacts courtesy of: The Civil War Library and Museum, Philadelphia, Pa

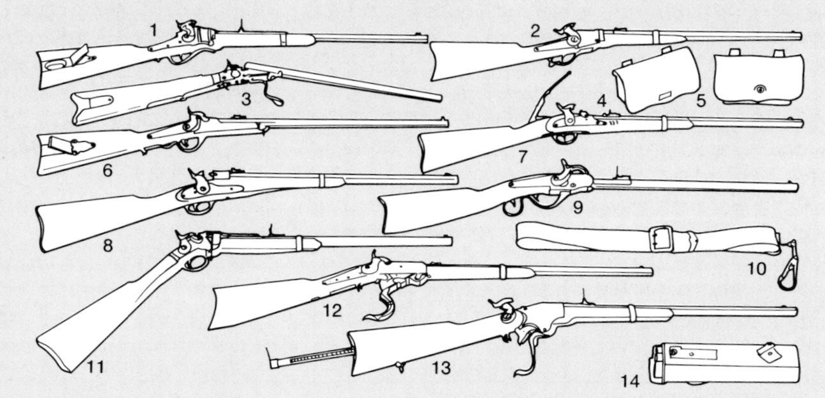

corps. Pope, himself a former cavalryman, also ended the policy of encumbering cavalry operations with baggage and supply wagons, effectively slowing horsemen down to the speed of their wagons. In future, troopers were to carry with them what they needed and take anything else from the countryside, thus achieving the dual benefit of speeding their expeditions and visiting a bit of hardship on the disloyal population of Virginia.[20]

The summer, however, still did not go well for them. In Pope's failed Second Bull Run Campaign, he again had too few cavalry and, though they did good work at picket and outpost duty, extended marching and counter-marching exhausted them. After his defeat, his cavalry went back to Washington to refit and rest. Though beaten once more they had at least learned self-reliance; how to move quickly in all weather; how to stretch three days' rations to six; how to forage in a land already scoured; and even how to start a blazing fire in the rain with wet wood if necessary. Further, they had learned that they did have a few good leaders, men like William Averell, Alfred Pleasonton, and John Buford – not perfect men, but good up to their limitations. With the experience that leaders and led were acquiring together, especially in the host of small skirmishes that summer and fall of 1862, they also learned that they could fight. And the style they evolved was a new one. While the mounted saber charge was still the most dramatic part of their repertoire, most often for a small action, especially against infantry, the cavalrymen used their horses only for mobility. Riding quickly to the point where they were needed, they dismounted, and while one man in four held the horses, the other three went into the action with their carbines, fighting on foot. By war's end it would be the dominant form of cavalry fighting.[21]

But they would do little of that in the next campaign. During Lee's invasion of Maryland in September, Federal cavalry played almost no role. Stuart, however, made yet another brilliant raid, adding to his luster. Only in its organization, as it looked for the right commander, did the Yankee horse slowly progress. "Our cavalry can be made superior to any now in the field by organization", declared General Alfred Pleasonton. "The rebel cavalry owe their success to their organization, which permits great freedom and responsibility to its commanders, subject to the commanding general."[22] By 1863 there was a single cavalry corps in the Army of the Potomac, following Pleasonton's suggestion. Soon thereafter, in March, the Yankee horsemen first stood their ground with their mounted foe and showed what they might do. At Kelly's Ford, on Virginia's Rappahannock River, a Union brigade commanded by William Averell forced a crossing of the river and then advanced toward a smaller body of Confederate troopers on the other side. Pistols blazing, the Rebels charged, and before they reached the Yankee line Averell's own men drew sabers and rushed forward. Back and forth they went. The men in blue stood their ground well, behaved like seasoned veterans, and for the first time showed the enemy that they had learned about war in the saddle now, and were ready to win their spurs. Though the battle was inconclusive,

Above: Specially envied were those Federals who carried the Spencer Carbine or, more infrequently, the Spencer Rifle, as does this Michigan sergeant. With his 1860 Colt .44 his fire-power would be formidable.

Below: Wherever the armies went, their cavalry was usually nearby. Outposts and small picket encampments like this one near Blackburn's Ford, Virginia, in July 1862, saw horsemen take their coffee and rest.

Averell's men had demonstrated that in an all-cavalry battle, almost all of it fought from the saddle, blue could stand toe-to-toe with gray.

Thus was the stage set for one great, and inevitable test between horsemen North and South, and it waited only three months to come. With Pleasonton now in command of the cavalry corps of the Army of the Potomac, his commander sent him on a raid toward Culpeper to "disperse and destroy the rebel force" believed to be there. That force was Stuart. In short, Pleasonton was ordered to bring on a major cavalry battle between his own 8,000 troopers and Stuart's 10,000.

He took Stuart almost completely by surprise in the early hours of June 9, and pushed his forward units back to the vicinity of Fleetwood Hill, near Brandy Station. Only a plucky defense by H.B. McClellan held the hill long enough for Stuart to reach the scene, and already charge and counter-charge had swept across its slopes before Stuart arrived. The greatest cavalry battle of the war had begun, and what followed was never to be forgotten by any who lived through it. "There now followed a passage of arms filled with romantic interest and splendor to a degree unequalled by anything our war produced", wrote one Confederate. Not a single trooper dismounted to fight, nor, he said, could he hear more than an occasional pistol and carbine shot. "It was what we read of in the days of chivalry, acres and acres of horsemen sparkling with sabers, and dotted with brilliant bits of color where their flags danced above them."[23] It was the dying gasp of an old mode of warfare.

In the next several hours, Fleetwood Hill was taken and lost repeatedly. Charge and counter-charge went on through the grim afternoon, yet some of the troopers, especially Yankees, found it all somehow exhilarating. Edward Tobie of the 1st Maine Cavalry never forgot the feel of his very first saber charge. "On they go, faster and faster", he remembered, "over fences and ditches, driving the enemy a mile or more. Oh, it was grand!" A man in the 6th New York rhapsodized over the "wild intoxication" of the mounted charge, "the most inspiriting, romantic, and thoroughly delightful kind".[25]

Before long, everyone lost count of the assaults, and many became disoriented. In what one New Yorker called "an indescribable clashing and slashing, banging and yelling", troopers lost almost all organization. In the mêlée, "we were now so mixed up with the rebels that every man was fighting desperately to maintain the position", though many were no longer certain of what their "position" was.[26] The dust kicked up by thousands of horses, the air filled with the cries of men who shouted themselves hoarse in the excitement, the bolting of panicked animals, the ceaseless raising and lowering of flashing blades, and the sounds of steel hacking into bone and flesh, created a scene almost surreal. "We could not tell friend from foe", a Pennsylvania cavalryman remembered, and after awhile many troopers simply slashed out at whatever came near them, unable even to see the colors of the uniform.[27] Though Pleasonton finally retired from the field, he left unbeaten, having achieved something of a moral victory by showing that Yankee horsemen could take the offensive against Rebel horse, give blow for blow, and stand their ground. One New Yorker called it "a glorious fight, in which the men of the North had proved themselves more than a match for the

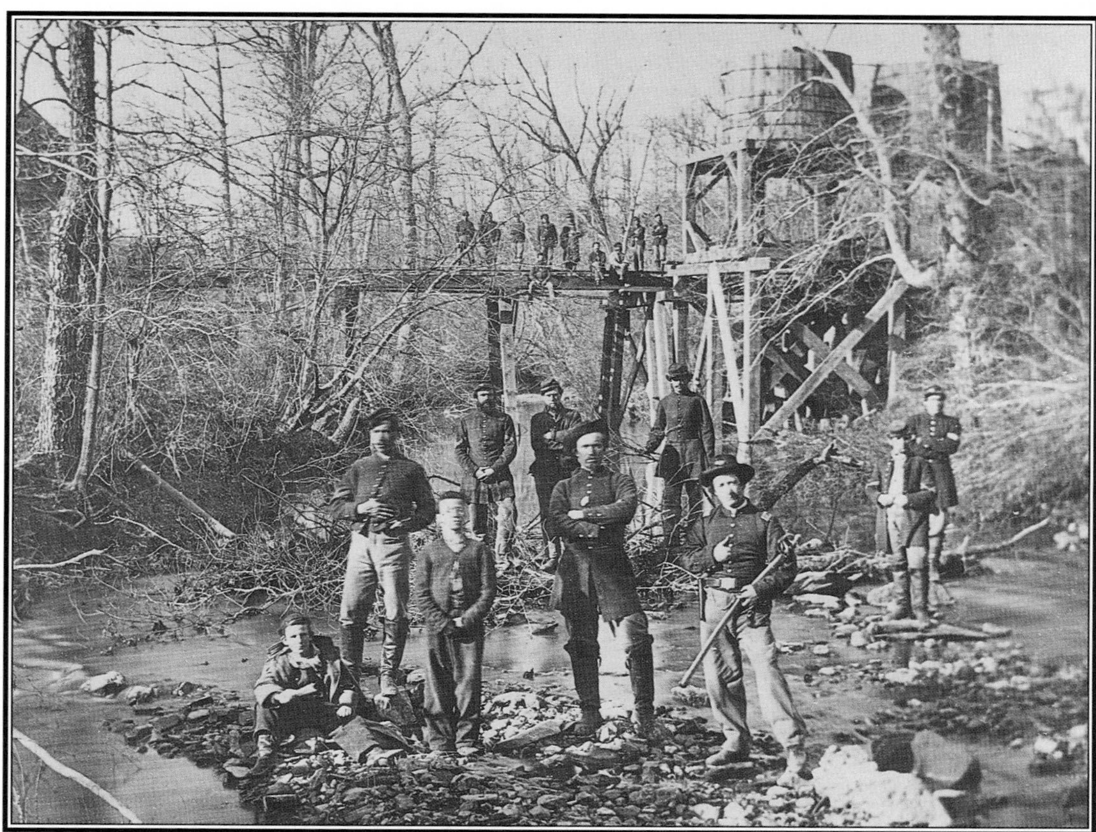

Above: Often the cavalryman's duty included garrison or guard duty along vulnerable railroad supply lines. This is a group of cavalry and infantry at a blockhouse on the Orange & Alexandria Railroad in 1864.

Below: The variety of weaponry carried on horseback can be seen on these men of Company I, 5th Ohio Cavalry. Five different models of pistol are evident, as well as their Sharps carbines and dragoon sabers.

boasted Southern chivalry".[28] Even the enemy agreed, Stuart's adjutant McClellan declaring that Brandy Station "*made* the Federal cavalry".[29]

Thereafter, Pleasonton's men performed as well as Stuart's, and the somewhat embarrassed Rebel chieftain resorted to yet another raid to redeem his reputation. Unfortunately, he did it when Lee needed him with the army fighting for its life at Gettysburg in July, and Stuart's reputation never completely recovered. The cavalryman's inherent desire for flash and dash lured him away from his real role of reconnaissance, screening, and protection for the main army.

It was the same west of the Appalachians, yet there were differences out there, not the least being that from the war's outset the Federals were every bit the equals of their foes. All of these western troopers were accustomed to riding and shooting, and all, as it developed, were more given to irregular warfare, even to plunder and pillage. Initially, the cavalry's role was small and organization varied. John Hunt Morgan, by 1862 the premier cavalry raider for the western Confederates, began the war commanding a squadron of Kentucky cavalry attached to the 1st Kentucky Infantry Brigade. Only by mid-1862 did North and South begin to expand their mounted commitments in the region, and then almost from the first they did so in a way different from their armies in Virginia. Difficult as the Old Dominion's landscape was for the traditional operations of cavalry, Mississippi, Tennessee, and Alabama were even worse, far too broken by woods and hills and rivers for the Napoleonic style. On the other hand, the myriad hidden back roads, the dense woods, the innumerable places for ambush, and the tenuous routes for maintaining supply lines and communications, all made this territory ideal for raids, though raids of a different sort than those of Stuart's. Out here they would be lightning quick, deep penetrations, speedy destruction, and hasty withdrawal. And out here they would, in the end, do far more real damage to the Federal war effort than all of Stuart's bold strokes combined.

Union Edged Weapons used by Confederate Forces

Like many other types of weapon, the South had to rely on its enemy in the North to supply at least some of its swords.

1 Model 1840 design of cavalry saber incorporating three-bar style of hand guard and housed in protective scabbard
2 Typical design of US officer's sword belt complete with straps and buckles for attachment to the sword's scabbard
3 Model 1812 design of Starr saber with simple stirrup style of hand guard
4 Model 1860 design of cavalry saber with variation in style of three-bar hand guard and complete with protective scabbard
5 Model 1850 design of Infantry Officer's sword with decorative pommel and hand guard and complete with protective scabbard
6 Relic of Model 1860 design of cavalry saber housed in protective scabbard. Hilt, grip and hand guard are missing, exposing tang while the scabbard features a partly obscured inscription that may refer to a military unit and which appears to read "15th th. loved the flashing of swords that struggled to be free"

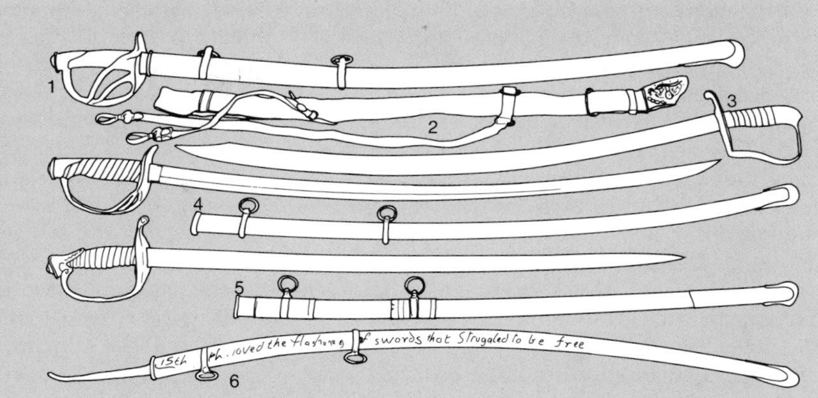

Artifacts courtesy of: The Museum of The Confederacy, Richmond, Va

Both sides turned raider early on. Morgan achieved a quick rise and maintained it through the war until his death in 1864. Nathan Bedford Forrest assumed prominence for a certain natural gift as a leader. Joseph Wheeler became, at 26, chief of cavalry of the Confederate Army of Mississippi, and a noteworthy – if often ineffective – raider behind Yankee lines. In the blue, Yankee generals turned to men like Albert Lee, David Stanley, and John T. Wilder. All of them operated on the same terms and with the same goals: get in the enemy's rear; burn railroad bridges and tear up track; hit supply bases and attack wagon trains; cut telegraph wires or, like Morgan, 'tap' into them to learn the foe's intentions; force the enemy to weaken his main army to deal with the raiders; gather information, and avoid a pitched battle unless certain of victory. Not every raid went this way, but every raid in the west began in whole or part for these reasons.

So it was in the spring of 1863 that General U.S. Grant, commanding the forces advancing toward Vicksburg on the Mississippi, sent Colonel Benjamin Grierson and 1,700 troopers on a 600-mile ride in sixteen days, from La Grange, Tennessee to Baton Rouge, Louisiana. "We are going on a big scout", wrote one of Grierson's men, "and play smash with the railroads".[30] So they were. Grant wanted them to cut rail lines, disrupt communications, and divert Confederates away from the defense of Vicksburg. It was a brilliant raid, perhaps the best of the war. With just two dozen casualties, the Yankee raiders inflicted about 600, tore up 60 miles of track and telegraph wire, destroyed 12,000 or more rifles and other Confederate supplies, and captured 1,000 horses and mules. William T. Sherman called it "the most brilliant expedition of the war".[31] More to the point, said Grant, "it was Grierson who first set the example of what might be done in the interior of the enemy's country".[32]

Grant would follow that example for the rest of the war. Meanwhile, farther west, beyond the Mississippi, lay an entirely different sort of war. The prairies and plains had been a nation of men

Confederate and Union Edged Weapons

Edged weapons were produced with varying degrees of sophistication.

1 Cavalry saber of unmarked and unidentified design
2 Unidentified cavalry saber complete with a scabbard made of sheet copper
3 Unmarked and still unidentified design of cavalry saber
4 Type of saber design as manufactured by the Nashville Plow Works, Nashville, Tennessee. Features distinctive style of grip guard
5 Unmarked and unidentified cavalry saber complete with a wooden scabbard
6 Unsophisticated style of short sword as used by members of Foot Artillery forces with the Confederacy. Sword is complete with a wooden scabbard

Union Edged Weapons (Insert)

7 US Model 1860 design of cavalry saber featuring three-bar type of grip guard
8 US Model 1840 design of cavalry saber featuring variation of three-bar type of grip guard
9 Imported Model 1840 design of cavalry saber, complete with scabbard featuring a hilt fabricated from iron

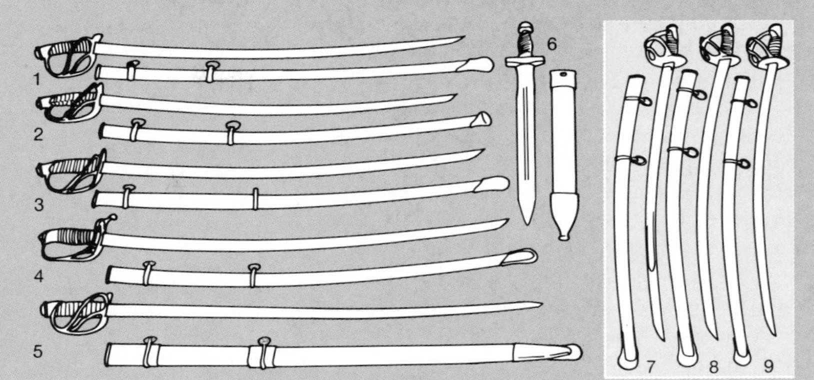

Artifacts courtesy of: Russ Pritchard Collection: 1-6; The Civil War Library and Museum, Philadelphia, Pa: 7-9

on horseback, already experienced at Indian fighting and handling firearms. As a result, the region was a spawning ground for legions of cavalrymen, North and South, and the wide and open landscape allowed for mounted operations on a grand scale. Indeed, the mounted arm rose to the greatest extent of its offensive potential out there. In the Rebel army commanded by General E. Kirby Smith in 1864, 22,800 of his 40,000 men were horsemen, making up fifty-seven percent. By contrast, in Lee's army the number was rarely more than ten percent. Indeed, cavalrymen were too numerous, and Smith actually strove to reduce his mounted arm.

These cavalrymen often went into battle mounted alongside infantry, reins in their teeth, pistols blazing from both hands. In that expanse only a very brave man, or a very great fool, risked being separated from his horse. Friendly lines could be a hundred miles away, and a merciless foe only too near.[33]

It was that merciless character for which the mounted fighting west of the Mississippi became most notorious. Both sides enlisted Indians, mostly Cherokee, and that alone introduced an element of occasional savagery into the fighting.

Corporal, Illinois Cavalry

Everything about the cavalryman of the Union, seemed to denote color and excitement. His short blue woollen shell jacket, gaily trimmed in yellow to denote the mounted service, stood out above his sky blue pants, all of it framed and trimmed by the polished black leather of his belt, boots, shoulder belts and black-trimmed blue kepi. While there were many variations, especially among privately raised and militia groups from pre-war days, most Yankee troopers looked like this cavalryman from Illinois. They rode on the same McClellan style saddle, carried the same regulation saber, wore the same Colt .44 Model 1860 Army pistol and, if they were fortunate, carried the same Spencer carbine repeater. Even their spurs were regulation issue, though the fitness of their horses varied widely. All they could not be issued was experience in combat, and that they would have to learn for themselves with a little help from Johnny Reb.

While stories of scalpings were greatly exaggerated, still it did occur, though it fell to whites to raise brutality on horseback to a science. Men like William C. Quantrill, George Todd, and William "Bloody Bill" Anderson, were nothing more than mounted Confederate terrorists, an embarrassment and sometimes a danger even to their own side. Across the lines, men like John Chivington and Charles Jennison were little better.

These men did do some good work, but most were in the war for themselves, using the civil dispute as a mere excuse for sanctioned pillage. Executions, tortures, scalpings and mutilations, all in the name of "the cause", revealed the guerrillas west of the Mississippi to be little else than criminals. If there was any doubt of that, then Anderson's Centralia massacre of September 27, 1864, offered the proof. In Centralia, Missouri, having captured a trainload of twenty-four unarmed Union soldiers on furlough, Anderson and his men shot them in the head one by one. Later the same day they rode over a dismounted detachment of 147 Yankees, killing 124, most of them as they surrendered or begged for their lives. Anderson's men took heads and scalps as trophies and decorations for their saddles.[34]

There were plenty of other excesses, not least the Lawrence, Kansas, "massacre" perpetrated by Quantrill in August 1863. While these cut-throats in uniform were by far the minority of the cavalry in the so-called Trans-Mississippi region, their depredations assumed such proportion in the public mind that they came to represent the cavalry service in general beyond the great river. By the end of the war, both sides were weeding out these elements in their own forces, though most would escape justice or punishment, and go on after the war to become local heroes or to ride the outlaw trail. Indeed, the so-called "Wild West" of the 1870s and beyond was largely the offspring of Civil War irregular cavalry service of the 1860s.

Fortunately, the mounted service east of the Mississippi River never took on the level of brutality that emerged west of the river, but as the spring campaigns of 1864 commenced, it was clear that the air of dash and derring-do was about spent, as the grim relentlessness of the war made itself felt more and more. Men like Forrest, who cared little for the pomp or flair of war, came increasingly to command. Pleasonton was replaced by Major General Philip H. Sheridan, a ruthless man with a killer instinct, and in his first battle, at Yellow Tavern, Virginia, on May 11, he won the day. During the same battle, Stuart received a mortal wound, his death and the demise of the dashing kind of service he had symbolized being almost simultaneous.

The Rebels were routed from the field, and finally Yankee horsemen had an undisputed victory. "From that time until the close of the war", wrote one, the Confederate cavalry "ceased to be distinguished for the enterprise and boldness in aggressive movement for which it was formerly remarkable".[35] For the rest of the war, the horsemen in blue relentlessly wore down their opponents, keeping them almost entirely on the defensive. The only brief glimmer of the old Cavalry Corps of the Army of Northern Virginia came in September 1864 when, led by General Wade Hampton, Rebel troopers rode out of their lines and in a wide swinging arc behind Yankee lines, captured a cattle herd of 3,000 beeves and brought it back to Lee's hungry men.

By contrast, the Confederate horse in the West remained active, mobile, and dangerous almost to the end of the war. Those who fought with Forrest used horses to get to battle, not to fight in

Above: The cavalrymen of both sides rode literally all across the divided country. This photograph, taken outside Baton Rouge, Louisiana by Southerner A.D. Lytle, captured images of Yankee horsemen encamped near the Mississippi River, their tents and campfires spreading almost to the horizon. It was troopers like these who rode on Benjamin Grierson's dramatic raid through Mississippi and Louisiana in 1863.

Below: Preparing to saddle and mount, or perhaps for a parade, hundreds of Federal troopers stand before their horses, while Lytle photographs them. There is probably a full regiment of men and animals in sight.

them. They rode quick, struck hard, then left just as fast. No one used sabers. Pistols were their weapons; pistols and carbines, and unflinching courage. And a willingness to kill. In the open spaces west of the Mississippi the Confederates carried on even more ambitious operations almost until the end. Given the expanse of territory to be covered when Rebels tried to raid or invade Arkansas and Missouri, only cavalry were practical for the task. Major General Sterling Price's raid into Missouri in October 1864, however, dwarfed all other such operations. He left Arkansas with 12,000 mounted men, the greatest assemblage of cavalry in Confederate history, hoping to drive the enemy out of Missouri. An army of 20,000 Yankees, 8,000 of them horsemen, assembled to meet him, and on October 23 at Westport, near Kansas City, the two forces met. Price's numbers by that time had dwindled to about 9,000, but still the resulting battle engaged about 17,000 horsemen on both sides, second only to Brandy Station among cavalry battles of the war.[36]

Price was defeated, largely due to his own poor leadership. Yet his loss also revealed the limitations of cavalry's usefulness on major campaigns over wide territory. Even after years of experience, many men still would not treat their animals properly. It was menial, dirty, smelly, and tedious work, the more so since a cavalryman had to care for his horse before himself. Many men simply could not adopt the proper attitude. As a result, they broke down their mounts, and when a horse was out of the campaign, so was its rider. Furthermore, even if well cared for, after traveling several hundred miles a horse was tired and unequal to the demands of charge and countercharge if a fight took place on horseback.

By this stage of the war, everything was different, and the men who had been in the mounted service since the beginning hardly recognized what it had become. If anyone on either side needed further demonstration that the role of the cavalry had changed in this war, and that its best use was for quick mounted raids,

Union and Confederate Handguns

1 Uhlinger pocket revolver as used by Union forces
2 Starr Army revolver as used by Union
3 Remington-Beals Army revolver as used by Union
4 Remington-Beals Navy revolver as used by Union
5 Remington New Model Navy revolver as used by Union
6 Manhattan Pocket Model revolver used by Union
7 Plant Third Model revolver as used by Union
8 Smith and Wesson No. 1 Second Issue revolver as used by Union
9 Colt Model 1862 Police revolver as used by Union
10 Model 1836 pistol alteration as used by Confederate forces
11 Confederate holster
12 Griswold and Gunnison late model revolver used by Confederates
13 Confederate holster
14 Rigdon, Ansley revolver as used by Confederates
15 Leech and Rigdon revolver as used by Confederates
16 Spiller and Burr revolver as used by Confederates
17 Revolver bullet mold used by Confederates forces

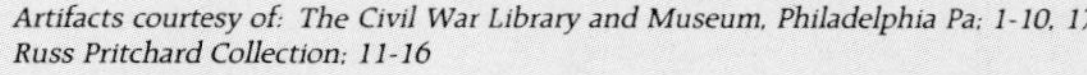
Artifacts courtesy of: The Civil War Library and Museum, Philadelphia Pa: 1-10, 17: Russ Pritchard Collection: 11-16

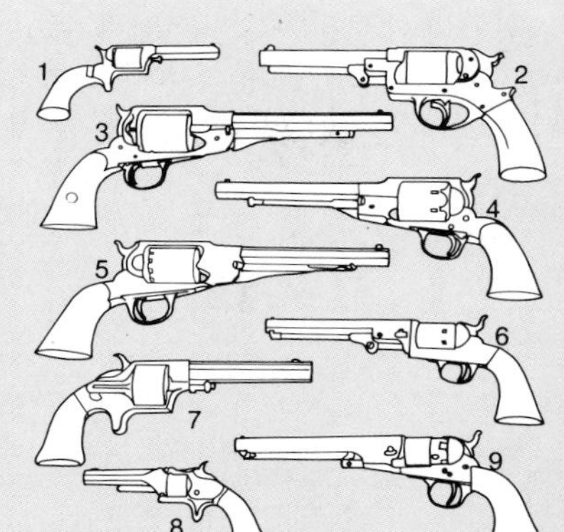

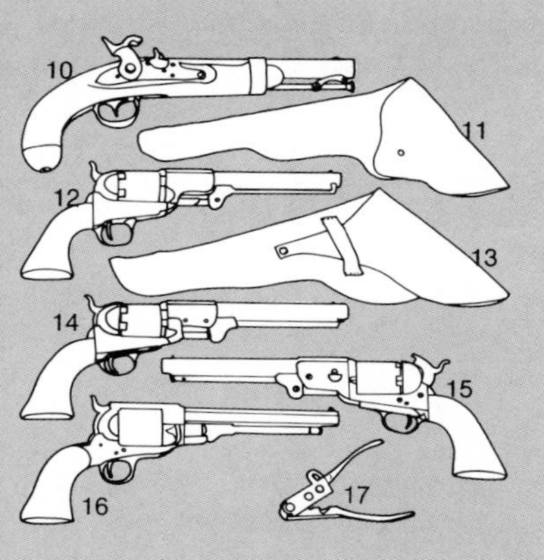

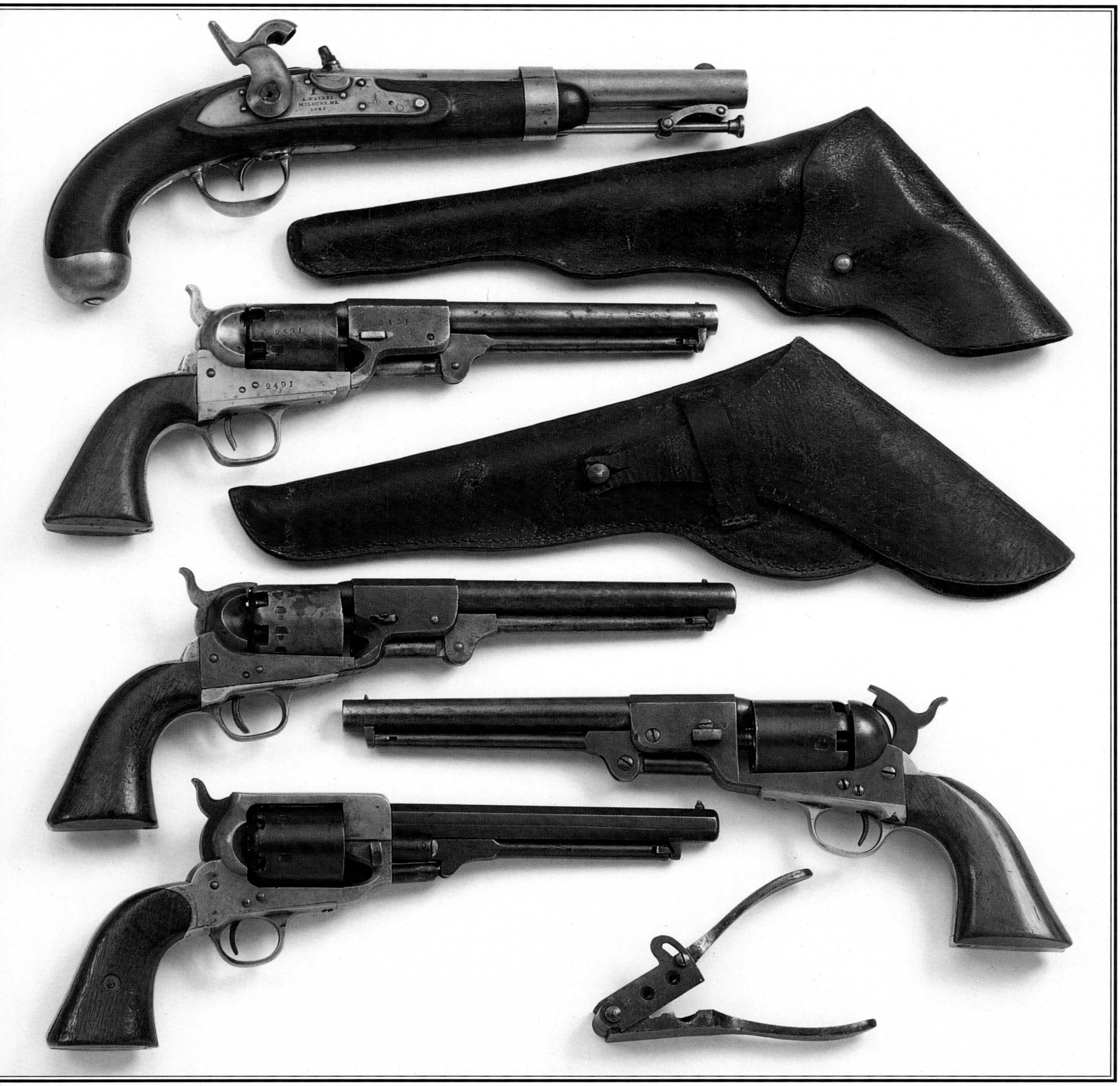

and for fighting afoot, then the last campaigns erased all doubt. On March 22, 1865, James Wilson, now a major general, led three divisions of cavalry across the Tennessee and into the heart of Georgia and Alabama. During the ensuing month, he moved swiftly to Tuscaloosa, and then on to the manufacturing center at Selma. Dogged and resisted by Forrest, Wilson and his 13,480 cavalrymen were simply too much for him. Wilson beat Forrest aside, destroyed Selma, and then moved on to Montgomery and the capital. By late April he had taken Columbus and Macon, Georgia.

In his wake he left a 525-mile march in which the bluecoat cavalry had beaten Forrest twice, captured more than half their numbers in prisoners and killed or wounded 1,000 more. Wilson destroyed seven iron works, seven foundries, seven machine shops, two steel rolling mills, five collieries, thirteen factories, three arsenals, a powder works, a navy yard, and five steamboats, not to mention thirty-five locomotives, 565 rail cars, and a host of other equipment. For sheer destructive force, it was the greatest raid of its kind, the ultimate in the potential of mobility combined with force, the new mandate of American cavalry. It destroyed the industrial ability of the Confederacy to continue. Before his campaign began, Wilson confided to his diary that, "In our next war our cavalry ought to play a proper part." By showing what cavalry could achieve, he wrote, "I desire above all things to be instrumental in bringing this about." Though American cavalry would never again fight in a war like this one, it is certain that Wilson helped provide the model for mounted doctrine in the future.[37]

Though resistance continued for a few weeks after April 9, 1865, symbolically Appomattox meant the defeat of the Confederacy. It reflected all the changes that had come about for the horseman in arms. The remnant of Stuart's once magnificent cavalry corps now answered to competent, but uninspired commanders, the men and animals worn to extremity. It was the failure of Lee's cavalry at the Battle of Five Forks on April 1 which in part helped make the Confederate position around Petersburg and Richmond untenable. Forced out into the open, Lee and his army had nowhere to go but a retreat to the southwest. Sheridan and his cavalry, already victorious at Five Forks, pursued Lee relentlessly while Grant and the infantry followed. At every point Sheridan cut off possible lines of march for the beleagured Lee. When Lee reached Amelia Courthouse, expecting to find vitally needed supplies sent ahead, he found nothing awaiting him. Sheridan had intercepted them. Marching on,

Above: Here at Brandy Station, Virginia, Yankee cavalry proved themselves equal to the Rebels. By February 1864, as the 1st US Cavalry posed on the old battlefield, Rebel horse were being hard-pressed everywhere.

hungry and exhausted, the Confederates were almost overwhelmed on April 6 by Sheridan's whole cavalry corps and elements of Union infantry. In fighting along Sayler's Creek, Lee lost a third of his army, including many of his generals, captured or dispersed.

From this triumph, Sheridan raced on to get ahead of the last remaining route open to Lee, and he did. On April 8, at Appomattox Station, Custer's division captured the only other supply train that might have helped Lee keep going, and then moved northeast to Appomattox Courthouse to find the remnant of Lee's army in position. That night, as darkness fell, Lee could see not only the campfires of Grant's army to his rear, but also those of Sheridan's troopers south and west of him. Lee was virtually surrounded. A spirited but doomed attempt to break out the next morning convinced Lee that there was nothing left for him but to surrender.[38]

Union cavalry did not win the war, and Rebel cavalry did not lose it. They played their part along with the other services, and to the degree

Above: By the end of the war, as Yankee cavalry emerged triumphant, massive regiments like the 13th New York Cavalry, on parade at Prospect Hill, Virginia, in July 1865, could fill whole plains.

Below: With his cavalry saber, his Sharps carbine, and his Colt .44 1860 Army revolver, this unknown horseman, like tens of thousands of his kind, had swept across the war-torn country and into legend.

that their efforts integrated systematically into the entire scope of their nations' war efforts, they made their contribution. But one thing is certain. The evolution of the cavalryman from idealized poseur and parade ground gallant, to swift, lightly-equipped, and unchivalrously destructive raider helped ensure that the war would end in the way it did. But for Wilson's havoc in Alabama and Mississippi, and Sheridan's in Virginia, the Confederacy might have had the ability to continue the war for months more.

As for the cavalrymen they led, the volunteers took home with them at war's end a powerful sense of pride. Indeed, men North and South would look back upon their days in the saddle as the best of their lives, forgetting in time the hardship, the heat and dust and hunger. They had been the last of the old and the first of the new, and fought a war on horseback entirely of their own making. No other cavalry service, anywhere, in any war to come, would be quite like theirs.

References

1 Stephen Z. Starr, *The Union Cavalry in the Civil War* (Baton Rouge, 1979), I, pp.48, 58.
2 *Ibid.*, pp.50-3.
3 *Ibid.*, p.60.
4 *Official Records*, Series III, Vol.I, p.77.
5 William C. Davis, *Battle at Bull Run* (New York, 1978), pp.207-8.
6 Starr, *Union Cavalry*, I, p.66.
7 *Ibid.*, p.78.
8 *Ibid.*, pp.104-5.
9 Richard Berringer, Herman Hattaway, Archer Jones and William Still, *Why the South Lost the Civil War* (Athens, Ga., 1986), p.170.
10 Heros Von Borke, *Memoirs of the Confederate War for Independence* (New York, 1938), I, p.39.
11 *Official Records*, Series I, Vol.II, Part 1, p.1042.
12 Von Borke, *Memoirs*, II, p.188.
13 Nannie Tiley, (ed.), *Federals on the Frontier* (Austin, Tex., 1962), pp.75-6.
14 Wiley, *Johnny Reb*, p.341.
15 Tilley, *Federals*, p.76.
16 India Logan, *Kelian Franklin Pedicord* (New York, 1908), p.114.
17 John S. Mosby, *Mosby's War Reminiscences* (New York, 1958), p.30.
18 *Ibid.*, p.30.
19 Starr, *Union Cavalry*, I, pp.258-9, 262-3, 282.
20 *Official Records*, Series I, Vol. XII, Part 3, p.581; Part 2, p.50.
21 Starr, *Union Cavalry*, I, p.303.
22 *Official Records*, Series I, Vol. XXI, pp.785-6.
23 William W. Blackford, *War Years with Jeb Stuart* (New York, 1945), pp.215-17.
24 Edward P. Tobie, *History of the First Maine Cavalry* (Boston, 1887), p.155.
25 Starr, *Union Cavalry*, I, p.395.
26 Noble D. Preston, *History of the Tenth Regiment of Cavalry* (New York, 1892), p.85.
27 *Ibid.*, p.85.
28 Willard Glazier, *Three Years in the Federal Cavalry* (New York, 1874), p.223.
29 H.B. McClellan, *The Life and Campaigns of Major General J.E.B. Stuart* (Boston, 1885), p.294.
30 Dee Brown, *Grierson's Raid* (Urbana, Ill., 1954), p.5.
31 *Ibid.*, p.223.
32 *Official Records*, Series I, Vol. XXIV, Part 1, p.58.
33 Albert Castel, "They Called Him 'Bloody Bill'", *Journal of the West*, III (April 1964), p.238.
34 Stephen B. Oates, *Confederate Cavalry West of the River* (Austin, Tex., 1961), pp.167-9; Castel, "Bloody Bill", pp.237ff.
35 Starr, *Union Cavalry*, II, pp.108-9.
36 Fred L. Lee, *The Battle of Westport* (Kansas City, 1976), pp.22-3.
37 James P. Jones, *Yankee Blitzkrieg: Wilson's Raid Through Alabama and Georgia* (Athens, Ga., 1976), pp.9, 28, 185-6.
38 Douglas S. Freeman, *Lee's Lieutenants* (New York, 1944), III, p.723.

CHAPTER FIVE

Rolling Thunder

The balance of 1862 saw the give and take of warfare more evenly balanced between North and South, though already there were signs of a slow turn of affairs in that Confederate victories only maintained the *status quo*, while Yankee victories had far-reaching impact on the course of the war. Hard after the Union defeat at Second Manassas in August, came the bloodiest single day of the war, when in September more than 2,000 men died in battle at Antietam, Maryland. Lee, attempting a raid into Maryland, was stopped and nearly overwhelmed, but was saved from disaster only by McClellan's timidity. It was the gray chieftain's first major defeat. It ended his raid, nearly shattered his army, and may have played a small role in preventing foreign powers from granting recognition and military assistance to the South. Psychologically, at least, Lee redeemed himself that December when McClellan's replacement, Ambrose Burnside, almost shattered his army attacking across the Rappahannock River at Fredericksburg in one of the most bloody and senseless repulses of the war. If he could not take Maryland, still Lee showed that he could hold northern Virginia.

Of greater significance was the failure of another major Rebel raid into Kentucky, led by General Braxton Bragg's Army of Tennessee. Initially successful, he captured the state capital before being forced out of the state by his defeat at Perryville in October, effectively ending Rebel hopes for a Confederate Kentucky. Meanwhile, Grant was on the move again, and enjoying initial success in his campaign to take Vicksburg, until a bold Rebel raid on his supply lines forced him to abandon his campaign for the season. Not so General William S. Rosecrans, who led his Yankee Army of the Cumberland into middle Tennessee after Bragg, and defeated him in a see-saw battle at Stones River as 1863 dawned. It was a battle whose climactic moment came when scores of massed Union cannon repulsed the greatest Rebel infantry charge of the war in the west.

IN DECEMBER of 1861 the Surry Light Artillery of Virginia was encamped near the James River, waiting out the winter, and waiting still to see some active service. Colonel Roger A. Pryor, its commander, really wanted the unit to serve as infantry, and apparently put quite a few roadblocks of his own in the way of his men receiving either serviceable cannon or training with the old pieces they had. But in the first week of December he finally decided to give the command "some sure enough practice at loading and firing", as Private Benjamin Jones put it. After six months in service, it was about time. "The Colonel wanted to see if our gunners could hit the broad side of a house", wrote Jones, and it turned out that that was literally what Pryor meant. Pointing to a farmhouse half a mile distant, the colonel challenged the battery to hit it, declaring that "he would be bound every one of them would miss it, clear and clean". In fact, there were soon four fine drafty holes in the side of the house, without anyone bothering to determine whether or not the building had occupants. For one of the Confederacy's premier batteries of artillery, it was hardly an auspicious beginning.[1]

In fact, rather few artillery units on either side began with much fanfare or good auspices. It was the forgotten branch of the service. In the first flush of enthusiasm, North and South, everyone rushed to get into the infantry. The foot soldier, carrying his mighty rifle with its gleaming bayonet, marching rank upon rank to war, was the

Though the artillery arm began life as impromptu as everything else, in time the artillery parks would seem to stretch forever and the big guns would thunder out all across America.

Gunners, Washington Artillery, CSA

The Washington Artillery of New Orleans was among the oldest and proudest of the private or fraternal artillery companies. All told it comprised five companies, four of which went to Virginia in the first days of the war and remained there thereafter. The fifth company served with the Army of Tennessee. Like many units, their uniforms and equipment evolved as the war progressed. Originally they wore dark blue frock coats or short artillery jackets with scarlet collars and cuffs over light blue trousers with scarlet stripes denoting the artillery arm. They wore scarlet kepis with blue bands and gold trim. Once in regular service the caps were all they retained, their blue uniforms being traded for gray after a few months. They also began by carrying sabers and pistols, but these too were given up in time. As inappropriate for a light artillery unit. Part of the Washington Artillery saw service at First Manassas.

image that captured the American imagination. For those with an extra quotient of dash, the cavalry beckoned, all leather and jingling harness, feathered caps and flashing sabers. The artillery, on the other hand, simply was not a romantic arm of the service, especially for volunteers. Hence the Virginia volunteer Colonel Pryor's anxiety to have the Surry Light become infantry instead.

Notwithstanding, there had been a number of private artillery companies before the war, some state militia, and other well-funded and organized "fraternal" outfits both North and South. The most famous was undoubtedly the Washington Artillery of New Orleans, formed in 1838, and already blooded by service in the war with Mexico. It enlisted the flower of New Orleans society into its ranks, and at times membership was almost mandatory if a young man wanted to rise. Yet by 1857 its strength had dwindled to a mere thirteen names on the rolls. Clearly, the rise of the infantry militia companies in the city had eroded its membership away to more popular forms of service. After all, cannon were dirty, noisy, heavy to manhandle around, and required almost constant maintenance.

Elsewhere in the nation before 1861 there were other such organizations as the Richmond Howitzers, the Washington Light Artillery of Charleston, the Norfolk Light Artillery Blues, and more. Yet compared to the burgeoning number of infantry and cavalry companies in pre-war America, their ranks were few. The fact is, there was no sort of artillery tradition in America, North or South. At West Point's Military Academy, every cadet studied the big guns, but artillery service was not one of the most favored postings for graduates, and much the same was the case at the several state and private military schools.

Consequently, when 1861 and war came there was no rush on either side to don the red stripes and facings of the artilleryman's uniform. Additional obstacles existed as well. Artillery service required of its enlisted men a greater degree of technical skill, frequently some mathematics, and no small degree of brawn. On top of that, it offered seemingly greater dangers than the other services. After all, cannon were the targets for other cannon, and it took a serene indifference to death for a man to stand at his gun impervious to the fact that the other side was hurling 12.3-pound iron balls at him at 1,440 feet per second. Furthermore, while infantry and cavalry regiments could be raised and even equipped within a small area, artillery batteries had to rely upon the state or Federal government for equipment, and many simply could not be raised locally.

From these and other causes, the artillery was always the smallest branch of the service North and South. By war's end, the Union would enlist 432 batteries, accounting for just twelve percent of all units that served. In the Confederacy, 268 batteries, battalions, and regiments numbered somewhat more, almost eighteen percent, but clearly neither army nor people were enthralled with serving the big guns.[2]

It is ironic, then, that once the new artillerymen were in their units, they often resisted strenuously the efforts of others to convert them to another branch. When the Washington Artillery of Augusta, Georgia, entered Confederate service and went to Pensacola, Florida, the commander, General Braxton Bragg, tried to switch them to infantry. The Georgians promptly arose in protest and requested transfer to another theater of the war before Bragg backed down. Similarly, Roger Pryor had to give up his designs on turning the Surry Light Artillery into infantry. The men would not have it. "We are born artillerymen", proclaimed Jones in September, 1861, "we are!" In fact, Pryor did not at first announce his intention, but the men soon divined it. In August they were "temporarily" assigned to the 3rd Virginia Infantry since no cannon had been assigned to them as yet. Consequently, they drilled with the infantry. The men grumbled, while officers assured them that their cannon would arrive before long. "The men shake their heads, and declare it is only a ruse to lure us piecemeal into the net, and fasten us to the infantry service for the war", wrote Private Jones. A month later they were finally given two old cannons for practice, which meant that while continuing their infantry training and drill, the men had to do double duty by commencing their artillerymen's routine. Pryor put Sergeant William Bloxam in charge, and he did even more to discourage their enthusiasm for the guns by making the men manhandle the ancient smoothbore six-pounders. "We are required to move the guns about by hand", wrote Jones, "over the field, to front and to rear, in echelon and in line, to sponge and load and fire in mimic warfare, until our arms ache, and we long for rest." But the men did not give up, so fixed had their determination become about being gunners. However much Bloxam and Pryor

Above: Nothing better illustrates the informal nature of the new Confederate artillery units than the chaos of uniforms worn by the members of this mortar battery near Pensacola, Florida in April 1861.

Below: By complete contrast, the members of the 1st Battery of Light Artillery, Massachusetts Volunteer Militia went off to war very well-equipped, including even a winning hand of poker posed for the camera.

pushed them, they did not complain. The Surry boys, Jones proclaimed, "will never cry out, 'Hold! enough of artillery for us'." And they never did.[3]

But for the monsters they tugged and loaded and fired, the gunners in blue and gray met with much the same experience as their counterparts in the infantry and cavalry in their first days in the armies. They had the same cheering send-offs from home, the same trips by water or rail to the training grounds, the same first encounters with camp life and camp death through measles. "Time passes lightly", wrote one artilleryman in 1861, "and we are getting used to drilling, and guard duty, and life in camp. These cloth houses are fairly good residences, and it is so easy to change them from one place to another. And there is need for so little furniture! or rather there is no room for it! We sleep and sit on the ground, with only some straw under us."[4]

Batteries in the Union Army were, as a rule, issued their guns, teams, and attendant equipment soon after their initial training and indoctrination into the military were complete. Across the lines, on the other hand, equipping a battery was all too often a gradual process, accomplished in unplanned stages. After receiving those two old smoothbores in September, the Surry Light Artillery waited until December before receiving another brace of guns, and sufficient horses to pull all four pieces. A Mississippi outfit left home with sixty-five horses, but only one cannon, and had to wait many months before another three field pieces arrived. It was March 1862 before the final guns arrived, making up its full six-gun battery complement, along with caissons, limbers, traveling forge, and battery wagon. Horses were in equally uncertain supply, with so many of the best being sold to the cavalry. "Our church bells even are being cast into field pieces", wrote an Alabama lieutenant, "but they are useless without horses. Can any one prefer the luxury or comfort even of keeping horses, to the preservation of our homes and lives?"[5]

Whatever they had when they began their service, the gunners looked forward to the same

Confederate Artillery Artifacts

In contrast to other arms, the nature of artillery often meant direct supply from state or government.

1 Typical trousers as worn by enlisted Confederate Army gunners
2 Pair of 20lb Parrott shells
3 Typical style forage cap as worn by enlisted gunners
4 Alternative style of forage cap as worn by enlisted gunners
5 50lb shell produced by the Confederate ordnance facility located at Dahlgren, Virginia
6 Representative shirt worn by Confederate gunners
7 Battleflag
8 Shipping crate used for movement of heavy projectiles
9 Short-style jacket as worn by enlisted gunners
10 Alternative short-style jacket as worn by enlisted gunners
11 6lb spherical solid shot
12 Model 1851 Colt Navy revolver with holster and belt
13 Wooden water canteen complete with strap for carrying
14 Haversack complete with shoulder strap for carrying
15 Model 1833 US Foot Artillery short sword encased in protective scabbard

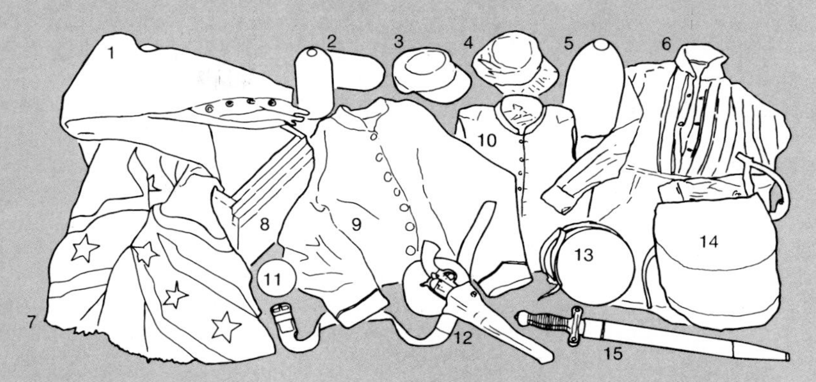

Artifacts courtesy of: The Museum of The Confederacy, Richmond, Va

endless round of repetitive drills as their compatriots the foot and horse soldiers. Officers divided their artillerymen into two groups, gunners and drivers, and drilled them accordingly. That exercise done, they might go through their full routine two or three times daily.

"What a time we had!", remembered Jones in later years. "What lessons we learned! What old Veteran does not recall the hard training of his early camp life, often under the command of men who were but little better than pig-headed martinets, regarding the private soldier as but a piece of putty, to be shaped into any form that might please them."[6] Yet there was purpose to the grinding repetition, and especially for the artillerymen. In the din of battle verbal commands could be garbled and unheard. Instead, they had to learn their tasks in a specific order, and by numbers so that even without orders the men would be able to function. The men were assigned numbers that designated their functions, and in little or no time the men themselves came to be referred to by their numbers, even among comrades.

North and South, most artillerymen could have been interchanged, and they would have been able to function without flaw. The routine was unvaried, unless the special nature of the gun required it. Gunner Number 2 was handed a "cartridge" of ball and powder, which he set inside the muzzle of the cannon. Gunner Number 1, who never let go his rammer, shoved the cartridge down the tube until it reached the bottom. Meanwhile Gunner Number 3 kept his thumb – sometimes protected by a leather sleeve – over the vent hole at the breech. Once the cartridge was in place, he jabbed a wire pick through the vent to open the cloth bag at the base of the cartridge, exposing the black powder within. Gunner Number 4, who sometimes wore a pouch on his belt which contained friction primers, rather like blasting caps, now placed a primer into the vent hole. A lanyard, several feet of braided cord, was attached to the primer and, at the proper command, a jerk at the lanyard ignited the primer

Union Artillery Artifacts

1 Light artillery shako hat complete with artillery insignia
2 Bugle
3 Parrott shell
4 12lb spherical solid shot
5 Forage cap as worn by Union gunners
6 Overcoat for mounted troops
7 Hardee hat
8 Union frock coat complete with rank insignia of a Sergeant
9 Musician's shell jacket
10 Artilleryman's shell jacket
11 Waist belt complete with metal fastening buckle
12 Model 1840 Light Artillery saber with scabbard and waist belt
13 Model 1860 Colt Army revolver complete with holster
14 Belt for carrying artillery fuse box
15 Artillery fuse box as affixed to belt *14*
16 Artillery fuse
17 Two packets of artillery fuses
18 Gunner's haversack complete with shoulder carrying strap
19 Artilleryman's service trousers
20 Non-commissioned officer's sash
21 Model 1833 Foot Artillery short sword and scabbard

Artifacts courtesy of: The Civil War Library and Museum, Philadelphia, Pa: 1-4, 12-13, 16-17, 19; J. Craig Nannos Collection: 5-11, 14-15, 18, 20-21

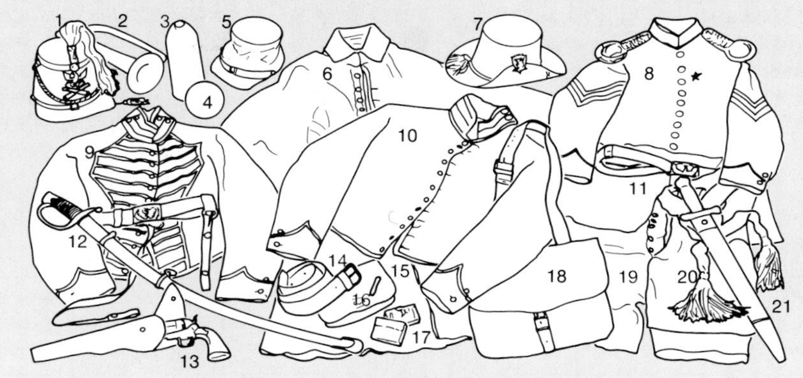

which, in turn, sent a blast of flame into the cartridge, discharging the piece. Immediately Number 1 reappeared, this time with a soaked sponge which he rammed down the barrel to put out any remaining embers or glowing fragments of the cartridge which might accidentally set off the next round prematurely. Gunner Number 5 ran forward with another cartridge and handed it to Number 2, and the whole process repeated itself. If the round happened to be an exploding shot, or shell, then Gunners 6 and 7 who manned the ammunition chest and handed cartridges to Number 5, cut the fuses according to the anticipated time of flight to the target.[7]

If it all went according to the numbers, a practised gun crew could get through the whole process twice in a minute, even given that many batteries had gun crews of only five or six men. A sergeant or corporal stood at the rear of the piece, in overall charge of the operation, including using the variety of generally inadequate tools then available to sight the gun on its target. "Indirect" fire, the technique of shooting over a hilltop or obstruction toward some unseen objective, was

Above: Standing in the mud and the rain after being unloaded from a supply train, these field pieces are covered for protection. To ensure a battery's efficiency in action, men and guns had to care for one another.

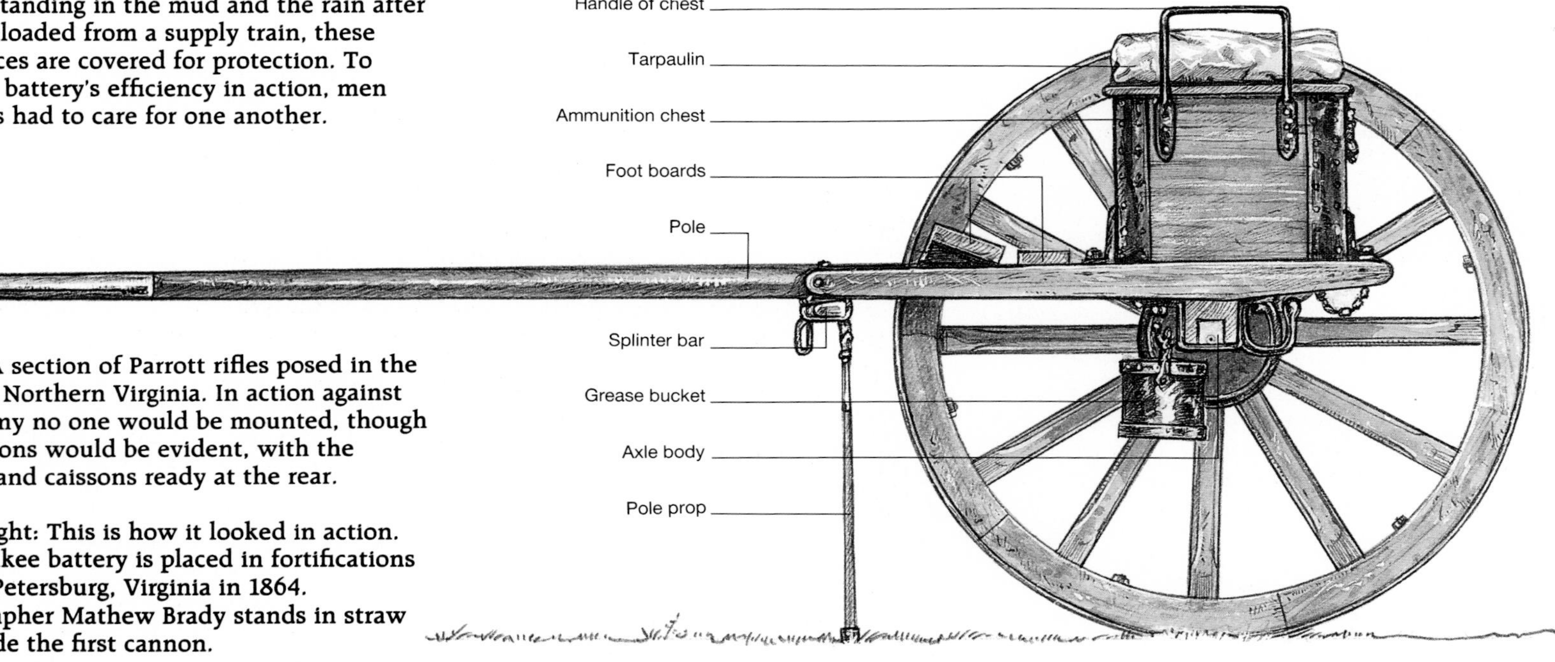

Below: A section of Parrott rifles posed in the fields of Northern Virginia. In action against the enemy no one would be mounted, though the guidons would be evident, with the limbers and caissons ready at the rear.

Below right: This is how it looked in action. This Yankee battery is placed in fortifications around Petersburg, Virginia in 1864. Photographer Mathew Brady stands in straw hat beside the first cannon.

still almost unknown. Men could only shoot at what they could see. That, and the limits of range of most cannon, meant that the sergeant had to sight on a target no more than a mile distant. Much of it was intuition and guesswork, and after every shot the process had to be done over again because the recoil of a firing field piece could send the gun rolling backward several feet. Indeed, it was the resighting, and not the loading steps, which kept the rate of fire to only two rounds per minute.

While all of this took place, the other half of the battery, the drivers, were concerned with other duties. Ideally there were six horses drawing every cannon and its attached limber, or two-wheeled ammunition chest. One driver managed each of the three pairs of horses, called lead, swing, and wheel teams. Similarly managed six-horse teams pulled each of the four-wheeled caissons, carrying more ammunition chests. Thus a fully equipped six-gun battery could require 72 horses at least, not counting those needed to draw the forge and battery wagon, carry the officers and act as replacements. It is no wonder that of a battery's full complement of 155 men including officers and non-commissioned officers, 52 were drivers. Another 70 served as gunners.[8]

It required good officers to make it all work, for the artillery was easily the most technically demanding of the combat arms. Like soldiers of all times, the Civil War artilleryman often thought all too little of his leaders. "The company drill was a profound enigma to him", one Rebel wrote of his lieutenant. "He could not give commands for the most simple movements. With the company on the drill ground he was completely befogged."[9] Yet others were happier with their leaders, and even the initially despised Bloxam won credit for his untiring efforts with Jones' own boast that "we are becoming quite expert in the artillery tactics".[10]

That considerable élan and self-confidence characterized many of the artillery batteries in the war, no doubt aided by the fact that, on average, the more intelligent enlisted men seemed to serve the artillery branch. The Richmond Howitzers, for instance, contained quite a number of college graduates, and many of the rest were businessmen, clerks, and the like, for "the flower of our educated youth gravitated toward the artillery", confessed Robert Stiles. "To my surprise and delight, around the camp fires of the First Company, Richmond Howitzers, I found throbbing an intellectual life as high and brilliant and intense as any I had ever know." Even allowing for exaggeration, the Howitzers were quite a remarkable outfit, with their own Glee Club, a Law Club that conducted mock trials and debates, and a host of young men who could declaim in Latin or Greek.[11]

Four prime attributes were necessary in a good gunner – intelligence, self-possession, comradeship, and loyalty to the gun. Of the first, little more need be said. As for self-possession, one need only consider the potentially terrifying effects of deafening explosions, torrents of flame shooting from the guns, and clouds of choking white smoke. A battery in action looked and felt like a scene from Dante's *Inferno*, and only men who could remain calm in the midst of that chaos could work the guns effectively. Comradeship was essential, for such a small group of men, six

12-Pounder Gun-Howitzer, Model 1857 (Napoleon)

The so-called "Napoleon" was the work-horse cannon for both sides throughout the conflict. Also cast in 6-pounder caliber this light, durable smooth bore weapon had a range of 2,000 yards and hurled more solid shot, case shot, grape and canister than all the other ordnance of the war combined. It was a simple piece, cast of bronze or iron, and mounted on an iron-bound wooden carriage on which was carried its own rammer, sponge, leather grease bucket and rope for hauling. Behind it stood its limber, really just an ammunition chest on wheels, and to which the piece was attached when pulled by its 6-horse team.

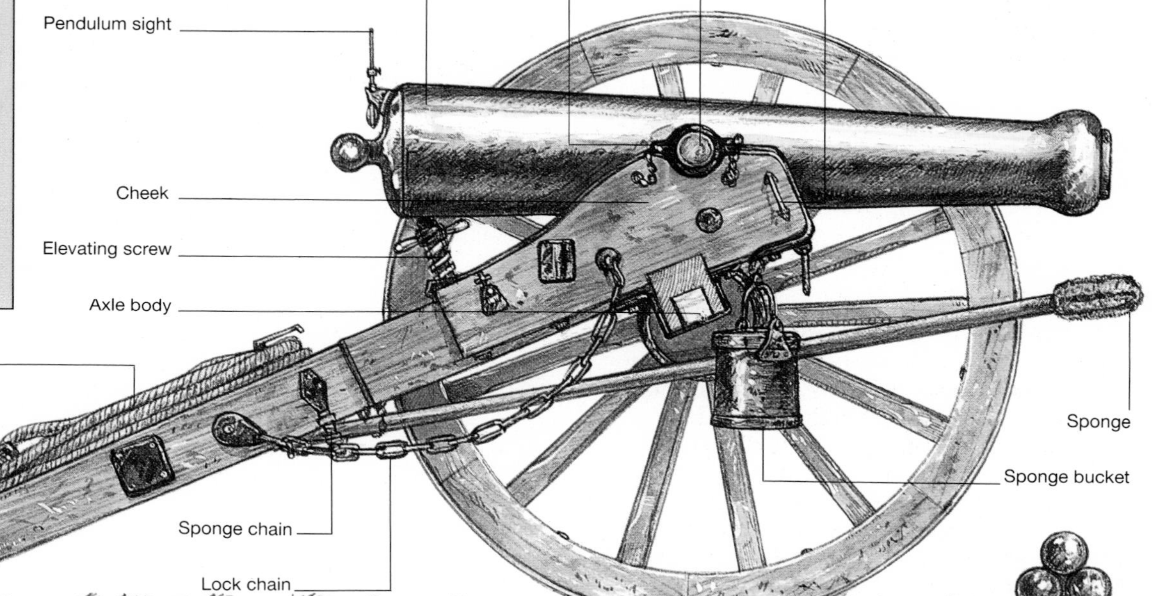

or seven on a gun crew at most, working tightly knit and vitally interdependent, had to get along with one another. A grudge, a hostile feeling between any two which might interfere with the efficiency of the battery as a whole, could endanger all their lives and lessen their effectiveness. Above all else loyalty to the gun was life to the gunner. Without his guns, an artilleryman was nothing, and nothing in the war would so wound the pride of a battery as the loss to the enemy of one or more of its cannon. Men would give up their lives to save their guns, and others seemed momentarily to forget even issues of loyalty and uniform in their devotion to a field piece.

In 1863 men of Samuel McGowan's Confederate brigade cut off and captured several pieces of a Yankee battery, along with their crews. Hastily the Federals tried to disable the guns to make them useless to the enemy, throwing away their lanyards, and adjusting the elevating screws so that the guns pointed high in the air and would require considerable time to retrain on their fleeing comrades. Nevertheless, some of McGowan's infantry managed to find a few primers, rig an impromptu lanyard, and send a couple of ineffectual shells over the heads of their retreating foes.

Looking on scornfully was the Yankee who, until moments before, had been the non-commissioned officer in charge of aiming the piece. After a few moments he dashed forward, shouting, "Stand aside, you infernal, awkward boobies! Let me at that screw!" In a trice he turned it up, depressing the muzzle until it bore down to the proper range. Grabbing the handspike extending from the trail or rear of the carriage, he turned the cannon until it pointed true, then shouted, "Now, try that! Let 'em have it! Fire!" The shot tore straight into the ranks of the retreating Federals, as did a few more which he directed the Confederate gunners in loading and firing. When it was all done, he stamped the ground and shook a clenched fist at his captors, crying, "Damned if I can stand by and see my gun do such shooting as that!" Even given his treachery, that was indeed loyalty to his cannon.[12]

Artillery Pieces

1 A full service history exists for this piece; the 3-inch Ordnance rifle, muzzle No. 1, made by the Phoenix Iron Co., Phoenixville, Pa in 1861. Issued to Reynolds Battery L, 1st New York Light Artillery, its first engagement was at Rappahannock Station in 1862. It fought at Second Manassas, Antietam, and Chancellorville before being captured by Rebels at Gettysburg, after the retreat through Chambersburg Pike on July 1. After that it was used by the Confederacy until it was recaptured by Federals at Spotsylvania in the spring of 1864
2 Horse-drawn Limber chest as used by Union forces to carry stocks of powder and shell into battle
3 Horse-drawn Model 1841 6-pounder field gun as used by Union artillery batteries. Tools associated with the use of this gun are also visible in this picture
4 Stack of 12-pound shot typical of Union ammunition expended by field artillery units engaged in battle throughout the Civil War
5 12-pounder Dahlgren boat howitzer of the type used by the Federal navy during the Civil War

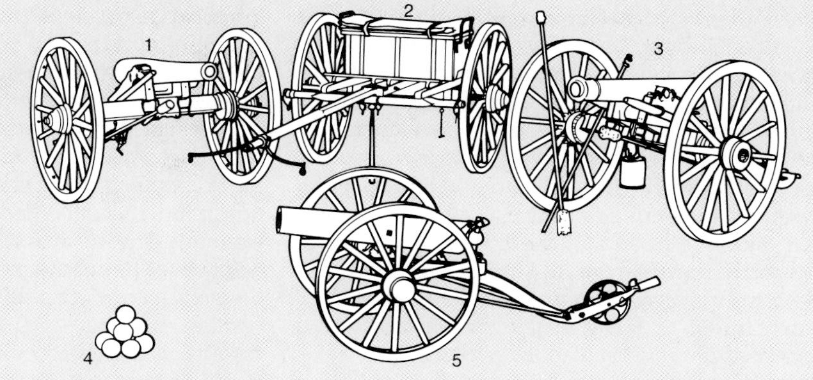

Artifacts courtesy of: Eugene Lomas Collection

There was considerable variety in the weapons that artillerymen both North and South were so devoted towards. The most widely used and respected gun of the war was the twelve-pounder gun-howitzer Model 1857, most commonly known simply as the Napoleon. It was a smoothbore whose tube alone weighed 1,227 pounds and measured five feet six inches in length. With a bore diameter of 4.62 inches, it took a cartridge consisting of a bag holding 2.5 pounds of black powder, attached to a 12.3-pound iron ball. Its effective range was up to 1,500 yards, though it was capable of firing well over a mile. It was named after Emperor Napoleon III of France, who adopted it for use in his army. When the Civil War began, the Union Army had only four of them. By the end of the war it had ordered the manufacture by private foundries of 1,157, making it far and away the most prevalent field piece in the Federal forces. A very few were rifled, at least one was made of wrought iron, but virtually all others were of cast bronze. Almost indestructable, they were the easy favorite of almost all gunners. They all could fire solid shot, round or conical hollow shells filled with powder for exploding, grapeshot – loads of round iron balls an inch or more in diameter – and canister, a virtual scatter-load intended to fire into oncoming ranks of infantry.[13]

The Confederates, too, made extensive use of the Napoleon, though with far more variations, due often as not to necessity. The best estimate suggests that Confederates manufactured around 535 Napoleons, some in bronze, some in brass, and nearly a quarter in cast iron. Many more came into Confederate service through the expedient of battlefield captures, and the Rebels were delighted to get them. The Union War Department in Washington valued a Napoleon at just over $600, but it was worth far more than that in a South whose industrial output was so overburdened as to be near exhaustion.

There were also a host of six-pounder field pieces used North and South, as well as field howitzers in six- and twelve-pounder calibers, intended primarily for the high trajectory flight of exploding shells into an enemy line or position. Far more popular and dramatic, however, was the new generation of rifled artillery. The Civil War was the first active testing ground for such weapons. They came in many sizes and under a host of names, mostly derived from their inventors, but quickly the armies seized particularly upon the Parrott and Ordnance rifles.

Rifling presented immediate problems. Bronze and brass were too soft. An iron shell driving its way down the tube would quickly wear away the rifling grooves which gave it its name and its accuracy. Cast iron was harder, but also brittle. The concussion could crack or even explode such a cannon. Robert Parrott of the West Point Foundry in New York achieved an ersatz solution to the problem by taking a cast iron gun tube, then wrapping a red-hot band of iron around its breech. As the band cooled, it contracted, forging itself to the tube and providing considerable extra support. Parrott manufactured up to 255 of them in a 2.9-inch ten-pounder bore, and another 279 in a full 3-inch diameter, also ten-pounders. He also turned out nearly 300 3.67 inch twenty-pounder Parrotts, and even a few monsters for seacoast fortifications, including 300-pounder rifles with ten inch bores that used twenty-five pounds of powder to fire a single projectile that weighed 250 pounds well over a mile.[14]

Confederates quickly copied the Parrott design, and in the same calibers, thus allowing the use of captured ammunition in their own guns. Like their Federal counterparts, they were trouble-prone, and frequently blew up at the breech, even with the iron reinforcing band. Much more reliable was the 3-inch Ordnance rifle, the beneficiary of a new innovation in manufacture. Wrought iron was stronger than cast, but by its very means of formation it could not be poured into a gun mold. Instead, wrought

Above: Robert Parrott's powerful breech-banded rifle appears here in two 100-pounder models in Fort Putnam, near Charleston. Stacks of massive shells stand ready to be hurled at Confederate lines.

Below: Confederates copied many of the enemy's cannon when they cast their own, even up to this massive Rodman 10-inch smooth bore, emplaced in defenses on the James River, protecting Richmond.

Below: Both sides even created an informal mobile artillery by mounting cannon on railroad flat cars. This giant 13-inch mortar nicknamed 'Dictator' was positioned at Petersburg between 1864-5.

iron rods were welded together to form a mandrel, and then four layers of wrought iron bars were wrapped diagonally around the mandrel, each in an opposite direction. A last layer of iron staves was welded to the outside, and the the whole was subjected to welding heat in a furnace. When the mandrel was then bored out and the tube rifled, a gun tube of incredible strength was the result. Experimental models could not be exploded until or unless loaded with powder and shell right up to the muzzle of the gun.

Almost 1,000 3-inch Ordnance rifles went to the Union armies during the war, and testimony to their accuracy came from all parties, including their targets. "The Yankee three-inch rifle was a dead shot at any distance under a mile", proclaimed a Rebel artilleryman.[15] No wonder that the Southerners emulated the weapon as best they could, but more often than not made use of captured guns and ammunition.

The weak point of all rifles was their ammunition, for time fuses were quirky, and often shells exploded in the air instead of on impact, and

Gunner, 1st US Artillery

Union artillery underwent considerable change during the war, especially in its uniform regulation. At the war's outset, it was the smallest branch of the service, as it would remain, and artillerymen were looked upon as infantry, with only a few companies actually equipped with cannon. This soon changed, with light or "field" artillery designed for active campaigning, horse or "flying" artillery accompanying cavalry, and heavy or "foot" artillery manning fortifications and sea defenses as well as serving the army's heavy caliber siege guns. Dress for the heavy artillerymen, as with the 1st US Artillery, remained what it had been before the war. They wore the same dark blue frock coat and light blue trousers as the infantry, a black felt Hardee hat, and black leather waist and cross belts. Since "heavies" also acted as infantry when not working their guns, they could also carry bayonets and cap boxes.

sometimes even before they had escaped the gun tube. As a result, experienced artillerymen generally preferred the simpler, more predictable, and dependable, Napoleon, which well accounts for their ubiquitous presence on every battlefield of the war.

A few gunners even had to deal with the leading edge of technology by adapting themselves to the new breechloading cannon. A number of inventors, chiefly British, experimented with guns which opened at the breech to accept their loads. The advantages could be many. More rapid fire, less time lost in forcing rifled shot down the tube, and the ability to place the projectile directly into the rifling grooves. A few 3-inch Armstrong rifles were shipped to the Confederacy, but not with great field success. Far more successful, though still limited in its field use, were the Whitworth rifles, in six- and twelve-pounder bores. There were several variants, but common to all was a hinged breech which unscrewed and swung to the side to allow loading. The Whitworths developed the highest muzzle velocity of all field pieces used during the Civil War, and could fire with telling accuracy farther than the gunner could see to aim. But they were easily disabled, and even General E.P. Alexander, Robert E. Lee's great artillery chief, confessed that "the United States three-inch rifle is much more generally serviceable".[16]

Whatever guns they served, the artillerymen North and South went through some of the same evolution of organization that their comrades in the saddle endured. At the war's outset, the Confederate artillery batteries were attached to individual brigades, usually in one or two batteries each. It was a cumbersome arrangement, for one general could jealously hold on to his artillery even though a fellow brigade commander elsewhere might desperately need it. By the end of 1862, the batteries were reassigned to the supervision of division commanders, who would order them about as needed among their brigades. It was a step in the right direction, and by 1864 they were all at the direction of the army corps com-

Field Artillery Projectiles

Pity the artilleryman working the big batteries who had to spend his war carrying 100lb shot. In the field artillery, projectiles rarely weighed more than 20lb and most commonly 6 or 12lb.

1 Union 20lb Parrott shell
2 Union 3-inch Absterdam solid bolt device
3 Union 10lb Parrott shell
4 Union 3-inch Hotchkiss canister device
5 Union 12lb solid shot
6 Union 20lb Schenkl shell
7 Union 10lb Schenkl shell
8 Union 6lb solid shot
9 Union 3-inch Hotchkiss solid bolt device
10 Confederate 10lb Parrott shell
11 Confederate 3-inch Mullane shell
12 Confederate 3-inch Reed-Broun shell
13 Confederate 10lb Parrott shell
14 Confederate 12lb British Britten shell (sabot portion is missing)
15 Confederate 3-inch Reed-Parrott shell
16 Confederate 12lb British Whitworth shell
17 Confederate 1-inch Williams solid bolt device
18 Confederate 12lb British Whitworth solid bolt device
19 Confederate 3-inch Burton shell (sabot portion is missing)

Artifacts courtesy of: The Civil War Library and Museum, Philadelphia, Pa

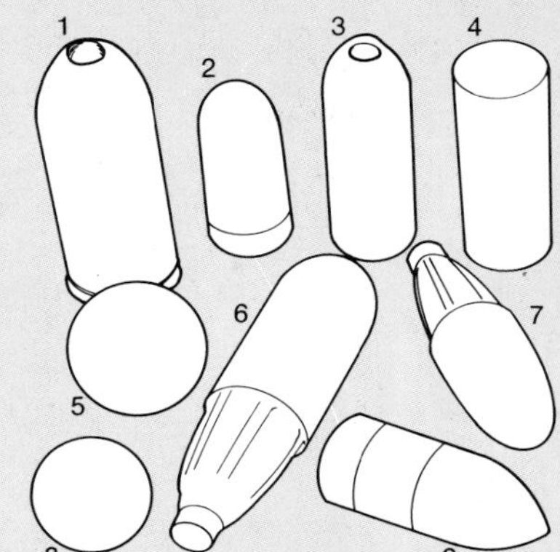

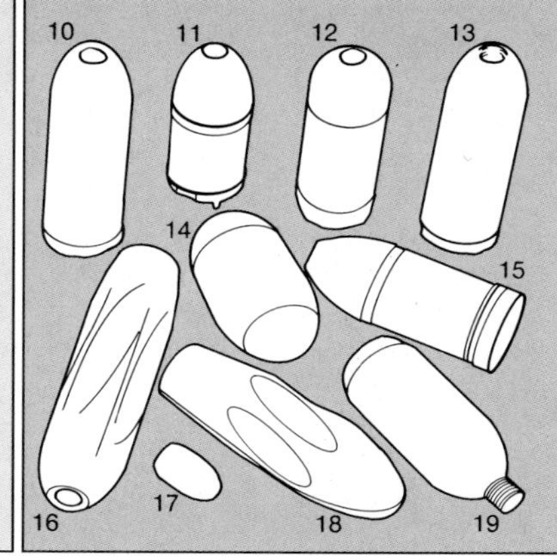

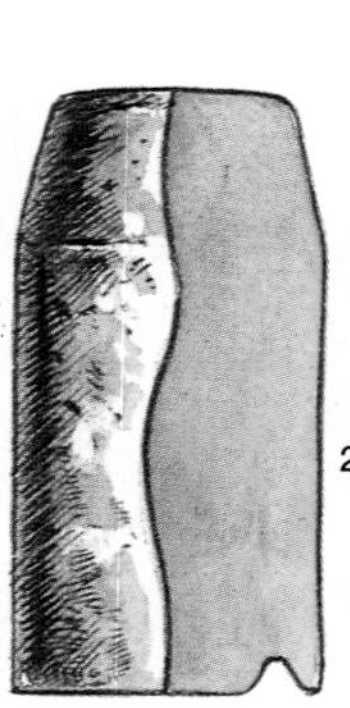
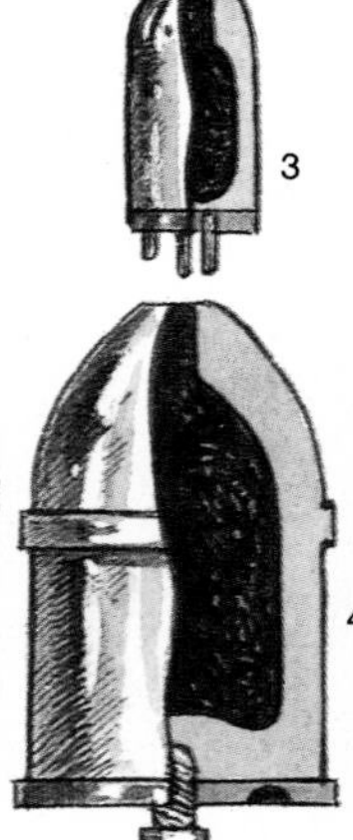
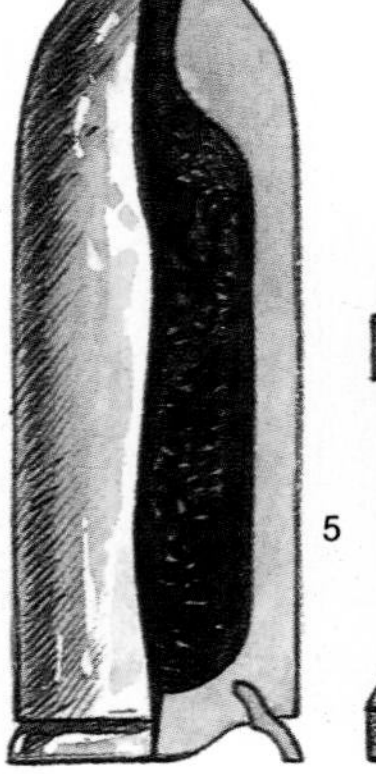
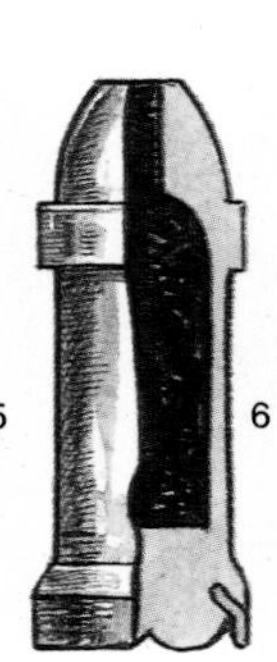
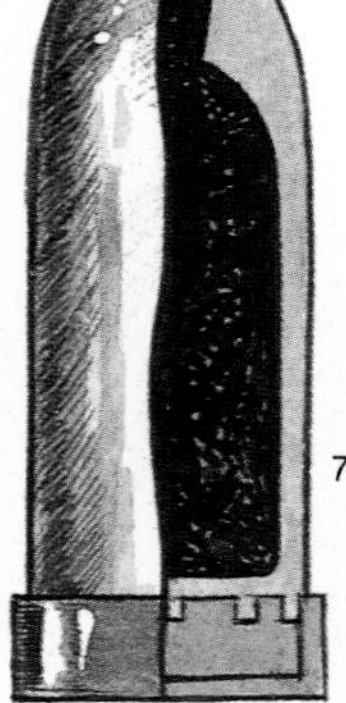
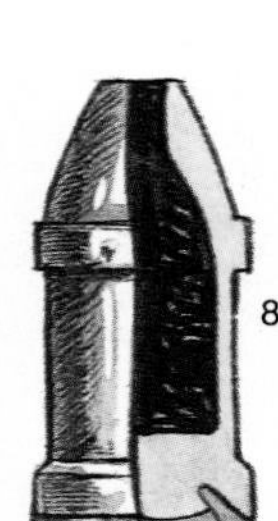
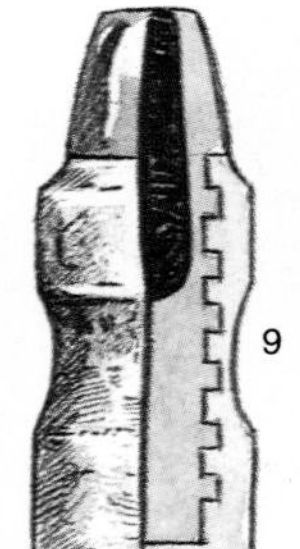
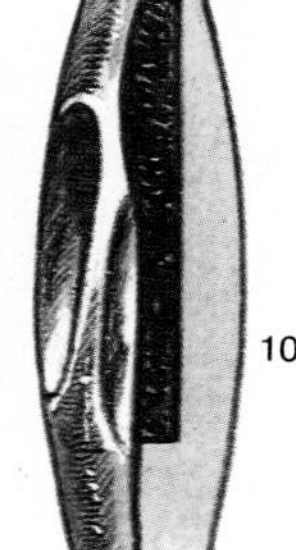

Confederate Artillery Projectiles

1 A 96lb shell with a copper base secured, and featuring radial grooves to grab rifling
2 Solid wrought iron 40.5lb bolt
3 31lb shell with copper plate base
4 58lb shell with copper plate base
5 Wrought iron 26lb shell with soft metal rings on base
6 Wrought iron 8lb shell with soft metal rings on base
7 Iron shell in 26lb caliber with copper rings at the base to grab rifling in barrel
8 Iron shell in 8lb caliber with copper rings to grab rifling
9 Lead-saboted 12.3lb shell
10 A 12.1lb wrought iron bolt for a Whitworth breechloading rifle

manders under chiefs of artillery. In the Union forces the batteries came to be brigaded together under the corps commanders as well, though with corps and army chiefs of artillery. Since the artillery, unlike the cavalry, was clearly and exclusively a support arm for the infantry, such formal organization, better than simply parceling it out among the several brigades, was imperative.

There was another sort of artilleryman in the armies, one whose service and weapons differed considerably from the men with the field batteries. All along the Atlantic seaboard stood masonry fortifications, some dating back to the turn of the century, built to guard river outlets, bays and harbors, and major cities like Charleston, Baltimore, and New Orleans. Several also guarded Boston, New York, and other Northern cities, and manning them was usually the task of "heavy artillery". These oversized regiments were intended to operate siege and seacoast guns, but often in the Union Army were rearmed with rifles and used as infantry. In the Confederacy, its forts were more frequently manned by displaced infantrymen or members of mobile siege and garrison units called siege trains. In the North it was a soft life, for no Yankee fort ever came under attack, or even threat. The men spent their war in garrison, practising at their guns, decorating their barracks, making gravel pathways around the parade grounds, and polishing their gear for the frequent inspection visits of dignitaries.

It was a different matter in the Confederacy, and especially at hot spots like Fort Sumter in Charleston Harbor, or Fort Pulaski near the mouth of Georgia's Savannah River. The constant object of Union attacks, these places afforded little enough rest to their occupants. Indeed, Pulaski was taken from the Confederates in 1862 when Union siege artillery simply battered a huge hole in one side of its massive masonry walls, and infantry prepared to swarm through. Other forts, like Jackson and St. Philip guarding New Orleans, came under the bombardment of heavy naval guns from the Yankee fleets.

No fort and its occupants, however, endured what Fort Sumter did. Sitting almost in the middle of Charleston Harbor, it was an obstacle no invader could go around. To take Charleston, the Union had first to take Sumter. It had fallen easily enough when the Rebels took it in April of 1861, but then its defenders were undermanned, and hardly put up even a show of resistance. By the time the Federals returned to attempt to retake it, the story was altogether different. Confederates had strengthened the fort, added to its firepower, and ringed the rest of the harbor with even more guns and fortifications. Thus when April 1863 arrived, and with it a fleet of conventional warships and several of the new ironclad "monitors", the Confederates in Fort Sumter were ready. On April 7 the Yankee fleet attacked, steaming straight into the harbor. The Confederates held their fire at first, and at the same time the sailors aboard the leading ships began to see peculiar bouys ahead of them in the water. The Rebels had previously placed these bouys as range-markers, and carefully sighted their cannon on them. As a result, once the Confederates opened fire, it was with telling accuracy. Before long there were at least 76 Southern guns concentrating their fire on the slender line of nine Yankee ships, mounting among them just 32 cannon. In the two-hour fight that followed, the Confederates fired some 2,209 shots, of which fully one-fourth found their marks. The monitor *Passaic* took a hit once per minute for thirty-five minutes, firing only four times in response. Within a few minutes the ironclad *Keokuk* took 19 hits that penetrated her waterline, and suffered 90 hits all told. She sank the next day. Other Federal ships collided with each other, and in the confusion the entire fleet managed to fire only 154 shots. Five of the nine ships were disabled, and the forts and their intrepid gunners stood secure.[17]

The defenders came in for even more gruelling experience later that year when the man who took Fort Pulaski came to try a hand at Fort Sumter. General Quincy Gillmore brought his siege guns with him, and for fifteen days in August bombarded Fort Sumter, hurling tens of tons of iron at it from long-range guns. Twice more he repeated the bombardment, largely reducing it to a pile of rubble. Yet, incredibly, the gunners inside the fort held out. Indeed, not until Gallipoli in 1915 would warfare witness such a defense

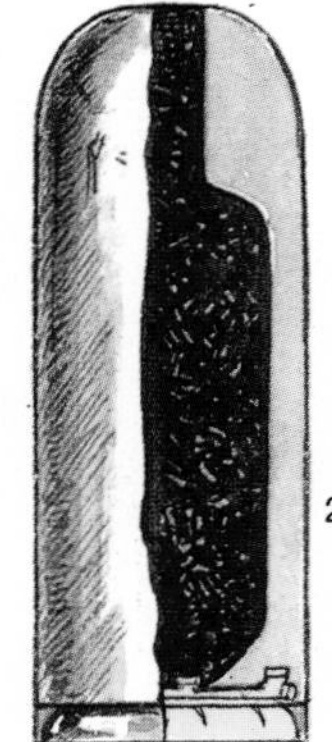

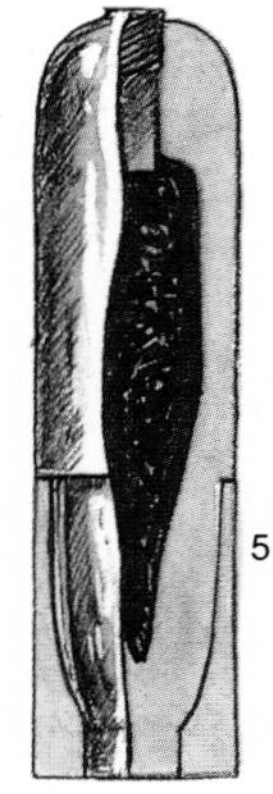
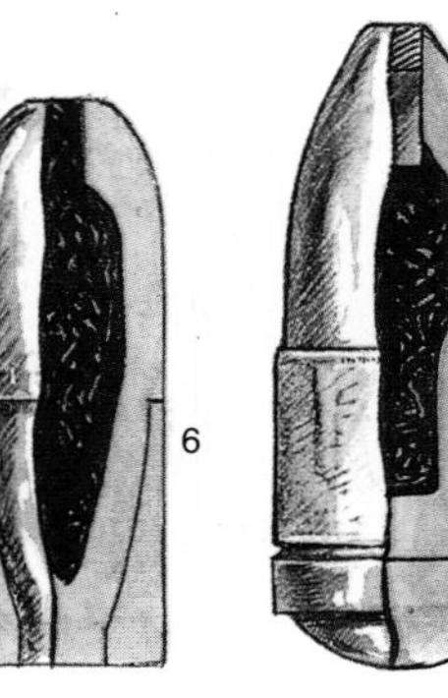
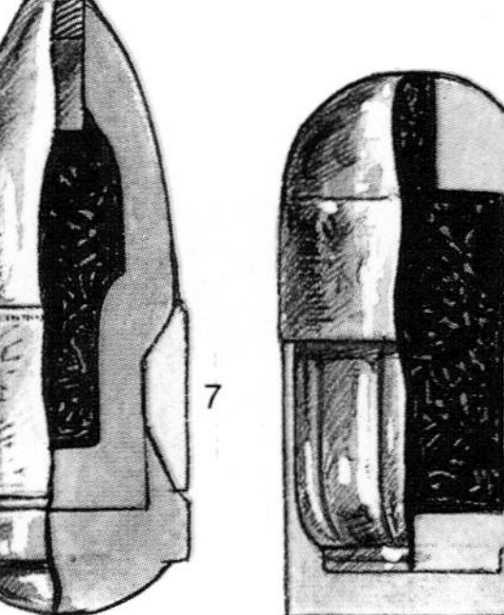
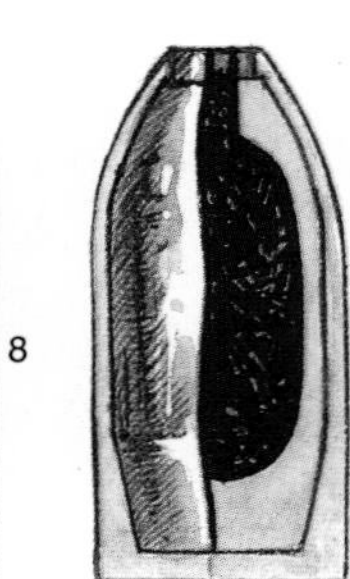

Union Artillery Projectiles

Enjoying a superior technological capability in iron, casting capabilities, powder making and more, the Union armaments industry produced a consistently higher grade of artillery ammunition than the Confederacy, with far more deadlier capabilities.

1 Brass ringed 81lb Parrott shell
2 Brass ringed 25lb Parrott shell
3 A 9.2lb Parrott case shot
4 A 24lb Schenkl shell with papiermache sabot
5 A 16lb Schenkl shell with papiermache sabot
6 A 7.8lb Schenkl shell with papiermache sabot
7 A 19lb lead-banded Hotchkiss
8 Lead sabot 23lb Dyer.
9 Lead-coated 13.2lb Sawyer shell

against combined military and naval attack. Bombarded by an ironclad fleet, by scores of enormous siege guns, attacked by amphibious parties, battered into a shapeless pile of brick and rubble, at times with every cannon in the place dismounted or out of commission, and sometimes with fevers and disease doing more damage to the garrison than the enemy, still it held out. At one time in 1864 the entire functioning defensive armament of Fort Sumter consisted of four shoulder rifles. Yet still it resisted.

The gunners burrowed inside the rubble, finding that it provided a wonderful defense. The loose mortar and brick absorbed the enemy shells better, more harmlessly, than had the standing walls. Deep within their tunnels, the defenders could sit out the bombardments in comparative safety. Indeed, the greatest loss of life in the fort in any single day came not from enemy shelling but, of all things, from whiskey. The gunners kept a barrel of it stored deep within the fort, and a candle flame – or perhaps a spark – came too near. The cask of spirits ignited, perhaps exploded, and soon set off a powder magazine nearby. The resulting blaze turned the underground passages into an inferno, killing or injuring 62 men, and forcing the rest to abandon the interior of the fort. It was ten days before the massive brick oven cooled enough for the gunners to re-enter. And Fort Sumter kept right on holding out until February 1865, after every other major Confederate city and fort had been taken.[18]

Wherever they served, whether in field or fort, the artillerymen of the Civil War were always in the thick of the action. It is no surprise that the very first shot of the war was an artilleryman's signal shell fired over Fort Sumter to commence the Confederate bombardment. If the account of one of Lee's officers may be accepted, the final shots fired by the Army of Northern Virginia came at Appomattox from the guns of Captain Valentine C. Clutter's Virginia battery. Two days later, with the war in Virginia over, an old colonel and his battery were guarding a pass in the Blue Ridge mountains when approaching Federals first tried to drive them out, and then passed on the news of Lee's surrender. When confirmation of the fact came to him, the old colonel formed his battery as if on parade, and ordered the men to run the guns up on to the bluff overlooking the Shenandoah River. The sun was setting in the west, the embers of their campfires dying out, as the colonel gave the order to fire. There was no target. It was simply a parting shot to the way of life they had known for four years. When the roar had ceased to echo in the surrounding mountains, he gave another command. "Let them go, and God be our helper. Amen!" Over the edge they all went, the guns splashing into the river's waters below.[19] All that remained were the men and the horses, and it is a fitting irony that, just as they had made war together, so now they would make peace. Federal terms allowed the men to take their horses home with them, and soon the animals that for four years had rushed their pieces to and fro in battle, were harnessed to the plow to turn soil for the rebuilding of the nation.

Left: Nowhere else in the divided country did the effect of artillery barrage show its true force than on Charleston's Fort Sumter. After its fall to Confederates in April 1861 it was battered but intact.

Below: Four years later, in April 1865 after its surrender, it had been reduced to a shapeless pile of rubble, artificially kept standing by baskets filled with earth. Yankee siege artillery had done all this.

References

1 Benjamin W. Jones, *Under the Stars and Bars* (Dayton, Ohio, 1975), p.20.
2 E.B. Long, *The Civil War Day by Day* (New York, 1971), pp.716-18.
3 Jones, *Stars and Bars*, pp.15-17.
4 *Ibid.*, p.13.
5 Larry J. Daniel, *Cannoneers in Gray* (University, Ala., 1984), p.12.
6 Jones, *Stars and Bars*, p.17.
7 Daniel, *Cannoneers*, pp.12-13.
8 *Ibid.*, p.13.
9 *Ibid.*, pp.13-14.
10 Jones, *Stars and Bars*, pp.19-20
11 Robert Stiles, *Four Years Under Marse Roberts* (Dayton, Ohio, 1977), pp.48-9.
12 *Ibid.*, pp.57-8.
13 Harold L. Peterson, *Notes on Ordnance of the American Civil War* (Washington, 1959), [pp.9-12].
14 *Ibid.*
15 Warren Ripley, *Artillery and Ammunition of the Civil War* (Englewood, N.J., 1970), passim.
16 *Ibid.*
17 Superintendent Naval War Records, *Official Records of the Union and Confederate Navies in the War of the Rebellion* (Washington, 1902), Series I, Volume 14, pp.4ff.
18 E. Milby Burton, *The Siege of Charleston* (Columbia, S.C., 1971), passim.
19 Jennings C. Wise, *The Long Arm of Lee* (New York, 1959), pp.956-7.

CHAPTER SIX

LIFE AT SEA

The year of 1863 was to be the one in which the tide undeniably turned. Despite all the defeats that had gone before, and those yet to come, it was evident that Union material and manpower resources were finally gaining the upper hand, while Yankee soldiers and leaders finally felt the confidence to face imposing men like Lee and Jackson on the field without fear.

In the west, Grant, ever relentless, resumed his drive toward Vicksburg. For nearly five months he moved and feinted toward the fortified river city, eventually moving his troops down the western bank of the river to a point below the city, then using Federal transports to get the men across the river to march on Vicksburg from below. In May he began what would be a 47-day siege of the city, slowly squeezing and starving its garrison. Confederate attempts to relieve the defenders were to no avail, and finally on July 4 the Confederates were forced to capitulate. Just four days later another major bastion, Port Hudson, Louisiana, also surrendered, and the Mississippi at last belonged to the Union from its source to the Gulf of Mexico, a crippling blow to the Confederacy.

Yet this crushing victory was overshadowed in the east by a less important but far more dramatic event: the Battle of Gettysburg. Once again Lee tried a raid into the north, and once again he faced a new commander of the Army of the Potomac, General George G. Meade. But Meade was different from McClellan or Burnside, or Joseph Hooker, whom Lee decisively defeated at Chancellorsville in May, though at the loss of Stonewall Jackson's life. Meade met Lee blow for blow, and in three days of hot bitter fighting shattered his proud army and forced him to retire into Virginia. So devastating was the battle to both armies that for over three months they campaigned little at all, and what action there was occurred on the rivers and seas as Lincoln's navy harrassed blockade runners and hunted Rebel privateers.

NOT SURPRISINGLY in a continent bounded by the seas, there were not a few Americans North and South who chose another kind of service in the rush to arms. The old Union, to a large extent, had always been a maritime nation. Yet, as was the case with its army, years of peacetime had allowed the United States Navy to dwindle dramatically. In 1861, out of a commissioned fleet of 90 vessels, some still uncompleted, the Union could count on just 35 modern vessels, with only three steamships readily at hand and not on some foreign station. That was not much of a force to cover some 3,500 miles of Confederate coastline, resupply isolated Federal outposts at Fort Pickens, Florida, and elsewhere, and maintain effectively the blockade of Southern ports proclaimed by Lincoln. Equally understrength was the manpower of the service, with just 7,600 seamen in uniform.[1] Of course, the Confederacy had no navy whatsoever at the outset, whereas the existence of a host of local militia units did give it an impressive headstart for its army. Thus for both North and South, there was a massive task ahead of the respective Navy Departments in acquiring ships and men to crew them.

Finding ships was, for both sides, a matter of building some, converting others to war purposes, and buying the rest. The South put into service perhaps as many as 500 vessels before the end of the war, though most were small, ersatz boats hardly equal to the demands made upon them. A few Rebel ships, however, achieved well-deserved notoriety, most notably the commerce raiders *Florida, Alabama, Tallahassee*, and others, and the river and harbor ironclads like the

Sailors both black and white, from every walk of life, relax on the deck of this Yankee river gunboat, revealing in perfect microcosm the makeup and pastimes of crews in Civil War navies.

Virginia (*Merrimack*), *Arkansas*, and *Albemarle*. As for the Union, by 1865 its Navy had seen service from 716 vessels, all but a few newly constructed specially for war.[2]

Finding the men to run those ships remained a constant challenge. A big problem, ironically, was the army. In the first rush of enthusiasm, everyone hurried to take up a rifle. No one even thought of the war lasting long enough for the navy to play a big role, nor did they really anticipate that there would be much need for naval engagement, even if the war did extend beyond the summer of 1861. Worse, the bounties offered to induce men to enlist in newly-forming regiments usually lured the few experienced seamen to try their hand at land service instead. So great did the shortage become that colonels of many regiments were urged to comb their ranks for men who had the skills to serve on boats, and to transfer them to the navy instead. Unfortunately, many officers used the opportunity not to transfer good men, but to get rid of undesirables. "Our Captain did some weeding out today", wrote a trooper of the 4th Illinois Cavalry in January 1862. A fleet of gunboats had asked for volunteers, "But the Captain took it upon himself to detail such men that he would rather spare and told them they had to go". One of the men so assigned was even then under arrest for drunkenness and attempting to kill his lieutenant.[3]

Before long, Congress authorized the payment of bounties for naval enlistments, though they were never as effective as with army enrollments, and by 1864 some volunteers were being paid as much as $1,000 per man to sign on. Though it never became a flood, Union naval enlistments rose sufficiently to crew every ship put into service, and during the course of the war some 132,554 eventually wore the blue. Across the lines, with far fewer ships of any size, and a fleet – such as it was – that was almost entirely confined to rivers and bays, the Confederate Navy had substantially smaller manpower needs. Even then, it was always hard-pressed for crewmen, and frequently had to borrow them from nearby army units when action approached. Probably not much over 5,000 men enlisted in the Southern navy during the war.[4]

However they came into the navy service, seamen North and South encountered much the same initial experiences as the youthful Alvah Hunter of New Hampshire. Unlike many young men, he actually wanted to get into the navy from the first, but when he appeared at a Boston recruiting office, he was repeatedly turned away. Just sixteen years old, he wanted to sign on as a "ship's boy", the lowliest of the enlisted grades, and essentially a fetch-all position for completely

Sailor, CSS *Alabama*

No vessel of the Civil War attracted so much attention or excited more fear than the Confederate commerce raider CSS *Alabama*. Its seemingly untrammeled depredations around the globe sent panic through the Union's merchant fleet and provided a morale boost to those at home. On board, unfortunately, Captain Raphael Semmes did not run the tightest of ships, largely because many of his crew were not Confederates at all, but adventurers from other nations including Britain; a factor that was to gravely effect the *Alabama*'s battle worthiness in her final fight with the *Kearsarge*. Still, he maintained discipline well enough and insisted that all his men be properly uniformed. CSN regulations called for gray cloth jackets and trousers in the fashion of the US Navy, or else a gray wool 'frock' or shirt with a white duck collar and cuffs. Other articles such as hats, silk neckerchiefs, and shoes or boots were to be all black.

inexperienced young men. The navy already had too many boys, he was told, and only his persistence won out in the end, when the intercession of an officer assigned to the new ironclad monitor *Nahant* got him his shipping orders.

Hunter appeared on the appointed day before the old commodore in charge of the assignment office and presented his instructions. Despite some grumbling about there being already too many ship's boys in the service, the commodore nevertheless enrolled Hunter as a First-Class Boy and sent him off to the surgeon for inspection. Apparently, it was not much different from the cursory lookover given to most army enlistees at the time, and Hunter concluded that "a 'boy' wasn't of sufficient importance to require a close examination". From the doctor he went to the outfitter's, and there drew his new uniform – two blue flannel shirts, trousers, socks and shoes, a clothes bag to hold them, two blankets, a crude mattress, and a hammock. He might also have drawn white cotton duck clothing, depending upon the officer commanding his ship. Thus outfitted, Hunter and others were taken out to the receiving ship for the initial training.[5]

The United States Navy had several old sailing ships-of-the-line still in commission in 1861, though clearly obsolete for the war at hand. Washington consequently turned them into receiving ships, virtually wharf-bound barracks and schools. Hunter went aboard the old *Ohio*, and there he changed into his new uniform, stowed his hammock and gear, and first heard the shrill whistle of the boatswain's pipe that would order his days for the rest of his service. That first call, incidentally, was the one most welcome – the call for supper. "With the eating of that first meal aboard ship", he recalled, "I began to feel that at last I was really shipped into the navy."[6]

Hunter spent three weeks on the old *Ohio*, though many new seamen spent longer periods of time before their posting orders arrived. To a landsman like him, one with no experience of the sea, it was all wonder at first. "I was so well content with having at last found a way into the navy I was quite satisfied to remain on board." Like thousands of other farmboys and clerks, he marveled at the massive wooden ship, with its "countless portholes for guns" and "her vast bulk". Crammed aboard with between 300 and 400 others, most of them his own age or a little older, he found no lack of fun and frolic. Hunter spent hours studying the ship's fittings and hidden places, looking at the smartly dressed marines who guarded the gangways and officers' quarters. Not a few of his fellow ship's boys were black, for the Union Navy was ahead of the army in enlisting Negroes. A ready camaraderie seems to have grown up between white and black in most instances, not the least because a ship could be a very small world to live in, and men inevitably had to set aside or unlearn prejudices in the interest of working and living together. However, this spirit did not always apply to the marines and many Civil War seamen adopted the age-old antipathy for the "lobster backs" whose duty it was to perform none of the ship's drudgery, but

Above: In 1861, the Union had to depend heavily upon its existing ships like the USS *Niagara*. More would come, however. By the war's end the Federal Navy would increase its size by over 600 vessels.

Below: Two years into the war, and on many ships, like this unidentified steam frigate, seamen crowded the decks preparing to work their guns, while the oft-despised marines stood armed and ready in line.

simply act as ship's police and – in the event of battle – take posts as marksmen or boarders. "One of the first things taught me", wrote Hunter, "was that a marine was the natural enemy of every sailor, and that all sailors were in duty bound to get ahead of the marines whenever possible." When postings finally came, no one was happier to see the new enlistees leave the receiving ships than the marines who made the ships their home.[7]

The common seaman's day, North or South, was much the same – one continuing routine, varied little except by the type of ship the man served, and the duty assignment of the vessel itself. Sometimes, if special duties like refueling or cleaning the ship were due prior to departure, the boatswain awakened the men well before dawn. More often, however, a bugler – a marine if the ship was large enough to carry a marine contingent – sounded reveille at 5 o'clock in the morning. While the bleary-eyed tried to clear their heads, the boatswain and others from the watch coming to an end ran along the berth deck shouting at the men and adding incentive by shaking or jarring their hammocks.

The first duty of the sailor was to stow his sleeping gear, wrap his blankets if any inside his hammock, roll it into a tight little ball, and stow it on the main deck in a special hammock netting behind the ship's bulwarks. There it served a dual purpose, for the netting and hammocks so placed could catch dangerous splinters sent flying about the deck by enemy cannon fire, and at the same time provide an obstacle to boarders in a close action. A seaman was expected to take only seven minutes from the sounding of reveille to the placement of his bedding in the netting, but depending upon the punctiliousness of his captain, and how much long, monotonous duty may have loosened discipline, he more often than not took longer.

With his bedding stowed, the sailor had more chores ahead of him before he was served his morning meal. He had to scrub his berth deck with seawater, and then use holystones to clean the main deck. That done, there were the guns to clean, with all exposed iron to be burnished to keep off rust. A ship carried lots of brass – bells, fittings, even ornamental hardware – and all of it had to be polished. Sails and rigging – if any – needed to be checked for mildew and wear, and the ship's ropes and tackle put in order. Only when his vessel glistened bright and clean in the morning sun did the sailor receive orders allowing him to wash and brighten himself.

By 7.30, all this behind him, the seamen dressed and waited for the sound of the boatswain's pipe calling them to breakfast. The men ate in "messes" of eight or more to a table, usually eating with others who shared their specific duty posts, such as gun crews, topmen on sailing ships, engineers, and the like. What they actually ate varied with the season and the climate of their station, as well as what might be locally available, but in the main every seaman was supposed to have a pint of strong coffee and a sizeable piece of hard, salted beef, called "junk" – and not without reason. Ordinarily the men took turns at acting as cook for their messes. The meal done, each man kept his cutlery and mug, while the mess orderly of the day stowed the cooking utensils and plates in the mess chest.

Happily, after a busy early morning, the sailor generally enjoyed a few hours of leisure after his breakfast, excepting perhaps a general call to

Above: The men who commanded the common seamen often had to call upon them to bear great hardship, though combat itself was infrequent. The crew of the USS *Kearsarge* were the exception. Their commander, Captain John A. Winslow, standing with his officers third from left, took them into battle off Cherbourg in France against that most feared ship, the CSS *Alabama*. Their victory immortalized their ship and themselves.

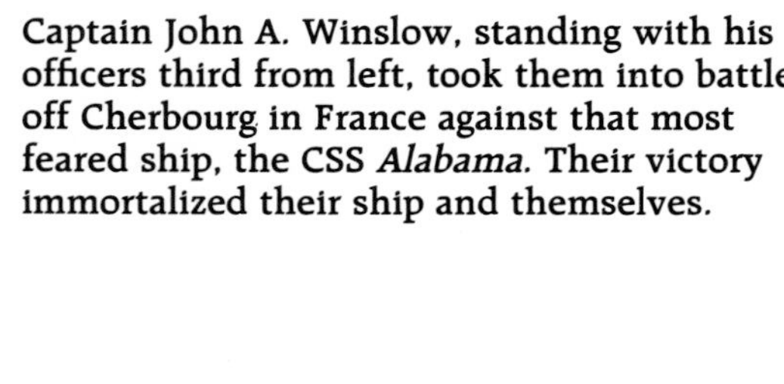

Above: The commander of the dreaded *Alabama*, Captain Raphael Semmes, here standing on board his ship against one of her massive pivot guns. Behind him is his executive officer John McI. Kell.

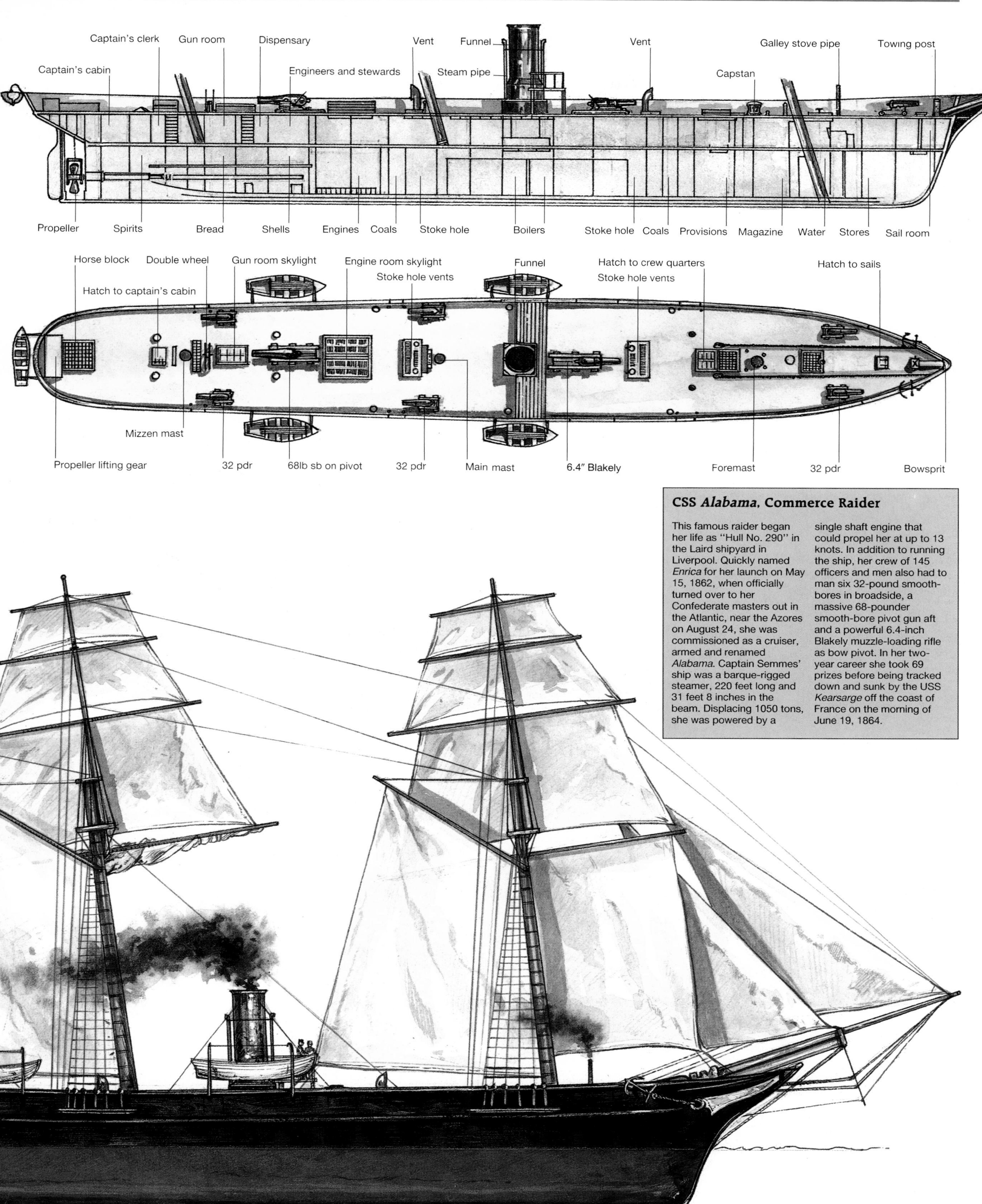

CSS *Alabama*, Commerce Raider

This famous raider began her life as "Hull No. 290" in the Laird shipyard in Liverpool. Quickly named *Enrica* for her launch on May 15, 1862, when officially turned over to her Confederate masters out in the Atlantic, near the Azores on August 24, she was commissioned as a cruiser, armed and renamed *Alabama*. Captain Semmes' ship was a barque-rigged steamer, 220 feet long and 31 feet 8 inches in the beam. Displacing 1050 tons, she was powered by a single shaft engine that could propel her at up to 13 knots. In addition to running the ship, her crew of 145 officers and men also had to man six 32-pound smooth-bores in broadside, a massive 68-pounder smooth-bore pivot gun aft and a powerful 6.4-inch Blakely muzzle-loading rifle as bow pivot. In her two-year career she took 69 prizes before being tracked down and sunk by the USS *Kearsarge* off the coast of France on the morning of June 19, 1864.

quarters for inspection. Otherwise, he wrote his letters – if he could write – mended his clothing, played cards or backgammon with his mates, and tried any other means available to escape what could be an endless round of tedium, especially for the Yankee sailors on blockade duty.

Noon brought yet another meal, this one more substantial, with salt pork or beef, vegetables, coffee, and whatever local produce might be available, especially eggs or cheese. Victuals varied greatly, with Union sailors enjoying a much more standard bill of fare, while Rebels ate in much the same ersatz fashion as their compatriots in the armies. Only the men aboard the commerce raiders like the *Shenandoah* or *Florida* enjoyed really ample tables, thanks to what they captured from the prizes they took. As the war wore on, many Confederate seamen received issues of meat rations only two or three times a week.

Training and drill occupied some of the afternoon, though there was little actual schedule or regularity about it. Indeed, one ship's boy on a Federal blockader in 1863 wrote that "the life of a sailor is not one of a real and regular work, his hours of rest may not be uniform but they are more or less regulated." The details of ship's routine might vary considerably from day to day, he observed, "yet its original outlines are the same day after day".

The one immutable factor, other than reveille and the early morning duties, was mealtime, and thus many sailors came to measure their days not by hours but by when they ate. Like all other meals, the 4 p.m. light supper came at the end of a four-hour watch, and here there could be a problem, for this was the final meal of the day, and it would be sixteen hours before the next day's breakfast. Men with late night watches could become painfully hungry.

Following supper, the crews had one more call to quarters for inspection at 5.30 before the ship was essentially finished with its active day – excepting, of course, vessels engaged in open sea steaming or on active blockade duty where most

Confederate Naval Arms and Accoutrements

In naval terms, the Confederacy ran at a disadvantage and had to rely a great deal on imported equipment.

1 Typical Confederacy Second National Bunting Flag as displayed by warships and other vessels of the South
2 British Pattern 1859 cutlass-type design of bayonet for use in conjunction with British Wilson breechloading naval rifle depicted below. Complete with protective scabbard
3 Thomas, Griswold and Company design of naval cutlass with belt, the fastening buckle of which displays an embossed CS motif
4 British Wilson breechloading naval rifle complete with ramrod in stowed position
5 Short-barrelled type of pistol used for firing of warning flares or colors of the day
6 Typical design of canvas sea bag as used by sailors on Confederate warships
7 Naval cutlass complete with canvas waist belt and protective scabbard
8 Firing mechanism for ship-borne cannon armament embarked on Confederate ships of the line

Artifacts courtesy of: Virginia Historical Society: 2-5, 7, 8; The Museum of The Confederacy, Richmond, Va: 1, 6

of the real action took place at dusk and after. Once their inspection was done, the crewmen had the rest of the evening to themselves. They retrieved their hammocks and slung them on the berth deck, and then lounged, slept, read, and secretly engaged in a variety of forms of gambling, though officially it was against regulations and offenders could be disciplined or fined. They threw dice, bet on dominoes and cards, tossed coins, and even bet on times and distances involved in their vessel's travels.[8]

But much more was available for those who craved recreation and entertainment. Banjos, guitars, fiddles, fifes, and more, came out on deck in the evenings, with some ships actually forming ensembles from their company. Even amateur theatricals were performed on the upper decks of men of war. Sporting contests, boxing, footraces, acrobatics, all played the same stage on many ships, depending largely upon the attitude of the captain as to what was acceptable. Until the grog ration was prohibited in 1862, Union seamen could have one gill – about four ounces – of whiskey mixed with water, while his Confederate counterpart received his ration only when it was available.

Once a week the men washed their clothes, hanging them to dry on lines stretched between the masts. Sometimes the ship's pumps were hooked up to hoses, and seawater was sprayed over the decks, which inevitably led to "much skylarking on the part of the boys and distress of the old sailors who directed the performance", wrote Hunter.[9]

It was partly because of the frolicsome nature of youth that the Union Navy in 1864 adopted regulations to govern enlistments, stipulating that no one under the age of eighteen was to be enrolled. It defeated itself, however, in that the only proof required of a young man was his own sworn oath as to his age. Further, for positions such as ship's boys, youths as tender as thirteen could be accepted providing they stood at least four feet eight inches tall. At the other extreme, no one over the age of 38 was to be enlisted under any circumstances unless specifically endorsed by the Navy Department. There were a host of

Above: Men gathered on every ship to make homespun music, just as the seamen on the deck of USS *Wabash* in 1863 did, to strum and fife and fiddle for their own entertainment and that of their comrades.

Below: Despite official regulations, many a young boy found his way into the navies, like this sea-wise looking 'powder monkey' aboard the USS *New Hampshire* lying off Charleston, South Carolina.

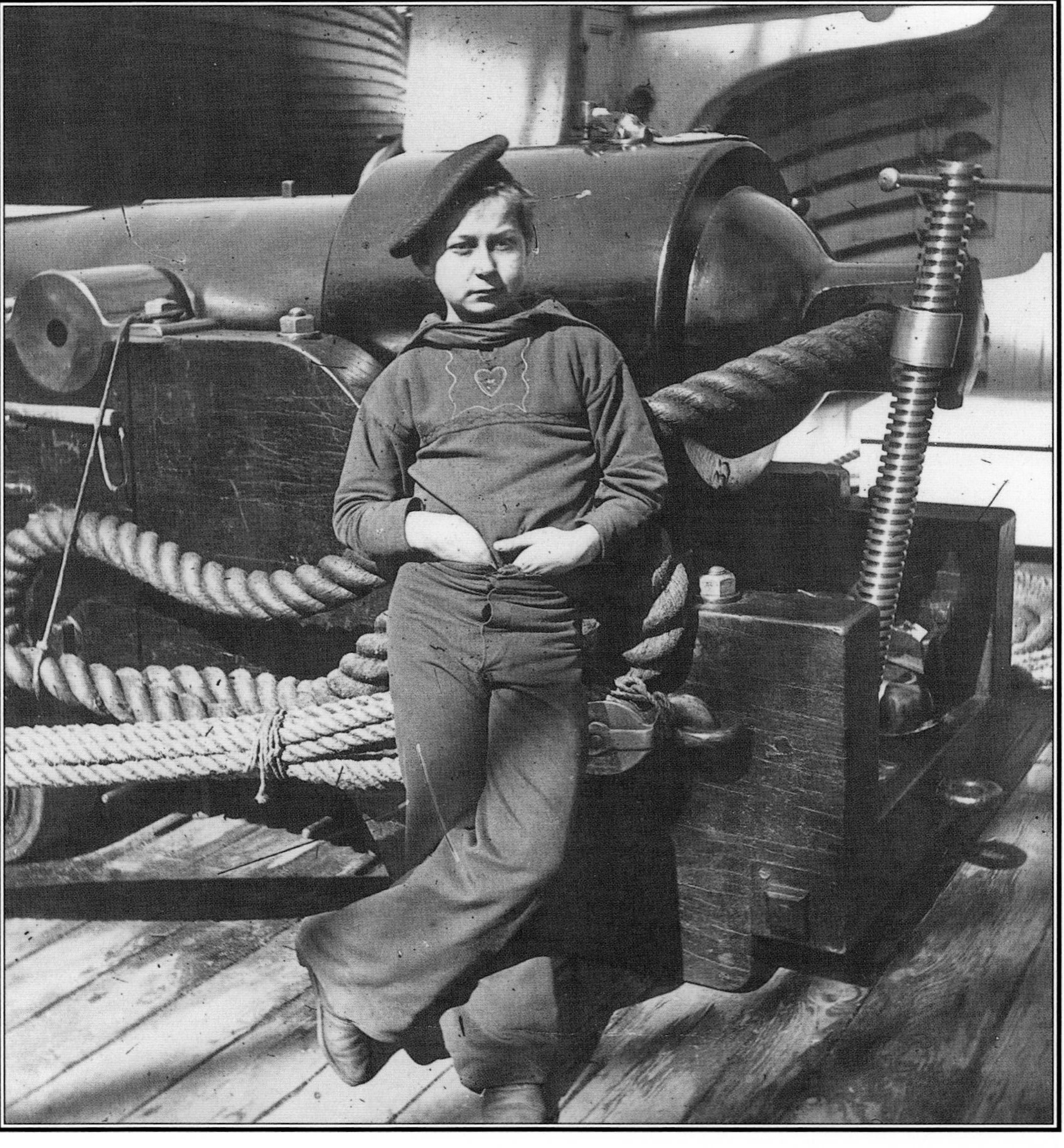

Above: What little excitement entered the lives of the Civil War sailors came from such things as chasing blockade runners and warships, like the CSS *Teaser*, which boasted this massive 100-pound bow rifle.

listed grades in both navies, ranging from the lowest, ship's boy, up to the yeomen and boatswains. Hunter received $8 a month; a boatswain might receive $120 when at sea; and all the grades in between – landsmen, musicians, cooks, nurses, coopers, painters, stewards, quartermasters, and more – received varying amounts prescribed by their length of service.

There was quite a mixture of men filling those grades. Negroes were enlisted into the Union Navy officially commencing in September 1861, and were given equal pay even while their counterparts in the army had to endure receiving smaller salaries than white soldiers. A host of other nationalities also went into the naval service, most of them northern Europeans who came from seafaring nations such as Norway and Sweden. In some cases, nearly one-half of a ship's crew were foreign born. In the Confederacy, by contrast, no blacks were officially enlisted, though many served as servants and cooks, and the bulk of the seamen were native born, most of them with little or no nautical experience since the South did not have much of a maritime tradition.

The provisions for food in the navies were specified by naval regulations, and in the North they were almost always met or exceeded, while the Rebel navy suffered some of the same shortages of its army counterparts, though rarely to the same extent thanks to proximity to seaports, and easier access to produce from blockade runners and captured Yankee vessels. In Lincoln's navy, official rations per man per day were to consist of a pound of salt pork and half a pint of peas or beans; or else a pound of salt beef with half a pound of flour and a quarter pound of raisins, apples, or other dried fruit; or one pound of salt beef with half a pound of rice and two ounces each of butter and cheese, along with tea and nearly a pound of hardtack or baked biscuits. Additionally, each week the men were to receive a half pound of cranberries or pickles, half a pint of molasses, and half a pint of vinegar. A number of substitutions were allowed by law, depending upon the availability of foodstuffs, but the basic quantities and proportions among the food groups remained the same.

Below: While most blockade runners escaped capture or destruction, many like the steamer *Robert E. Lee* did not. Captured and renamed the *Fort Donelson*, she ended her days in service to the Federal Navy.

It was a diet heavy in salt and starch, with an absence of citrus or fresh green vegetables to help prevent scurvy. Recognizing that it was not sufficient to sustain the stamina and health of the seamen on long blockade duty, Union Secretary of the Navy Gideon Welles early authorized supplementation of the ration where possible. In practice, the cooks at sea managed to prepare a number of variations out of the stocks in their larder, though the daily menu hardly varied enough to make the men relish their meals. Pork and beans became a staple, and a very popular dish, called 'duff', was a simple boiled pudding of flour and water sweetened with molasses and given variety by mixing with it dried fruit or nuts. But this diet could be overdone. Charles Brother, serving aboard the USS *Hartford*, recorded in his diary his daily dinner ration, and just the month from March 14 to April 14, 1864, shows that he had pork and beans on twelve days for dinner, duff on seven days, and what he called 'bullion beef' and coffee on six other occasions. At least the cooks refrained from serving the same dish more than two days consecutively. And on only two days did he note a special occasion when "fresh grub" – whatever that was – was presented to his mess. Sometimes special concoctions of the cook's came out of the pots, a few of which still defy description, such as 'dandyfunk', a stew of hardtack soaked in water and baked with salt pork and molasses. Sometimes there was 'sea pie', a multi-layered dish of meat and crust. It is no wonder that being served the same usually bland dishes over and over, the sailors developed a host of not very complimentary sobriquets for them. In both navies, for example, salted or pickled beef was invariably known as 'salt horse', denoting not only its lack of savor and tenderness, but also the sailors' wry suspicions as to its source.[10]

The seaman's monotonous daily diet was only part of what proved top be an almost ceaselessly tedious existence. It is a fact that the average sailor saw substantially less real action than most soldiers, and many seamen never actually went into battle at all. Without an occasional chase of a blockade runner or privateer to break the tedium in the Union navy, without the rare excursion of a Rebel ironclad against a Yankee gunboat or block-

ading fleet, the sailor's life was an unbroken routine in which one day was no different than the next. Further, shore leave was painfully infrequent, in part because most ships were on station, sometimes hundreds of miles from port, and also in part to prevent desertion, for few men who endured the boringly unvaried existence of the sailor failed to entertain the thought, at least, of running away.

It is no wonder, then, that just as in the army, drinking became a major release, and a major disciplinary problem. For decades, the regulations had provided for a spirit ration, just enough to give a man a little ease, but not enough to get him intoxicated. The problem was that many men did not drink and either gave or sold their ration to others. Some men also hoarded their rations, saving it for one big evening, and now and then managed to smuggle a few bottles aboard after a shore leave. And when they drank too heavily, the men would misbehave. "All insubordination, all misery, every deviltry on board ships", wrote the Union Assistant Secretary of the Navy, "can be traced to *rum*".[11] Alvah Hunter had only been aboard his new ship *Nahant* a few days when he went below one evening and and came upon "one of the most distressing sights I have ever seen". Some "despicable creature" had smuggled whiskey aboard, and sold a couple of quarts to some of the men, "and half a dozen of our best sailors were fighting-roaring drunk".[12] Aboard the CSS *Alabama* in November 1862, a troublemaker escaped the ship, swam to a nearby vessel in the harbor of Martinique, and returned with "a great quantity of spirits", which he passed out among the crewmen. They became so drunk that one threw a belaying pin at an officer who tried to control them, and soon Captain Raphael Semmes had a small-scale mutiny on his hands. Because of instances like this, the Union Navy Department, acting on Congressional mandate, abolished the grog ration entirely on July 14, 1862, substituting an additional five cents per day per man as compensation. Never popular, this act itself nearly led to mutiny, especially when the Bureau of Medi-

Union Naval Arms and Accoutrements

From a minor force, the USN would grow to become a major player in the Confederacy's defeat.

1 Typical National Bunting Flag as displayed by warships of the Union Navy during the Civil War
2 Type of pike used to facilitate the boarding of Confederate warships during close-order naval engagements
3 Parallel ruler of type used as an aid to navigation by Union naval personnel when at sea
4 Presentation case containing 1862 design of Navy Medal of Honor as awarded to Union sailors for conspicuous gallantry in battle
5 U.S. Navy Model 1842 muzzle-loading type of percussion pistol complete with integral ramrod
6 Typical design of box containing primer
7 Stand of grape shot of type used in sea battles of the American Civil War
8 Dahlgren-manufactured example of bowie type of bayonet complete with protective scabbard
9 Union Officer's naval cutlass of Model 1860 design
10 Union Officer's naval cutlass of Model 1841 design

Artifacts courtesy of: The Civil War Library and Museum, Philadelphia, Pa

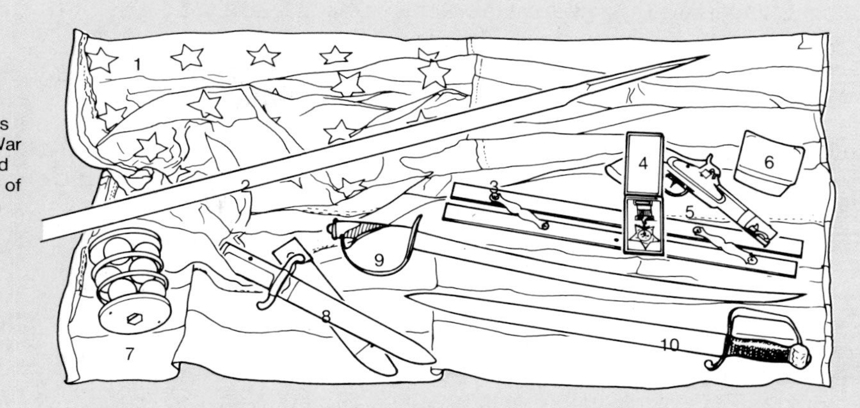

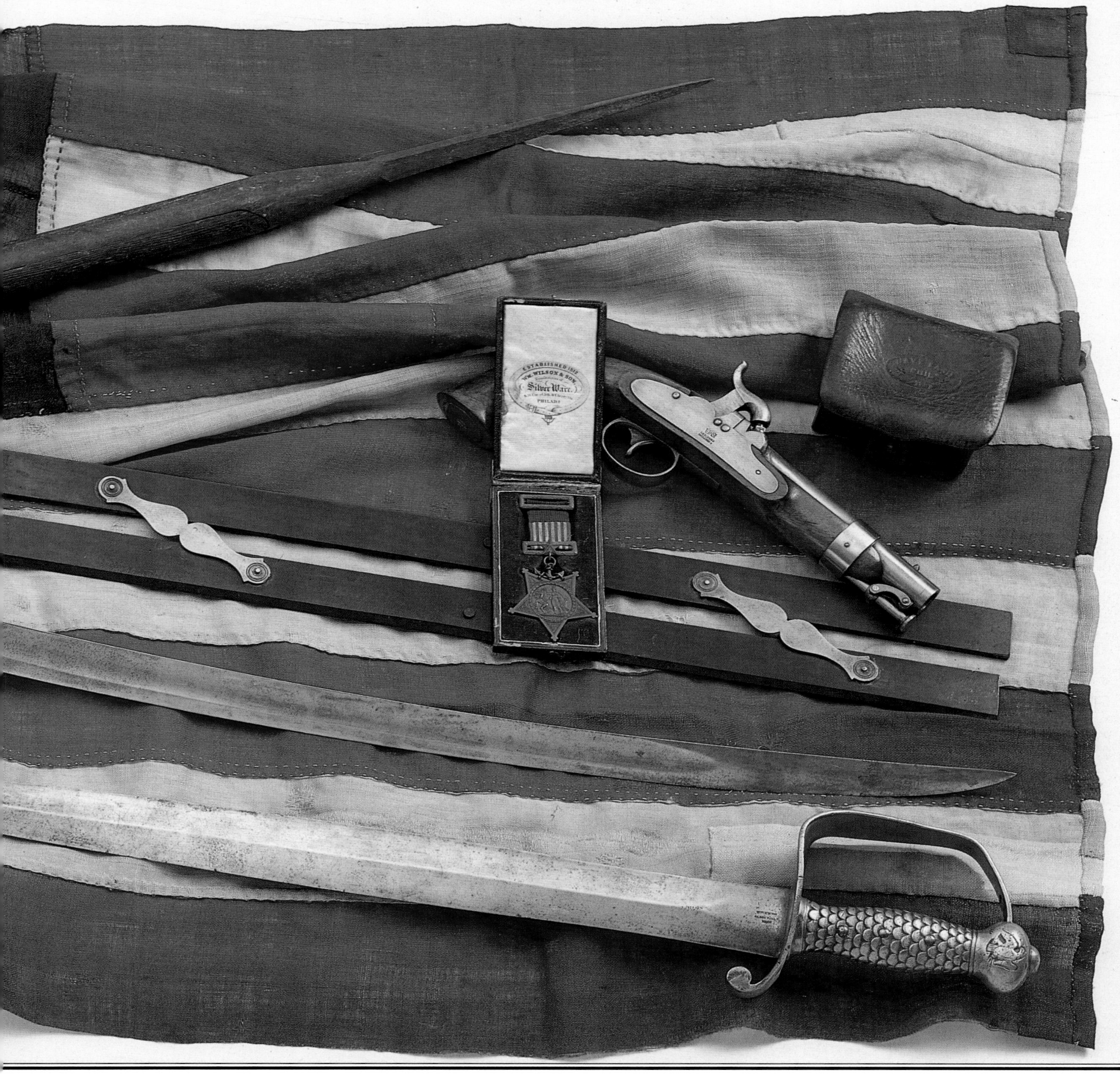

cine and Surgery suggested that the men might like iced tea instead, or even oatmeal![13]

Obviously, because men would misbehave, there had to be means of punishment for offenders, though this presented special problems in the confines of a ship at sea or on station in a river in enemy territory. Serious offenses like mutiny, disobeying orders, desertion, treason, and the like, were to be dealt with by courts martial. Even seemingly minor infractions like swearing, drunkenness and gambling could be thus tried, as could duelling.

Other than flogging, which was outlawed entirely, almost any penalty an officer could devise was allowable. A man could be demoted, his pay reduced accordingly. He could be confined in the brig – or the ship's hold or coal bunkers if there was no brig – for as many days as needed, with or without hand and leg irons, and on bread and water if the captain chose. He could be denied shore leave or punished with extra duty. And if he committed a more summary offense, he could be confined for up to two months, one month of it in irons and on bread and water, or even dismissed from the service. Lesser offenses were disciplined at the will of the captain or his officers, and serious crimes could be punished by death.

Generally, the seamen encountered less formalized punishments for their misbehavior, as officers suited the penalties to the crimes. When Semmes's mutineers were under control on the *Alabama*, he had them taken one by one to the gangway and ordered shipmates to douse them with buckets of water. At first the inebriates howled in derision at the paltry punishment, yelling at the quartermasters to "come on with their water". But the water came faster and faster, incessantly, leaving a man no time to catch his breath between one dousing and another. After a time, choking, sick, near to fainting, they begged to be forgiven. Then Semmes released them and sent them to their hammocks. He never experienced another mutiny.[14]

There was a considerable variety in the conditions experienced by seamen, depending upon their posting. Yankees stuck on blockade service endured, arguably, the most tedious life of all, spending months at a time patrolling back and forth a few miles outside a harbor or river mouth, waiting to catch an occasional runner. If the seas were down and the winds were low, it could be hot and sticky. When the weather rose, the

Above: It was aboard lightly armored converted river steamers like the Mississippi raider USS *Rattler* that most seamen saw real battle action. Up and down the waterways, these gunboats fought a steady war for complete control.

Below: Far more impressive than the ersatz gunboats were the mighty river ironclads. Resting here in the Mississippi off Cairo, Illinois, the USS *Baron DeKalb*, USS *Mound City*, and USS *Cincinnati*, promise deadly combat for any Rebel ship willing to fight.

churning seas battered ships and men alike, leaving the latter sea-sick and debilitated. It was somewhat better for the sea-going cruisers that plied the oceans in search of the Rebel commerce raiders. Though they spent months at a time on cruise, at least they encountered unusual or exotic ports, and more shore leave when available. The same was true of the men aboard the ships they hunted.

Sailor-for-sailor, there was far more real action, and much more relief from the tedium, for the men stationed aboard the river gunboats. Hundreds of these plied the Mississippi and its tributaries, as well as all the major navigable rivers along the eastern seacoast. Smaller, shallow-draft vessels, they usually operated out of bases in the interior, or else in a harbor, and returned frequently to refill their small coal bunkers. That meant many more opportunities for the men to get leave to go ashore. Additionally, water, wood, and foraging parties often left the vessel while on patrol, spending a few hours or even days on the riverbank and in the interior. It was still hot service, and muggy along the Southern waterways, but foul weather presented much less of a hazard.

The tedium was further relieved by the very real hazard of action, for a river gunboat might frequently encounter enemy shore batteries, an attack from shore-based boarders, even an occasional raid by cavalry. And now and then, especially on the Mississippi, there could be a major fleet battle or attack upon some fortified city like New Orleans or Vicksburg. For every blockade sailor who died of sea-sickness or scurvy, a river seaman died in action.

Ironically, the safest service of all was also the most uncomfortable. The rush of building of ironclads – called "monitor fever" in the North – led to the commissioning of scores of the ungainly monsters. The Confederate *Virginia*, con-

Petty Officer, US Navy (USS *New Hampshire*)

The petty officers were the men who, some said, really ran the ship. They were the boatswain's mates who passed and carried out the orders that saw that the captain's instructions were met. They were the gunner's mates who managed each cannon. They were the carpenter's mates and sailmaker's mates, ship's steward and cook; each man giving a vital task the personal oversight required to get each important job done and keep the ship in perfect running order. These men wore much the same type of uniforms as the common seamen, blue wool or white duck trousers and frocks with blue striped cuffs and collar. An embroidered foul anchor was to appear on the sleeve of their jackets as a mark of rank. The boatswains carried pipes or whistles, and all petty officers could carry weapons such as pistols and cutlass as sidearms.

USS *Monitor*

Most famous of all Yankee warships was the so-called "cheese box on a raft", the USS *Monitor*. Designed by Swedish inventor John Ericsson, the ironclad was really an amalgamation of many previous ideas. Ericsson's genius was in combining them all into an effective warship. Most noticeable on the vessel was her armored turret, a 20-foot wide cylinder, 9 feet high, protected by 8 inches of iron plating. It mounted two 11-inch smooth-bore cannon and was operated by a steam engine which also ran ventilators. The hull itself was 172 feet long at the waterline and was covered with 4½ inches of armor on the sides and 1 inch on the deck. Heavy and unwieldy, she could make barely 6 knots, but it was enough for her to stymie the CSS *Virginia* (*Merrimack*) in their epic duel in Hampton Roads, Virginia. Nine months later, however, her unseaworthiness became her undoing, and she went to the bottom in a storm on December 30, 1862.

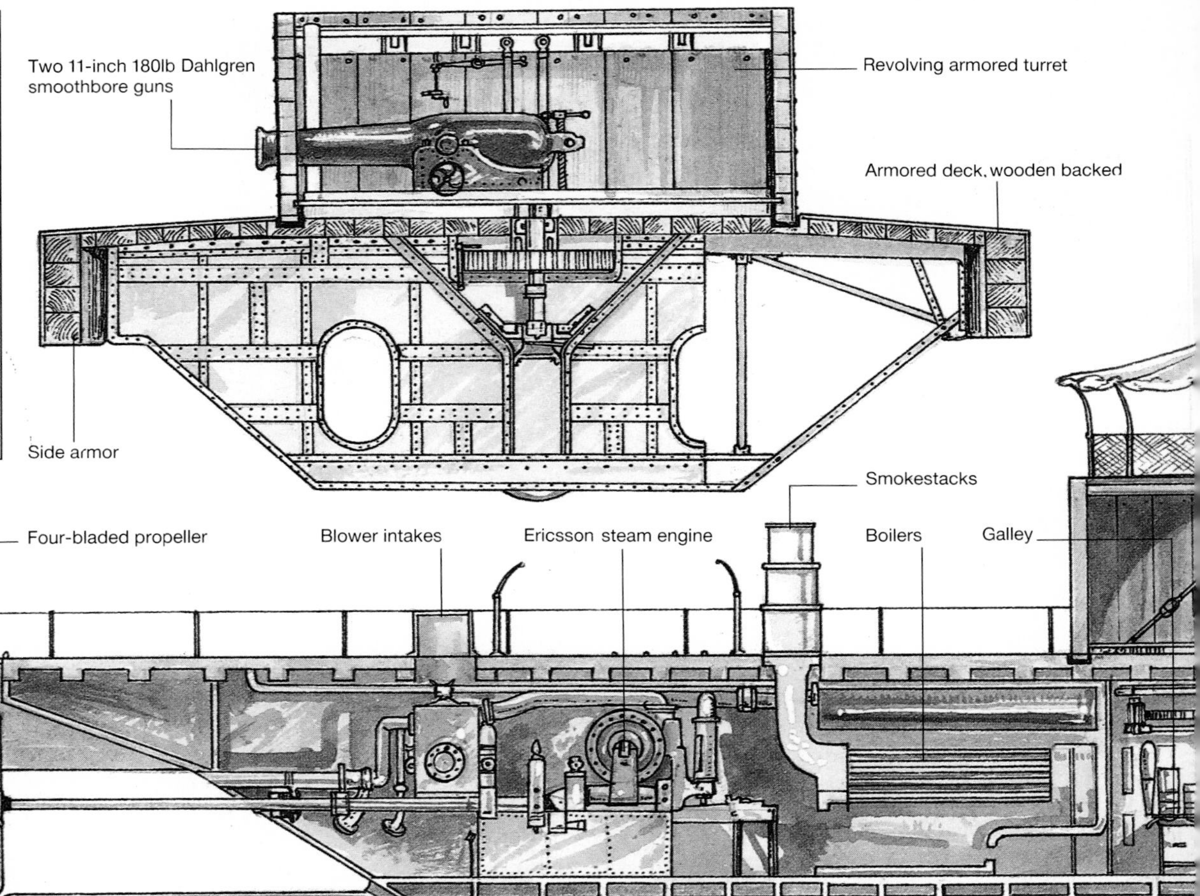

verted from the old *Merrimack*, was not the world's first ironclad as is often supposed, but it was the virtual prototype for almost every other Rebel ironclad of the war. Its foe the USS *Monitor* was likewise the precursor of a host of others, most with one turret, some with two, and even one with three gun towers. The Union also built several other river gunboats that were iron-sheathed to protect the crew and machinery from shore batteries. Most were effective, a few were not. But all of them were absolutely miserable to serve aboard. Ventilation was almost non-existent, and in the hot and humid Southern summers, temperatures beneath the iron sheathing on decks and turrets could rise well over 120°F during the day. With no windows to cool the interior, or to let in light, the men lived in a damp, dark, fetid, nightmarish underworld. "I began to think that in our Navy [comfort] does not exist", wrote a man aboard the CSS *Baltic*. Even worse was the Rebel ironclad *Atlanta*, serving in the sounds of Georgia. "I would defy anyone in the world to tell when it is day or night if he is confined below without any way of marking time", wrote a man aboard the ship. "If a person were blind folded and carried below and then turned loose he would imagine himself in a swamp."[15] The only remedy the Confederates found was to berth their ironclad crews ashore at night when possible, and almost all ironclad sailors soon learned to abandon the steamy berthdeck for the top deck at night. "Hot, hotter, hottest", wrote a man aboard the *Monitor* in Virginia's James River in August 1862. "Could stand it no longer, so last night I wrapped my blanket 'round me & took to our iron deck – if the bed was not soft it was not so insufferably hot as my *pen*."[16]

No wonder every shipboard surgeon had to worry about a host of ills, from diarrhoea and dysentery, to typhoid, malaria, and simple exhaustion. Quinine was liberally dosed when available, and canned tomatoes were the only

Below: During the so-called 'iron-clad fever' that swept the Union, some absolute behemoths were constructed, among them the mighty armored steamer USS *Choctaw*, one of the biggest vessels on the rivers.

Bottom: While giants like the *Choctaw* dominated the Mississippi Valley, the more conventional monitors like USS *Saugus* made life hardly bearable for crews who served inside their furnace-like iron hulls.

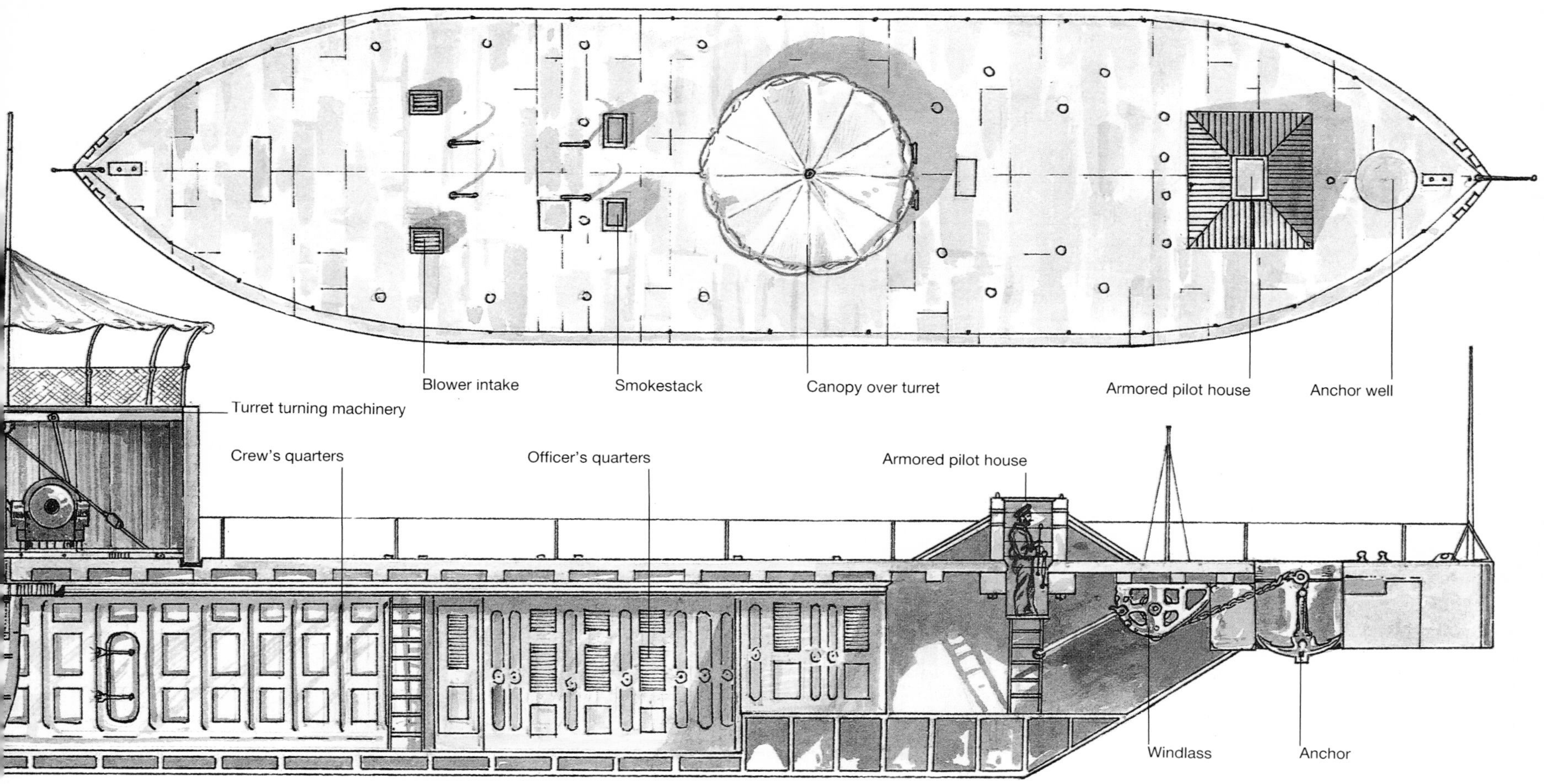

Blower intake
Smokestack
Canopy over turret
Armored pilot house
Anchor well
Turret turning machinery
Crew's quarters
Officer's quarters
Armored pilot house
Windlass
Anchor

Below: When the Yankee sailor had to go into battle aboard a monitor, the ship usually protected him well. The gun turret of USS *Passaic* reveals the ordeal through which she passed in the attack on Charleston, South Carolina, in April 1863. Despite being hit numerous times, and failing in her assigned mission, the *Passaic* still withstood a terrible hail of iron, her men inside remaining unscathed.

answer for scurvy when fresh vegetables and fruit were unavailable. As for sea-sickness, the sailors had their own remedies. When Alvah Hunter first fell ill with it on the *Nahant's* initial voyage, an old salt persuaded him to drink sea water and, incredibly, he immediately felt better.

If the burden of boredom was greater for the sailor than for his counterpart in the armies, at least he carried a lighter load. The footsoldier lugged nine or ten pounds of rifle and another twenty or more of other impedimenta wherever he marched. Happily, the seamen had no knapsacks, nor any assigned rifles or other weapons to husband. Every vessel in the Union Navy carried arms racks of muskets or carbines, pistols, and the traditional cutlasses. While every man at one time or another spent his share of duty at cleaning and caring for the weapons stores, still he did not have a specifically assigned weapon that was regarded as his own, other than pocket or clasp knives which the Navy Department issued to every man. On shipboard, in time of action, most men served either the engines or the guns. If there was a prospect of close-in fighting between ships' companies, then the racks disgorged their cutlasses, revolvers, and sometimes even boarding pikes. Yet such actions were almost nonexistent in the Civil War, restricted to a few stealthy night actions and cutting-out expeditions where a brave few tried to take an enemy vessel by surprise. In fact, many naval crews saw more action ashore, either as armed parties carrying shoulder arms, or else manning shore batteries.[17]

What fighting the seaman did engage in was usually ship-to-ship or ship-to-shore manning the cannon of his vessel He worked a variety of guns almost as great as that of the artillerymen in the army, though generally the ship's guns came in more awesome sizes. There were rifles that fired projectiles ranging from twelve up to 150 pounds, most of them Parrott's, though also a number of the newly designed Dahlgren rifles, often called "soda pop" guns thanks to their shape resembling that of a bottle. aboard some of the biggest vessels, and especially on ironclads expected to combat forts or other ironclads, massive smoothbores firing projectiles up to fifteen inches in diameter and weighing 440 pounds or more, were also served by the gun crews. And there were a lot of them. By the last year of the war, the Union Navy alone carried over 4,600 guns aboard its ships. Numbers for Confederate vessels are far less precise, but certainly more than 2,500 saw service. Regulations differed according to the gun and the availability of men, but in general it took sixteen seamen to operate one muzzle-loader, most of them performing functions that corresponded closely to the duties of the artillerymen with the army forces. In addition, the massive guns had to be manhandled forward by rope and tackle after every recoil, and that task alone could occupy nine seamen.

The experiences of sailors both North and South were quite apart from those of the soldiers, and distinct to the kinds of ships they manned. Rarely did any man ever have to face the ultimate test of a hand-to-hand, face-to-face encounter with an enemy. Most of the water-borne action of the war took place on the rivers and harbors of the South, between gunboats and ironclads, or such vessels and Confederate forts. In either case, most of the time the gun crews enjoyed the protection of an iron casemate or turret in the case of the ironclads, and at least some kind of iron reinforced wood, or even cotton, bulwarks aboard the gunboats and converted river steamers. As a result, the seaman's view of the action was limited to what he glimpsed through his gun-port. Fighting was for him a methodical repetitive performance of the functions necessary to load and fire. Unless his ship took a bad hit, the most common enemy was the smoke, choking heat, and deafening noise inside the gun deck.

Of course, the protective bulwarks of iron or whatever else surrounded the ship above the

Above: It could take several seamen to operate one of the main cannon aboard ship, though the little 12-pounder deck howitzers like the Dahlgren shown here aboard the gunboat USS *Hunchback* required far fewer.

Below: It was the massive Parrott rifles like the huge one below, on the deck of the USS *Mendota*, which could take a complement of 16 men or more. Every seaman had his assigned task, every one of them dangerous.

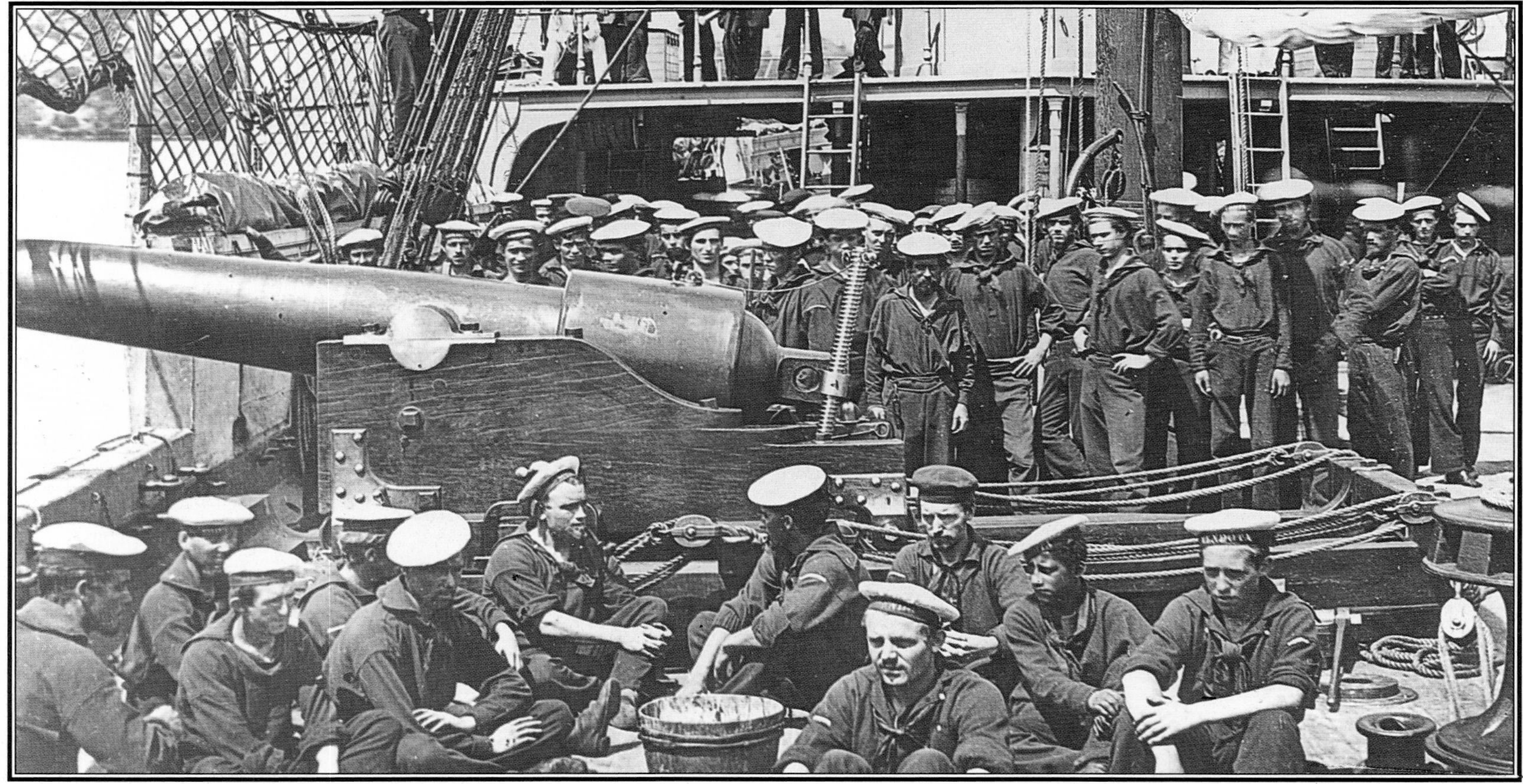

water-line, varied greatly in effectiveness. A really accurate shot from one of those massive 15-inch smoothbores, or a heavy solid 'bolt' or projectile fired from a big rifled cannon, might penetrate any but the strongest armor, and then a ship's crew was in trouble. Flying splinters of wood and iron could become deadly missiles inside a gun deck. And if an enemy shot penetrated through the protective hull and punctured the steam engines' boilers, then the ship's interior could become a scalding inferno.

Nevertheless, while advancements in warfare had made fighting increasingly more dangerous for the footsoldier, for the seaman the Civil War was comparatively the safest conflict to date. Consequently, of more than 132,000 Yankee sailors, just 1,804 were killed in action or died as a result of wounds, and of them nearly one-fifth were scalded to death by burst boilers. Perhaps another 3,000 died of other causes, but total deaths still amount to less than four percent. Confederate naval casualties are difficult to ascertain, though their overall percentage was likely greater, since Southern protective armor was less effective than that of the North, and considerably more Rebel vessels were battered into submission.[18]

Still, when compared to a better than one-in-five chance of meeting death in some form or another for the soldiers, the sailors' hopes of survival were immeasurably greater. As for the men aboard the Confederate commerce raiders, the few naval blockade runners, or the Yankee ships that chased both, injuries in action from enemy fire were almost non-existent. The commerce raiders took on only unarmed merchant vessels, and the blockaders the same. And when they did fire, often as not their target was only a dim smudge of sail or a column of smoke on the horizon.

Indeed, for most sailors, Blue and Gray alike, the real action of the war was invariably a dot on the horizon – an event dimly seen, indistinctly heard, and peripherally experienced. That they did their part cannot be denied, nor is it arguable that the control of the rivers, harbors, and coast-lines for which they vied, was not ultimately crucial to success or failure. Yet for the men who often endured a year of inaction for every day of battle in those ships and boats, theirs was a war on the margins of the greater conflict.

Above: Assisted by a white-belted marine, sailors of the USS *Miami* work at gun drill with their 11-inch Dahlgren gun. Practice at these drills was as close to combat as many seaman ever came in their boring war.

Below: Compared to the hazards of war on land, naval service looked splendidly safe. Even in cranky oddity ships like the Confederacy's torpedo boats, or "Davids", seamen encountered few dangers.

References

1 Long, *Day by Day*, p.719.
2 *Ibid.*
3 Francis Lord, *They Fought for the Union* (Harrisburg, Pa., 1960), p.286.
4 Long, *Day by Day*, p.720.
5 Alvah Hunter, *A Year on a Monitor and the Destruction of Fort Sumter* (Columbia, S.C., 1987), pp.7-8.
6 *Ibid.*, p.8.
7 *Ibid.*
8 William C. Davis (ed.), *Fighting for Time* (New York, 1983), pp.366-71.
9 Hunter, *Monitor*, p.8.
10 Lord, *They Fought for the Union*, p.287; C. Carter Smith, Jr. (ed.), *Two Naval Journals: 1864* (Birmingham, Ala., 1964), pp.19ff.
11 Naval History Division (comp.), *Civil War Naval Chronology* (Washington, 1961), Book II, p.67.
12 Hunter, *Monitor*, p.20.
13 Davis, *Fighting for Time*, p.373.
14 Raphael Semmes, *The Confederate Raider "Alabama"* (Greenwich, Conn., 1962), pp.138-40.
15 William N. Still, *Iron Afloat* (Nashville, 1971), p.100.
16 Robert W. Daly (ed.), *Aboard the USS Monitor: 1862* (Annapolis, Md., 1964), p.205.
17 Lord, *They Fought for the Union*, p.293.
18 Long, *Day by Day*, pp.710-11.

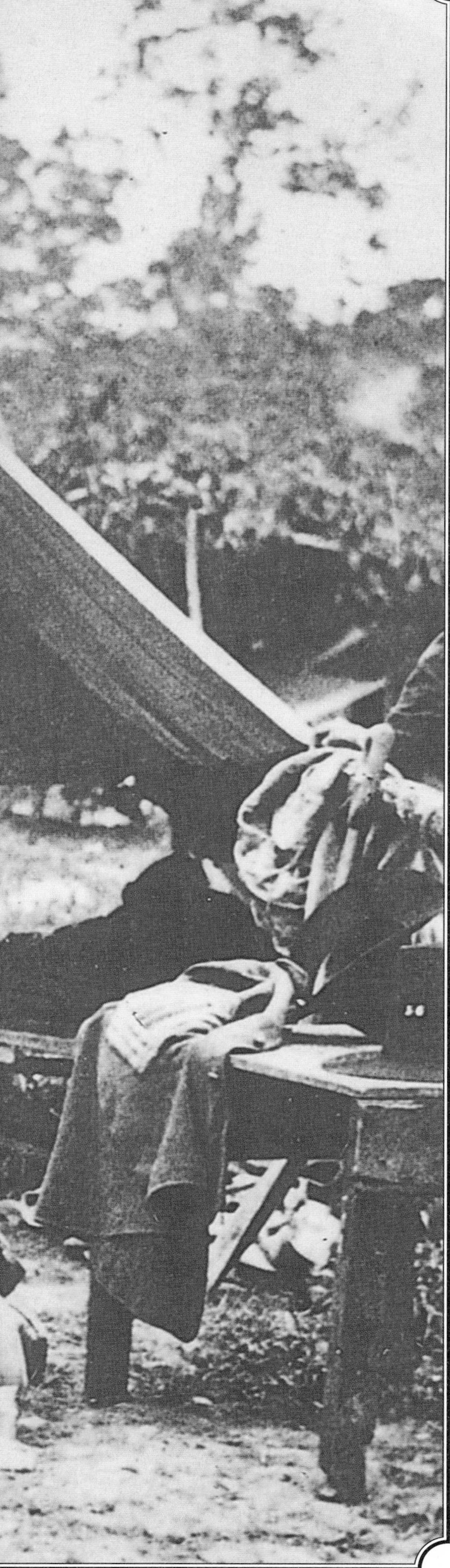

CHAPTER SEVEN

TENTING TONIGHT

Only late in 1863 did Lee and Meade move against each other again, and then only in indecisive and desultory campaigns in northern Virginia that saw little action. The real activity was all in Tennessee and northern Georgia. After the Tullahoma Campaign, in which Rosecrans feinted Bragg's army out of Tennessee altogether, the Federals occupied the key rail center at Chattanooga. But in September Bragg decided to strike back, and on September 18 he moved north to meet Rosecrans along Chickamauga Creek. The two-day battle that followed was one of the most ferocious of the war. By the end of the first day, no one seemed to have the advantage, but then on the next, September 20, a miscarried Federal order resulted in a hole in Rosecrans' line just as Bragg launched a massive assault at that very spot. The Federal army broke in two, most of it running in panic back to Chattanooga, along with Rosecrans, in what was the most complete defeat ever inflicted by a Confederate army. Bragg, realizing the size of his success, almost immediately followed up on his victory, and soon had Rosecrans besieged.

Within a few weeks Lincoln put Grant in charge, and he replaced Rosecrans directly with General George H. Thomas. At once Grant broke the blockade of supplies to Chattanooga, then began rebuilding the army for a break-out, which began on November 23, when Thomas took Orchard Knob, in front of the impressive Rebel positions atop Missionary Ridge. The next day the Yankees, under William T. Sherman, took the northern end of Bragg's line at Tunnel Hill, while Hooker stormed and took Bragg's southern anchor on top of Lookout Mountain. On November 25, Thomas' army moved straight up the slopes of Missionary Ridge and put Bragg's forces to disgraceful rout. A few days later a Confederate corps besieging Knoxville, Tennessee, was also driven back, leaving the Union in full mastery of eastern Tennessee. But then the coming of cold forced both armies into the huts and cabins – and monotony – of camp life in winter quarters.

THERE WAS, said an old Confederate Carlton McCarthy, a "fancy idea [that] the principal occupation of a soldier should be actual conflict with the enemy". The recruits of 1861 "didn't dream of such a thing as camping for six months at a time without firing a gun, or marching and countermarching", not to mention "the thousand commonplace duties of the soldier".[1] There, however, lay the true essence of Civil War soldiering. For every day spent in battle, Yank and Reb passed weeks – even months – fighting other enemies: heat and cold, hunger, deprivation, bad sanitation, foolish officers, the allurements of the devil, and worst of all boredom.

Out of it all came their most enduring memories of the days of their youth. "Let us together recall with pleasure the past!" exclaimed McCarthy years later; "once more be hungry, and eat; once more tired, and rest; once more thirsty, and drink; once more cold and wet, let us sit by the roaring fire and feel comfort creep over us".[2] They were simple pleasures all, but to the men in blue and gray they were triumphs in themselves, adversities conquered in the unending battle to make the campgrounds of North and South homes away from home.

The new soldiers came ill-prepared for their lives in camp. Hometown oratory charged their emotions to expect an immediate rush headlong

Of the many things that the soldiers both Blue and Gray would remember in later years, their fondest memories would be of those hours spent taking their ease with comrades in camp.

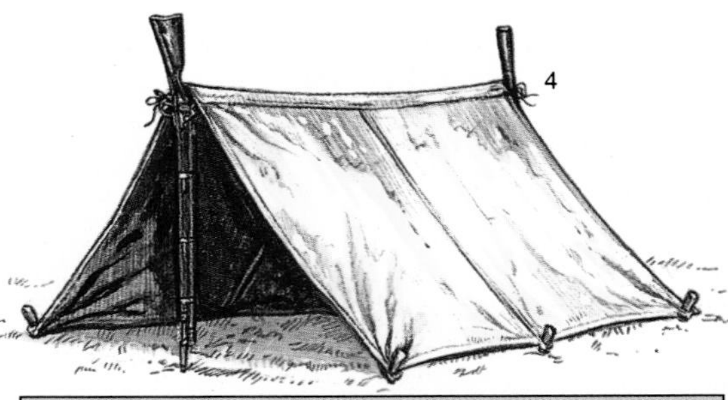

Tent Types

The soldier took such shelter as he could, or as much as the quartermaster allowed him. The tents the men used varied in size and shape, though they all succeeded in being mostly cold, drafty and cramped.

1 The wall tent was the best, though difficult to erect.
2 Wedge tents offered speed of assembly, but far less space
3 The Sibley tent, though more comfortable for soldiers on the march also proved too cumbersome on the march
4 In the end, it was the lowly dog tent which most soldiers used. Two men each carried half which they buttoned together at night.

into glorious battle, fight day in and day out, and then, the war won, return home again in triumph. Their first scanty drill and training in the rendezvous camps gave little hint of what would really come once they joined the armies in the field. No one taught them to cook, or pitch tents, or not to dig their latrines upstream of their camps. No one told them what to expect – because no one *knew* what to expect – when suddenly thousands of men from all stations of life were thrown together – saints and sinners, bullies and milktoasts. Sometimes those who had gone before sent back warnings of what lay ahead for the new recruit in camp, but in the end every man had to learn for himself.

The new soldier learned rather quickly that his only real place of refuge from the parade ground was his tent, his home for three seasons of the year. As with his weapons, a considerable variety of shelters first appeared in the summer of 1861. Some units like the Washington Artillery of New Orleans came with candy-striped tents. Others showed up with nothing at all, and the governments had to cast about for what would suit their regiments the best. Wall tents were initially popular, canvas dwellings shaped exactly like a small house. But they proved too expensive to manufacture, too cumbersome to pitch and carry, and eventually found themselves inhabited only by those too weak or too exalted to do the work of erecting them – hospital patients and officers.

Much more popular and efficient was the Sibley tent, named for its inventor Henry H. Sibley, now a brigadier general in the confederate service. One Reb likened it to "a large hoop skirt standing by itself on the ground".[3] Indeed, it resembled nothing so much as an Indian teepee, a tall cone of canvas supported by a center pole. Flaps on the sides could be opened for ventilation, and an iron replica of the tent cone called a Sibley stove heated the interior – sort of. Often more than twenty men inhabited a single tent, spread out like the spokes of a wheel, their heads at the outer rim and their feet at the center pole. Yet regulations called for no more than a dozen inhabitants, and while some soldiers found the Sibleys more healthy and comfortable than a regular barracks, that only applied on days when the weather was fair. When the cold or rain forced the men to keep the tent flaps closed overnight, the air inside became unbearable. John D. Billings, a Massachusetts artilleryman, never for-

Above: Confederates like these men of the 9th Mississippi near Pensacola in early 1861 had to contend with hotter climates. They erected brush-cover arbours, called "shebangs", to protect them from the sun.

Below: The soldiers of both sides showed considerable imagination in the ways they adapted their campsites and tents to suit their needs. These Yankees have built their Sibley tents off the ground.

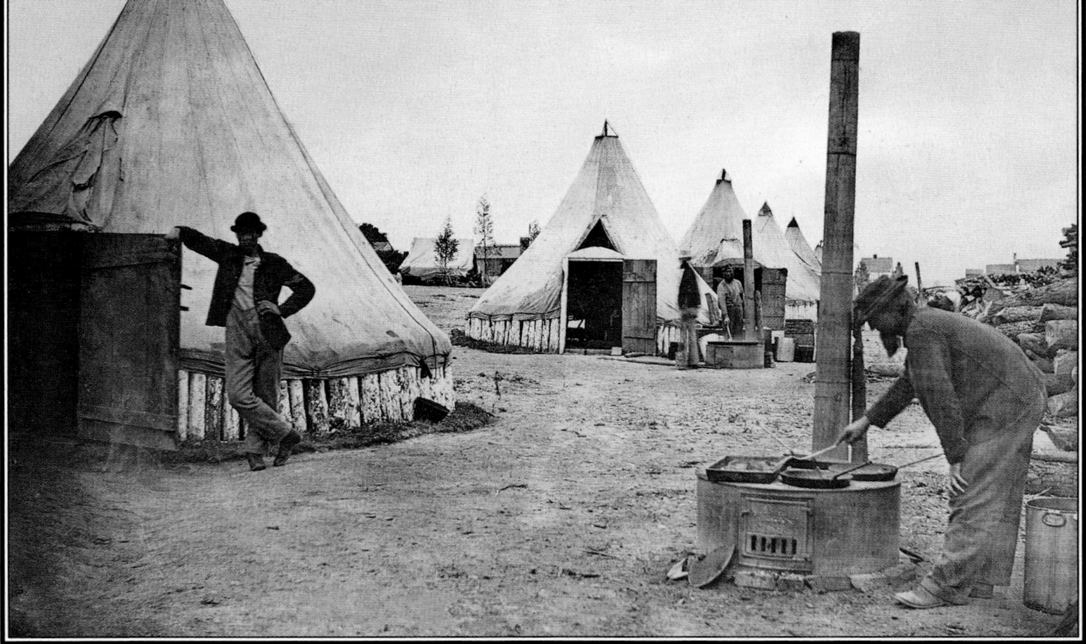

got what it was like to enter a Sibley after such a night "and encounter the night's accumulation of nauseating exhalations from the bodies of twelve men (differing widely in their habits of personal cleanliness)". It was "an experience which no old soldier has ever been known to recall with great enthusiasm".[4] Eventually, Sibleys also proved too cumbersome for extensive field operations.

Rapidly the tents became simpler, lighter, and as a rule less comfortable. For a time Billy Yank tried sleeping in the wedge tent. Exceedingly simple, it was little more than a six-foot length of canvas that its four to six occupants draped over a center pole. Stakes held its sides to the ground, and end flaps closed the openings, allowing some privacy, but absolutely no comfort. With only about seven square feet of space per man on the ground, the men had to sleep "spoon" fashion. When one turned in his sleep, all the others had to do the same. And with the ridge pole only five feet off the ground, even the shorter soldiers were forced to stoop to enter.

Private, 56th US Colored Infantry

It was inevitable that the Union government would find a way to take the ex-slaves, whose cause had been so great a part in starting the war, and turn them into a weapon for winning it. Thousands wanted to take up arms to fight for their brothers still in bonds in the Confederacy, and eventually several tens of thousands were enlisted in more than 100 all-black regiments; though at the beginning they were regarded more as laborers than combat soldiers. The uniforms and equipment for these units was virtually the same as that for this private of the 56th United States Colored infantry, and in fact, no different from that of the average white soldier. Dark blue wool jacket, light blue wool trousers, blue cloth kepi, Springfield rifle and accompanying bayonet were all standard issue. Most glaringly different was the fact that for most of the war, until at least 1864, black soldiers were paid less than their white counterparts.

If that were not bad enough, by the latter part of 1862, and for the balance of the war to follow, an even smaller soldier shelter came into use. "It would only comfortably accommodate a dog, and a small one at that", said Billings. So that is what they called it – the dog tent.[5] It differed little in nature or name from the pup tent of later wars. Two men shared it, and it took two to make it, each one carrying with him a half of the canvas. They buttoned their halves together, slung it over a center pole, and then lay down side-by-side in the cramped interior to contemplate what little impediment, if any, their shelter offered to the elements since it had no end flaps to hinder cold and wind. In 1862 the Yankee Asa Brindle told his family that the dog tent reminded him "forceable of a hog pen". He deeply lamented that its inventor had not been "hung before the invention had been completed".

Confederates suffered continually from want of proper shelters, as they suffered with a shortage of just about everything else. Captured Yankee tents were often all they had, for wartime shortages affected canvas as well as weapons and ammunition. Lacking tents, the Southerners improvised crude shelters as best they could, often piling brush or stretching oil clothes over fence-rail frameworks to make so-called "shebangs". However crude, still inhabitants pronounced them "very comfortable in warm weather".

However it was that fourth season of the year, the winter's chill, that most challenged the Reb's and Yank's ability and imagination. When the leaves began to turn and the north winds freshened, the men in the tents took their axes and saws out into the neighboring woods and virtually mowed them down. If timber was in sufficient abundance, whole log cabins rose up. More often, however, the soldiers blended earth and trees, their tents, even scavenged portions of local buildings, to produce their winter quarters. Before the ground froze, they dug into the earth a foot or so, then they built their log walls another four or five above the pit, capping them with flat roofs of brush or boards, or even tents slung over

Confederate Camp Artifacts

Homespun garments, a few trinkets, a pipe carved from soapstone, all were the sorts of items to be found in any Confederate's knapsack. These he augmented, when he could, by appropriating from the dead whatever they would no longer need. Few as his camp belongings might have been, many a Southerner would fight and even kill to keep them safe from other hands.

1 Blanket
2 Tin cup
3 Wooden personal effects box
4 Shaving kit
5 Pipe and handmade tobacco bag
6 Wallet
7 Match safe
8 Tent lantern
9 Piece of hardtack
10 Tin cups
11 Handmade pipe
12 Mess tin
13 Leather cup
14 Ladle
15 Skillet
16 and 18 Folding combination eating utensil
17 and 19 Tin cups
20 Nut bowl
21 Personal effects bag
22 Lighting device
23 Candle
24 Candle holders
25–28 Matches and lighting devices

Artifacts courtesy of: The Civil War Library and Museum, Philadelphia, Pa: 1, 5-10, 14, 16-28; J. Craig Nannos Collection: 2-4, 11-13, 15

a center pole. They waterproofed their roofs by spreading their own ponchos or rubberized blankets over the canvas, and kept the wind and rain from whistling through the walls by packing the chinks between the logs with mud. For many of the upper-crust soldiers from the affluent cities, it was like a return to the pioneer homes of their forebears. For the boys from the wooded hills and mountains of Appalachia, it was often just like home.

Every winter hut was as individual as the men who built it. They made fireplaces of sticks and mud, with an old barrel for a chimney. More ambitious men foraged brick to erect true masonry masterpieces. Furnishings came from whatever might be found – and more often liberated when in enemy country. No farmer's barn was safe, and any abandoned house presented a true emporium of domestic possibilities. Straw and pine needle mattresses covered bunks along the walls. Boxes and log ends made serviceable stools to set before their rough wood or crate tables. Bayonets thrust into the logs became candlesticks, and more straw spread upon the floor absorbed the mud from outside tracked in by visitors.

Nothing in the Civil War could escape the soldiers' penchant for nicknames, and certainly not their winter dwellings. A Louisiana unit dubbed two of its houses "Sans Souci" and "Buzzard's Roost". Some New Englanders called their's the "Swine Hotel", "Hole in the Wall", and "We're Out", while a Bostonian recalled the glories of home naming his domicile the "Parker House". Even the streets bore names, and not always just patriotic titles like "Lincoln Avenue" or "Lee Boulevard". Many an encampment had its "Mud Lane" and "Starvation Alley". Some, like one admiring Indianian, might declare that "Instead of appearing like a camp of rusty soldiers, it looks like a city of magnificent splendor", but few found winter quarters so delightful. The huts were not that much better than tents, and whether freezing in the snow or drowning in the rain, the whole camps were generally a mess.

Union Camp Artifacts

The scanty personal items possessed by the common soldier assumed greater importance to him as the war went on. They were some of the few items that were truly his and which set him apart from his messmates, and he guarded them jealously.

1 Patent coffee boiler
2 Haversack
3 Tin cup
4 Model 1858 canteen
5 Porcelain cup
6 Coffee boiler
7 Housewife
8 Sewing kit
9 Handkerchief
10 Folding candle stands
11 Haversack
12 Knapsack
13 Tin cup
14 Sibley stove
15 Rubber blanket
16 Chess set
17 Model 1858 canteen
18 Folding cup
19 Hardtack
20 Tin plate and spoon
21 Eating utensils
22 Coffee pot
23 Pipe and tobacco
24 Matches
25 Tintype
26 Diary and pocket bible
27 Pocket watch
28 Straight razor and case
29 Pocket mirror
30 Manuals
31 Playing cards
32 Folding combination eating utensil
33 Haversack

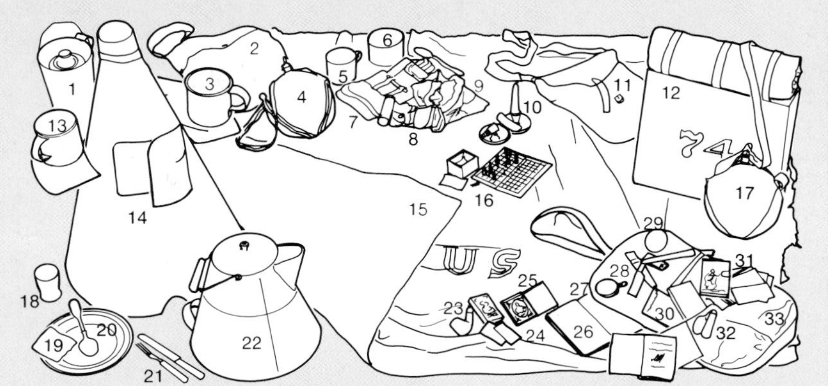

Artifacts courtesy of: The Museum of the Confederacy, Richmond, Va

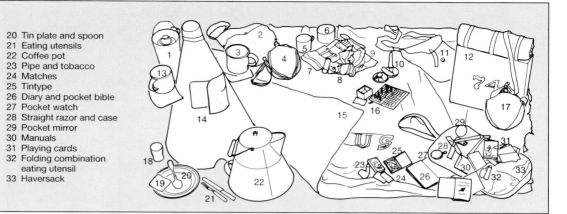

Above: In winter a soldier's camp home could be a perfect mire, the muddy "streets" little more than swamps, while only "corduroyed" walkways, covered in branches, offered a dry place to step.

Above: To pass their free time, men like this Georgian of the "Clinch Rifles" read and wrote incessantly, sending home letters like the one under his pen, and keeping diaries such as the one at his left hand.

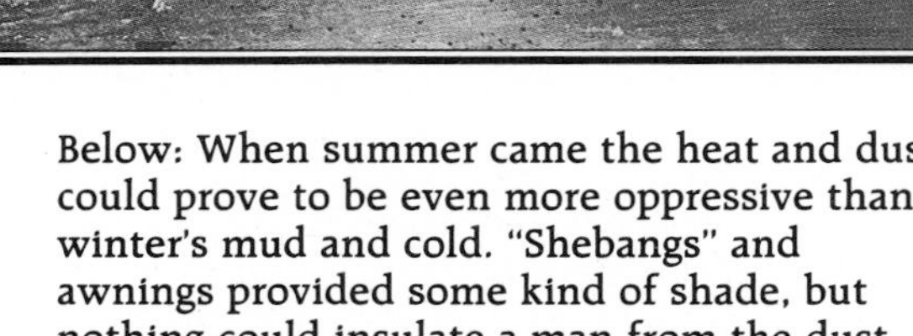

Below: When summer came the heat and dust could prove to be even more oppressive than winter's mud and cold. "Shebangs" and awnings provided some kind of shade, but nothing could insulate a man from the dust.

"This plain became a wallow-hole", complained one Bay State soldier; "the clay surface freezing at night and thawing by day, trampled by thousands of men, made a vast sea of mud."[9]

Confederates fared no better. In the first winter of the war, a Reb at Manassas spoke of the place as "literally a lake of mud. Wherever you go the ground is so soft that you have to hold your breath to keep from sinking. Men and horses are often completely buried in driving over roads, and you see their heads protruding above the mire." Perhaps he exaggerated just a bit, but it was no stretch of the imagination to look on the filth and inconvenience, the fleas in the mattresses, the lice in their clothes, and the mud caked everywhere, and see why he would "be perplexed whether to laugh or sympathize".[10]

Making matters even more difficult for the men, winter or summer, was that they were left entirely on their own to fill their idle time, and as the war went on, they had more and more of it to fill as drill was relaxed. Neither government made a concerted effort to provide systematic recreation or diversion. Worse, furloughs or brief releases from camp to return home for a visit were extremely limited. Men from the North were too far away from home to get much use from a furlough, and Confederates were too few in the first place to allow them to go to the rear. General Daniel Harvey Hill sarcastically declared that "if our brave soldiers are not occasionally permitted to visit their homes the next generation in the South will be composed of the descendants of skulkers and cowards."[11]

While they were required to remain in camp, almost like prisoners, the soldiers had to contend with the ever-present mud in winter and dust in summer. In the latter season of 1864 one Connecticut soldier likened a walk through camp to a stroll through an ash heap. "One's mouth will be so full of dust that you do not want your teeth to touch one another."[12] A Yankee cannoneer wryly remarked that whenever a grasshopper jumped up, it raised such a cloud of dust that Confederate lookouts reported the Union army was on the move again. The dust blew through the holes in their worn clothing and caked to the sweat on their bodies. "I have no seat in my pants", lamented a Virginian, "the legs are worn out, have had but one pair of socks which are worn out completely, my shirt is literally rotted off me."[13] A new issue shirt proved to be so louse-ridden that he could not bear to wear it. Relief societies like the United States Christian Commission and several state societies, North and South, did what they could to bring a little comfort to the soldiers' lot, but it was ever a losing battle.

Filling all those countless thousands of hours of unoccupied time proved to be the greatest challenge facing Yank and Reb alike. Not surprisingly, so many men being away from home for prolonged periods for the first time in their lives, it was the common soldiers' preoccupation with the folks at home which afforded the most popular camp pastime. "Everybody is writing who can raise a pencil or sheet of paper", one Virginian wrote to his own dear loved ones in July 1861. Never before had such massive numbers of Americans been away from home for a prolonged period. Instinctively, they sensed that they were living through something unusual, an epoch worth remembering and reporting to their families. Letter writing, too, was the only contact that many could have with their loved ones, given the restrictions on furloughs. As a result, they sent letters back and forth that taxed the Postal Department as never before. In some regiments

of 1,000 or more men, it was estimated that 600 letters a day were written and posted.[14]

There was a remarkable sameness to what men in blue and gray wrote home about. They talked of their battles, to be sure, but those were few and infrequent. More often they told of their friends, their day in camp, the marches, the heat, the weather, sickness – virtually anything that came to mind – as if the very act of writing was the bond with their loved ones, and not what was written. They used ink and pencil, even crayons. They wrote on foolscap and parchment, in the margins of newspapers and on the back of wallpaper. When a precious sheet of paper was filled, if there was more to say they gave the sheet a quarter turn and cross-wrote over what they had already written. "They is a fly on my pen", wrote John Shank of Illinois: "I just rights What ever Comes in my head."[15]

They wrote as they spoke, and those who could not write dictated letters for their friends to scrawl for them. Quaint as their spelling and grammar appear today, it is testimony not so much to the limits of model literary skill then prevailing, but rather to the surprising degree of at least communicable literacy among a host of men, many of whom had barely the rudiments of schooling. They were earthy, as in their speech, and they had their share of slang terms, many of which took on lasting meaning. "Snug as a bug in a rug", they wrote of their quarters. "Let 'er rip", "scarce as hen's teeth", "red tape", and a host of other idioms went through the mails. Just as a later world conflict would spawn such expressions as "snafu" for an operation gone awry, the Civil War soldier said that something bungled had "gone up". There was a certain homespun eloquence to their metaphors. One Ohio boy called a recent letter from home "Short and Sweet just like a rosted maget", and when another soldier complained to his wife about his spartan camp, he said "To tell the truth we are between sh-t and a sweat out here."[16]

But the most common element in all letters sent home by the boys in the field was the earnest desire for their family and friends to respond in kind. Nothing livened a day like mail call. "Those who received letters went off with radiant countenances", said Confederate John Worsham. "If it was night, each built a fire for light and, sitting down on the ground, read his letter over and over. Those unfortunates who got none went off looking as if they had not a friend on earth."[17] Private E.K. Flournoy lamented to his wife that he "was almost down with histericks" to hear from home.[18] When a Minnesota boy got a letter after a long silence, he confessed that "I can never remember of having been so glad before. I cried with joy and thankfulness."[19]

Above: A big reason for writing all those letters was the hope of receiving some in reply. The day when the mail wagon arrived, like this one of the II Corps, Army of the Potomac, was a blessed one.

Below: Offering other opportunities for reading, and keeping up with national events, the news vendors sold the latest papers from the major cities. Especially popular were the illustrated papers.

They saved their letters and read them again and again. And when there were no letters to peruse, the literate men consumed anything else they could find in print. "Everybody has taken to reading", wrote a Yank.[20] Some better-funded regiments actually established camp libraries. The 13th Massachusetts had its own library at Williamsport, Maryland, in 1862. In 1864 Colonel John C. Wickliffe of the Confederate 9th Kentucky even detailed one of his orderlies to forage for books in Georgia, and built a camp library with rather eclectic holdings. They included Hugo's *Les Misérables*, Dumas' *Three Musketeers*, an encyclopedia of geography, a French reader and grammar, and even a volume of the 1859 *Patent Office Report*. The orderly also produced what he styled a "purty good book", though apologizing for the "damned *bad print*", that happened to be a volume of Cicero's works. "I don't know whether you can read it or not", he told Wickliffe. It was in Latin.[21]

Surprisingly, there were a few soldiers who could read Latin and Greek, and the classics were not at all unknown in the camps. The works of

Shakespeare and Milton were read around many campfires as well, though Sir Walter Scott was far more popular. Popular novels of the day, as well as patriotic literature, were consumed with equal relish, not to mention the rapidly growing genre of works actually inspired by the war they were fighting. By 1862 the first memoirs of service began to appear, highly dramatized and often more than a bit fictional, still they enjoyed considerable popularity. Also popular was more serious fiction, like Edward Everett Hale's *The Man Without a Country* which appeared in 1863, and was widely believed to have been inspired by the story of Ohio Democrat Clement Vallandigham, who was expelled from the North for treason. Most popular of all, however, was the Bible. The US Christian Commission distributed tens of thousands of copies in the Union camps, and even more found their way to soldier hands North and South through private means.

Newspapers proved ever in demand, especially the illustrated press of the day. The *New York Illustrated News, Frank Leslie's Illustrated Newspaper, Harper's Weekly*, and for a brief time the Confederate *Southern Illustrated News*, provided the men with weekly accounts of the course of the war and events at home, illustrated with crude and often very inaccurate woodcuts. Literary magazines like *Harper's Monthly* and the *American Review* also came to the camps, but far more popular were booklets created especially for soldier consumption, the "dime" novels and paperback "penny dreadfuls" that the sutlers sold. Thousands of copies circulated among the soldiers. There were even a few copies of what a chaplain termed "licentious books" and "obcene pictures" to be had, most of them imported from Europe.[22] Entrepreneurs distributed flyers in the camps advertising their "spirited and spicy scenes", usually showing scantily-clad maidens and captioned with heavy-handed puns about "storming the breastworks".[23] In the end, the men simply read or looked at whatever they could find, and if that was not sufficient, they sometimes created their own reading material.

Enterprise Ms
May 28
Mr A. V. Montgomery
Camden
Madison County
Mississippi

A. V. Montgomery
Camden Miss
Madison County

Spotsylvania
County Va
10th May (1864)

Dear Father
This is my last letter to you. I went into battle this evening as courier for Genl Heth. I have been struck by a piece of shell and my right shoulder is horribly mangled & I know death is inevitable. I am very weak but I write to you because I know you would be delighted to read a word from your dying son. I know death is near, that I will die far from home and friends of my early youth but I

Heth's Divn Line of Battle
Spottsylvania C.H. Va
A. V. Montgomery Esq May 15th 1864
Dear Sir
The painful task has devolved upon me of communicating the sad tidings of the death of your noble son James R. Montgomery who fell mortally wounded in the engagement of Tuesday the 10th inst about five miles from this point.
During the series of battles that have taken place during the last ten days the Signal Corps of this Division have been called upon to act as couriers to Genl Heth. It was in the performance of this duty that my dear friend received his wound.

to tender my deepest sympathy.

Heth's Divn

A. W. Hyatt Esq
Care W S Chapman
Nashville
Tenn

Camp Walker, January 1862
Boomerangs, 13 Va. Reg.
Manassas Station, Va.,

Dear Aunt Annie:— I received your letter and was glad to hear from home, I am very sorry that Vir is sick, but I hope she will soon be well, Aunt Annie I will only write you a short business letter this time, you must not consider this an answer to your long and interesting letter, I want you to send me the little trunk and key, with my socks or (yours rather) in it, I think I can sell them now for a good price, put in also Annie Liste that I drew off, I want to showe it to some of the boy's. Also the smallest cake of Red and Blue paint and a camels hair brush, I am drawing pictures here for some of the boy's and they want them coloured, you need not send any more. get me severall boxes of French Mustard if it can be had, if not the common mustard will do— and if they have neither get me the seed mustard, the Drs say it is healthy to eat on meet, and I am so fond of it, If you can get it for me I will remit you the money Aunt Annie, as soon as I am paid off. I have not a cent of money now.
Well Aunt Annie I forgot to tell you how you can get the trunk to me, you can send it to me by the Southern Express Company get it to Charlestown and put it on the cars there, Uncle Joseph can do it for me, and then it will go straight to me. The wagon for the 13th Regiment will bring it to our Company. Do not

Miss M W Skelton
Genito P. O.
Powhatan Co
Virginia

Manassas C.H. Va
Jany 13/64
Mr George C. Tabb Jnr
Richmond
Va
Box 955

Confederate Correspondence

A few words from home gave the soldier in the field more cheer than any other release, except perhaps the far more infrequent arrival of pay day. Of course, some of the plaintive pleas of suffering and want from those at home hardly encouraged the soldier to stay in the ranks, but mostly the folks tried their best to bolster their men's morale. The soldiers for their part sometimes wrote anything and everything that came into their heads. They drew pictures, maps of their bivouacs or recent battles, even crude portraits of their messmates. The main point was simply to keep in touch with home, which, given the haphazard nature of postal delivery in the Confederacy was not always an easy task.

1–2 Soldier's postmarked letter covers and correspondence
3 Letter of condolence, Spotsylvania, May 1864
4–6 Letter covers
7 Letter from the 13th Virginia Regiment, Manassas, Va, 1862
8 Sketch of a camp scene, captioned as being near Bunker Hill, 1862
9 Official Confederate Government letter cover
10 Soldier's letter cover
11 Hand drawn battle map, Mississippi, 1863

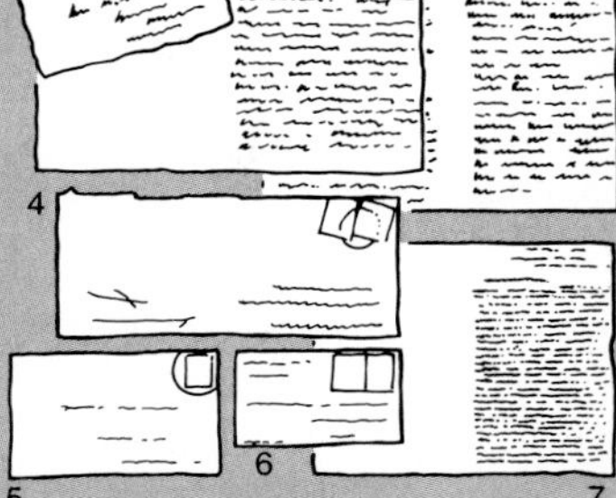

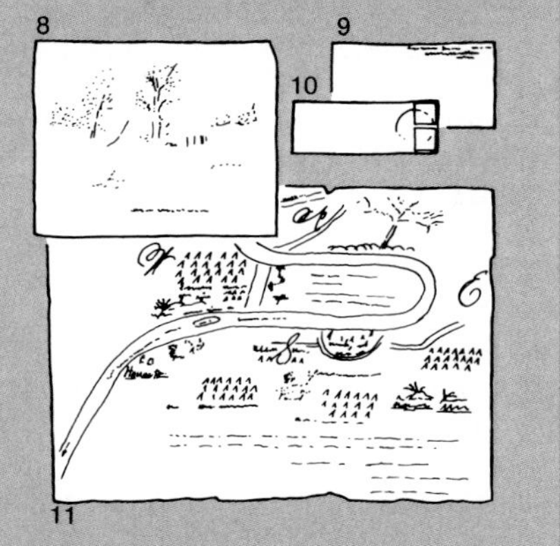

Artifacts courtesy of: The Museum of the Confederacy, Richmond, Va

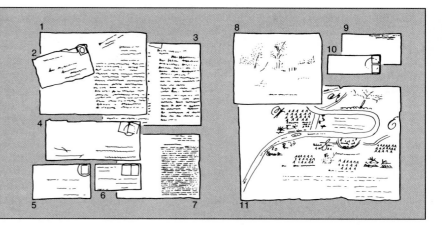

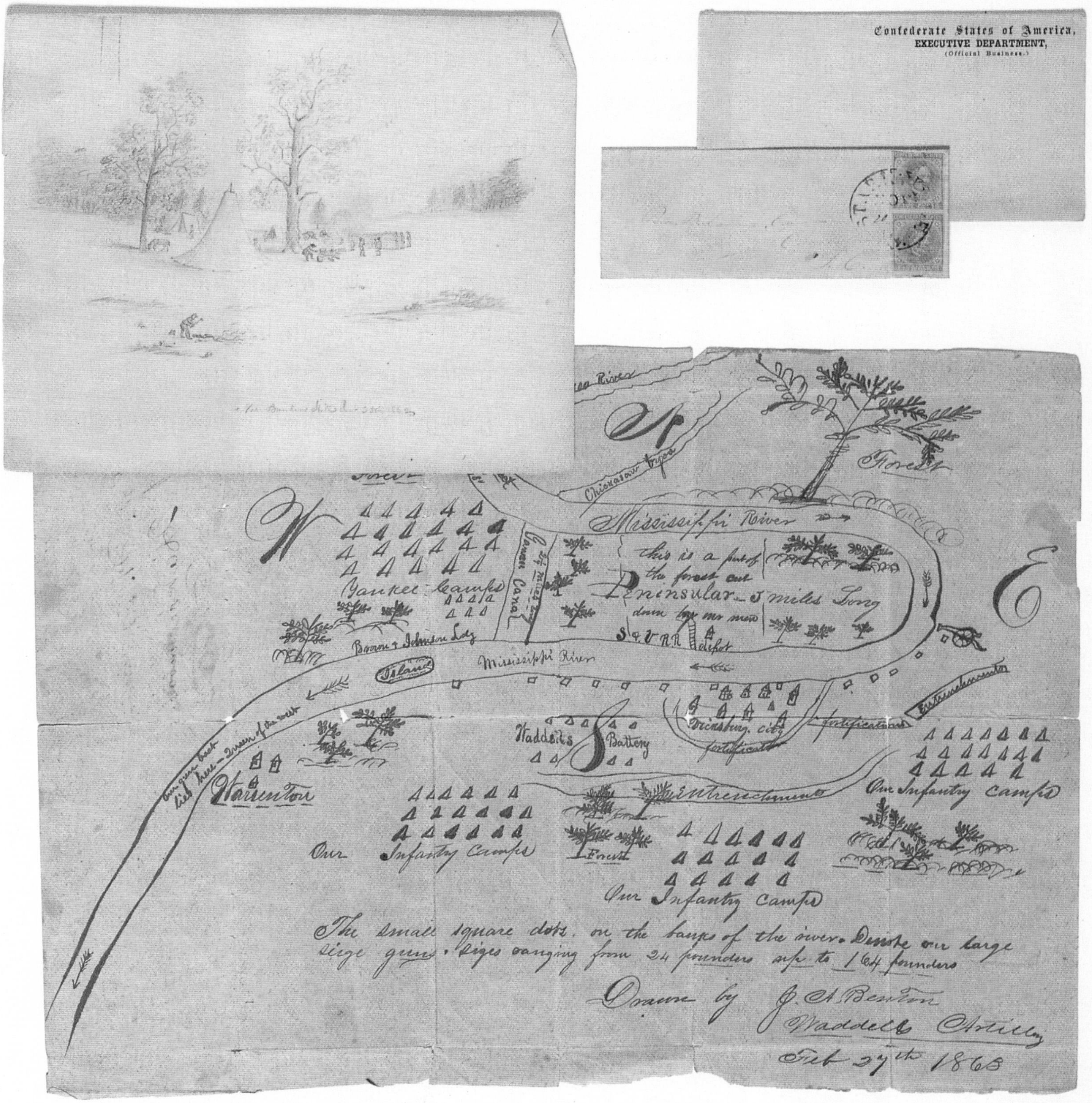

Scores of regiments edited and printed their own newspapers. General John Hunt Morgan's renowned Confederate cavalry issued the *Vidette* sporadically for two years, as much to badger the Yankees as to entertain the men.[24]

Music quickly came to occupy a special placed of importance in the soldiers' life. It was a musical era. In the absence of other entertainments, family song fests around the piano were a cultural norm in the middle class of both North and South, augmented by public concerts and participation in church hymns available to everyone. Their songs, like their times, were highly sentimental, maudlin, demonstrating extremes of emotion, but especially concerning romantic love, the sorrow of loss, and patriotism. Stirring national songs helped rally men to enlist all through the war, especially at its outset. Often they learned their march steps to the tune of snappy martial airs, and later moved off to battle with songs in their ears. Sales of sheet music and song books were at their highest level in American history, and except in the bitterest of weather or the depths of depression after defeat, every camp North and South gave rise to hummed and sung melodies every night.

Most regiments, especially from the North, brought some kind of band with them to the war. The instruments were often indifferent in quality, and their players little better, though time and practice made some quite proficient. Many regimental and brigade ensembles, however, simply made a lot of noise. One Texas band was described by a dismayed auditor as "braying", while another listener described Confederate bands in general as so wretched that "their dismal noises are an intolerable nuisance".[25] Discordance was hardly the exclusive realm of Rebel brass, however, for many would have argued that the 6th Wisconsin band was the worst of the war. It knew only one song, "The Village Quickstep", and even hearers who knew the song could never recognize it when the Wolverines played. It did not help that the regiment's colonel looked on his band as a punishment assignment.[26]

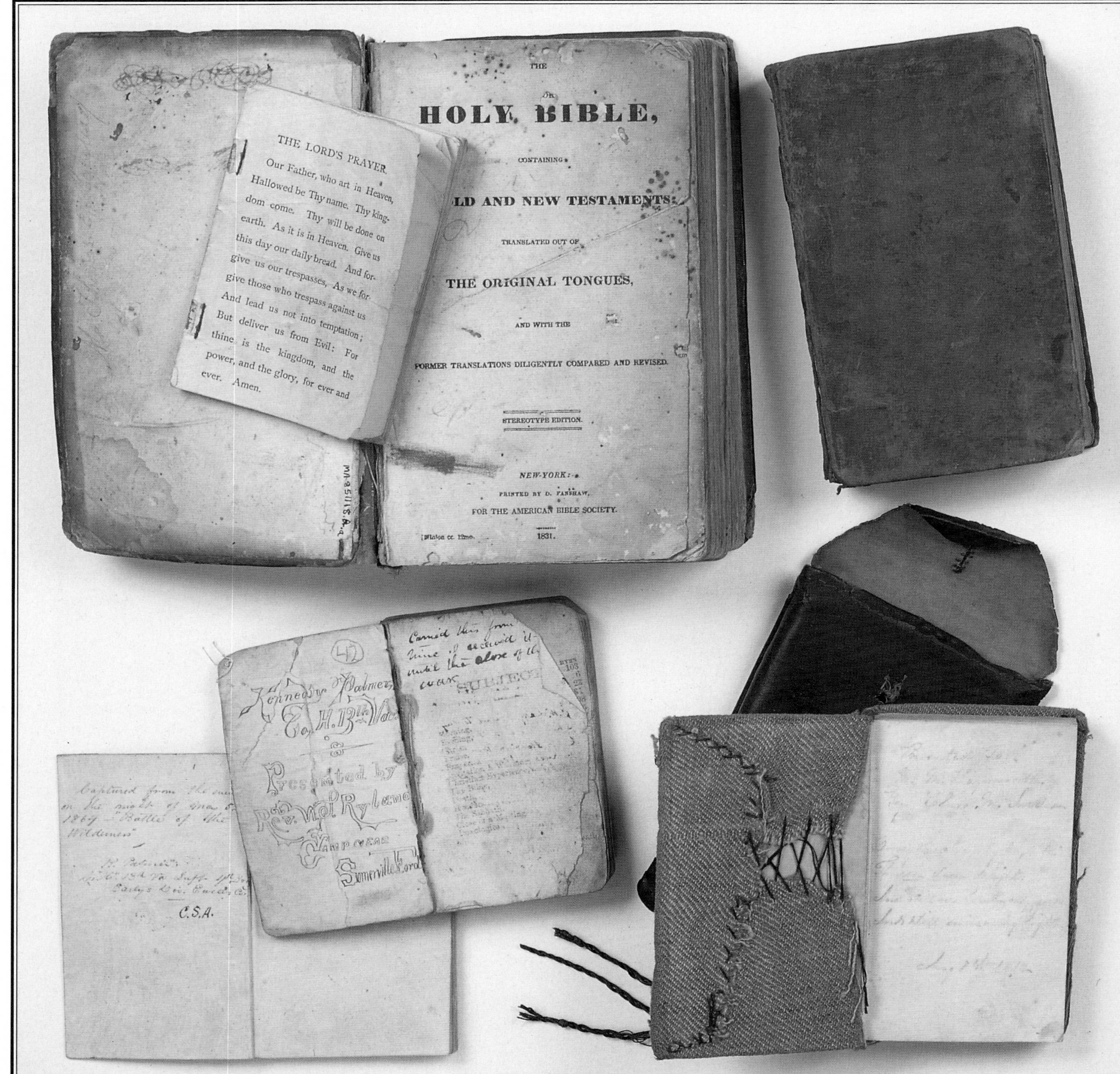

Confederate Books and Journals

Despite a comparative low literacy rate, particularly within the Southern armies, the war witnessed the production by the troops of thousands of journals, as well as an enormous outpouring of printed material that flowed into the camps. A great deal of this was devotional, though illustrated newspapers like *Harper's* or the *Southern Illustrated News*, were all eagerly read.

1 Bible printed for the American Bible Society, New York, 1831
2 Copy of the Lord's Prayer
3 Prayer Book
4 Prayer Book owned by Kennedy Palmer, Company H, 13th Va, presented to him at Camp Mead and carried by him throughout his service
5 Book inscribed as having been captured on the night of May 5, 1864 during the Battle of the Wilderness
6 Protective wallet for 7
7 Sacking-covered book
8 Personal journal
9 Journal, embossed: "P. McPherson"
10 Personal journal covering the period during the outbreak of the war
11 War journal inscribed: "Tucker Randolph April 8th 1861"

Artifacts courtesy of: The Museum of the Confederacy, Richmond, Va

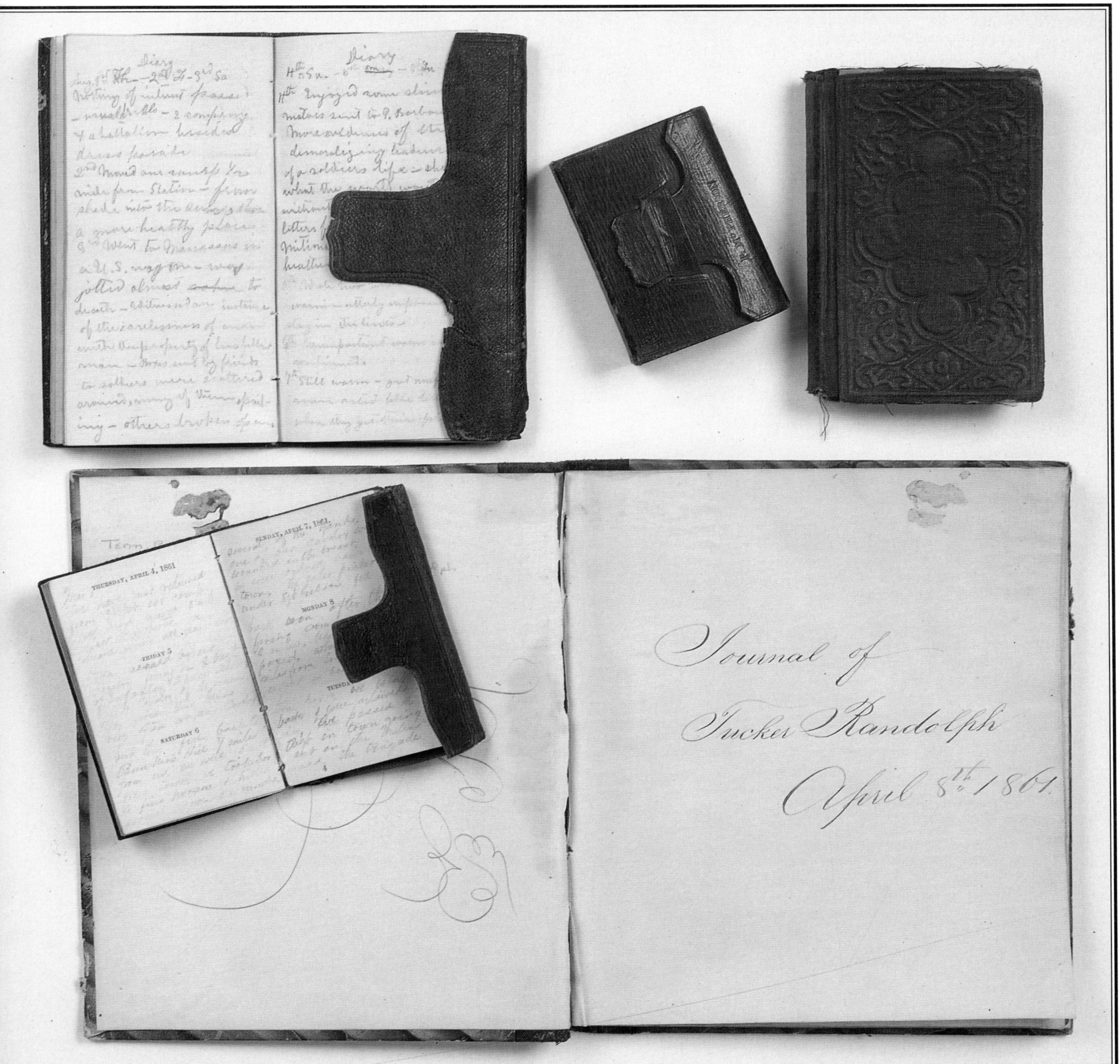

Good or bad, still these bands were welcome in the camp as they brought relief from the tedium of daily life. Thousands did not wait to depend upon the bands however, and instead made their own music. Every company, and indeed many messes, had one or more men who could saw out a few tunes on the fiddle, strum a guitar, play a flute, or even just twang a Jew's harp. Singly or in ensemble, they entertained themselves with "Hell Broke Loose in Georgia", or the "Arkansas Traveler", or "Billy in the Low Grounds". Even more festive than this was the occasional banjo picker, whose ringing strings could join with a good fiddler to provide a genuine hoedown for the men to dance.

Cheerful instruments were necessary, too, because the natural bent of the individual was toward more sad and sentimental songs, reflecting his longing for home. They sang songs like "The Empty Chair", "All Quiet Along the Potomac", "When This Cruel War is Over", and "Just Before the Battle Mother". Ironically, a favorite on both sides was "Auld Lang Syne". "My Old Kentucky Home" and other Stephen Foster tunes brought tears to blue eyes and gray, and looking forward to the day when peace would come, Yanks and Rebs alike sang of "When Johnny Comes Marching Home Again". Just as their songs could serve to stir their martial ardor, so could the mournful melodies depress low spirits even further. "Home, Sweet Home" was banned from the camps by commanders in the winter of

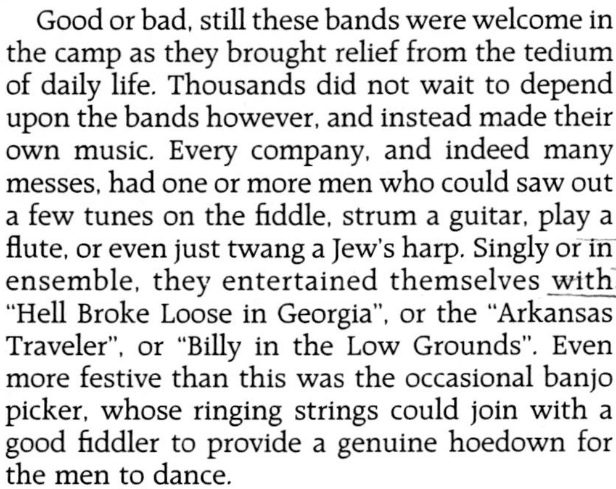

Commissary Sergeant, 30th Ohio Volunteers

Few non-commissioned officers could be more important to the enlisted man than his quartermaster who supplied him with his uniforms and equipment, or even more so, his commissary sergeant. He was the man, like this commissary of the 30th Ohio Volunteers, who kept the men supplied with their "dessicated" vegetables, their "blue" beef, and their "worm castles", or hardtack. Johnny Reb and Billy Yank may not have liked the food they grumbled and complained about so, but when they did not get it, they groused even more. The commissary sergeant was distinguishable only by his sleeve markings. Otherwise, he appeared as any other NCO of the company. When his unit went into battle he might even pick up a weapon and take a hand himself, but if not, he had quite enough of a battle of his own settling the company ration accounts.

1862-3 after the Army of the Potomac had suffered the demoralizing defeat at Fredericksburg on December 13.[27]

Chaplains tried to boost morale with stirring hymns instead. They led the men in choruses of "Rock of Ages" and "All Hail the Power of Jesus' Name". "Amazing Grace" even then had a special appeal to the military. Moreover, there were a host of happy secular tunes available when someone could start the tune going. The old song "John Brown's Body", already a favorite in the North before the war, became an informal anthem, with a host of different lyrics invented by the men, including the popular "We'll Hang Jeff Davis from a Sour Apple Tree". "The John Brown song was always a favorite, at all times and seasons", wrote the commander of a black regiment, and its stirring, moving melody became even more inspiring when Julia Ward Howe wrote yet another new lyric for it, and called her version the "Battle Hymn of the Republic".[28]

They sang "Yankee Doodle" and "The Girl I Left Behind Me", "The Star Spangled Banner", and in the South were heard "The Yellow Rose of Texas", "The Bonnie Blue Flag", and of course "Dixie". The Rebels teased their peanut-eating soldiers from Georgia with a song that told how, just prior to battle, the general heard an awful racket of popping and cracking, and believed it was the Yankees attacking, only to see that it was "the Georgia militia, eating goober peas".

Some men sang in battle, probably more to steady their own nerves than to inspire their comrades. They sang their old marching songs, or rousing patriotic airs like "Rally Round the Flag". During the fighting in the Virginia Wilderness on May 6, 1864, one solitary Yank began shouting the tune as his brigade struggled to regain its formation after a brutal Rebel attack. In a few minutes there were a hundred or more joining in with him, "Shouting the Battle-cry of Freedom!"

The most enduring musical contribution of the Civil War, however, was a bugle call. The soldiers' lives were ordered by the sounds of the bugle. The one that signalled an end to the day, the order to "extinguish lights" and go to bed, had been the "Tattoo", a call in constant use in the United States Army since at least 1835. One evening in July 1862, however, while General McClellan's army lay in bivouac at Harrison's Landing, Virginia, Brigadier General Daniel Butterfield called a bugler to his tent. He had heard the "Tattoo" that night, as on innumerable evenings before. As he later recalled, "it did not seem to be as smooth, melodious and musical as it should be". With the bugler before him to test his alterations, Butterfield slowed the tempo of the call, changed its rhythym, and extended a few of the notes. The only note that he actually changed in pitch was the first one. Once Butterfield had "got it to my taste", the new call was quickly adopted through most of the army, and eventually all of it. He would later receive erroneous credit for composing the piece, when he merely tampered a bit with an old call, but the resulting version of "Taps" became one of the most haunting, evocative melodies ever played, one that touches the souls of Americans of all times.[29]

As sobering as many of their songs were, the common soldiers were not the maudlin, doleful characters that their verses implied. They were raw, earthy, fun-loving men who valued a laugh above all else. Fun and pranks helped many a dull day in camp pass by. If a gullible civilian came into the bivouac and asked for Company B, some-

Above: Informal musical groups quickly formed in the camps, as musicians who could play guitars, fifes, violins or banjos gathered to pass the idle hours by making entertainment for their messmates.

Below: Every kind of prank imaginable was practised by the boys of Blue and Gray. In Washington DC in 1861, these lads of the 7th New York Militia found time to build a human pyramid for the camera.

where down the line would arise the cry "Here's Company B", to be repeated all over the field. Just as often, some bored soldier decided to mimic a cow or a chicken. Within minutes, men all over the camp joined in a barnyard chorus that set officers on their ears.

Teasing was a chronic release, with practical jokes as commonplace as drill. In winter quarters someone could always count on a soldier dropping a handful of gunpowder down a chimney for some explosive fun, or else covering the chimney over with a blanket or boards to smoke the inhabitants out into the cold. If a new recruit went out on his first sentry duty, veterans would sneak up upon him in the dark. When he challenged their approach with "Who goes there?" the reply could prove to be anything from a blue streak of oaths, to "A flock of sheep". And when a new boy came to camp and was issued his first uniform, the old timers liked to tell him that he had been cheated by the quartermaster, sending the young Horatio scrambling back to the supply tent to demand that he be issued his regulation umbrella, too.[30]

Soldier fun took a more stately, ceremonious turn in some of the camps, especially those which were more permanently established. Fraternal orders and secret societies enjoyed a popular wave in the 1850s before the war, and many of their members brought their lodge ritual and dogma with them to the army. Masonic lodges thrived in many of the camps, North and South, with more than one recorded case of combatants ceasing hostilities temporarily in order to join in some fraternal ceremony. Several Yankee Masons who died in camp or combat were buried in Southern cemeteries with Confederate Masons presiding. Several camps were entertained by literary and debating societies. The 50th New York Engineers built their own theater out of timbers at Petersburg in 1864, in order that their dramatic club , the "Essayons", might perform. South of the lines, in the winter of 1862-3 a handful of well-educated men and officers of the 9th Kentucky Infantry staged their own production of *Bombastes Furioso.* The battle-hardened veterans who

Confederate Musicians' Equipment

As battle began, the men of the Confederacy would march to the guns, flags flying and band playing.

1 Typical example of Confederate First National Pattern Flag as carried by Army bands
2 Typical style of forage cap as worn by musicians of the Confederate Army
3 Bugle with attachment points for carrying strap
4 Snare drum complete with carry strap and drum sticks
5 Snare drum and drum sticks
6 Typical design of frock coat as worn by Confederate musicians
7 Clarinet as used by Confederate Army bands
8 Alternative type of bugle used by armies of the Confederacy
9 Alternative type of bugle used by armies of the Confederacy
10 Small horn insignia as worn on uniform of some Confederate musicians
11 Militia waist belt complete with metal belt plate
12 Fife as used by Confederate Army bands
13 Alternative type of fife used by Confederate musicians
14 Alternative type of fife used by Confederate musicians

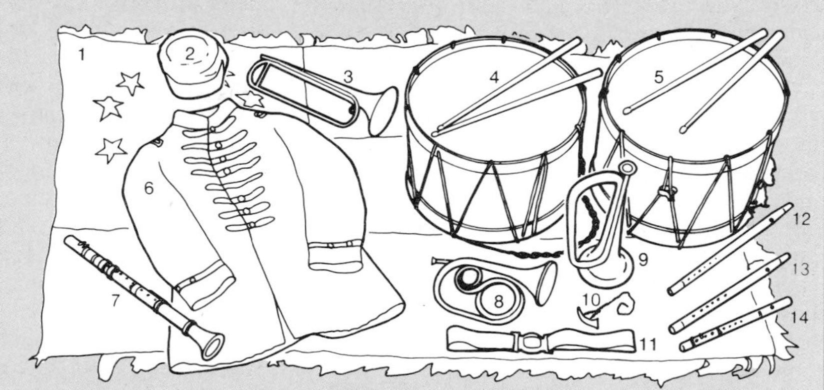

Artifacts courtesy of: The Museum of the Confederacy, Richmond, Va

took the female roles had to go around Manchester, Tennessee, borrowing dresses from the local belles.[31]

The 48th New York and 45th Massachusetts were admired for their stage plays as well, and minstrel shows and burlesques were much in demand from anyone who could perform them. A mock court martial provided good fun, and any opportunity to parody officers drew huge crowds, especially the dress parade with officers marching in the ranks while enlisted men, wearing huge comic opera epaulettes and medals the size of canteens, strutted and barked orders.[32]

Perhaps the soldiers' ways of finding fun were the more inventive because more conventional entertainments cost money, and the boys of 1861-5 were not very well financed. Indeed, even pay day itself was one of the happier diversions in camp, though rarely for long. When a paymaster was on the way, said one Illinois Yank, "a thousand pairs of eyes anxiously watched the road for the approach of the man who carried the panacea for all ills".[33] Even more emphatic was the Massachusetts private who declared that "A paymaster's arrival will produce more joy in camp than is said to have been produced in heaven over the one sinner that repenteth".[34]

They were not paid much. Privates on both sides at first received $11 monthly. North and South increased the pay somewhat, but especially in the Confederacy, uncontrolled inflation more than eradicated any benefit from the raise. By 1864 in the South, a pair of shoes could cost $125, seven months' pay. Worse yet, payday on both sides came with alarming irregularity. General John B. Floyd complained in 1862 that half of the men in his 51st Virginia Infantry had not been paid in six months. "They have not a single dollar to purchase the least little comfort, even for the sick."[35] Later in the war some Confederates would go a year and more without receiving a dollar. Families back home that needed a share of a soldier's pay became desperate, and thousands of disillusioned and bitter men deserted to return and care for their wives and children.

Union Musicians' Equipment

1 Tuba brass instrument used by Union musicians
2 Snare drum complete with carrying strap and decorative trim
3 Bugle complete with attachment points for lanyard
4 Eagle style of snare drum with carrying strap and decorative trim
5 Fife made of rosewood as used by Union musicians
6 Eagle style of snare drum complete with carrying strap and drum sticks. Like the other snare drums, this is handsomely decorated and is a marked contrast to those of the opposing Confederate forces
7 Saxhorn brass instrument as used by Union musicians
8 Pair of drum sticks complete with carrier and body harness
9 Model 1840 Musician's long sword complete with scabbard and shoulder harness belt for carrying
10 Baton as used by Union band leaders
11 Key type of bugle as used by musicians on the Union side
12 Bugle complete with lanyard as used by Union musicians

Artifacts courtesy of: The Civil War Library and Museum, Philadelphia, Pa: 1-7, 10-12; J. Craig Nannos Collection: 8-9

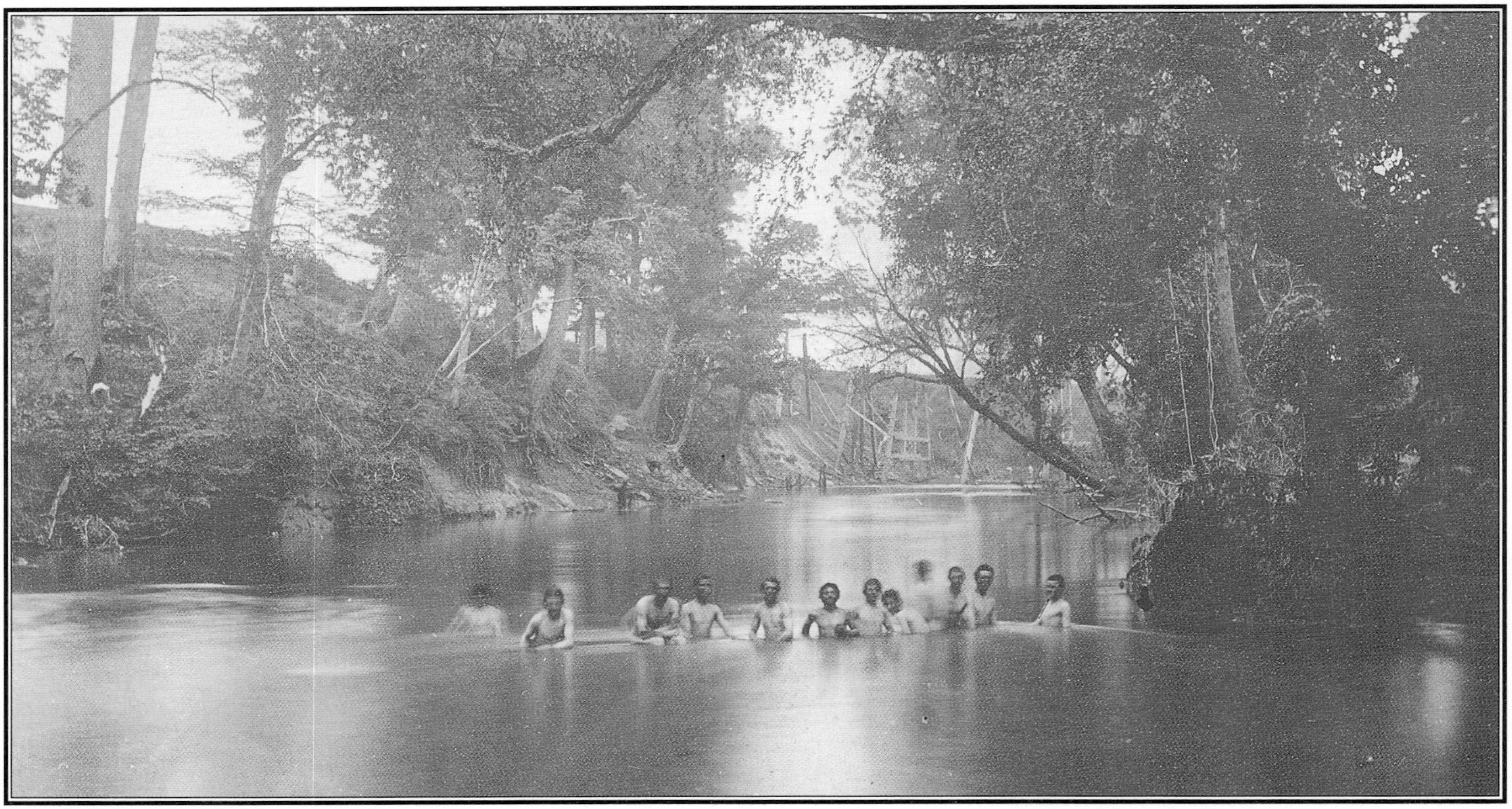

It is no wonder that the frustration of poor pay and harsh living environments often produced a ruggedness in soldier fun that sometimes had its roots in anger and frustration. Every winter saw snowball fights, usually on a small inter-personal scale. But occasionally a little good-humored – or not-so-friendly – contest could expand rapidly into a small-scale battle of its own. Many units felt a strong rivalry, especially when well-equipped and supplied regiments were bivouacked near outfits from some poorer locale. Jealousies smoldered until some vent for release presented itself, and a snowball fight proved ideal. One winter two New Hampshire regiments, the 2nd and the 12th, gave battle with the icy missiles. "Tents were wrecked, bones broken, eyes blacked, and teeth knocked out", recalled a participant; "all in fun".[36] Most famous of all was the Great Snowball Battle of March 1864, when the Confederate Army of Tennessee in winter quarters at Dalton, Georgia, began an impromptu contest that eventually turned into a full-scale battle. Even generals joined in, personally leading whole regiments in charges, taking prisoners and giving no quarter. Among the spoils of battle were hats and frying pans "and 4 or 5 pones of corn bread".[37]

Above: Most of all the men in the armies sought diversion and a little fun from the serious business of fighting a civil war. Who could resist a swim, like these yanks in Virginia's North Anna River in 1864.

Below: Whether they were on the Tennessee River or in Virginia, they could of course just simply sit and talk; fight anew all those old battles and boast of what they would do in the ones to come.

At Vicksburg, Mississippi, in 1862, Rebels staged a hog race between two such noble steeds. Unfortunately, one of them ran off a bluff carrying its rider on its back. The hog survived, the "jockey" did not, and his bereaved friends mourned him that night by cooking and eating his porcine charger with a grim sort of humor.

Soldiers raced with wheelbarrows, wrestled, boxed, leaped hurdles, and more, but probably their favorite sport proved to be the infant game of baseball. Contrary to later myth, it was not the invention of Abner Doubleday, then a Yankee general. The game used a soft ball then, and the base runner was only put out when actually hit by a batted or thrown ball. Consequently, high scores were the rule, the 13th Massachusetts once beating the 104th New York by 62 to 20. Some put too much gusto into throwing a man out. "He came very near knocking the stuffing out of three or four of the boys", a Texan wrote of a team-mate. "He could throw harder and straighter than any man in the company . . . and the boys swore they would not play with him."[38] Even cricket was played, and now and then, with ironic humor, the men would try bowling, knocking down the pins with rolling cannon balls.

As much as anything, the men, as soldiers of all times and places, simply sat and talked. Politics, philosophy, the progress of the war, reminiscences of home and family, any topic could draw a conversation to pass an afternoon or evening. Camp gossip filled most of their talk; what officer was a coward, which one was overlooked because he did not have the right connections, where the next battle would be fought, when the war would end. Rumors flew like flies in such an environment. "Every one tries to see what kind of rumor he can start", confessed a Virginia private, "so when our bodys are still we have our minds puzzled and harrassed".[39] Others did not appreciate the promiscuous spread of half-truths and gossip. "I never heard so many lies in my life as are told in camp", one complained. He determined to stop his own lying and rumor-mongering, and discovered happily that "I find I get along as well as usual" without it.[40]

Above: For all their ferocity against the enemy on the battlefield, in camp they could be gentle and considerate. It was not unusual for boys with packages from home to share their contents with messmates.

Below: Those long-distance camps are what they recalled, the days of "tenting tonight". Times of camaraderie, of surcease from the blood of war, when men gave their youth gladly and it was good to be young.

That last man was emblematic of all of the common soldiers of the war. Somehow amid the privations and disruption in their young lives, they made do and got along "as well as usual". A surgeon of the 5th New Hampshire might come to the field in Virginia in 1862 and recoil at "the bare-faced boys, the sallow men, the threadbare officers and seedy generals, the diarrhea and dysentery, the yellow eyes and malarious faces, the beds upon the bare earth in the mud, mist and the rain", and confess that the sight destroyed his "pre-conceived ideas of knight-errantry".[41] But through it all, the men got along with humor, open generosity, and the adaptability that became their trademark.

Of course they all wanted to go home. All of their games and pranks and pastimes were but ways of making the days go by until, the victory achieved, they could become civilians again. It showed itself most of all in their songs. "Many are the hearts that are weary tonight, waiting for the war to cease", went one air. "Many are the hearts that are looking for the right, to see the dawn of peace."

As in that song, they all, North and South, had their share of "Tenting Tonight on the Old Camp Ground". They all spent many an evening, telling the old stories, playing their fiddles, carving at a bit of wood, or merely staring into the glowing embers of their fires, watching them

Dying tonight, dying tonight,
Dying on the old camp ground.

But for all the sadness and melancholy, in after years, with the forgiving memories of age, they all took genuine pleasure in their days in the field. Even earlier, after four years of hard campaigning, many of the boys had to confess that they revelled in the soldier experience. Like Charlie Wills of Illinois, they could say in their hundreds of thousands that "I never enjoyed anything in the world as I do this life".[42]

References

1 Philip Van Doren Stern (ed.), *Soldier Life in the Union and Confederate Armies* (Bloomington, Ind., 1961), p.301.
2 *Ibid.*, p.325.
3 Bell I. Wiley, *They Who Fought Here* (New York, 1959), p.84.
4 John D. Billings, *Hardtack and Coffee* (Boston, 1888), p.47.
5 *Ibid.*, p.49.
6 Bell I. Wiley, *The Life of Billy Yank* (Indianapolis, 1951), p.56.
7 John Worsham, *One of Jackson's Foot Cavalry* (New York, 1912), p.91.
8 James I. Robertson, Jr. (ed.), "An Indiana Soldier in Love and War", *Indiana Magazine of History*, LIX (1963), p.253.
9 John L. Parker, *Henry Wilson's Regiment* (Boston, 1887), p.219.
10 Stephen A. Repass to Mrs. Peter Shirley, February 16, 1862, in private collection.
11 McHenry Howard, *Recollections of a Maryland Confederate* (Baltimore, 1914), p.254n.
12 Bruce Catton, *A Stillness at Appomattox* (New York, 1953), p.201.
13 W.G. Bean, *The Liberty Hall Volunteers* (Charlottesville, 1964), p.155.
14 Wiley, *Billy Yank*, p.187.
15 Edna Hunter, *One Flag, One Country, and Thirteen Greenbacks a Month* (San Diego, Calif., 1980), p.97.
16 Wiley, *Billy Yank*, p.187.
17 Worsham, *Foot Cavalry*, p.98.
18 Bell I. Wiley, *The Life of Johnny Reb* (Indianapolis, 1943), p.193.
19 Wiley, *Billy Yank*, p.190.
20 *Ibid*, p.153.
21 William C. Davis, *The Orphan Brigade* (New York), 1980), pp.202-3.
22 "Diary of Charles Ross", *Vermont History*, XXX (1962), p.135.
23 "Spirited and Spicy Scenes", *Civil War Times Illustrated*, XI (January 1973), pp.26-7.
24 Wiley, *Johnny Reb*, p.170.
25 Arthur Fremantle, *Three Months in the Confederate States* (London, 1863), p.71; *Battlefields of the South* (London, 1863), II, p.101.
26 Bruce Catton, *Mr. Lincoln's Army* (New York, 1951), p.19.
27 S. Millett Thompson, *Thirteenth Regiment of New Hampshire Volunteer Infantry* (Boston, 1888), p.104.
28 Wiley, *They Who Fought Here*, p.150.
29 Russell H. Booth, "Butterfield and 'Taps' ", *Civil War Times Illustrated*, XVI (December 1977), pp.35-9.
30 Wiley, *Billy Yank*, pp.171-2.
31 Davis, *Orphan Brigade*, pp.168-9.
32 Wiley, *Billy Yank*, pp.163-74.
33 George Parks, "One Story of the 109th Illinois", *Journal of the Illinois State Historical Society*, LVI (1963), p.286.
34 Charles E. Davis, *Three Years in the Army* (Boston, 1894), p.15.
35 O.R. Series I, 52, Part 2, p.252.
36 Martin A. Haynes, *A History of the Second Regiment, New Hampshire Volunteer Infantry* (Lakeport, 1896), p.212.
37 Wiley, *Johnny Reb*, pp.64-5.
38 *Ibid.*, p.159.
39 Worsham, *Foot Cavalry*, pp. xxi-xxii.
40 Wiley, *Johnny Reb*, p.169.
41 William Child, *A History of the Fifth Regiment New Hampshire Volunteers* (Bristol, N.H., 1893), p.99.
42 Charles W. Wills, *Army Life of an Illinois Soldier* (Washington, 1906), p.14.

CHAPTER EIGHT

Willing Spirits & Weak Flesh

The long winter of 1863-4 was one of the most trying of the war. There was no campaigning at all in the east, while out west the only operation of major significance was the abortive Red River Campaign of March-May 1864. Led by the inexperienced General Nathaniel Banks, the expedition was intended to move up Louisiana's Red River into Texas, while Federal troops from Arkansas marched overland to join Banks. Such a move, it was believed, would carve the Confederate Trans-Mississippi department, already isolated from the eastern Confederacy, in two pieces.

It went wrong almost from the first. Banks was late with his part of the scheme, and when he first met the foe at Sabine Cross Roads, he was soundly beaten. Withdrawing, Banks' problems were further compounded by low water on the Red River which almost trapped his supporting fleet. For ten days in May the Federal line of retreat was almost completely blocked before Banks finally managed to extricate himself and his army from near-disaster. The campaign was an utter failure.

Elsewhere, U.S. Grant had taken over command of all Union armies as general-in-chief. United command of the forces in Tennessee and Georgia went to his trusted subordinate Sherman, and while Meade retained command of the Army of the Potomac, Grant himself chose to accompany Meade in the coming campaign in Virginia. Grant planned to press the enemy everywhere, sending Meade against Lee and Richmond, Sherman against the vital rail center at Atlanta, Banks up the Red River, and other forces against the Shenandoah Valley.

As spring came the war was entering its third year. Major religious revivals swept the armies, and a sober reflection on what lay ahead of them replaced the soldiers' previous light-heartedness. They were tired of the war and of the army, and did not mind saying so. Some did more than talk.

"THERE IS some of the onerest men here that I ever saw", Virginian Adam Rader wrote home, "and the most swearing and card playing and fitin and drunkenness that I ever saw at any place". An Alabama boy invited his brother to visit his camp, but advised him to bring with him a shotgun for his own protection. In general, few who lived with the armies North or South would have disagreed with the Louisiana Confederate who counseled others not to follow him into the army, "for you will smell hell here".[1]

"They have every temptation to do wrong", wrote an Iowan, "and if a man has not firmness enough to keep from the excesses common to soldiers he will soon be as bad as the worst". With all that time on their hands in the camps and on the march, the men made their own diversions to take their minds from their condition, and it is no surprise that many of their pastimes ran toward the seamy and insubordinate. "There is no mistake", said the Yank from Iowa, "but the majority of soldiers are a hard set".[2]

A number of leaders on both sides tried to do something about the language in the ranks, and the Washington War Department even made it a punishable offense at one point, valuing one infraction as worth a dollar, more than two days'

Woe to the soldier who broke the army's rules. Even at the best he could face a humiliating punishment; riding the wooden horse for hours, the object of the camp's derision and jest.

pay. It was a pointless attempt. "Oaths, blasphemies, imprecations, obscenity, are hourly heard ringing in your ears until your mind is almost filled with them", a Mississippi recruit complained, and a fellow Confederate chaplain lamented that in camp he "heard more cursing and swearing in twenty-four hours than in all my life before".[3] It was a soldier's form of release. He could not talk back to an officer, but he could curse him back in the semi-privacy of his tent. It did not make the mud any thinner, the cold any less chilling, the food any better or the lice any the less numerous, but somehow it helped. As a result, wherever and whenever soldiers gathered, the air rang with "profanity of the worst form from morning till night".[4]

A good reason for a soldier's profanity might have been his losses at wagers, for gambling of every kind was as common among the men as their colorful language. Every army camp was a virtual casino, with games of faro and "chuck-a-luck", "sweet blanket" and poker of all sorts in near-constant operation. Many liked to roll dice, but far and away the men preferred card games. The sutlers did a good business in card decks, in part because of the popularity of the games, but also because before battle many a suddenly fearful and pious soldier threw away his deck, not wanting it on his person should he be killed and have to face an angry Maker. Officers as well as enlisted men joined in the games, "taking a twist at the tiger" as they called it, and even a few chaplains dealt the cards, though most of the latter complained of the Sunday morning games that drew men away from their services.[5]

Both sides attempted to put a stop to it, but they might as well have tried to make the soldiers drink pink tea instead of coffee. "Open gambling has been prohibited", a Confederate noted in 1862, "but that amounts to nothing".[6] And once a battle was done, the survivors, suddenly forgetting their earlier resolutions to reform their ways, could be seen scouring the countryside for the dice and cards they had so readily thrown away before the fight.

For all too many, the next stop down the ladder of degradation became an easy one. Theft in the camps was a common occurrence, and not too surprisingly, since it was an almost natural outgrowth of the "foraging" – essentially condoned theft – which they were encouraged to participate in along the march. A few individuals exhibited a natural talent at the craft of foraging. Sam Nunnally of the 21st Virginia would just vanish from camp for a few days, to reappear laden with booty. He was especially skilled at playing dead on the battlefield, and then rifling the pockets of the real slain after the fight. Perhaps the most accomplished plunderer in any army was Billy Crump of the 23rd Ohio. As orderly to Colonel Rutherford B. Hayes – future 19th President – he borrowed the colonel's horse, spent two days looting in West Virginia, and came back carrying fifty chickens, two turkeys, one goose, over twenty dozen eggs, and upwards of thirty pounds of butter.[7]

When not plundering the countryside, or their own messmates, many soldiers found sport in robbing the sutlers who followed the armies. Many regarded it as simply tit for tat, assuming that the sutlers were gouging them heavily by selling shody products at inflated prices. "He is always on hand promptly when his financial interest is benefitted thereby", an Iowa boy said of the army sutler, "and never to be found when most needed". When soldiers looted a sutler's stores, they might confess that it was, indeed, undisguised theft, but averred that "the sutler's business in many cases is not much better".[8]

Frequently bored or frustrated soldiers turned their misbehavior on each other. Fighting was commonplace in the camps, stemming from causes as simple as a personal insult, to resentment of being bivouacked next to despised immigrant regiments of Germans or blacks. Some outfits, especially the Irish units, became famed for their combativeness, and the 7th Missouri once had 900 fights break out on a single day, among just 800 men in the regiment.

Every kind of bad conduct had causes that were legion, but the most common of all was simple drunkenness. The stuff the soldiers drank was called "mean" whiskey, and not without reason. It was vile by any standard, and the attitude of the men who drank it is evidenced by what they called the stuff. "Rock Me to Sleep Mother", "Old Red Eye", "Rifle Knock-Knee", "Bust Skull", "Rot of Pop Skull", and "Oh, Be Joyful", are but a few of its sobriquets. A boy from Indiana described it as "bark juice, tar-water, turpentine, brown sugar, lamp-oil and alcohol". To consume it, many advised first warming it over the fire, while others put a match to it and let some of the alcohol burn off first. They could all agree that "it was new and fiery, rough and nasty to take".[9]

Given the opportunity, the men sometimes made their own drink, fermenting anything they could find, even pine boughs. Its effects were deadly. One Vermont boy remembered that he "saw snakes and devils and howled in terror"

Above: When frustration, or the penchant for misbehavior became too great, the army sutler was deemed fair game. Believed to be a parasite and cheat in his own right, he was usually regarded as a logical target.

Below: Gambling was one of the most popular recreations available to Johnny Reb and Billy Yank, and the variety of games of chance they devised was incalculable. All were frowned upon but all were played.

after an evening at the jug. The colonel of the 126th Ohio and most of his officers became completely incapacitated after several buckets of egg nog and whiskey, and the colonel of the 48th New York was actually found dead in his tent the morning after a bender. No wonder that General George B. McClellan charged in 1862 that "no one evil so much obstructs this army as the degrading vice of drunkenness." Could he but keep the liquor out of his bivouac, "it would be worth 50,000 men to the armies of the United States".[10] His more sober officers would have agreed, for drink caused more insubordination than all other influences combined. When he had had enough of "the creature", a soldier thought little at all of talking back to a superior. Men were on record as calling their officers "damned puppy", "whorehouse pimp", "skunk", "bugger", and "sh-t-house

Sergeant, 6th Pennsylvania Cavalry "Rush's Lancers"

Oddly enough, Pennsylvania became known during the war for some of its unruly cavalry regiments. Arguably the worst disciplined regiment in the Union army was the 3rd Pennsylvania cavalry, with more than its full complement of courts-martial, desertions, insubordinate enlisted men, and incompetent officers. Perhaps it was in reaction to such a poor reputation that the 6th Pennsylvania Cavalry strove so hard to create a distinguished record with the Army of the Potomac. Of course, part of its reputation derived from its distinctive – indeed, in the Union army, unique – weaponry. Originally uniformed and equipped like any other cavalry regiment in the army, the 6th – called Rush's Lancers after its colonel, Richard Rush – later adopted to fight with a nine-foot lance. These wonderful weapons were quite useless against the poorest Rebel firearm, and were discarded.

adjutant". "You kiss my arse, you God damned louse", one Yankee told his captain, while another confronted his commander with "You ain't worth a pinch of sh-t". Most often of all, they bought themselves time in the guard house by calling someone in authority a "son of a bitch".[11]

Drinking, swearing, and all the attendant vices, would be constant companions of the Civil War soldier, despite all efforts to the contrary – despite the influences of frequent revivals and temperance movements. These were red-blooded men who needed to give vent to their boredom and anxieties. There was an additional frustration that led to yet another kind of misconduct. The men were far from wives and sweethearts, and this in an era of exaggerated sentimentalities, when the courting ritual was almost medieval, and outward expressions of love and sexuality strictly confined. More than anything else, Civil War soldiers' letters were filled with protestations of love and fidelity and anxious promises of the reception to be met when "Johnny came marching home again".

Many women had actually been the catalysts in getting their men to enlist in the first place, and thereafter their role was to sustain their men's patriotism and morale by mail. As for the men who went to war without a girl waiting back home, the competition to find a lady friend became keen. Indeed, when women were in short supply, one girl might often give her attentions to more than one suitor. And when a boy did find a girlfriend, he could become ecstatic, if not poetic. "My girl is none of your one-horse girls", proclaimed a jubilant Yankee. "She is a regular stub and twister. She is well-educated and refined, all wildcat and fur, and union from the muzzle to the crupper."[12]

Some wrote simple home or camp news, while others penned poetry, some if it of no mean caliber. But generally the men's minds were on more elemental matters. "I aint hugged a gal for so long I am out of practice", complained one soldier, and most men and women managed to turn the subject to fidelity sooner or later. Some

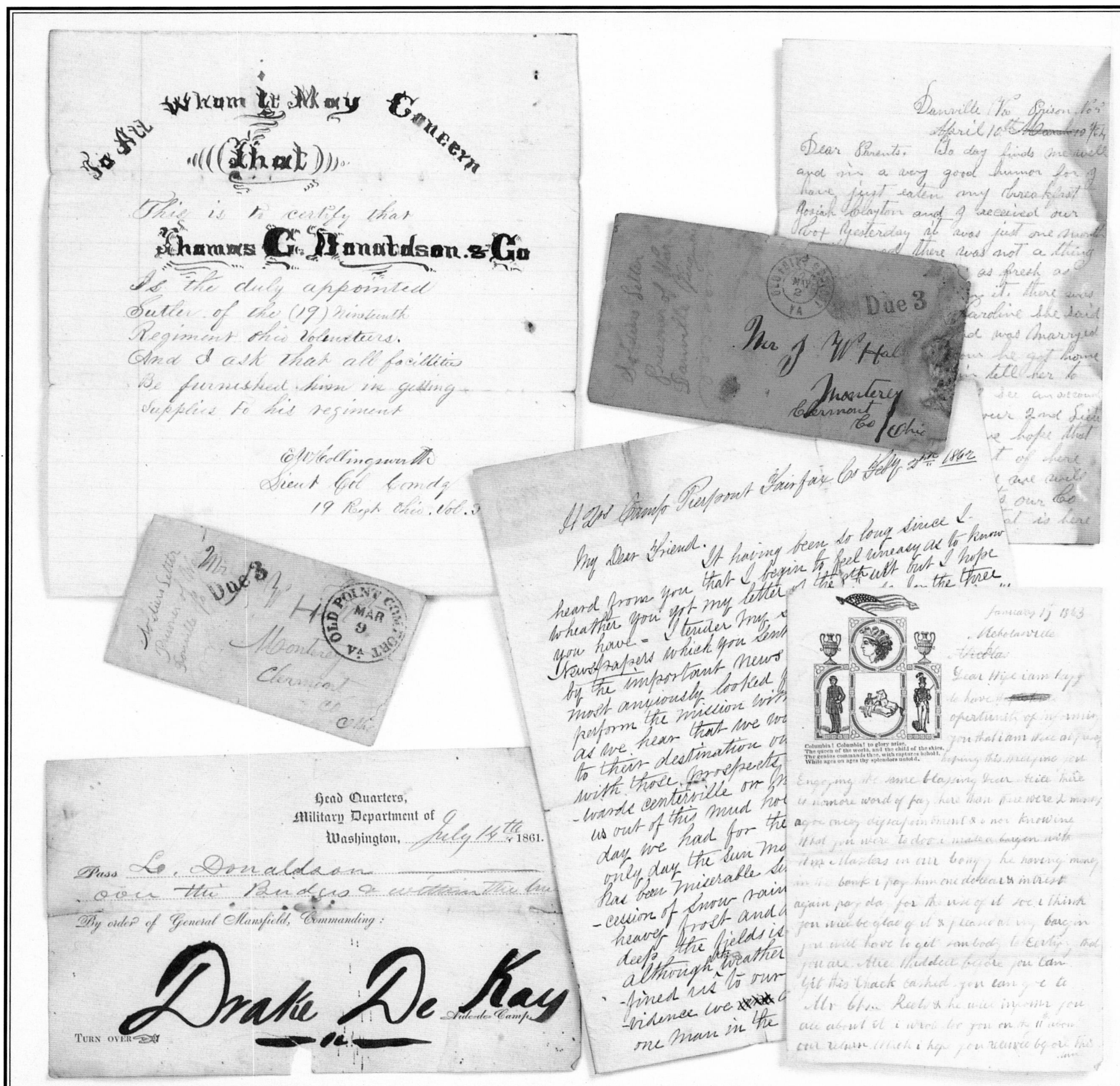

To All Whom It May Concern
That
This is to certify that
Thomas G. Donaldson & Co
Is the duly appointed
Sutler of the (19) Nineteenth
Regiment Ohio Volunteers.
And I ask that all facillities
Be furnished him in getting
Supplies to his regiment

E. W. Hollingsworth
Lieut Col Comdg
19 Regt Ohio Vol.

Head Quarters,
Military Department of
Washington, July 14th 1861.
Pass L. Donaldson
over the Bridges & within the lines
By order of General Mansfield, Commanding:
Drake De Kay
Aide-de-Camp
TURN OVER

Mr J. W. Hal
Monterey
Clermont
Co Ohio
Due 3

Mr J. W. H
Monterey
Clermont
Ohio
Due 3
OLD POINT COMFORT
MAR 9
VA.

H Qrs Camp Pierpont Fairfax Co Feby 2nd 1862
My Dear Friend. It having been so long since I heard from you that I begin to feel uneasy as to know wheather you got my letter of the 8th ult but I hope you have - I tender my ... Newspapers which you sent ... by the important news ... most anxiously looked ... perform the mission with ... as we hear that we ... to their destination ... with those prospects ... -wards centerville or ... us out of this mud ... day we had for the ... only day the sun ... has been miserable ... -cession of snow rain ... heavy frost and ... deep the fields is ... although the weather ... -fined us to our ... -vidence we ... one man in the

January 1, 1863
Dear Wife i am happy to have the opertunity of informing you that i am well at present hoping this may find you Engaying the same blessing

Columbia! Columbia! to glory arise,
The queen of the world, and the child of the skies.
Thy genius commands thee, with raptures behold,
While ages on ages thy splendors unfold.

Union Correspondence

In an era when hundreds of thousands of Americans were illiterate, the number of soldiers who either wrote letters themselves or else had literate friends write home for them is truly remarkable. Even when there was little to say, they still sent their letters to wives and loved ones, as if aware that they were living through the greatest adventure of their generation. As well as correspondence, in this organized war, the written word became important to Billy Yank because the pass that let him go into town, or the furlough that sent him home were all written to form. It was a war that moved on words as well as marching feet.

1 Sutler's appointment document issued by the 19th Ohio Volunteers
2 Letter from a prisoner, in Danville, Va
3 Letter cover for *2*, and addressed to Ohio
4 Letter cover of the same correspondence
5 Soldier's letter
6 Pass issued by Provost Marshal, July 14, 1861
7–9 Letters featuring patriotic vignettes
10 Further letter from the prison in Danville
11 Soldier's letter
12 Cover for *10*
13 Letter from camp

Artifacts courtesy of: The Civil War Library and Museum, Philadelphia, Pa

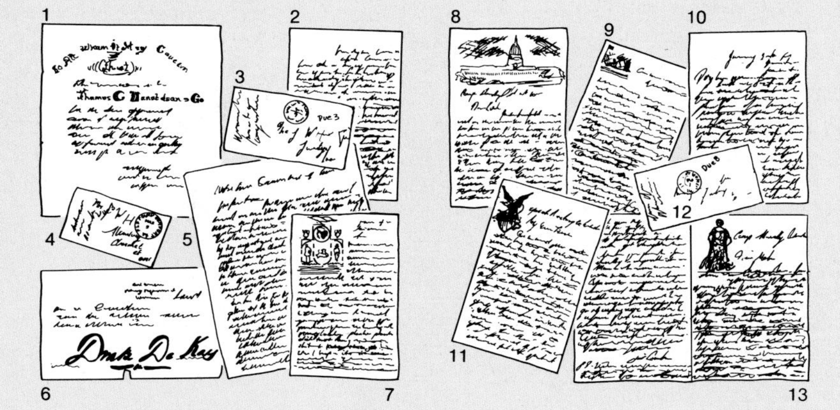

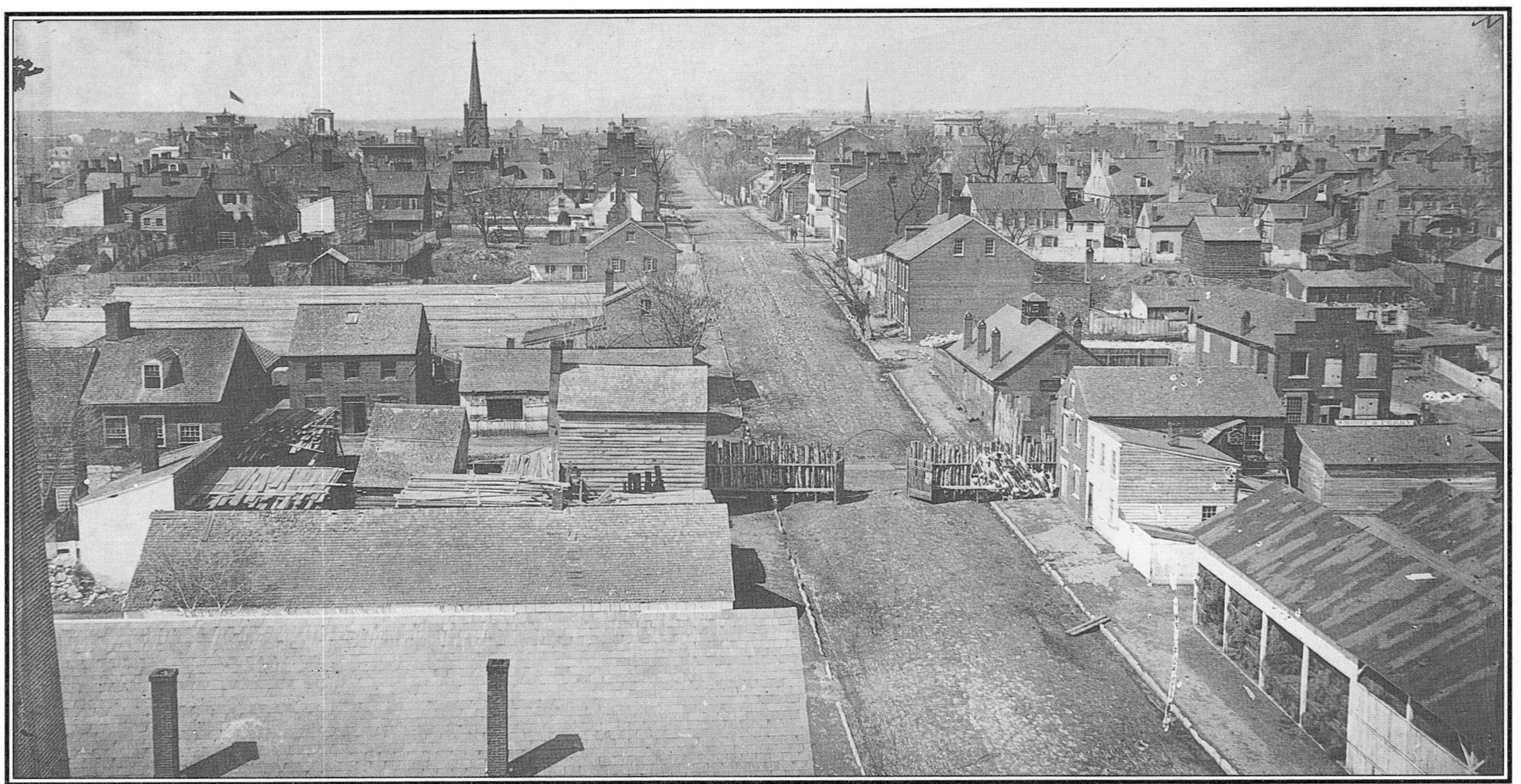

joked. "I don't feel much like a maryed man", Leander Stilwell wrote to his wife, "but I never forgit it sofar as to court enny other lady", adding that "if I should you must forgive me as I am so forgitful". When a Reb from Tennessee chided his wife on giving birth to a girl nine months after a furlough, she teased him that "I think you give your boys to some body else".[13]

Occasionally, despite the mores of the time, the letters from home were positively inflammatory. "Remember me when you lay on your hard bed", one wife wrote her man, and another warned her husband to store up his sleep, for "you would not sleep in a weeak when I got my arms around you".[14] When James Goodwin received a letter from his wife around Christmas on 1862, he must have squirmed on his camp stool when she described in detail their recent honeymoon and "the night when first we retired to the mid night couch, one by one to enjoy the highest streams of pleasure that the soul and body ever knows".[15] This was no cringing violet. And with the pleasures of the flesh on the minds of the women at home, and with them writing about it to their husbands and sweethearts, how much more so did the men in the field feel their enforced abstinence. "I have not seen a gal in so long a time that I would not know what to do with myself if I were to meet up with one", wrote a Rebel from Virginia, "though I recon I would learn before I left her".[16]

It should hardly come as a surprise, then, that many men sought the companionship of local ladies of rather casual acquaintance to relieve their loneliness. "I had a gay old time I tell you", one Massachusetts soldier wrote from Virginia in 1863. He drank during the day, and "in the evening Horizontal Refreshments or in Plainer words Riding a Dutch gal".[17] Alluring opportunities were everywhere. Washington alone had more than 450 bordellos in 1863, employing 7,000 or more prostitutes. Pennsylvania Avenue teemed with whole blocks of fancy houses, many with names like "Hooker's Headquarters", "the Ironclad", "Madam Russell's Bake Oven", and more. "It is said that one house out of ten in the city is a bawdy house", an Indiana boy wrote of Alexandria, Virginia, just over the Potomac from Washington; "it is a perfect Sodom".[18]

Similar temptations waited for the boys in gray. After the war the old veterans tried to deny any such behavior, claiming that "Confederate soldiers were too much gentlemen to stoop to such things", but the fact is they felt the same needs as their enemies in blue. Richmond fairly teemed with prostitutes, openly walking the streets and sometimes soliciting customers on the park around the Capitol itself. Prices became competitive. "I have not got but three tast[e]s since I have been in Va.", a Johnny Reb wrote home, "and I got that from two fine looking women. I tell you the three goes cost me but eleven dollars."[19]

Above: Almost every major city in the path of the armies saw a burgeoning of camp followers. Alexandria, Virginia so teemed with brothels that a soldier termed it, "a perfect Sodom". Richmond was no better.

Right: The men on both sides were red-blooded, young, with a healthy interest in matters of the flesh. Prostitutes did a fair share of business when armies were near, and "exotic" photos sold well.

For the soldier who did not or could not get to the city, there were more than enough camp followers near the armies. Some even donned uniforms and got away with pretending to be solders, their comrades helping with the charade in order to keep the ladies handy. Of course a man took a chance with a prostitute, and many found themselves the losers. "You can get plenty of Grous here", one Confederate wrote from Petersburg in 1864, "but you will get wounded nine times out of ten".[20] Venereal disease was always a hazard, and occasionally an epidemic. The problem began at the very beginning of the war. In 1861 one out of every dozen Yanks was diagnosed with some variant, a percentage that held up throughout the conflict. Confederates fared no better, and some regiments were particularly prone, like the 10th Alabama, which contracted no fewer than 68 cases in a single month.

Cures varied widely, and were almost all completely ineffectual in those days before antibiotics. A Confederate surgeon west of the Alleghenies gave his patients whiskey-soaked silk weed root, along with pills derived from pine resin. Others dispensed silver nitrate, zinc sulfate, mercury, and a host of herbal remedies. None of it worked, of course, and the more strait-laced came to regard the afflictions as divine punishment for their comrades' conduct. "If there is any place on God's fair earth where wickedness 'stalketh abroad in daylight'", wrote an Illinois private in 1862, "it is in the army".[21]

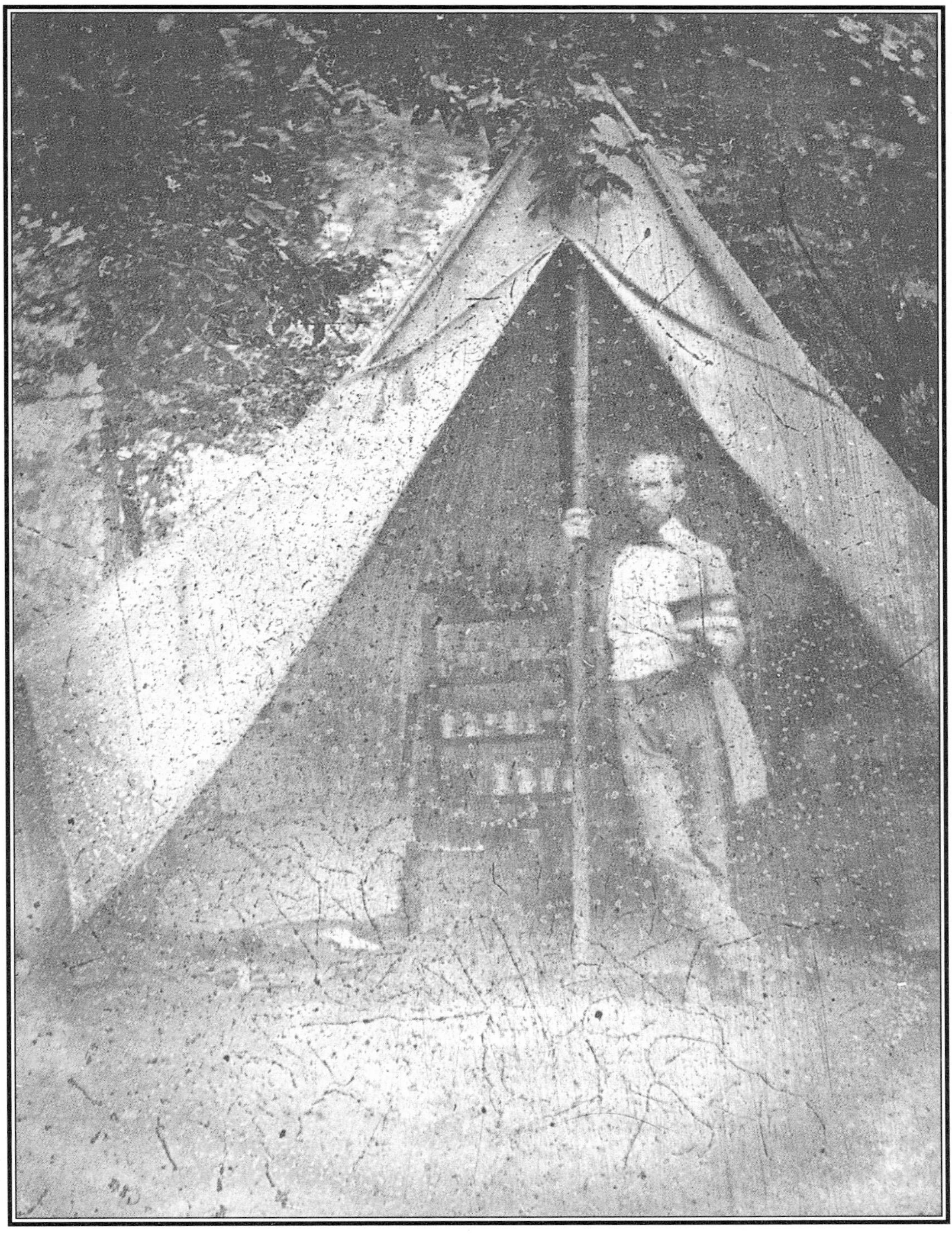

Above: For the poor soldier who got more than he bargained for in his amorous escapades, surgeons could do little. This Confederate surgeon could offer only the bottles of ineffective remedies behind him.

In the end, many officers would have agreed with Lieutenant Colonel H.E. Peyton, when he reported to the Richmond authorities in September 1864 that "the source of almost every evil existing in the army is due to the difficulty of having orders properly and promptly executed".[22] The fact is that neither side in this war ever completely accomplished the task of turning raw civilians into soldiers. "There is not that spirit of respect for and obedience to general orders which should pervade a military organization", concluded Peyton. "We had enlisted to put down the rebellion", wrote an Indiana private, "and had not patience with the red-tape tomfoolery of the regular service". "Furthermore", he went on, "the boys recognized no superiors, except in the line of legitimate duty".[23] In battle, the men looked to their officers for leadership, but when it came to the ways they used – and misused – their leisure time, it was no one's business but their own. These men were products of the days of Jacksonian America, highly individualistic, independent, deeply imbued with the American ideal that one man was as good as another. They would not be ordered about like cattle, and such discipline as officers were able to maintain came at the enlisted men's sufferance, and only after the officers earned their respect. No wonder that at the war's outset, foreseeing the problems ahead, Confederate General Joseph E. Johnston lamented that "I would not give one company of regulars for a whole regiment" of volunteers.[24]

As a consequence, discipline in this war would never reach a point at which it could predictably deter the men from doing what they pleased, whether it be gambling, drinking, thievery, or whoring. They had no use for the pomp and ceremony of soldiering, nor for its artificial etiquette.

There were good leaders, to be sure, and the men in the ranks were not sparing in paying tribute to those whom they respected. An Alabama soldier wrote with pride when he boasted of his regiment's leaders that "a more impartial set of officers . . . cannot be found in any company in the army". His captain was so loved that hundreds "would defend him to the last, and follow him into the most imminent danger".[25] Good officers could elicit that kind of admiration and devotion from their men, and with it they had little difficulty in maintaining discipline and keeping them out of trouble.

Yet there were all too many wearing shoulder straps who did not enjoy such respect. Thousands of officers on both sides used political or family influence to obtain commissions, or else won election to their posts by buying votes or bribing the men with liquor. Others received commissions thanks to earlier service in Mexico or against the Indians on the Plains, but that experience was no guarantee of ability. At the same time, while these often incompetent seniors tried to impose some discipline on their men, there were many more fresh, inexperienced young men with commissions who were hardly older than their enlisted subordinates. An Iowa Yank bemoaned that "I never saw so many green officers as are in some of the new Reg[iment]s. There is fun for us to see them go through their maneuvers. It is rather a funny operation for one man to teach another what he don't know himself."[26]

A few of the new officers sensed that they were the object of a good deal of sport among the men because of their inexperience. Some studied, while others like Lieutenant Samuel Craig stole away to the woods to practise drill by shouting commands at the trees. One colonel dealt with his own uncertainty by writing all the necessary commands on bits of paper he kept inside his uniform blouse. It worked well enough until they all fell out on the parade ground one day, and as he snatched them up they were out of order. Completely flustered, he simply cancelled further drill for the day.[27]

The enlisted men soon developed a disdain for many of their incompetent officers, and they did not hesitate to grumble to any who would listen. "I wish to God one half of our officers were knocked in the head by slinging them Against A part of those still left", an Illinois soldier groused in 1864, and a Pennsylvanian was even more emphatic. "If there is one thing I hate it is the Sight of a shoulder strap", he grumbled. "For I am well convinced in My own Mind that had it nor been for officers this war would have Ended long ago."[28] When complaining about specific leaders, the men became even more emphatic. A Florida Rebel declared that his officers were "Not fit to tote guts to a Bear". Another Confederate thought his colonel "an ignoramus fit for nothing higher than the cultivation of corn", and when a Federal general died, presumably of alcoholism, not a tear was shed at his military funeral, and one of his men privately declared that he was "in hell pumping thunder at 3 cents a clap".[29]

Inevitably such insubordinate thoughts occasionally found expression to the officers' faces, and then there could be hell to pay. When a man with a commission heard himself being called a "vain, stuck-up illiterate ass", or when another officer was told "you are God damned trash" by a common soldier, the response was not likely to be amicable. An Irishman called his captain a "God damned low-lived son of a bitch", and when another son of Erin was berated by an officer, he shouted that "you are a God-damned, white livered, tallow-faced skunk, and if you say that again I will knock every tooth down your throat and kick your arse through the company streets."[30]

Some men did not stop at words. Pranks and humorless practical jokes awaited the pompous or unpopular officer. A North Carolina captain who had sent a private to the guardhouse, later dozed off in an alcoholic stupor on a troop train, only to wake up and find himself locked in the privy. Sometimes a disgruntled soldier went even further, and took out his frustrations with his fists, a club, and occasionally even a musket. In the Battle of Cedar Mountain, Virginia, on August 9, 1862, a Federal shell hit and terribly savaged Confederate Brigadier General Charles Winder. He died in a few hours, and it is probably just as well, for several of his men were already plotting his death. A hated martinet, he so infuriated his soldiers that some of them "spotted" him, meaning that they intended to kill him given the first opportunity. "We could hear it remarked by someone near every day", wrote one of his men, "that the next fight we got in would be the last for Winder".[31]

Fortunately, the most extreme form of insubordination was very limited. Nevertheless, it is one of the ironies of the Civil War that the common soldier often thought a good deal better of his enemies than he did of his own officers. From the beginning of the war to its end, the most prevalent form of insubordination of all was fraternization with the foe, which is hardly surprising. Bonds of language, friendship, sometimes even blood, linked thousands of Rebs and Yanks. "Although intercourse with the enemy was strictly forbidden", one Pennsylvanian wrote after the war, "the men were on the most friendly terms, amicably conversing and exchanging such commodities as coffee, sugar, tobacco, corn meal and newspapers."[32]

"It was a singular sight", wrote one Yank, "to see the soldiers of two great hostile armies walking about unconcernedly within a few yards of each other with their bayonets sticking in the ground, bantering and joking together, exchanging

Confederate Personal Artifacts

Life in camp was made immeasurably more bearable by the personal belongings in Johnny Reb's knapsack or blanket roll. His inspiration, his entertainment, romance, almost everything for his soul might be found there. These personal belongings made life more bearable.

1 Pocket Bible and hymnal
2 Pocket Bible
3 Eye glasses
4 Pocket Bible
5 Pocket hymnal
6 Personal effects bag
7 Photograph album
8 Water bottle
9 Bullet molds
10 Gunpowder can
11 Percussion cap tin
12 Pocket watch
13 Case for eye glasses
14 Wallet
15 Carved spoon
16 Carved pin
17 Percussion cap tin
18 Chess board and set
19 Paint box
20 Pocket knife
21 Hammer
22 Housewife. (Soldiers were required to repair their own uniforms, and these small sewing kits contained needle and thread.)
23 Miniature shoe ornament
24 Flute
25 Change purse
26 Deck of playing cards
27 Guitar
28 Powder horn

Artifacts courtesy of: The Museum of the Confederacy, Richmond, Va

the compliments of the day and even saluting officers of the opposing forces with as much ceremony, decorum and respect as they did their own. The keenest sense of honor existed among the enlisted men of each side. It was no uncommon sight, when visiting the picket posts, to see an equal number of 'graybacks' and 'bluebellies' as they facetiously termed each other, enjoying a social game of euchre or seven-up and sometimes the great national game of draw poker, with army rations and sutler's delicacies as the stakes."[33]

The private soldiers were little concerned with the philosophical, economic, and other weighty issues that had brought about the war. For them it was simply something that seemed to drag on interminably. While they could muster their hatred of the enemy before and during a battle, it was difficult to sustain this emotion during the long lulls that generally followed an action. Instead, facing each other for weeks or months across a field or from opposite sides of a river, it was only natural that the men would start shouting a few epithets and jokes at each other. That led to familiarity, and familiarity bred fraternization. They traded scarcities for scarcities: Yankees always wanted good Virginia tobacco, the Rebs never had enough real coffee. When a river divided their lines, they made little sailboats and passed them back and forth with the precious cargoes. When only a field or wood lay between, the soldiers met in the middle. A certain kind of etiquette even evolved in such dealings, one of its strictest rules being the one "that forbade the shooting of men while attending to the imperative calls of nature".

When the prospect of a fight loomed, the men unconsciously began to work up their hatred once more. "All I want to do is to lick these Sons of B--ches across the river", one Yank private vowed before a battle.[34] Nevertheless, except for such times, acts of mercy and friendship across the lines – even during battle – became commonplace in every major conflict of the war. Despite all the efforts and threats of their officers, Johnny Reb and Billy Yank could not help liking one another now and then.

Faced with all these varying forms of insubordination and misbehavior, the best the officers on either side could do was to use punishment as an example and hope that it worked. It did not. The problem was the complete lack of uniformity in dealing with miscreants. Punishment was not specifically prescribed for most offenses by military code, and so the officers in charge used their own judgement in selecting appropriate atonement. As a result, glaring inequities existed from the outset. One poor fellow, possibly dull-witted, found himself sentenced to three years of hard labor just for being absent from camp without leave for five days. At the same time, six Rebels who actually deserted the service were caught and, instead of facing prison or worse, were simply stood before their colonel, given "a little fatherly advice", and returned to the ranks of their regiment.[35]

It is hardly a surprise, therefore, that when offenders of capital crimes got off with a lecture, while others guilty of minor infractions could find themselves treated like heinous criminals, most men in the ranks simply ceased to regard punishments as a deterrent. Worse, for the serious offenses that required courts martial, the military justice system was overwhelmed with cases. Witnesses necessary for prosecution and defence could always fall in battle before testifying, and the officers needed to sit on the courts were more urgently required at the front. A trial could take months, even years, to take place, and to avoid the delays, many commanders simply did not resort to the regular system. Instead, they passed judgment and meted out punishment on their own.

Below: When a soldier overstepped the boundary of military law, he was likely to meet with an officer of the Provost Marshal either from his brigade or from army headquarters. That was just the beginning.

This instantaneous form of justice could prove dangerous for the offender, for a ranking officer handing out his own sentences immediately after an offense was likely to be angry, and his sentencing thus influenced. When Union General Jefferson C. Davis had to sentence five soldiers just caught molesting a Tennessee girl, he first fumed and then as they were stripped and tied to a cannon wheel, he ordered the man who gave witness against the others to himself wield the whip and flog the other four fifty lashes each.

The guardhouse was the most common punishment, the number of days inside determined by the severity of the offense, from only a few hours to a month or more. Whatever the sentence, the guardhouse – often just an open field marked by ropes and watched by sentries – was hardly a hardship. Bread and water could make it less bearable, but in fact many offenders looked upon it as a respite from regular duty. In the 2nd Kentucky Infantry, Confederate Colonel Roger Hanson found infractions so frequent that on some days the guardhouse became more an informal bivouack for his regiment, and he began making daily visits to lecture the men sternly about their behavior.[36]

Commanders used their imaginations a bit more when it seemed necessary for the punishment to fit the crime. For several hours messmates saw one Federal cavalryman walking about their camp carrying a saddle on his back, only to learn that this was his sentence for stealing the saddle. A Rebel who sold whiskey in camp against regulations, spent the better part of the day straddling a fence rail and riding around the camp with bottles tied to his feet and a sign saying "Ten Cents a Glass" hanging from his neck. A Confederate who shot a stray dog was ordered to run around the camp with the dead animal in his arms as punishment, and another Southerner who fired his rifle in camp against orders had to carry a log for three hours.[37]

Insubordination could bring several hours of the ball and chain, usually a thirty-pound cannon ball on a few feet of heavy chain attached to the offender's leg. Wherever he went he had either to carry the ball or else drag it behind him, an exhausting exercise after a surprisingly short time, even for the most robust of offenders. For cowardice or unauthorized absence, soldiers tied the transgressor's hands in front of him, shoved his knees up and inside his arms, and thrust a stick over one elbow, under the knees, and over the other elbow. A gag placed in his mouth completed his being "bucked and gagged" and several hours in the hot sun in this very uncomfortable position was a punishment fit for all but the most serious of crimes.

Ironically, what most soldiers dreaded more than many other forms of punishment was being ordered to perform extra hours of guard duty, and yet it is the punishment that they most infrequently received. Many officers felt, as did General Thomas C. Hindman, that "standing guard is the most honorable duty of a soldier, except fighting, and must not be degraded".[38] Yet this attitude did not mean that commanders were overly inclined toward mercy in judging their men. "There was a class of officers who felt that every violation of camp rules should be visited with the infliction of bodily pain in some form", John D. Billings of Massachusetts lamented.[39]

Certain special crimes such as cowardice, desertion, insubordination, rape, murder, trea-

son, and the like, were regarded almost uniformly by all officers, and nearly all shared the same notions of proper punishment. The lucky man was simply discharged from the service dishonorably. His head shaved, his uniform stripped of its buttons and insignia, he was drummed out of camp in sight of his comrades while the regimental band played the "Rogue's March". All the while his former mates showered on him the vilest sort of verbal insults, and on these occasions, at least, no attempts to curtail profanity were made. When this punishment seemed insufficient for the offense, a man could be branded, to carry his shame with him for life. His cheek, or forehead, or hip, would feel the red-hot iron imprint the appropriate letter for his crime – "c" for cowardice, "d" for desertion, "t" for thievery, and so on from crime to crime.

In a few cases, even this was not adjudged to be enough, particularly for desertion. It was a crime that, left unpunished, could demoralize whole regiments and cripple an army. The inducements were many, and ever-present. "My dear Edward", a North Carolina wife wrote to her soldier husband with the army. "I would not have you do anything wrong for the world, but before God, Edward, unless you come home we must die. Last night I was aroused by little Eddie's crying. I called and said 'What is the matter, Eddie?' and he said 'O Mamma! I am so hungry.' and Lucy, Edward, your darling Lucy; she never complains, but she is growing thinner and thinner every day. And before God, Edward, unless you come home, we must die."[40]

Such appeals from home were many and persuasive, especially in the South where civilians felt the war as much as soldiers. The desertion rate stayed low at the war's outset thanks to patriotism, but as the conflict wore on, the number of absentees rose dramatically. One of every nine Rebels would desert during the war, and in the Union army one out of seven took "French leave", some soldiers deserting again and again after being returned to the army. During 1864 and

Above: Some officers had a positive genius for devising innovative sentences for infractions of the rules. Outside impromptu guardhouses all manner of punishments could take place, some painful, all humiliating.

Below: Men like these prisoners at Maryland's Point Lookout, could be made to wear barrels and forced to parade to and fro with placards hanging from their necks saying "thief", "drunk" or worse.

beyond the influx of draftees and men who enlisted to receive bounty payments introduced an undermotivated element into the Union forces, which further aggravated the desertion rate. And the seemingly interminable war itself put the severest tests upon the resolve of men and homefolk on both sides. "It is useless to conceal the truth any longer", a Confederate wrote from the Petersburg trenches in 1865. "Many of our people at home have become so demoralized that they write to their husbands, sons and brothers that desertion *now* is not *dishonorable*".[41] By the time he wrote those words, over 420,000 Rebs and Yanks combined were on the rolls as being absent without leave.

From the start, military law provided for the death sentence to deal with deserters when caught. However, commanders were reluctant to impose capital punishment early in the war, not realizing the necessity of the example, and still feeling the personal sympathy for the volunteer soldier which several years of war would eventually replace with a more strictly professional military attitude. When the sentence of death was imposed, it was often commuted to life imprisonment, or incarceration for the duration of the war. But finally, in cases of rape, murder, spying, severe theft and, of course, desertion, the death penalty was more and more frequently imposed. Edward Cooper of North Carolina, whose wife sent him that heart-wrenching letter, was saved from the death penalty by producing his wife's plea. Few hearts were hard enough not to sympathize in such a case. Indeed, in the Union Army fewer than ten percent of all desertion convictions eventually led to death sentences, and only a quarter of those so sentenced failed to receive a commutation. The rate of executions in the South ran somewhat higher.

But occasionally the sentence had to be carried out, publicly, usually by firing squad, though hanging was sometimes employed for specially unsavory offenses such as rape. The regiment – sometimes the entire brigade – was drawn up on three sides of a square, while the condemned

Confederate Prisoner of War Handicrafts

Johnny Reb showed off a lot of his natural inventiveness in the face of adversity by the ways in which he filled his time in prison camps, making what he needed for himself, and souvenirs for the happy days after he would be released. It filled in the time and let him forget his dilemma. Religious, entertainment, practical items, all were produced by his deft hands and active imagination.

1 Wooden box
2 Wooden box
3 Covered bowl
4 Covered cady
5 Chess set with box
6 Game box
7 Candle stands
8 Comb
9 Woven palm fan
10 Keepsake box
11 Chess set and box
12 Jewelry box
13 Chess set and box
14 Chess set and box
15 Water ladle
16 Uncarved coconut shell
17 Weaving shuttle
18 Carved chess set and box
19 Chess set and box
20 Game of Jackstraws with box
21 Chess set with box
22–27 Various hand-made tools
28 Carved coconut shell
29 Carved religious objects
30 Game of jackstraws
31 Hand carved fork and spoon

Artifacts courtesy of: The Museum of the Confederacy, Richmond, Va

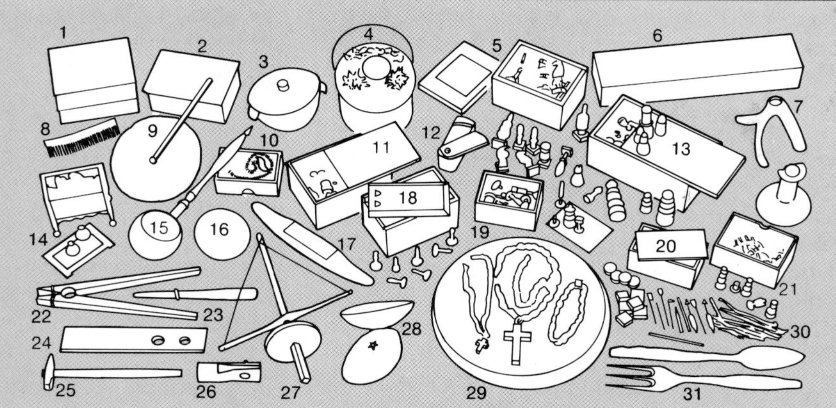

man, to the tune of a funeral dirge, rode on top of his coffin or walked to the open side of the formation. Standing beside his own freshly-dug grave, he heard the sentence of the court read aloud one last time, spoke with a chaplain if he wished, and accepted or declined a handkerchief for his eyes.

Then the sentence was carried out. "It was hard to bear", wrote a witness to one execution. "Faces paled and hands shook which were not accustomed to show fear; and officers and men alike would have welcomed a call to battle in exchange for that terrible inaction in the sight of coming death."[42]

Adding to the apprehension were the stories which many of the men had heard, of muffed executions. The average soldier was not an able marksman, and when about to shoot a defenseless comrade his aim could be even more unsteady. When Frank McElhenny deserted in 1862, going over to the enemy, and then deserted them to go back to his own lines, he had the misfortune to run right into his own old regiment. Tried and convicted, he was set for execution on August 8, 1864. His hands bound, his eyes blindfolded, he stood before a firing party a scant few paces away. When they fired, he fell to the ground with five bullets in him. But still he lived. Another squad sent another eight slugs into his chest before he died.

Others fared even worse. In the Army of Tennessee in 1862, twenty Confederates stood twelve paces from a man and only slightly injured him. Four more soldiers came forward and fired and still he breathed. Finally all twenty-four reloaded and managed to kill him with a volley that might have mowed down a whole squad of the enemy. When a Pennsylvanian was being executed, he was still sitting upright on his coffin after the first volley. When a second squad fired, he fell, but then got up and gamely sat on his coffin again. Only the third firing party finally managed to kill him.

Perhaps worst of all was the execution of two "bounty jumpers", men who enlisted to be paid a few dollars, and then deserted, probably intending to enlist yet again under different names to collect yet more bounty money. George Elliot and Edward Latham of the 14th Connecticut were tried and convicted, September 18, 1863, being set for their execution. All the usual ritual, blindfold, prayers, reading of the sentence, passed without event. Pluckily the condemned men shook hands with each other and the officer in charge, and then sat down upon their coffins. When the smoke from the volley cleared, they could see that Elliot had fallen, apparently killed. Latham, however, still sat upright on his coffin, and feverishly ripped the blindfold from his eyes to see

Private, "Wheat's Tigers"

Of all the unenviable reputations in the Confederate army, probably none was more widely known than that of the 1st Special Battalion, Louisiana Infantry, known as "Wheat's Tigers" after their commander, Major Roberdeau Wheat. Raised in June 1861 from the sons of planters, soldiers of fortune, and riff-raff of the New Orleans back streets and shanties, the battalion won its nickname of "tigers" for its unmanageable behavior: "so villainous", wrote one officer, "that every commander desired to be rid of it." Yet their battle record was excellent and during actions such as First Manassas they suffered such heavy losses that the battalion was disbanded in August 1862 after Wheat's own death at Gaines' Mill in June. The man had held the unit together and without him it collapsed. "Wheat's Tigers" were easily recognized by their colorful zouave costume of blue and scarlet, and their Model 1841 rifles.

Above: For the soldier who transgressed too far against the military system, there could await a court-martial, on which a board of officers sat to decide his fate from a few days' punishment to execution.

Below: For the worst crimes of all, such as murder or desertion there awaited hanging or the firing squad. The man being shot here is Johnson, a Confederate spy, but the scene was much the same for others.

what had happened. At once two men were ordered forward to dispatch him as he sat there "wildly staring them in the face". Both rifles misfired, and Latham's old comrades back in the ranks began to wish that he would get up and simply run away. He had faced death twice, and that was enough. Apparently he was too consumed with fright to move. Finally the officer in charge ran to him and put his pistol against the man's temple. Again it misfired, and still Latham sat there like a panicked rabbit. At the next try, the officer finally put a bullet into his brain.

And all the while, George Elliot, far from being dead, was standing up watching the proceedings and bleeding from a painful wound in his abdomen. "Blow my brains out!" he begged the firing party, and the officer in charge tried to so do, but at point-blank range his pistol botched the job, and only two more rifle balls in Elliot's chest finished the job. Even then, so thoroughly shaken by the macabre events of the past few minutes that he could not be sure anyone was really dead, the officer ordered two more riflemen to continue firing. One slug took away half of Elliot's face, and the other was fired into his heart from such a close range "that his clothes took fire from the powder flame".[43] It was a disgusting exhibition for everyone involved, yet still they had to file past the dead men and look at the price of justice before the two were placed in their coffins, face downward so they could not look toward heaven, and then covered over with earth and no marker.

Capital punishment was meted out to about 500 Yanks and Rebs in the Civil War, more than in all other American wars combined, and two thirds of them for desertion. Yet the fate of men such as Elliot and Latham never came close to curbing the volunteers' natural bent for insubordination, their rejection of military regimentation, and the urge to leave the army when they chose. "Shocking and solemn as such scenes were", concluded Billings, "I do not believe that the shooting of a deserter had any great deterring influence on the rank and file".[44] There were always those willing to risk getting away, just as there were always those who would not find any sort of punishment a hindrance for misconduct of any kind.

The offenses that led to these punishments, like the punishments themselves, attracted a great deal of attention then and later, but they were happily the exception in soldier life. Relatively few Yanks and Rebs were ever seriously insubordinate, and far fewer still suffered any rigorous retribution for their occasional antics. As for their attitude toward the military, and their grumbling and grousing about it, that would never change, and if disliking officers and wishing to be somewhere other than in the service were adjudged to be crimes, then every army in history has been populated with "criminals".

References

1 Wiley, *Billy Yank*, p.26; James I. Robertson, Jr., *Tenting Tonight* (Alexandria, Va., 1984), p.56.
2 "Peter Wilson in the Civil War", *Iowa Journal of History and Politics*, XL (1942), pp.402-3.
3 Wiley and Milhollen, *They Who Fought Here*, pp.190-1.
4 D.E. Beem to . . . , May 20, 1861, David E. Beem Papers, Indiana Historical Society, Indianapolis.
5 Robertson, *Tenting Tonight*, p.62.
6 Wiley, *Johnny Reb*, p.39.
7 William C. Davis, ed., *The Guns of '62* (New York, 1982), p.216.
8 Mildred Thore, ed., "Reminiscences of Jacob Switzer", *Iowa Journal of History and Politics*, LV (1957), p.325; Charles D. Page, *History of the Fourteenth Regiment, Connecticut Volunteer Infantry* (Meriden, Conn., 1906), pp.131-2.
9 Robertson, *Tenting Tonight*, pp.59-60.
10 Wiley, *Billy Yank*, p.252.
11 *Ibid.*, pp.199-201.
12 Francis Lord, *They Fought for the Union* (Harrisburg, Pa., 1960), p.215.
13 Wiley, *Johnny Reb*, p.271; Bell I. Wiley, "A Time of Greatness", p.6.
14 Bell I. Wiley, *Confederate Women* (Westport, Conn., 1975), p.171.
15 Jane Goodwin to husband, n.d., *Civil War Times Illustrated* Collection.
16 Wiley, *Johnny Reb*, p.271.
17 Robertson, *Tenting Tonight*, p.60.
18 Wiley and Milhollen, *They Who Fought Here*, *passim*.
19 *Ibid.*
20 *Ibid.*
21 *Ibid.*
22 O.R., I, 42, Part 2, p.1276.
23 Bruce Catton, *America Goes to War* (Middletown, Conn., 1958), p.53.
24 Douglas S. Freeman, *Lee's Lieutenants* (New York, 1945), I, p.13.
25 James G. Hudson, "A Story of Company D, 4th Alabama Infantry Regiment", *Alabama Historical Quarterly*, XXIII (1961), pp.156-7.
26 "Peter Wilson", p.301.
27 Evan R. Jones, *Four Years in the Army of the Potomac* (London, 1881), p.45.
28 Wiley, "A Time of Greatness", pp.11-12.
29 Wiley, *Billy Yank*, pp.185-6; Wiley, *Johnny Reb*, p.235.
30 Wiley, *Billy Yank*, pp.199, 201.
31 *Ibid.*, p.199; Wiley, *Johnny Reb*, p.242; John O. Casler, *Four Years in the Stonewall Brigade* (Dayton, Ohio, 1971), p.102.
32 Gilbert A. Hays, *Under the Red Patch* (Pittsburgh, 1908), pp.270-1.
33 *Ibid.*
34 Wiley, *Billy Yank*, pp.350-1.
35 *Ibid.*, p.213.
36 Davis, *Orphan Brigade*, p.53.
37 Wiley and Milhollen, *They Who Fought Here*, p.178.
38 O.R., I, 32, Part 2, p.654.
39 Billings, *Hardtack and Coffee*, p.146.
40 Ella Lonn, *Desertion During the Civil War* (New York, 1928), pp.12-13.
41 George D. Harmon, (ed.), "Letters of Luther Rice Mills", *North Carolina Historical Review*, IV (1927), p.307.
42 O.R., IV, 3, p.1182; A.S. Roe, *The Twenty-Fourth Regiment Massachusetts Volunteers* (Worcester, 1907), p.428.
43 John H. Silverman, "The Excitement had Begun!", *Manuscripts*, XXX (1978), pp.276-7.
44 Billings, *Hardtack and Coffee*, p.161.

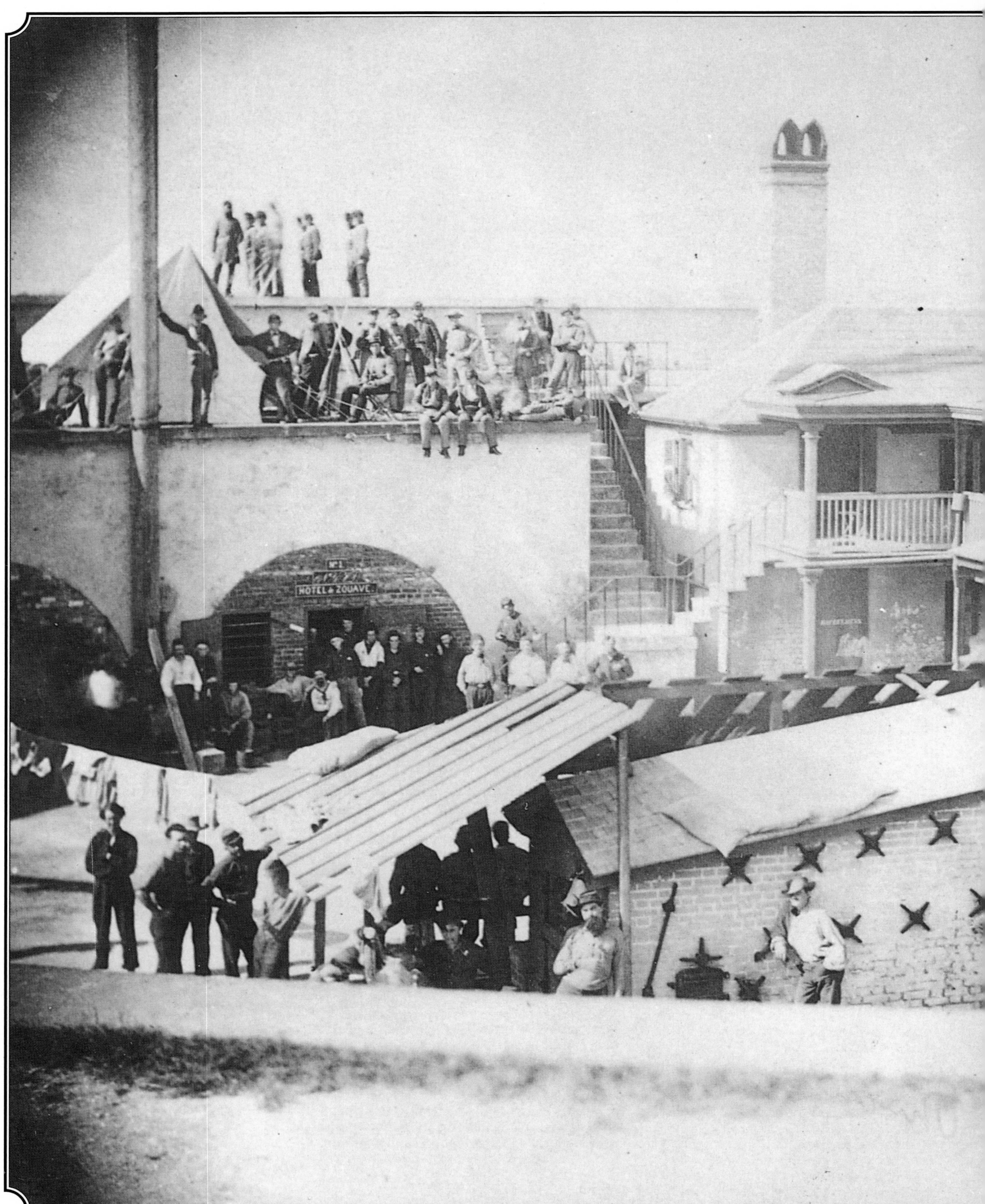
No 1
HOTEL de ZOUAVE

CHAPTER NINE

IRON BARS A PRISON MAKE

All at once that first week of May 1864, the continent seemed to erupt in smoke and gunfire. On the fourth, Grant and Meade crossed the Rapidan River in Virginia, moving into a dense wooded area known locally as "the Wilderness". There, just one day later, they met Lee in what became one of the bitterest and most confused battles of the war, two brutal days of slugging back and forth, often at enemies unseen in the underbush. When it was over nothing had been gained, but unlike his predecessors, Grant did not pull back. He pushed around Lee's flank and met him again in vicious fighting spread over two weeks in and around Spotsylvania Court House. Stymied there, Grant kept on the move still, meeting Lee again and again on the North Anna River in late May and at Cold Harbor in the first three days of June. The intensity of the fighting was like that never before encountered in Virginia. Still Lee held, and finally on June 14 Grant stole a march on Lee, secretly took his army across the James River, and began to move on Petersburg, back door to Richmond.

Simultaneously Sherman was marching through north Georgia, steadily pushing Joseph E. Johnston, back in command of the Army of Tennessee, before him until the Confederates stopped Sherman temporarily at New Hope Church. In the Shenandoah valley, the first Yankee invasion was stopped cold on May 15, when a Confederate army half its size routed it at New Market. But another campaign would come in its wake in a few weeks. On the Virginia peninsula, more Federals pushed toward Richmond, attempting to pinch it between themselves and Grant. On the high seas, the dreaded Rebel commerce raider *Alabama* was finally hunted down and sunk.

So constant was the fighting that besides the killed and wounded, the numbers of captured soon exceeded everyone's expectations. In Georgia, captured Yanks began streaming into a compound called Camp Sumter. It was soon to be known everywhere as Andersonville.

"WILL NO one send a little word to cheer us in our gloomy hours of activity?" bemoaned one Confederate. "Oh, God! how dreadful are these bitter feelings of hope deferred. Thus we linger, thus we drag the slow, tedious hours of prison life."[1]

That lonely Southerner spoke volumes for all the hundreds of thousands of men, blue and gray, who survived the rigors of camp life, the dangers of battle, even the horrors of illness and wounds, only to fall victim to an enemy just as insidious and deadly. Johnny Rebs and Billy Yanks went off to war with a host of naive hopes and genuine fears: new friends, novel sights, camp life, hard marches, battle, martial glory, perhaps even wounds and death. But none of them went expecting capture or the nightmarish lot of the prisoner of war. None who went through that experience would ever forget it.

As so often in this war which everyone had been predicting for years, North and South were entirely unprepared to deal with captured enemies. As was so often the case, that lack of foresight led to tragedy. When 1861 dawned, not a single military prison existed on the continent capable of holding more than a few ill-behaved enlisted men. Even when the guns spoke at Fort Sumter, both sides immediately expected the conflict to last barely through the summer, and thus no preparations for prisoners were made.

The war's first prisons were nothing more than hastily converted warehouses. Yankees captured at First Manassas were kept in Charleston's old Castle Pinckney, their guards on the parapet.

The release of Major Robert Anderson and his entire garrison from Sumter, with all courtesy and honor, seemed a matter of course.

Yet even as the Federals left the smoldering fort amid an air almost of gaiety, there were hundreds of forgotten comrades in blue, over a thousand miles to the west, who had been virtual prisoners of war for two months, and still the Confederate authorities did not know what to do with them.

It was on February 18, 1861, that Major General David E. Twiggs surrendered his Department of Texas to the New Confederates. His command included 2,648 United States Regulars, all of whom, he was assured, would be allowed to keep their arms and equipment. Further, they were to be left to march out of the state free and unmolested. "They are our friends", declared a Confederate decree exhorting Texans to show courtesy to the Yankees; "they have heretofore afforded to our people all the protection in their power, and we owe them every consideration".[2]

Yet confusion set in immediately. Authorities became fearful of so large a body of armed Federals. Transport that was to take them from a Gulf coast port to the North was delayed. Then Confederate leaders decided that Twiggs' men should not be allowed to leave before an attempt was made to recruit them to Southern arms. Special recruiting officers were dispatched, among them Colonel Earl Van Dorn. When Van Dorn took command in Texas, the Confederacy reversed its policy completely. Going back on the agreement, they now decided that the roughly 1,600 Yankees remaining in the state constituted a hazard. "Officers and men must be regarded as prisoners of war", were Van Dorn's orders.[3] Those instructions went out on April 11, just as final orders were going to Charleston to open fire on Fort Sumter. With war coming at last, there must, at last, be prisoners of war. The Yankee officers were released on parole and sent home, but their men in the ranks would spend the next two years in Texan prison camps. The first to suffer from administrative shortsightedness, they were only the first of legions to follow.

It is indeed fortunate that the balance of 1861 saw so little action. With no major battles other than First Bull Run in the East and Wilson's Creek out in Missouri, Union and Confederate authorities did not immediately face massive numbers of prisoners. After the débâcle at Manassas, Confederates found no more than 1,100 Yankees on their hands, and the Federals' captures were less than a dozen. Combined prisoners of war on both sides out in the Missouri battle barely exceeded 200. Numbers like these were manageable, placed little strain on resources, and afforded North and South both time to evolve some kind of policy for dealing with prisoners. Alas, even with this breathing space, neither side moved with dispatch or imagination.[4]

In fact, it took some time before Lincoln even recognized Confederates as prisoners. Since he maintained all along that the South never left the Union, and was instead in a state of insurrection, there was, therefore, no "war", and only in a war could there be prisoners to be accorded the standard treatment for captured enemies. Confederates were involved in a treasonous rebellion, subject to being dealt with as traitors, not as prisoners.[5]

As a result, in the months following Bull Run, when both sides might have been erecting prison camps and setting up the administration necessary to care for prisoners, they devoted more time instead to posturing and blustering. Lincoln intended to try captured Confederate privateers as traitors, for whom the punishment was well known. So Jefferson Davis declared that he would execute an equal number of Federal prisoners for every Southerner hanged. Only after heavy public and administrative pressure did Lincoln finally back down and agree to consider the privateers as legitimate prisoners. And all the while, as additional – though small – numbers of men were taken prisoner, they joined the hundred of others languishing in hastily improvised military prisons. In 1861, if the boys North and South had any awareness of the indecisiveness of their governments on the prisoner issue, and of the woefully inadequate means of caring for prisoners of war even at the most basic level, they might have marched off to battle with a little less spring in their step.

When they did go to battle and suffer capture, they soon found themselves standing for hours in holding pens, or in a gully surrounded by armed guards, while officers recorded their names and units. Provost marshals issued orders for sending the prisoners to established compounds far behind the lines, and then the prisoners were off. The lucky ones traveled by boat or rail, but as the war went on such transportation, especially in the South, was most needed for other proposes, and so more often than not the prisoners walked into captivity.

Above: For the soldier who was captured, his first stop on the road to prison would be a holding area behind the battle line, such as the one in which these Confederates are being held near Belle Plain, Virginia.

Below: Men like these Confederate prisoners were sent to depot prisons like Point Lookout, Maryland, where their paperwork was processed and a decision made as to which prison camp would receive them.

Those who rode found it less than pleasant. After Lieutenant Alonzo Cooper of the 12th New York Cavalry was captured at Plymouth, North Carolina, on April 20, 1864, he was marched in full uniform for several days before he and his men reached the railroad at Tarboro. There they were crowded into cattle cars, forty to the car, and the rolling stock had not been cleaned out since the last 'beeves' departed. "It was, therefore, like lying in a cow stable", complained Cooper. Things got worse, however. "We now began to realize what short rations, or no rations, meant." While some of their guards and the local citizens performed acts of comfort and kindness, others sought immediately to profit by their adversity. Cooper had to pay ten dollars to buy nine sandwiches for himself and some comrades. Later on a pie cost him five dollars. "At this rate a millionaire could not long remain outside the poor house", he lamented. And when rations were issued, they were soft bread and spoiled bacon.[6]

Yet in the days ahead, most of the prisoners would look back on such fare as princely compared to what awaited them. After leaving the front, many arrived first at depot prisons like Point Lookout, Maryland, or Richmond's later infamous Libby Prison. From these points they were sent deep into the interior, where they were to spend the balance of their prison days. And once at their ultimate destinations, the men's names were once again checked against a list, like bills of lading.

Private and Corporal, US Veteran Reserve Corps

The enormous manpower demands of the Union Army's many functions behind the lines became so great that Washington had to attempt to place less able-bodied men in some postings, in order to free the fitter men for active service. Thus in 1863 was created the Veteran Reserve Corps. It was to be composed of men who were disabled or hospitalized and divided into two battalions – one for men able to use weapons, the other for those missing a limb. Eventually, veterans whose terms of enlistments had expired were also allowed to serve in the corps, with or without disabilities. Men of the Reserve wore uniforms of sky blue kersey, with dark blue cap and trimmings, the jacket cut short in the cavalry pattern, even though they were strictly an infantry service. Their weapons were usually old or worn out models, which like their owners were no longer needed on the front line.

Early in the war the captured Yanks and Rebs did not necessarily feel any great apprehension, even when they saw the old tobacco warehouses or the hastily erected tent compounds that were to be their prison homes. They did not expect to be there for long. Indeed, the practice up to Bull Run had been to release prisoners on their parole, that is, to send them home under an agreement not to take up arms once again until properly "exchanged". Prisoner exchange was an old practice in warfare. Paroled prisoners remained free at home, though still members of the military and subject to its orders. However, they could not fight again until formally traded – exchanged – for a like number of paroled prisoners on the other side. A paroled man who fought again before being exchanged was subject to harsh punishment if discovered, even death.

It came as a rude shock, then, when the Yankees taken at Manassas found themselves spending several months in prison after their capture. Lincoln's refusal to recognize that a real war existed precluded any prisoner exchanges. To negotiate with the Confederates would in effect, he feared, constitute recognition of the Richmond authorities as a legitimate government, which could have grave diplomatic implications. Only under considerable pressure did Lincoln finally designate General John Dix to arrange a formal exchange system with the enemy. The agreement allowed for the man-for-man trading of private soldiers as well as officers of equivalent rank. Within the hierarchy of officers, trading was to take place on the basis of a cartel with the British made back in 1813. A corporal was worth two privates. A captain was equal to two lieutenants. A major general required 30 enlisted men for exchange. If there were not enough men available for exchange on one side or the other, those remaining unexchanged were to be paroled pending exchange. "Friendly discussions" were to take care of any disputes, but in any case the process of exchange was to continue uninterrupted. If it had worked, there would have been no Civil War prisons.[7]

Above: Colonel William Hoffman, who took charge as Union commissary general of prisoners in 1861, and speedily brought effective – and hard-edged – economic efficiency to the welfare of Rebel prisoners.

Unfortunately, it did not work. Neither side was ready for the overwhelming load of record-keeping required, nor for the scale and pace which the war would quickly assume. Worse, some generals believed that the system impaired morale, actually encouraging men to get themselves captured in order to be paroled home with slim prospect of exchange. The system only worked well for the first few months before it steadily broke down. Both sides launched accusations of bad faith, and when black soldiers entered the equation after 1863, the Confederates refused to treat them on an equal basis with whites in the exchange. That same year the whole agreement fell apart amid accusations and recriminations.

Even when the cartel was still in effect, North and South began to take halting steps toward dealing with the prisoner problem, though their solutions betrayed little genuine long-range planning. In October 1861, Colonel William H. Hoffman was appointed commissary general of prisoners in the Union Army, charged with keeping record of prisoners taken, managing any exchanges, transporting supplies to Union prisoners in the South under truce agreements, and, of course, maintaining and administering the camps established to hold captured Confederates. Hoffman proved to be admirably efficient. His initial task was to establish the first specially created prison on Johnson's Island on Lake Erie, near Sandusky, Ohio, and he did so with speed and skill. He also did it with something that characterized all his operations for the rest of the war – spartan thrift. Intended solely for the sake of wartime economy, Hoffman's stinginess would unintentionally lead to considerable hardship and suffering for many Rebel prisoners.[8]

That measures were short-sighted is all too clear in the fact that Hoffman's prison at Johnson's Island was originally designed for only 1,000 men, this in a war that would see hundreds of thousands captured. The fall of Fort Donelson alone, in February 1862, just two weeks after Johnson's Island opened, funneled 15,000 new prisoners into Hoffman's system. The captives from this one engagement forced the ersatz creation of four new camps in Indiana, Illinois, and Ohio, as well as swelling numbers in other established compounds. After the cartel gave way in May and July 1863, Hoffman was never entirely able to keep up with the rapid influx of prisoners.

The story was even worse south of the Potomac. Management of Confederate prisons was put in the hands of Brigadier General John H.

Below: At first, prisoners like these Yankees at Castle Pinckney in July 1861, could adopt a gay and jaunty air, fully expecting the war to be a short one, and themselves to be exchanged or freed very quickly.

Winder, a sixty-one-year-old Marylander who began the war as provost of Richmond. Gradually his authority spread until, on November 21, 1864, he was finally made commissary general of prisoners. Where Hoffman's economy was self-induced, Winder had no choice but to cut corners. He established a few new camps, notably Camp Sumter near Andersonville, Georgia, but most Yankee prisoners were stuffed wherever he could find room, whether on a barren island in the James River, or in Libby's tobacco warehouse in Richmond. Like Hoffman, Winder never intentionally set out to mistreat or harm the prisoners entrusted to him, but suffer they did.

Filthy, unsanitary, riddled with vermin, the prisons of the Civil War were all, in varying degrees, hells on earth. "It is useless to attempt a description of the place", declared an Alabamian incarcerated at Fort Delaware; "a respectable hog would have turned up his nose in disgust at it."

Above: Hoffman's model prison was Johnson's Island, near Sandusky, Ohio. Local troops like the Ohio National Guard 8th Light Artillery, performed guard duty in the prison, whose stockade appears behind them.

Bedbugs inhabited every mattress and dark place. Confederates in Washington's Old Capitol Prison occasionally joined forces against the insects and had "a promiscuous slaughter, regardless of age or sex". Yet when it was all done, the bugs were back, and the Rebs had to conclude that "they must recruit from the other side, like the Yankee army, as we can notice no diminution in the forces".[10] A Rhode Islander held prisoner in the South declared that "the vermin was so plenty that the boys said they had regimental drill".[11]

Perhaps worst of all were the fleas. "The beasts crawled over the ground from body to body", wrote a New Yorker, "and their attacks seemed to become more aggravating as the men became more emaciated".[12] By daylight they could be found and killed, but in the dark of night the men had no choice but to suffer. "We hunted them three times each day but could not get the best of them", wrote John Adams of Massachusetts. "They are very prolific and great-grandchildren would be born in twenty-four hours after they struck us."[13]

The constant scratching helped make a shambles of the prisoners' already tattered clothing. Many, and particularly Confederates who were hardly well clad to start, often wore little more than rags when they first reached the prisons. A few months in a warm climate where the mildew could rot the fabric from their frames might leave the poor men virtually in threads, often reducing them to the humiliation of scavenging rags from the bodies of their dead comrades, vermin and all. Happily, if they had to wear rags, at least the prisoners held in the South faced winters less harsh than the Rebels incarcerated at Johnson's Island and the like. There the gales of winter tore through open stockades and drafty barracks. Hoffman recognized the problem, but dealt with it in his usual miserly fashion by acquiring ill-made or wrong sized Federal uniforms which had been rejected for field service. With these he equipped such of his prisoners as he could, in the process also managing to find blankets for most of them.

On both sides of Mason and Dixon's line, with little else to occupy their day, prisoners spent much of their time thinking about their rations. Eating them, such as they were, provided the only break in the monotony of the day. What they ate matched their surroundings for miserliness and contamination. Meat rations came spoiled and fly-and-worm infested, while bread was moldy and full of maggots.[14]

Below: Washington's Old Capitol Prison was just one of the many civilian buildings converted to prisoner of war needs in the Union capital. The only ones to benefit from the place would be the fleas and lice.

Ration quantities were often such as merely to whet appetites, not satisfy them. A South Carolinian tallied his daily fare as a half-pint of "slop water" coffee for breakfast, a half-pint of "greasy water" soup for dinner, and with it a three or four ounce piece of meat. "The writer has known large, stout men to lay in their tents at night and cry like little babies from hunger", he said.[15]

The prisoners went after any source of meat, be it dog, cat, bird or rat. "We traped for Rats and the Prisoners Eat Every one they Could get", wrote an Arkansan at Johnson's Island. He captured and ate a "mess of Fried Rats" himself, finding that they tasted like squirrels and "was all right to a hungry man".[16]

Before long rumors swept the camps that prison authorities actually intended to starve the men to death, and the accusations were often repeated after the war. There was no truth in it on either side. War demands simply limited what was available, especially in the South. As a rule the Yanks held there ate almost as well – or as badly – as Confederate soldiers in the field. Yet when he heard reports of starvation in Southern prisons, Colonel Hoffman ordered a cutback in rations to his own prisoners in retaliation. By the end of the war he could proudly return to the Federal Treasury nearly $2 million that he had saved by ration reduction. A move which no doubt made the plight of his prisoners worse.

Drinking water matched the food, coming from polluted wells, or camp streams fouled by prison waste.[17] In such a situation, sickness on a massive scale was inevitable. Immediately apparent was scurvy. First the skin discolored and lost its resiliency. Then hair and teeth fell out – then came weakness, lethargy and death. In the camp at Elmira, New York, in its first three months over 1,800 cases occurred, while at Fort Delaware more than ten percent contracted it. A terrible suffering made all the more horrible by the fact that the fresh vegetables that could have prevented the disease were readily available. But Colonel Hoffman regarded them all as luxuries, and after his retaliatory cutback in rations for

Confederate Prisoner of War Handicrafts

Johnny Reb spent hours making these trinkets, as symbols perhaps of hope.

1 Bone napkin ring
2 A bone book
3 Hinged case with ornately carved lid
4 Carved box
5 Carved jars
6 Carved necklace
7 Carved bracelet
8 Carved devotional bracelet
9 Carved acorn
10 Carved acorn container
11 Carved brooch
12 Carved pair of earrings
13 Carved pipe bowl
14 Carved eating utensils
15 Fishing line handle
16 Stick pin
17 Heart-shaped stick pin
18 Carved Maltese cross
19 Carved buttons, monogrammed
20 Carved box
21 Pendant with masonic insignia
22–26 Carved rings
27 Carved spoon
28 Spoon, carved with the name of its owner, W. B. Davidson
29 Miniature boots
30 Miniature tables and chairs
31 Candlestand
32 Miniature shoes
33 Carved link necklace
34 Comb
35 and 36 Watch chains
37 Carved link chain
38 Woman's collar made from macramé

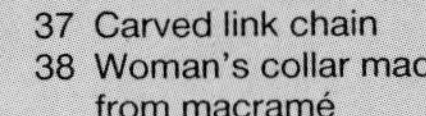

Artifacts courtesy of: The Museum of the Confederacy, Richmond, Va

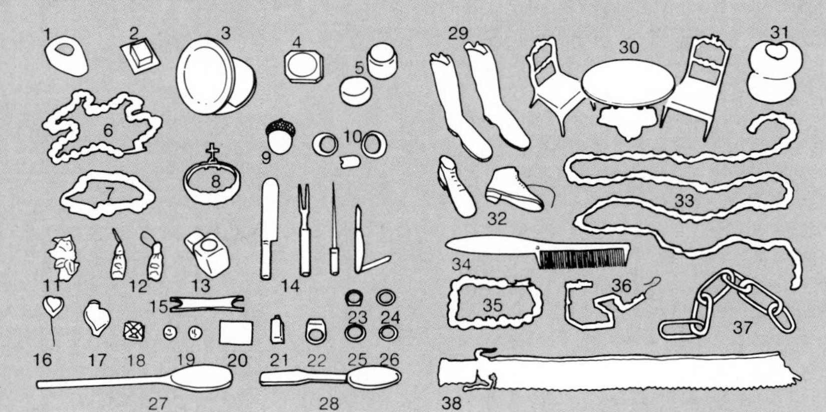

Confederate prisoners, no "luxuries" were to be allowed. As a result, while thousands of men suffered from the disease, the $23,000 appropriated for vegetable purchase lay dormant in the Fort Delaware relief fund.

Conditions were just as bad in the South. Surgeon Joseph Jones at Andersonville reported that "from the crowded conditions, filthy habits, bad diet and dejected, depressed condition of the prisoners, their systems had become so disordered that the smallest abrasion of the skin, from the rubbing of a shoe, or from the effects of the sun, the prick of a splinter or the scratching of a mosquito bite, in some cases took on a rapid and frightful ulceration and gangrene."[18] All the prisons had hospitals, but Andersonville's was the worst. It comprised five acres of open ground outside the main stockade, and there stewards tended to men who languished under the sun on straw piles and boards. Even in Northern prisons like Camp Douglas in Illinois, the death rate in a hospital could be six a day. At Camp Sumter it was far worse. Stewards cleaned wounds with dirty water poured on them, forming pools on the ground where insects bred in the moist filth. Inevitably, millions of flies swarmed over the helpless patients, relentlessly laying eggs in their open wounds and sores. Scores of men went mad from the pain of maggots eating their way through their inflamed flesh.

Men who formerly had faced enemies with guns and bayonets, now had to contend with a new sort of foe, sometimes just as fatal: boredom. The hours of confinement crawled past, even more tedious, more empty, than the long days of winter quarters. No prisons provided any sort of organized occupation for their inmates; the men were left entirely to their own devices for recreation. Most of them wrote as often as they could, in part to pass the time, and in part in the hope that they would receive mail in response.

Above: While the overcrowding in Civil War prisons was universal, nowhere was it as apalling as in Georgia's Camp Sumter, or Andersonville. In all, 33,000 men were crammed into its 26 acres of open ground.

Below: For a prisoner of war, simply being locked-up in a more plentiful region was no guarantee of better health. Camp Douglas, near Chicago, had a high death rate among Confederates like these Rebels.

Paper, especially in the Rebel prisons, was in short supply, with many men asking their loved ones to send them blank foolscap with their replies. Censorship by authorities was so rigid that often letters were barely decipherable after the censor's eye had passed over them. Offending words or passages were blacked with ink, or sometimes even cut out with scissors, leaving the missive in tatters. In time, some prison commanders even had to limit the quantity of outgoing mail because of the overloading of work for the censors. "I found it impossible to permit them to write to everybody as they please for the reason that four clerks in the post-office could not read 2,000 letters a day", wrote the commandant at Fort Delaware.[19]

Commandants could not deny the prisoners religion, however, and the Almighty found thousands of friends and converts in the camps. Like prisoners of all places and all times, Johnny Reb and Billy Yank could take some measure of succor in faith. "Often while walking the floor of the prison", wrote a Reb on Johnson's Island, "I repeat the Lord's Prayer, and I find my whole mind absorbed upon the subject of my future state of existence or my appearing before God." In the

Above: At Camp Morton, Indiana, as in every other prison, the inmates had to fight all kinds of psychological enemies, including boredom, that malaise which came from the countless hours hoping for release.

Below: The tattered uniforms and weary demeanor of these Yankees, newly-released from Confederate prisons in Texas in 1865, shows clearly how the privations of prison could debilitate a once healthy soldier.

prison hells, meeting their Maker seemed all too imminent to the captives.[20]

For a few of the prisoners, nothing, not faith or singing or writing or games, could maintain their spirits. At Camp Sorghum, South Carolina, a New York prisoner looked upon men who sat "moping for hours with a look of utter dejection, their elbow upon their knee, and their chin resting upon their hand, their eyes having a vacant, far-away look".[21] After a time all of the miseries and hardships weighing them down simply became too heavy. Faced with their condition, short food and bad clothing, crowding, filth, the suffering of comrades, and the ever-present specter of death, some men simply gave up their grasp on reality or their will to live. "The sufferings of the body were not equal to the tortures of the mind", wrote a prisoner from New Hampshire. Uncertainty, isolation, ignorance and despair, "all had a depressing effect upon the mind, and finally many became insane."[22] Many more simply gave up and died.

For those who held on to their reality and their hope, it was endless talking that got them through the days, and they discoursed on everything. Newly arrived prisoners, "fresh fish" as they were called, were pumped mercilessly for what they knew of the war, of affairs at home, and most of all – the unceasing topic – of the prospect for an exchange. "There is considerable excitement this morning about Paroling", wrote a Minnesota private at Andersonville, "but it is all gass I reckon for there never was so ignorant a lot of men to gether since the World stood".[23] Yet for every hope dashed, another surfaced soon in its place. It was all they had.

When they tired of talking of the prospects for release, the prisoners turned their tongues toward the men who held them captive. Ironically, only two prison commandants of the war were later honored with memorials, though for very different causes. One was Colonel Richard Owen, in command of Indianapolis' Camp Morton. So well liked was he that after the war his former prisoners commissioned and paid for a bust of the colonel that still stands in the Indiana capitol. Equally admired was Colonel Charles Hill, commandant at Johnson's Island, a "good friend to the prisoners, all of whom esteemed him very highly for his kindness of heart".[24] Indeed, so kind of heart was Colonel Robert Smith, in charge of the Confederate prison at Danville, Virginia, that he is reputed to have become an alcoholic when he could not endure seeing the suffering of his ill-supplied charges.

Far more common, of course, were the commanders regarded as evil incarnate by their prisoners. It was a natural, if not always deserved, opinion, and the men delighted in telling sometimes exaggerated stories of Point Lookout's Major Allen Brady trampling prisoners under his horse's hooves, of Lieutenant Abraham Wolf at Fort Delaware exhibiting "all the mean, cowardly, and cruel instinct of the beast from which his name was taken", or of that "vulgar, coarse brute", Richard Turner of Richmond's Libby Prison, who kicked dying men for the fun of it.[25]

The men who told these stories had probably never even seen their prisons' commandants, much less witnessed the outrages alleged. Yet there were genuine atrocities enough, most often as a result of the incompetence of the men put in charge of the prisons. It was not, after all, the kind of position which tended to attract either the most gallant or the most able of officers. Indeed, unfitness for field service was precisely the criterion which determined that some men should serve as commandants. Political influence could also get a man a commission and a safe place running a prison, far from the dangers of battle. Colonel Charles W.B. Allison, commanding at Camp Chase in Ohio, was found "entirely without experience and utterly ignorant of his duties", by an inspector from Washington. Worse, "he is surrounded by the same class". However, the inspector noted, not without perception, "he is a lawyer and a son-in-law of the Lieutenant-Governor".[26]

Much worse were the guards. "We are under the Malishia", an inmate wrote of his guards, "& they are the Dambst set of men I ever had the luck to fall in with yet". Prisoners did not fail to comment on the fact that most guards were either men too old to serve in the regular forces or else too young, and most were looked on as "the worst looking scallawags". In Camp Sumter, Captain Henry Wirz reported that the carelessness and inefficiency of his guards was "on the increase day by day".[27]

With such a low opinion of guards prevalent throughout the prisons, it is no wonder that before long greatly exaggerated stories of their cruelty and brutality began to circulate. Guards shot men for no reason, went the rumors. With the vivid paranoid imagination common to the helpless in any situation, prisoners soon came to maintain that rewards were offered to guards who mistreated or even killed prisoners. Everyone heard tales of the escapees whom the guards hunted down with vicious dogs which were allowed to savage their victims. Most of the stories were unfounded, but it is certain that no

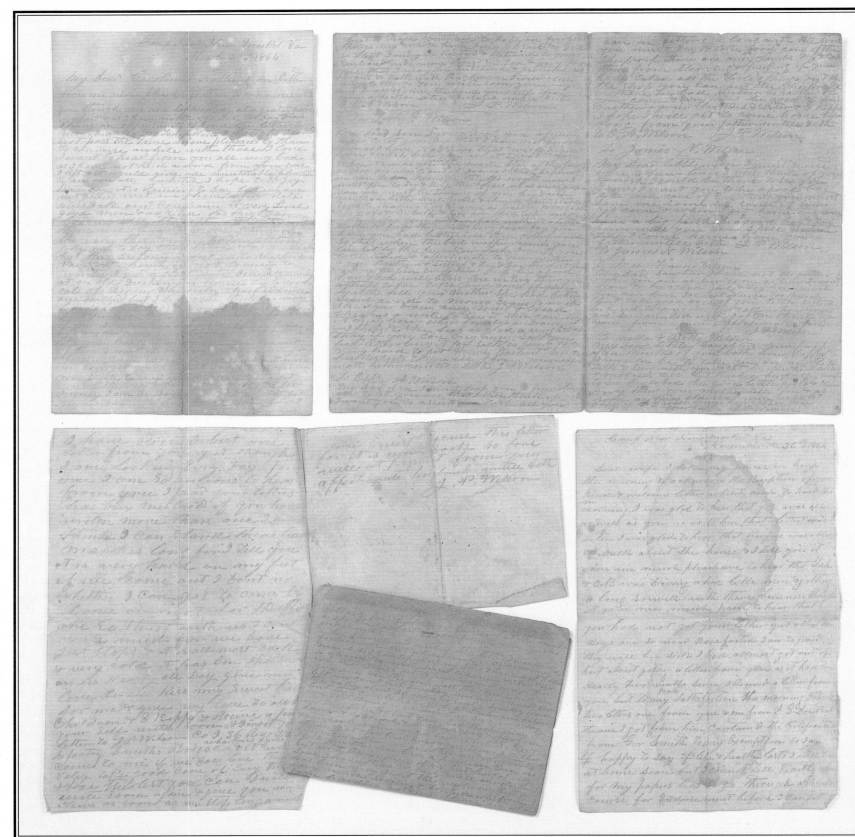

Confederate Soldier Correspondence

Letters written home from camp and prison by Corporal John P. Wilson, Company I, 36th Virginia Infantry during 1864-5

John P. Wilson was a typical Johnny Reb, only unusual in that his time in service was relatively short. He entered the war late, enlisting in October 1864, in Company I of the 36th Virginia Infantry. Just a month after this he was detailed home to serve as a county constable, but then rejoined his regiment and served with it until captured at the Battle of Waynesboro on March 2, 1865. Like so many other prisoners poor Wilson died of disease, after less than two months at Fort Delaware. Tragically, his death on April 28, 1865, came just as most other prisoners were being sent home. During his brief service, however, Wilson left behind a valuable legacy of his letters written home both from his regimental camps and from his prison cell. Like most soldiers, his primary words were expressions of longing for home and love for his family. Within them too can be read the concern of a soldier for his dying cause, and his anxiety at seeing the world he had known changed forever; changes though that he would never live to see.

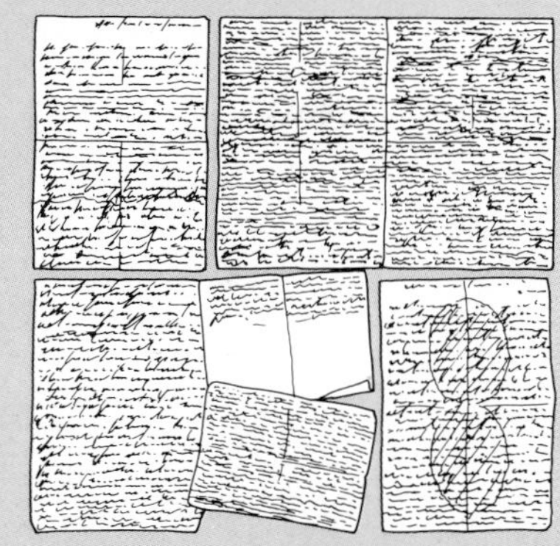

Artifacts courtesy of: The Museum of the Confederacy, Richmond, Va

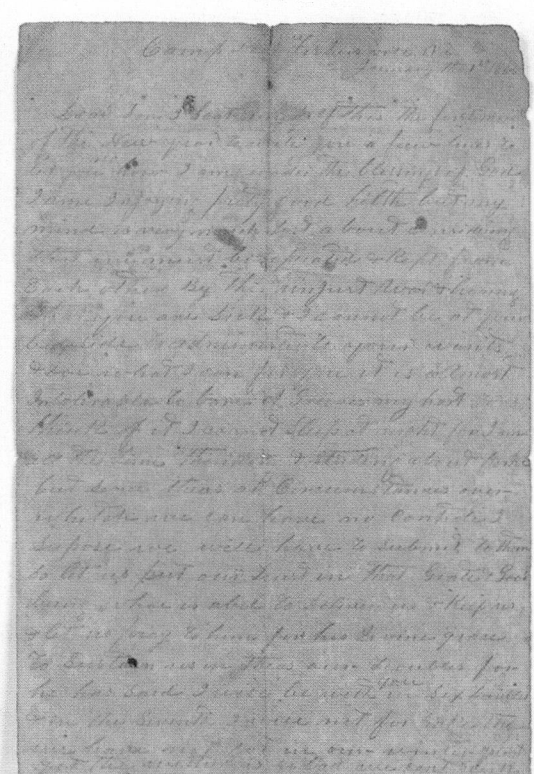

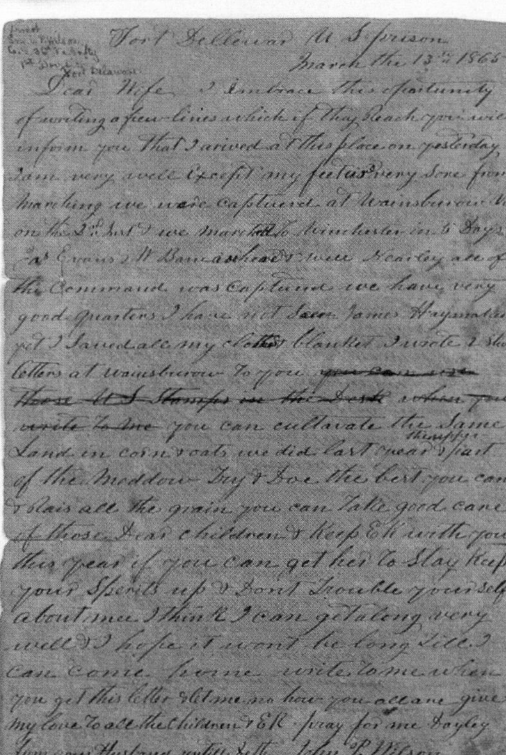

Fort Delaware U S prison
March the 13th 1865

Dear Wife I embrace this opertunity of writing a few lines which if thay reach you will inform you that I arived at this place on yesterday I am very well except my feet as very sore from marching we ware captured at Wainsburow Va on the 2nd inst & we marched to Winchester in 6 days [illegible] Evans & W [illegible] & [illegible] nearly all of the command was captured we have very good quarters I have not seen James [illegible] yet I saved all my clothes blanket I wrote 2 short letters at Wainsburow to you ~~[illegible]~~ when you ~~write to me~~ you can cultavate the same land in corn & oats we did last year & part of the meddow [illegible] & doe the best you can & rais all the grain you can take good care of those dear children & keep E[illegible] with you this year if you can get her to stay keep your sperits up & dont trouble yourself about mee I think I can get along very well & I hope it wont be long till I can come home write to me when you get this letter & let me no how you all are give my love to all the children & E[illegible] pray for me dayley from your Husband untill deth John P. Wilson
to E A Wilson

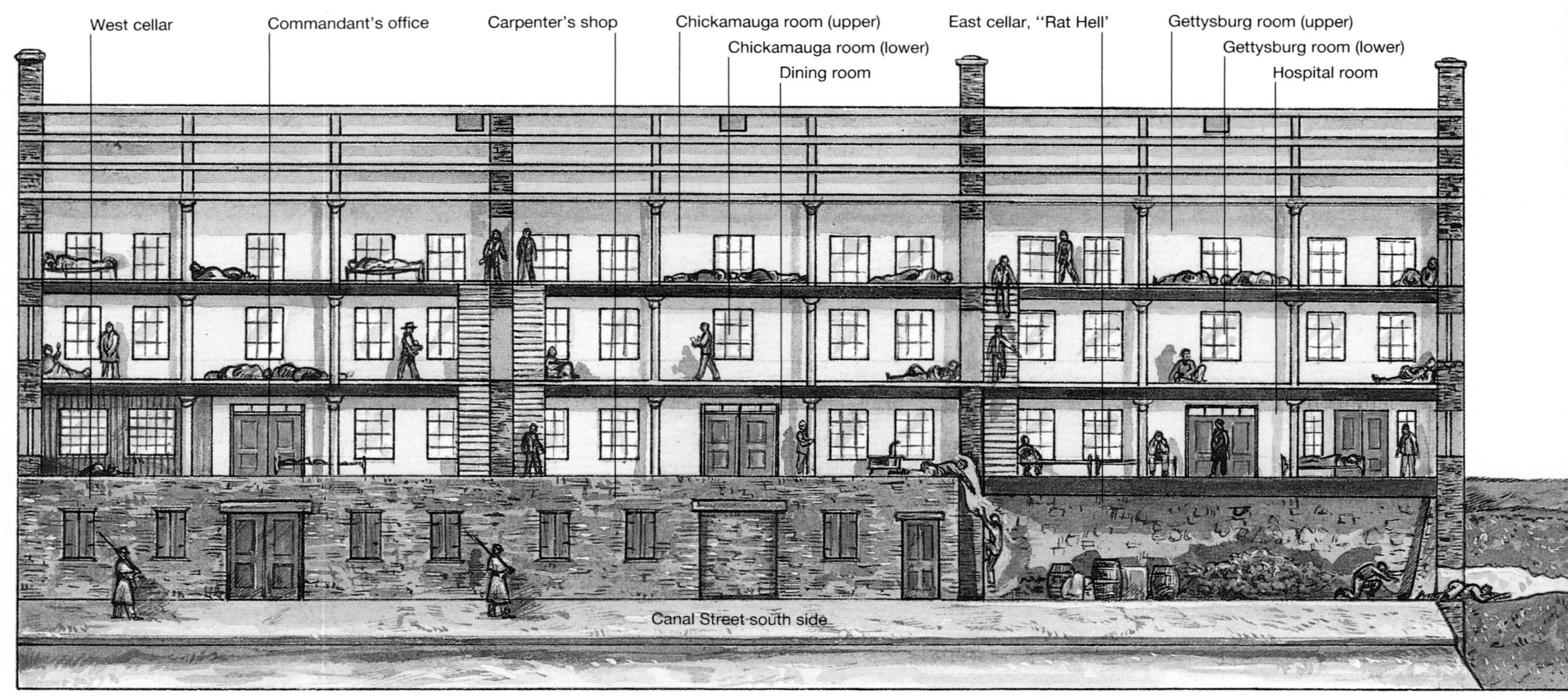

prisoner loved his jailor overmuch. The opportunity afforded to the guards to commit petty tyrannies without retaliation did indeed lead to frequent excess. "An ambitious coward", wrote one Texan in prison, "loves authority where he is secure from danger and can vent his fiendish nature on his fellow man". No Civil War prisoners later felt moved to erect statues of their guards.[28]

It is hardly surprising that, with all he faced from unintentional neglect to wilful mistreatment, many a prisoner decided not to wait around for exchange. "Freeedom was more desired than salvation", wrote a Yankee, "more sought after than righteousness".[29] Many men escaped soon after their capture and before reaching prisons. Once in the pen, thousands more were not deterred from making the attempt. Every prison had its breakouts, and many were successful, though more were not.

By one's and two's, several hundred prisoners made good their departure, though often only to be recaptured. Attempts of larger proportions usually failed because of the enhanced risk of discovery. In December 1864 the war's largest attempted escape involving enlisted men took place at Danville, but it went wrong almost from the start. Led by General Alfred Duffie and Colonel William Raulston, the men intended to overpower their guards, rush out of their warehouse barracks, free the rest of the prison's inmates, and then destroy the Confederate supply base at Danville and disappear into the Shenandoah Valley to rejoin the Federals. Unfortunately, an outcry arose as soon as Duffie grabbed a guard, and the warehouse was quickly locked from the outside. A warning shot accidentally gave Raulston a mortal wound, and the rest of the would-be escapees flocked back to their bunks. That was all there was to it, and Danville never experienced another escape attempt. Some tries were more successful, most notably Confederate General John Hunt Morgan's break from the Ohio State Penitentiary with several of his cavalrymen, but these were basically exceptions to the rule, for most of those who walked through a prison gate, the only way they left again was by release – or death.

Above: None of the prisons were pleasant places, but a few became infamous as "hell holes". In the North, Elmira, in New York, won such a reputation. One fourth of its Confederate inmates never left alive.

Below: Matching Elmira in infamy, and symbolic of the worst kinds of prison hardship, was Andersonville. Its horrid, primitive conditions are more than evident in this Confederate image of 1865.

Escape from Libby Prison, 1864

Beyond any doubt, the best known prison break of the war involved officers, and was led by Colonel Thomas E. Rose of Pennsylvania. Held in the old warehouse and ship chandlery of Libby & Son, and inhabiting large, spare floors empty of any comforts beyond a few ineffectual fireplaces, Rose and others planned a daring escape. Chiseling down behind a first floor fireplace, they managed to break into an unwatched basement room. From there, they broke through the building's foundations and began the long and tedious business of digging a tunnel out beneath an empty yard towards the apparent security of the buildings opposite. Every evidence of digging had to be carefully concealed from their Confederate captors. Due to a miscalculation, the tunnel was brought to the surface several feet short of their objective. Luckily, however, they managed to conceal the opening and frantically continue digging until the tunnel was complete. On the night of February 9, 1864, Rose and 108 others escaped through the tunnel and spread out through Richmond's streets on their dash to freedom. A total of 58 escapees managed to reach their own lines, while 48 of the rest including Rose himself were recaptured. Two of the escapees, however, were drowned trying to cross the James River. The only fatalities in this escapade.

Below: Many prisoners managed to escape, though rarely in significant numbers. An exception, though primarily among officers, was the daring break from Richmond's Libby Prison, shown here with its guards in 1862.

Most prisoners never attempted to escape. Their conditions simply wore them down mentally and physically to the point where they simply languished away in places little heard of before the war, but which rapidly became storied scenes of hardship and suffering. Probably the worst of all in the North was the prison camp located outside Elmira, New York, on the Chemung River. "If there was a hell on earth", wrote a Texan, "Elmira prison was that hell".[30] Badly located where the receding waters of the river left a stagnant pool in the compound after a flood, its condition was made the worse when the prisoners dumped their garbage and camp sewage into that pool. This "festering mass of corruption" went unremedied for months while Hoffman obtained careful estimates of the expense of draining it. When it was drained, he spent a modest sum to allow the prisoners to build their own sewer. Yet elsewhere the barracks were falling apart due to cheap green wood being used in their construction. Worse, Hoffman built a prison for half the numbers he was told to expect, with the overflow frequently having to sleep out in the open. When winter came, there was but one stove for every 100 prisoners. Morning roll call sometimes made 1,600 or more Rebels stand barefoot and ill-clad in the snow. As a result, one man in five had scurvy, and men died at the rate of ten a day. In October 1864, when the post surgeon almost boasted that deaths were down to forty per week, a guard lamented that prisoners were dying "as sheep with rot". Before it closed at war's end, a quarter of all of Elmira's prisoners died within its confines.[31]

Elmira and all the others could not match the infamy attached to a Confederate prison which was opened in Georgia early in 1864 to hold the overflow from Virginia's camps. Camp Sumter, it was called, but it quickly came to be known generally by its proximity to Andersonville. Poorly located and hastily built, it afforded to its inmates only such shelter as they could themselves built out of scanty materials. The South's transportation woes denied a sufficient supply of anything from reaching the camp. Its only water came from a sluggish stream which served as latrine, garbage dump, breeding ground for millions of insects, and drinking water for up to and exceeding 33,000 prisoners. It is no wonder that fully half of the prison population was on the sick list every month. Indeed, it was more a huge hospital than a prison, and its sheer size worked against the men it held. In population, it would have ranked as the fifth largest city in the Confederacy, behind New Orleans, Richmond, Charleston, and Montgomery, yet its 33,000 "citizens" were crammed into a 26-acre space that allowed each man a bare twenty-five square feet to live on.

The stories of apalling suffering that emerged from that dreadful prison are among the most heart-rending of the entire war. Some greatly exaggerated, many simply invented, still the substance beneath them all was more than sufficiently horrifying to earn the camp a place in the annals of infamy.[32]

All the anguish of Andersonville required someone to blame, someone to hate. And all the blame was laid upon its commander, Major Henry Wirz. He was an easy man to hate, a foreigner who spoke poor English, a man of quick temper and little patience. Unspeakable atrocities were laid at his feet. He paraded before his prisoners with a pistol threatening to shoot them at random. He intentionally withheld food and clothing and medicines. He lured men over the "dead line" inside the prison's stockade, a line beyond which no man was to step without being shot by guards. He was a fiend incarnate, they said. Few realized that he was nearly as much a victim as his prisoners. He had not built the prison. Winder, not Wirz, bore what responsibility there was for shortages, and he, worn down by the war and his responsibilities, died on February 7, 1865, before the conflict ended. As a result, many a prisoner in Camp Sumter turned all his hate upon Henry Wirz, and vowed vengeance if ever the war should end.

At last the suffering came to an end. Federal authorities recommenced the exchange system early in 1865, even while advancing Yankee armies were taking whole states from the Confederates and thereby freeing prisoners by the thousands. Finally the Rebel government stopped trying to hold on to their prisoners. Thousands were simply paroled where they were and released. After the surrenders of April and May, prison doors everywhere opened at last. For the returning Southerners, there was nothing to do but try to forget. But for the winners came the opportunity for justice against their tormentors. Hysteria and exaggeration of prison excesses in the South soon swept the Yankee press and pulpit. "I have seen prisoners knocked down by the guard with iron bars and clubs", asserted one New Englander, "and have seen Union men stripped of their clothing and ducked in the freez-

Guard, Salisbury Prison Camp

Just as in the North, where unfit men were used as prison guards to free the more able-bodied for the field, the Confederacy tried to assign convalescents to its prisons as guards. Sometimes, however, it simply was not possible, in which case, units understrength or otherwise not sufficiently organized for the field were given the duty instead. Salisbury Prison Camp in North Carolina was one such facility. For a time men of the 42nd North Carolina Infantry served as guards before being combined with the remnants of other regiments in order to make up an almost full-strength unit. Clad in regulation gray or butternut trousers and short jacket, their shoes, hats and overcoats were whatever they could find and scavenge. Most of them were no more happy to be at the prison than their prisoners. Except for the fact that they were armed they could have been on the other side of the stockade.

ing cold water".[33] Tales of every sort of torture were told, many of them imagined, more greatly exaggerated, but the public listened and believed.

Inevitably someone had to pay for the horrors. Winder was dead, and that left Wirz. In May 1865 he was arrested and taken to Washington where he was subjected to a sham of a trial before a military tribunal. Admittedly an unsympathetic man, probably not an able administrator, Wirz became the classic victim of circumstances. Protesting that he had been simply a soldier following orders, he was convicted of "murder in violation of the laws and customs of war". There had never been any doubt of the verdict, or of the sentence. On November 10, 1865, in a carnival atmosphere, surrounded by soldiers chanting "Andersonville, Andersonville" over and over, he mounted a scaffold at Old Capitol Prison and became the last victim of Andersonville.

Unfair as it was, Wirz' death was symbolic of unbelievable restraint on the part of the North, for he was the only Confederate to be executed after the four years of bloody, bitter war. Forty years later he became the second Civil War prison commander – along with Richard Owen – to be memorialized. A simple marker went up to his memory just outside Andersonville, commemorating his innocence of the crimes charged against him. Ironically, today, over the spot where he died, symbolic of the justice which he was denied, stands the United States Supreme Court.

So many had died. Over 211,000 Billy Yanks were captured during the war, and of them at least 194,000 went into Southern prisons. Of their number, 30,218 never came home again: more than fifteen percent. About 214,000 Confederates were sent north to Union prisons, and there 25,976 were to die. Over 56,000 Americans, thus, had expired painfully, isolated, cut off from the comfort of friends and family, locked away in the cold and festering prison hells of North and South. "Abandon hope, all ye who enter here", was supposedly inscribed above the sallyport of the prison at Fort Jefferson in the Dry Tortugas. It might as well have applied everywhere that soldiers languished in captivity.[35]

When hope did spring forth, it came in strange guises and often so unlooked for that it gave to the poor unfortunates a rare glimmer of good in what must have seemed to them an evil world. At Andersonville, where there was the least cause for hope, the crowding and lax sanitation polluted most of the compound's water. But then in August 1864, after a heavy downpour, a spring suddenly bubbled up from the ground. It was pure, clear water, and its seemingly miraculous appearance was taken by the hapless inmates as a sign from the Almighty that they had not been forgotten. They called it Providence Spring, and it flows still, long after the stockades and huts and all the other vestiges of that squalid horror have long since disappeared.

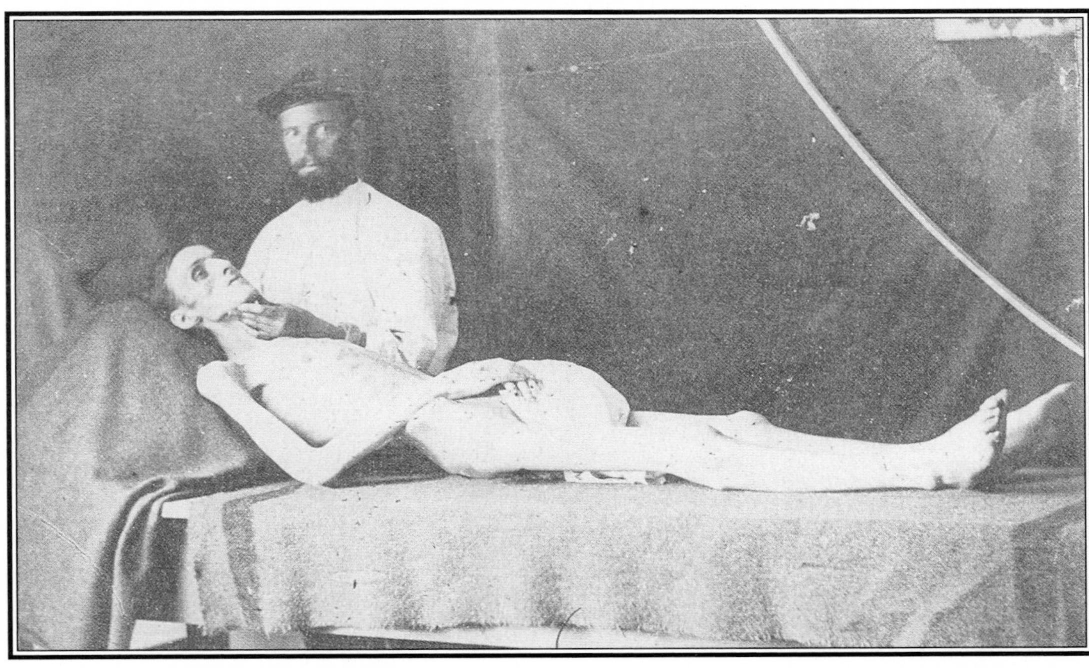

Above: So bad did conditions become at Andersonville and elsewhere that many refused to believe that the sufferings of men like this prisoner happened by chance. Accusations flew of deliberate cruelty.

Below: Over 56,000 prisoners, from both sides, met death in the camps from hunger, disease, cold or loss of the will to live. Their graves, like those at Andersonville, gave mute testimony to their suffering.

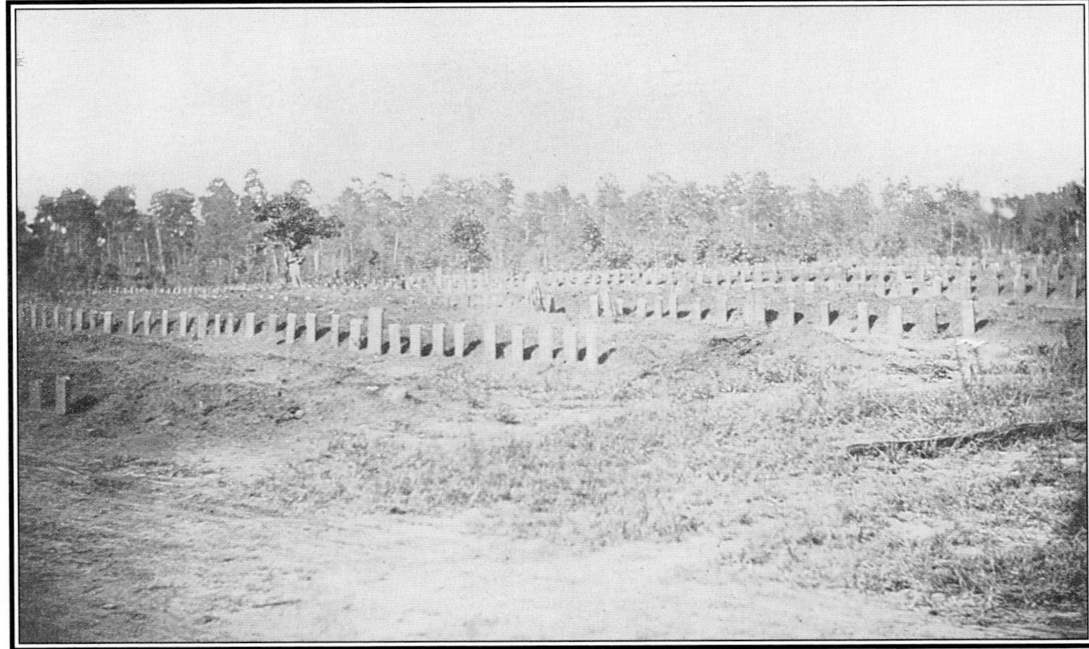

References

1 Walter Clark, ed.,*Histories of the Several Regiments and Battalions from North Carolina . . .* (Goldsboro, N.C., 1901), IV, p.677.
2 O.R., Series II, Vol. 1, p.6.
3 William B. Hesseltine, *Civil War Prisons* (Columbus, Ohio, 1930), pp.3-5.
4 William C. Davis, *Battle at Bull Run* (New York, 1977), pp.245, 253.
5 Hesseltine, *Prisons*, pp.7-14.
6 Alonzo Cooper, *In and Out of Rebel Prisons* (Oswego, N.Y., 1888), pp.39-40.
7 O.R., Series II, Vol. 4, pp.266-7.
8 Hesseltine, *Prisons*, pp.38-46.
9 Edmund D. Patterson, *Yankee Rebel* (Chapel Hill, N.C., 1966), p.120.
10 James J. Williamson, *Prison Life in the Old Capitol* (West Orange, N.J., 1911), p.68.
11 Frederic Denison, *Sabres and Spurs* (Central Falls, Iowa, 1876), p.196.
12 George Putnam, *A Prisoner of War in Virginia* (New York, 1912), pp.40-1.
13 John G.B. Adams, *Reminiscences of the 19th Massachusetts* (Boston, 1899), p.140.
14 *The Papers of Randolph Abbott Shotwell* (Raleigh, N.C., 1931), II, p.140.
15 James T. Wells, "Prison Experience", *Southern Historical Society Papers*, VII (July, 1879), pp.327-8.
16 Ted R. Worley, ed., *The Memoirs of Captain John W. Lavender* (Pine Bluff, Ar., 1956), p.132.
17 Anthony M. Keiley, *In Vinculus* (Petersburg, Va., 1866), pp.66-7.
18 O.R., Series II, Vol. 8, p.602.
19 *Ibid.*, Series II, Vol. 6, pp.809-10.
20 William N. Norman, *A Portion of My Life* (Winston-Salem, N.C., 1959), p.205.
21 Cooper, *Rebel Prisons*, p.267.
22 Leander Cogswell, *A History of the Eleventh New Hampshire* (Concord, N.H., 1891), p.531.
23 Ovid Futch, "Prison Life at Andersonville", *Civil War History*, VIII (June 1962), p.123.
24 Hattie L. Winslow and Joseph R.H. Moore, *Camp Morton, 1861-1865* (Indianapolis, 1940), p.262.
25 Military Historical Society of Massachusetts, *Civil War and Miscellaneous Papers* (Boston, 1913), p.181.
26 O.R., Series II, Vol. 4, p.197.
27 Futch, "Prison Life", pp.129-30; O.R., Series II, Vol. 7, p.708.
28 Val Giles, *Rags and Hope* (New York, 1961), p.221.
29 Abner Small, *The Road to Richmond* (Berkeley, Calif., 1939), p.175.
30 James I. Robertson, Jr., "The Scourge of Elmira", *Civil War History*, VIII (June 1962), p.184.
31 *Ibid.*, p.191.
32 J. Waldo Denny, *Wearing the Blue in the Twenty-fifth Massachusetts Volunteer Infantry* (Worcester, Mass., 1879), p.366.
33 Denison, *Sabres and Spurs*, p.317.
34 Holland Thompson, "Treatment of Prisoners", in Francis T. Miller, comp., *Photographic History of the Civil War* (New York, 1911), VIII, p.180.
35 O.R., Series II, Vol. 8, pp.946-8.

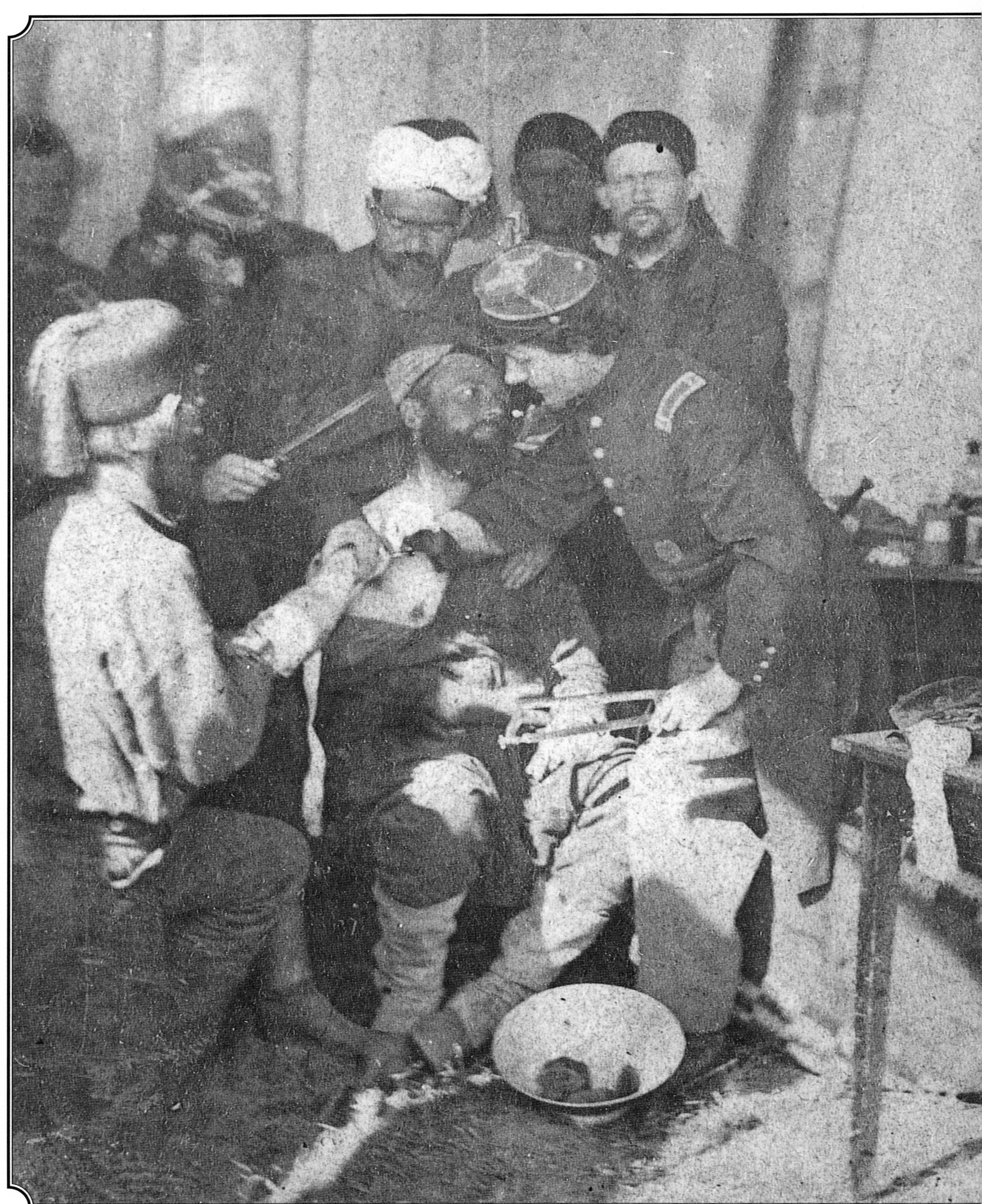

CHAPTER TEN

THE DEADLIEST ENEMY

The summer of 1864 was one of the worst of the war. Almost constant fighting between the armies produced casualty lists that staggered North and South alike, and severely damaged Union morale, even leading Lincoln to fear that he might not be re-elected in November. Worse, his armies were seemingly stalemated.

After crossing the James River, Grant narrowly missed taking Petersburg unawares, thanks only to the sluggishness of his subordinates and the brilliant defense of a scratch force assembled to meet him while Lee rushed to the scene. Futile assaults soon convinced Grant that there was no alternative but to lay siege to the city, and soon the most elaborate system of offensive and defensive earthworks ever seen in American warfare stretched around Petersburg and Richmond. Hoping to break the stalemate, Grant even approved a bold plan to tunnel from Yankee works across the no-man's-land to explode a huge mine under the Rebel works. It succeeded brilliantly until botched orders and timid commanders failed to exploit the hole blown in Lee's line. With that failure, Grant turned his attention to strengthening and tightening the siege, and cutting off one by one Richmond's supply lines by rail.

Sherman, too, had his problems, especially when he met a bloody repulse at Kenesaw Mountain in June. But then Johnston was replaced in command for his unapproved retreats, and General John B. Hood took charge, rashly leading a series of bold but unsuccessful assaults of his own. Sherman pushed him back, laid siege to Atlanta, and in early September forced its surrender. It was a success vital to Union morale, and made better by the victories of Philip H. Sheridan's cavalry as it laid waste to the Shenandoah.

But it came at a terrible price. Hospitals North and South overflowed with the sick and the wounded from all the fighting, turning America into a continent of suffering.

LURKING IN the shadows behind the pomp and glory, beneath all the patriotic fervor, the thrill of the battle, and even the serene camaraderie of the campfire, awaited enemies more dread and sinister than all the bullets on the continent. Ignorance and disease lay in store for everyone. The common soldiers of the war faced each other only infrequently. Yet every day they risked their lives in battle with the unseen minions of corruption and decay, sometimes the result of their wounds, more often from the simple act of living through another day in camp. They entered the lists armed only with superstition, protected chiefly by neglect. So pitiful was their armor that the Union Army, which enlisted more than two million men during the course of the war, went out in 1861 to administer to sick and injured – who would number in hundreds of thousands – with no more than twenty thermometers. No wonder that poet and nurse Walt Whitman would cry out that "future years will never know the seething hell and black infernal background, and it is best they should not".[1]

The kind of medical examination given to new recruits was often their introduction to the kind of medical care they could expect in the army, and was itself the first inferior obstacle that disease frequently vaulted in making its way into

Even though this scene depicting an amputation is almost certainly staged for the camera, the real operation would have looked little different to the terrified soldier facing surgery.

the camps. All too often the examining physicians seemed to pay little more attention to the man in front of them than that necessary to ensure that he had both arms and legs. One physician, a "fat, jolly old doctor", told jokes to the men he examined, then gave them "two or three little sort of 'love taps' on the chest", and squeezed their back, shoulders, and limbs. "I only wish you had a hundred such fine boys as this one!" he would say to the enrolling captain. "He's all right, and good for the service."[2]

In fact, thousands of soldiers entered the armies without ever seeing a doctor at all, while others were pronounced sound by men who knew nothing at all about medicine. If a man had been able-bodied enough to walk behind his plod or wield a shovel in civilian life, then so far as they were concerned, he could shoulder a rifle. Consequently, lax or ignorant examinations – or none at all – allowed thousands of ill and frail men to come into the military, many of them bringing their infections and infirmities with them to pass them along to their messmates.

No wonder that a short time after organization, the regiments began to suffer a high rate of attrition from sickness. Most units started the war around 1,000 strong. But by the time the 1st Connecticut went to its first battle, a few months later, it counted only 600 fit for duty. And the 128th New York suffered even more, numbering barely 350 men after only a year of active service. Some 200,000 men, over twenty percent of those enlisted in 1861 and 1862, had to be dismissed and sent home after their illnesses and handicaps manifested themselves in the field. Even then, the state of sophistication in dealing with unsound bodies was such that the best authorities hardly knew what to look for. In the South, always hard-pressed for manpower after the first year of the war, instructions governing who should serve and who should be rejected cautioned doctors to "exercise a sound and firm discretion and not yield your judgment in favor of every complaint of trivial disability".[3] Wisdom suggested that an active outdoor life in the army might even be a curative, and that many ailments were "strengthened and improved by the exposure incident to the life of the soldier". If a man had a short leg, a weak heart, bad eyesight, a stutter, bladder trouble, haemorrhoids, a hernia, even a missing eye or absent fingers, still however interesting his case might be to the doctor's "professional" curiosity, so far as the army was concerned he was fit for service.

Above: In every major city North and South hastily converted buildings soon became hospitals. Like Philadelphia's General Hospital, they saw thousands of soldiers arrive with every affliction imaginable.

Very few of these men had ever congregated with large numbers of others in their lives. Indeed, many had never even attended school, nor experienced sufficient exposure to others in childhood for them to contract and survive even the most rudimentary childhood diseases. Mumps, chicken pox, measles, whooping cough, scarlet fever, were entirely new to them, and what was usually a two-week inconvenience to a child, could prove to be fatal to an adult.

In three regiments from Mississippi in 1861, camp measles killed 204 men in just three months. A surgeon visiting the hospital found 100 or so men stuffed into a room with the patients lying on the hard floor, without mattresses or even straw, with nothing but blankets for comfort. Several were obviously close to death, vomiting, some with blood poisoning, while their condition was "something that astonished everyone, even the surgeons".[4] It was the same everywhere. In one Yankee outfit from Iowa, almost half its men fell out of duty with measles.

While there was nothing anyone could have done to prevent the epidemics of such childhood diseases that ravaged the camps, much of the other sickness that plagued the soldiers might have been avoided but for the ignorance of the era. What the campsite itself did not contribute to ill health, the carelessness of the men themselves supplied. Incredibly, it took years for some regiments to grasp the simple fact that sickness might be reduced – and the palatability of their water greatly enhanced – if only they stopped locating their latrines upstream of their camps. Often their campsites were chosen for an officer's convenience, or in some place where another regiment had bivouacked before, thereby saving them the trouble of clearing land. In winter they even sometimes inhabited the huts left by the previous winter's occupants, oblivious to the presence of the previous occupants' lice, fleas, fouled water, and fetid waste dumps.

Sanitation was a foreign word to almost all soldiers, and the men paid for their ignorance. Indeed, their behavior made their naivety even more costly. In an era of often exaggerated modesty, many men objected to using the regimental latrines, which were usually located out in the open. Others were too lazy to walk to the "sinks" as they were called. Instead, thousands simply relieved themselves where they stood, even in their own camps, or else walked behind a

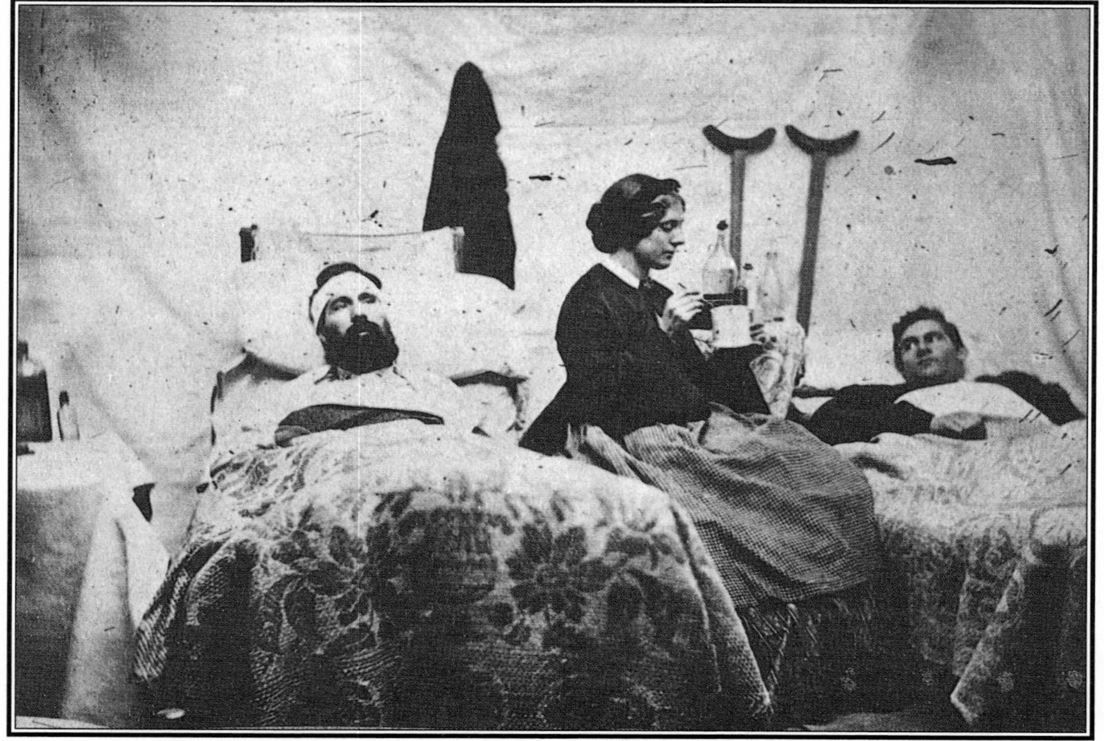

Left: To care for those who could no longer care for themselves, a women's nursing corps was formed. These nurses brought tenderness and sympathy as well as medicine and rest to the wounded and the ill.

Ambulance Corpsman and Hospital Steward, US Army

Circumstances very quickly dictated that a large number of special support services be created to help the enormous numbers of sick and injured. Out on the battlefield an ambulance corps was organized in an attempt to get the wounded speedily to the surgeons in the rear. Men too short or otherwise unfit for active duty became ambulance corpsmen, like the boy on the left. Their uniforms differed little from those of regular soldiers except for an occasional insignia. More specialized training was required for the hospital stewards like the man on the right. Given at least a smattering of medical education, their tasks were to tend the wounded, assist the surgeons and perform a number of other necessary functions several of which would be later taken by female nurses in the bigger general hospitals. Only the medical chevrons on his uniform jacket denote his branch of service.

tree. New men soon learned to watch where they walked, and even where they slept. One Virginian awoke one morning and rolled up his bedding only to discover that "I had been lying in – I won't say what – something that didn't smell like milk and peaches".[5] A Federal camp inspector in 1861 reported most Yankee bivouacks awash in litter, garbage, and decomposing trash of every description, "slops deposited in pits within the camp limits or thrown out broadcast; heaps of manure and offal close to the camp".[6] The excrement and castout garbage of hundreds of thousands of men turned the camps – especially in the heat of summer – into an olfactory nightmare. However tragic the war was for the human beings who had to endure it, for untold numbers of microbes and vermin it was a bonanza, a five-year feast with the soldiers themselves destined to be the dessert.

Army regulations did provide some instructions for covering the latrines and for camp cleanliness. But then, Union regulations also required men to wash their hands and feet daily, and to bath completely once a week, though in reality soldiers went months at a time without bathing. Consequently, Johnny Reb and Billy Yank simply learned to live with their unwelcome companions. They joked about the mosquitoes, claiming they could be heard to bray "like mules". Lice were reputedly found in clothing with the letters "I.F.W." ("In For the War") on their backs. Even in battle the men were sometimes seen using one hand for their weapon and the other busy swatting flies or scratching bites. "I get vexed at them and commence killing them", one Confederate said of the swarms of flies, "but as I believe 40 of them comes to every one's funeral, I have given it up as a bad job."[7]

Above: Sometimes whole regiments could find themselves hospitalized, or so it seemed. Those too seriously ill to be treated and released near the front went to general hospitals like this one in Washington.

Considering this world in which they lived, it is no wonder that the soldiers suffered staggering losses to the pestilences thriving in their midst. Malaria took a respectable toll, though the men knew it variably as "the shakes", the "ague", or "intermittent fever". "We are more afraid of the ague here than the enemy", an Illinois boy wrote home. Almost half of the 38th Iowa was hospitalized or killed by it, and over one million cases were diagnosed before the war was done.[8] At morning sick call, malaria on average accounted for twenty percent of those who fell out. No one suspected the pesky mosquitoes that bit them. Instead, doctors and men alike attributed the disease to the "poisonous vapors" arising from swamps and ponds.

Typhoid was an even greater threat. "We would rather die in battle than on a bed of fever", a Federal colonel protested, yet this was the fate of all too many.[9] The colonel could see them "jabbering and muttering insanities, till they lie down and die", but he could not find out why they died. They called it "camp fever", and never traced it to its origins in tainted water. In the Southern armies it may have claimed as many as a quarter of all who died in the war.

But of all diseases, the one the soldiers feared most, and the one to which their own habits most contributed, was the alvine flux. Typically they endowed it with a host of sobriquets – "diarrhea", "dysentery", "the debility", "the runs", "Virginia Quick Steps", "Tennessee Trots", and so forth. Most often they simply called it what it most demonstrably was: "the shits". More than one wag quipped that in this war "bowels are of more consequence than brains", and it was only part jest. Intestinal disorders killed more men than all the bullets fired in four years of combat. Soldiers lived in mortal fear of the diseases, and well they should have, for contracting one or more of them was a virtual certainty. One and three-quarter million cases were reported in the Union Army during the war, and that does not include the untold thousands that went unreported thanks to the soldiers' well-founded contempt for the remedies and doctors available to them.

It was no wonder. Often as not, the doctor did not make an examination, but rather left it to the patient to perform his own diagnosis by asking "what is the matter with you". For those who complained of dysentery, the standard prescription was a dose of "salts", a cathartic which, in fact, acted as a laxative, only making matters worse. Complaints that it had not been effective often produced nothing more than another, larger, dose of the same, and on top of that castor oil. The result was predictable. "You are realy now subject to disease", wrote one who went through the treatment, "and that is just the way that we had so many sick." Worn down by ineffectual treatment that reduced their resistance, many men only contracted other diseases. "Sick dogs are treated better than this", a bitter Yankee complained such treatment.[11]

All of these maladies were aggravated by the want of proper clothing and equipment. The soldier had but one uniform, and replacements

Above: Vast numbers of hospital tents arose, particularly in the North. This group at Kendal Green, near Washington, served men whose illnesses were not serious enough to require interior confinement.

Below: One of the sights that every man became used to was the cemetery, often located not far from the hospital. This one at City Point, Virginia, is pitiful evidence of the number of unidentified.

came infrequently. The result was worn garments, inhabited by all manner of insect guests, and not much inclination to bathe when a man was forced to put his dirty old clothes on once again.

Exposure out in the field, especially in the cold months, killed thousands. Many men simply froze to death. "It is really pitiful to see our boys at night sitting around their fires, nodding and almost asleep", wrote a Rebel officer. "The ground is too cold for them to lie down on, and their blanket is not warm enough for them to cover with".[12] Such exposure opened the door to infection even wider.

Below: Rebels had the same hospital experiences as Yanks, except that the scarcity of medicines made their ordeal much worse. Moore Hospital, in Richmond, suffered a want of everything but patients.

The soldiers' diet only added to the problem, for the concept of nutrition was as foreign as the commands in the French drill manuals. Reb and Yank alike received rations that were ill-balanced, ill-preserved, and ill-prepared. Surviving their own food was often a greater feat than escaping the enemy shot and shell. Most desirable was meat, but it was one of the least plentiful elements of the soldier fare. Perhaps that was a blessing, for whatever its form or manner of preservation, the meat came tough, old, and sometimes virtually rotting. So bad was it that one Yank declared, "one can throw a piece up against a tree and it will just stick there and quiver and twitch for all the world like one of those blue-bellied lizzards at home will do when you knock him off a fence rail with a stick."[13]

Much of the beef came pickled, but the men called it "salt horse". It was so tough, briny, rank when cooked, that one bunch of Yanks reacted to a particularly ripe issue of pickled beef by parading it through camp on a bier, then giving it a funeral complete with a military salute and volley over the grave. A Confederate joked that his men needed an issue of files to sharpen their teeth if they were to eat the the petrified beef issued to them. In fact, many ate their beef raw, for it was less tough that way, and many feared that it was only a matter of time before they were fed hooves and horns.

Yanks ate their meat pretty much as it came, but Rebs seemed to prefer frying several chunks of it in the ubiquitous grease in which they cooked everything. They added water, and sometimes vegetables to make a stew, crumbling into it some cornbread and calling the resultant mush "cush". The grease content only further contributed to the stomach ailments already besetting them, but the Rebs liked it just the same. Besides, the mixture helped disguise another feature of the meat ration North and South: passengers. Men joked that they never had to carry their own meat, for the maggots infesting it made it travel on its own, adding that "we had to have an extra guard to keep them from packing it clear off".[14]

Vegetables provided just as much opportunity for derision, and just as many chances of disease and malnutrition. Shipment of raw vegetables to distant armies was impractical in most cases, and so Yankee commissaries supplemented the soldier diet with dehydrated shredded vegetables packed into tight hard cakes. Called "dessicated" by the issuing sergeants, the men in the ranks dubbed them "desecrated vegetables", and more often referred to the cakes as "baled hay", for many believed that not a little grass and straw found its way into them. Prescribed procedure was for the men to immerse the cakes in boiling water, but the rate of expansion was so great that tall tales inevitably arose of men who ate their cakes dry, then began writhing in agony on the ground, in imminent peril of explosion as the cakes expanded within them. Consequently the men took fresh produce whenever they could get it, and few farmers' fields were safe in the harvest season.

Most prevalent of all in the soldier diet was hardtack, a large, dense cracker made of shortening and flour. Too stale to eat whole, it was generally broken up with a rifle butt or soaked in water or fried in grease to soften it. The men called the crackers "sheet-iron crackers", "teeth-dullers", and "worm castles" in reference to the weevils and maggots all too often found in the cracker boxes. "All the fresh meat we had come in the hard bread", on wag quipped, "and I preferring my game cooked, used to toast my biscuits".[15] A few playfully fired bits of hardtack across the line at the enemy.

Confederates also ate hardtack crackers, though wheat flour was in shorter supply in the South, and most Rebs ate cornbread instead. Yet it, too arrived in the mess tents barely palatable, sometimes full of mold and cobwebs. When the men in either army got their hands on actual flour itself, they had a field day baking their own soft bread, although not all of them knew how to go about it. In the 101st Ohio an issue of a barrel of flour sent the men wild. Some added water to it and kneaded it on their rubber blankets while others balled the dough on to their bayonets and tried to roast it over the campfires. "Some pegged the stuff to trees near the fire and swore at it", and most of it wound up wasted, though "we had lots of fun if we did go hungry".[16]

All of these privations could be borne so long as the men had their coffee. Most men were issued the beans themselves, either raw or roasted. It was up to them to find a way to grind them down for brewing. Some crushed them on rocks, and a few regiments were even issued special Sharps rifles that had coffee grinders built into the stocks. However ground, the brew was a ubiquitous companion. Rarely did a column halt for more than a few minutes before someone started a fire and made a pot of coffee. Billy Yanks had by far the best of it, for their supply was unlimited during the war, while their foe had to make do much of the time with substitutes like chicory or parched corn. Both sides drank it strong and without sugar and milk.

The men enjoyed few opportunities to better their diet beyond what the commissary provided. Most permanent camps had sutlers, licensed civilian vendors whose rates were all too often usurious in the absence of competition. Enlisted men came quickly to notice that the sutlers arrived with their pies and cakes and other delicacies just about the same time as the paymaster. The goodies stayed in camp, but the soldiers' hard-earned pay disappeared overnight. Packages from home also augmented camp diet, though what arrived in the boxes was usually stale or beaten about from travel, and frequently raided by government "inspectors" along the way. Generous boys often shared these prizes from home with their tent mates.

Whatever the sutler or homefolk could not provide, the soldier found for himself, usually at the expense of the farmers in the vicinity of his

Confederate Medical Equipment

Fighting for a cause in which everything was in short supply, the Confederate surgeon's collection of instruments, medicines, and accessories was always pitifully limited. Most of it was imported, and all of it was precious. Needles and scalpels could mean men's lives in surgery. And primitive though that equipment may seem, it was all that stood between the soldier and the grave.

1 Field medical kit
2 Surgeon's valise
3 Regimental medical chest
4 Surgeon's shirt
5 Forage cap
6 Surgeon's frock coat
7 Medical chest
8 Medicine kit
9 Medicinal bottles
10 Medicinal bottles
11 Stretcher for casualties
12 Leather case for *13*
13 Surgical kit for major amputations including: several large scalpels; a bone saw; several tourniquets; two or three probes; two or three curved needles; thread and a pair of bone cutting pliers
14 and 15 Two medical saddlebags
16 and 17 Tourniquets
18 Surgical pocket kit
19 Surgeon's pocket drug kit
20 Field bandage supplied by a ladies aid group
21 Surgeon's traveling bags

Artifacts courtesy of: The Museum of the Confederacy, Richmond, Va

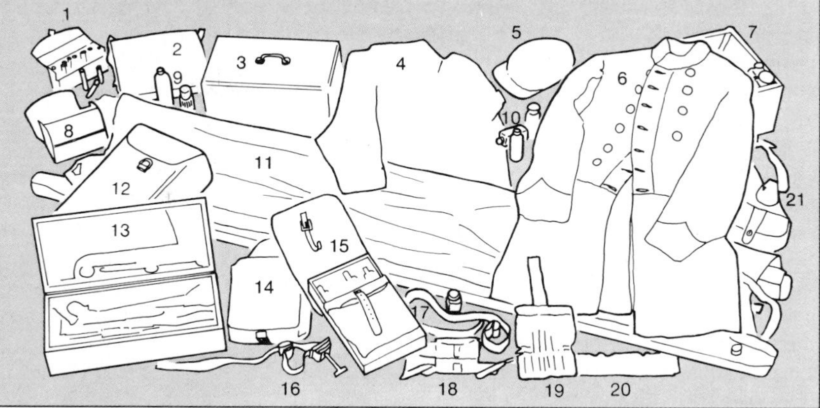

camp or march. Foraging was a universal pastime in both armies, and though sometimes actually punished by officers, it was most often tacitly allowed, and sometimes even encouraged. Men would often ask a hog to take the oath of allegiance to the Union. When it naturally refused, or else simply did not answer, the loyal Yankees had little choice but to kill it and serve it at their mess. Confederates felt the same way about chickens, jesting that on the march "we would not allow a man's chickens to run out in the road and bite us".[17] Consequently, chicken bite was one form of malady rarely if ever reported to the surgeons. The thinking on both sides in the war was that if the government supplied the basic foodstuffs in sufficient quantity, the men would get by satisfactorily. However, such was rarely the case. On the march or in battle, food became rare and of suspect quality. Sometimes men even scavenged corn from the feeding sites of army animals, hoping the beasts' rations might be less tainted than their own.

Hope, of course, was not enough. The rate of disease from all causes was epidemic and the endless sick reports and the bulging hospitals were ample testimony to the persistent problem. Keeping in mind that a single soldier could step out at sick call several times for different maladies, still the Union Army's sick rate for the first full year of the war was well over 3,000 cases reported for every 1,000 men in service. By the end of the conflict it had declined somewhat to 2,273, still a staggering figure. The burden this placed upon the armies' medical departments would have been overwhelming even if they had been well prepared for it.

No one was prepared, and once again it was the common soldier who paid the price. Attitudes were so ill-informed that in 1861 the Union's chief doctor actually believed that some theaters of the war did not need hospitals at all – thanks to their healthful climates. The physicians who served under him were equally ignorant. In that era a man became a doctor by spending at most two years in medical school, and often as not the second year consisted of nothing more than repetition of the first. Furthermore, anyone who could pay qualified for attendance. As for the rest of the practising doctors in the army, they had learned their trade by apprenticeship, learning

Above: Little more than a two- or four-wheeled open wagon, the battlefield ambulance came into its own in this war. Obviously posed, this image gives little sense of the urgency of its work.

the age-old myths and misapplications by watching older doctors who were just as ill-informed. Germs were yet unheard of, and understanding of asepsis lay years in the future. Most medications were useless, and some methods of treatment had not seen improvement since the days of Caesar. Surgeons looked upon bodily temperature as so unimportant that there was rarely a call for those twenty thermometers.

For a "violent Conjestion of the Stomach", poor Ben Pearson of the 36th Iowa endured "about all it was possible for me to suffer & live". The surgeons put hot bricks at his feet and oil cloths on his abdomen, thinking the heat would "draw out" the illness. "Cold clamy Sweat ran out at every poar cold as death", he remembered. "Oh such hours of suffering".[18] When pneumonia baffled physicians, they prescribed liquor and quinine, even laudanum, a tincture of opium. That failing, they might slash a patient's wrists to bleed him, or even pour burning alcohol on his chest. For intestinal disorders, in addition to the salts, calomel, turpentine, mercury, chalk, and even strychnine, were dosed. Watermelon juice helped a cold, so they thought, and tree bark and whiskey relieved malaria.

Army medicine could turn a man's stomach inside out. A New Hampshire boy sent a sample of a stomach powder administered to him home to his family. "It will cure any ails that flesh is heir to", he said, "from a sore toe to the brain fever".[19] So indiscriminately did surgeons administer opiates that they indirectly created a substantial post-war problem: the nation's first real bout with drug addiction.

Faced with these bogus remedies, many soldiers tried treating themselves, with about equal success. Morphine was available to anyone who could purchase it, and many men used it for a variety of ills. Whiskey and mustard plasters were even more popular. Miraculously, some hardy souls simply got better despite what they gave themselves, reinforcing the determination of thousands of sufferers to go "*anywhere else*

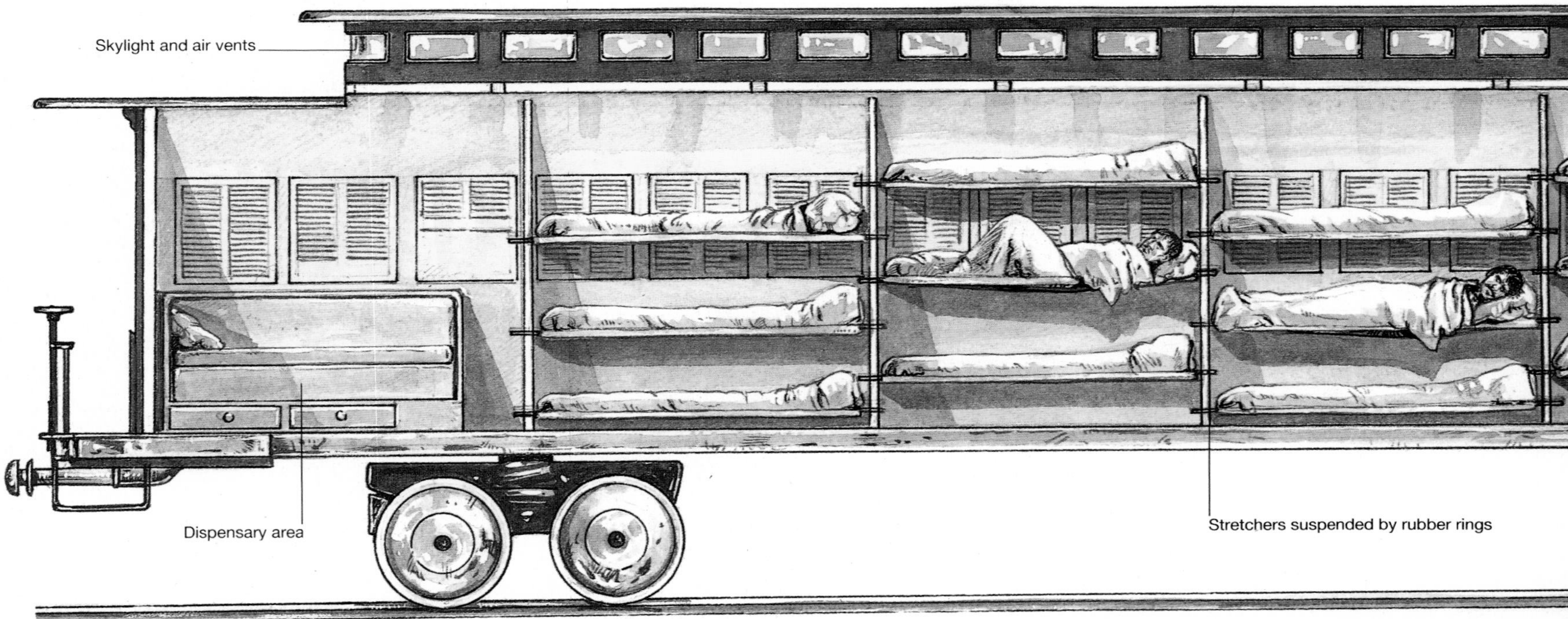

first" before entering a camp hospital.[20]

In their defense, the surgeons, so heavily outnumbered by the sick and injured, were dreadfully overworked. In the North there was but one doctor for every 133 men in the ranks, and in the South it was worse – one for every 324. These massive case loads could be death-dealing, and it is no wonder that alcoholism was a common complaint lodged against the doctors. Drink was their only relief, yet it also led to harmful myths that eroded the soldiers' confidence, such as the story of the drunken surgeon who went to set a broken leg, but performed his operation on the wrong limb, leaving the patient to die of shock. Worse, military bureaucracy frequently misused the few good enlisted men, sending those with no experience at all to the front line operating tables, while keeping many men with several degrees and years of practical expertise behind the lines rolling bandages.

No wonder the soldiers coined a host of epithets for their doctors, from "sawbones" and "Old Quinine", to "Loose Bowels". Yet when a man felt that he needed his physician, when he was wounded and bleeding, in pain, he wanted whatever treatment was available, and quickly. It was a veritable bedlam. "The horrors of the war are best witnessed after a battle", said a Vermont sergeant, and he was right.[21] Every building and tent available became a hospital. Wounded and screaming men were lying everywhere in their own blood and filth. Doctors were in short supply, medicines and opiates often the same, and even water to cool the parched tongues of the wounded and dying might be contaminated and so offensive that men retched at the smell of it. "The foul air from the mass of human beings made me giddy and sick", wrote a resident of Corinth, Mississippi, after a battle in April 1862 turned the city into a Confederate hospital. "And when we give the men anything we kneel in blood and water".[22]

Above: Once removed from the field by ambulances or comrades, the wounded went to a field hospital where immediate attention was given. Groups of wounded and amputees were a common sight at such places.

Rifle bullets caused more than ninety percent of all Civil War wounds, and artillery accounted for most of the rest. Whatever the agent of his injury, the soldier at first felt little pain on being struck – just a staggering impact that frequently sent him sprawling on the ground in a momentary daze. Then began an ordeal of one crisis after another.

Those fortunate enough not to fall between the lines, where they might lie for the duration of the battle or be overlooked in the confused aftermath, were carried from the field either by friends or litter-bearers. Their feeling was returning by then, and the pain could quickly escalate to agony. Clumsy bearers could make it worse as they jolted and often dropped their litters, on top of which all too many of the bearers were practised thieves whose first interest was in rifling the pockets of the helpless wounded on their stretchers. Ambulances were little better, with inadequate springs and uncaring drivers; the excruciating pain exacted by a rough ride could itself send a soldier out of his pain and on his way to the next life.

At the field hospital itself, a sort of triage separated the slightly wounded from those needing immediate attention, and from those beyond help. The first and last were placed aside, the former to wait, the latter to be made as comfortable as possible as they died. They were given opium or whiskey if available, and then ignored while the surgeons went to work with their probes, their knives, and their saws.

The size of the bullets that struck men in the Civil War, ranging from .36 caliber all the way up to a massive .75, ironically made some of the surgeon's work simple, insuring that any abdominal or chest wound was almost invariably fatal. Men with head or serious body wounds were usually set aside. Amazingly, about a quarter of these men actually recovered, very likely a better result than if the physicians had actually tried to save them. For the rest, any limb wound that did not shatter the bone had probably done irreparable damage to the nerves, tendons, or arteries, leaving the surgeon only to find the bullet and stop the bleeding, and three times out of four, amputate the limb.

The lucky soldier received some anaesthesia before the knife sliced into him. Doctors preferred chloroform when they could get it, putting a soaked sponge or cloth over the patient's nose

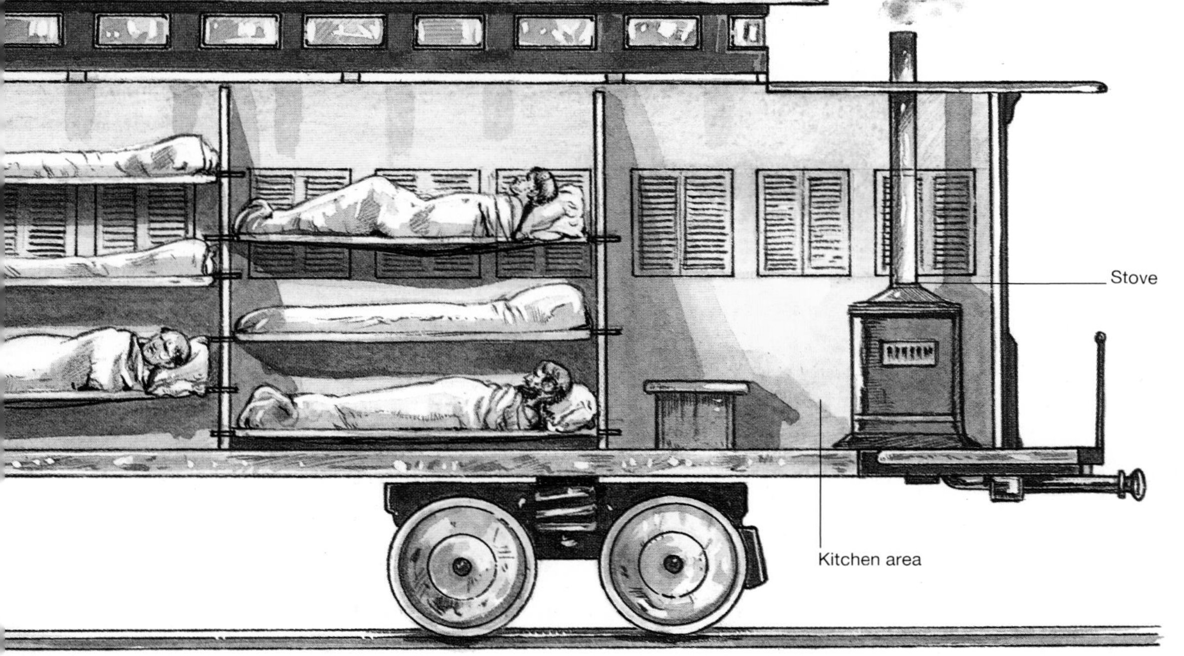

US Army Hospital Railway Car

Never before in an American war had there been such enormous numbers of sick and wounded, most of whom would require removal far to the rear for a lengthy period of treatment and recovery. Never before had America fought a conflict on such a huge geographic scale which would require the movement of wounded over vast distances. Just as the movements of the armies would come to depend more and more upon the railroad, so did the removal of the sick and injured. At first simple box cars or freight coaches were converted to accommodate wounded on litters, even flat cars were used for those deemed well enough to hold on. As the number of wounded increased and their condition became more and more serious, however, a more effective and comfortable means of transportation became necessary. The US Military Rail Road and army medical establishment finally came up with this hospital car, which in a number of variations saw wide usage wherever Union armies and railroads went. Some cars held thirty or forty men, borne on stretchers or litters arrayed along each side of a center aisle. Space was limited, but the car was ventilated through skylights in the roof, and was heated by one or more stoves. Suspension springs made the ride a little more bearable for those in pain, and attendant nurses on board could care for the basic and immediate needs of the men. The wounded had to be as comfortable as possible during journeys that could take days to complete.

until he went limp and limber. Ether, too, saw use, as well as laudanum. But all anaesthetics, especially in the Confederacy, could suddenly fall into short supply if the surgeons were not prepared for a major battle and its attendant casualties. Stories of men being given a dose of whiskey and told to bite on a bullet or a stick were widely told and exaggerated, but it happened just the same. Meanwhile, outside the operating tent, those awaiting amputations of their own could only lie and listen to the screams of those not fully anaesthetized, and watch the results of the knives' and saws' work accumulate. After Gettysburg some men told of seeing piles of severed limbs five feet high.

"The surgeons and their assistants, stripped to the waist and bespattered with blood, stood around, some holding the poor fellows while others, armed with long bloody knives and saws, cut and sawed away with frightful rapidity, throwing the mangled limbs on a pile nearby as soon as removed", wrote a Confederate cavalryman.[23] The sight was too much for many of his men, who vomited in their saddles when they passed by. The surgeons had little time, and often no inclination, to clean either their hands or their instruments, unknowingly spreading a host of diseases from one man to another. With hideously contaminated hands, they handled the raw flesh of new wounds, probing deep with their fingers. After the Battle of Perryville, Kentucky, in October 1862, one whole Yankee hospital was filled with cases of meningitis, osteomyelitis, and peritonitis, almost all certainly caused by the surgeons' filthy hands. Their diagnosis, however, was "poisonous vapors" once again, and their treatment was simply to open the hospital windows.

"Oh it is awful", a surgeon cried after the fighting in the Wilderness in Virginia in May 1864. "It does not seem as though I could take a knife in my hand to-day, yet there are a hundred cases of amputation awaiting for me. Poor fellows come and beg almost on their knees for the first chance to have an arm taken off. It is a scene of horror

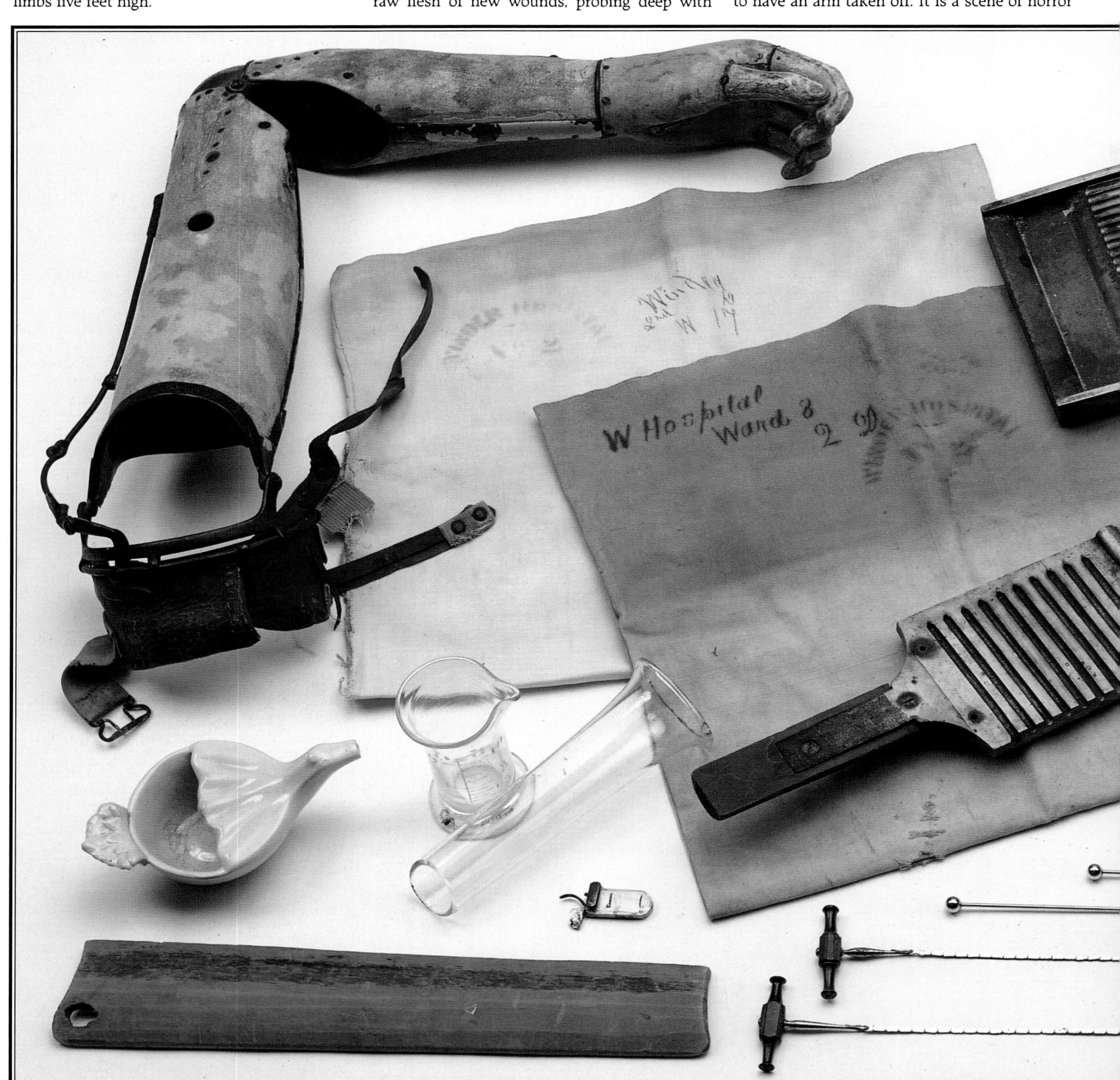

Confederate Medical Equipment

Much of what the Rebel surgeon and his nurses had to use was made by themselves. Most had to concoct their own pills and tablets, cut their own splints, sometimes even making their own crutches. Even the professionally manufactured equipment in their hands – as with their Yankee counterparts – was pitifully inadequate and ineffective, if not downright dangerous to the patients.

1 Prosthesis (or false limb), for left arm
2 and 3 Hospital linens
4 Pill mold
5 Measuring scales
6 Feeding cup for an invalid
7 and 8 Medicinal measuring beakers
9 Chemist's mold
10 Prescription scales with tin case
11 Pill tile, for handmaking pills, inscribed, "Dr R. B. Richardson"
12 Medicinal spoon
13 Scale weights
14 Surgical thread
15 Pocket surgical kit
16 Wooden splint
17 Spring-activated fleam (or bleeder)
18 Folding scalpel
19 Scissors
20 Probes
21 Surgical chain saws
22 and 23 Bone saws for undertaking operations such as major limb amputations

Artifacts courtesy of: The Museum of The Confederacy, Richmond, Va

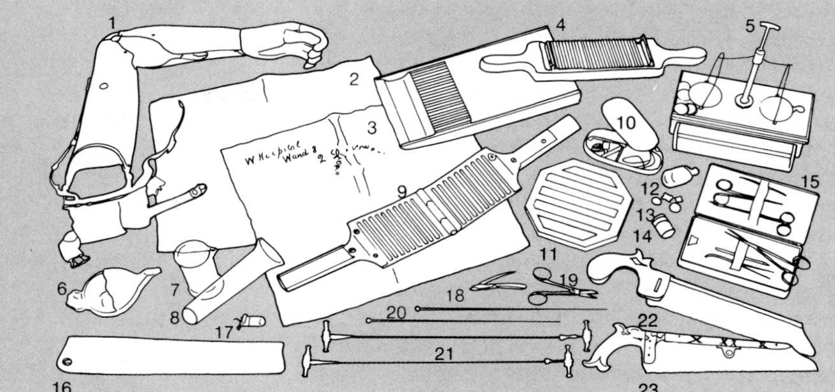

such as I never saw. God forbid that I should see another."[24] Most surgeons, despite their ignorance, tried their best for their men, and the pressure and the overwork took its toll on their own wellbeing. They could not rest so long as there were wounded, and after a battle like Gettysburg or the Wilderness, the men needing immediate attention could number in the tens of thousands. "We are almost worked to death", Surgeon George Stevens of the 77th New York wrote, "yet we cannot rest for there are so many poor fellows who are suffering". All too many they had to watch die. "They look to me for help, and I have to turn away heartsick at my want of ability to relieve their sufferings." "All my friends", he grieved, "and all thought that I could save them".[25] No wonder doctors took to the bottle.

Even if they survived the field hospitals, the wounded had another ordeal to endure as they were taken to the rear to the hundreds of general hospitals that grew up in most of the cities of North and South. Here, where the fatal infections and gangrene most often surfaced, they might spend months, even years, slowly recuperating. Richmond was a city of hospitals, with thirty-four of them in operation. One, Winder Hospital, held 4,300 beds, and Chimborazo was even bigger,with a capacity of up to 8,000, as well as a number of its own support operations including bakeries and factories, and even its own cattle and fields. Chimborazo alone treated some 76,000 wounded and ill during the war. Across the lines, Washington nurtured even more. There were twenty-five military hospitals in the Yankee capital, and even more in its environs.

The doctors running these established hospitals ranged from those too old for field service, to those too inexperienced. The nursing staffs were little better. Volunteer women helped, especially in the Confederacy, but in the North a gradually developing professional nursing corps took over those duties left to them. It was here that Whitman acquired his insight into the dark side of warfare's byproduct of suffering. "I go every day or night without fail to some of the great government hospitals", he told a friend. "O the sad scenes I witness – scenes of death, anguish, the fevers, amputations, friendlessness, hungering and thirsting young hearts, for some loving presence." He had to keep himself constantly busy to keep from weeping, though the kindness and comfort he could give to the suffering rewarded him for his turmoil. "I find I supply often to some of these dear suffering boys in my presence and magnetism that which nor doctors, nor medicines, nor skill, nor any routine assistance can give."[26]

With men in short supply, and needed in the armies, women came forward to help treat the wounded and ill. While most went through the war unnoticed, some like Dorothea Dix and Clara Barton achieved considerable fame, and began careers which led to great strides in health care after the war. Mostly, they were volunteers, though Barton organized a corps of nurses to her exacting standards, which included the stricture that no nurse should be too pretty.

The situation in Richmond remained less formal throughout the war, and the male opposition to female nurses was harder to overcome. A middle-aged Jewish widow named Phoebe Pember was not to be deterred, however. Refusing to take no for an answer, she was appointed Chimborazo Hospital's first female hospital matron and worked there for the rest of the war. She

Above: What bullets did not do, infection often did. This boy will shortly lose his foot due to the gangrenous infection that has set in. It will save his life, but for many amputees that was small consolation.

Below: For all too many the amputation of a limb was the only way to deal with shattered bones and torn flesh. For an unfortunate few, more than one limb was lost. In the 1860s, his future was grim.

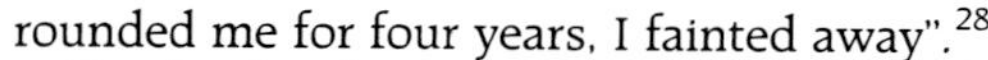

found herself, "in the midst of suffering and death, hoping with those almost beyond hope in this world; praying by the bedside of the lonely and heart-stricken; closing the eyes of boys hardly old enough to realize a man's sorrows." Faced with all that, she could not be bothered with nineteenth-century conventions of propriety in caring for a man's body. "A woman *must* soar beyond the conventional modesty considered correct under different circumstances", she said. The ordeal of a woman's experience would place her above these pedestrian considerations. "If the fire through which she passes does not draw from her nature the sweet fragrance of benevolence, charity, and love – then indeed, a hospital has no fit place for her!"[27]

Certainly Phoebe Pember earned her place at Chimborazo. Nothing so typifies the sacrifice and anguish of those treating the men, as a cold night in 1863 that she spent with a boy named Fisher. He was a special favorite on her ward, a boy badly wounded in the leg who had escaped amputation and, ten months later, was taking his walk up and down between the rows of beds. "He had remained through all his trials, stout, fresh and hearty, interesting in appearance, and so gentlemannered and uncomplaining that we all loved him", she wrote. But this night she was called to his side to find a jet of blood spurting from his leg. The walk had unsettled a jagged bit of bone and severed an artery. At once she put her finger on the wound to stop the bleeding, then called for the surgeon on duty. He came, shook his head, and pronounced the artery too deeply encased in the fleshy part of the leg to be repaired. The boy must perish.

"Long I sat by the boy", she later wrote. At length she told him what the doctor had confided to her, that in the prime of life, young Fisher was going to die. He took the news with his usual equanimity, gave her instructions for informing his mother, then looked in her eyes.

"How long can I live?"

"Only as long as I keep my finger upon this artery", she replied.

For a long pause he was silent, while she wondered what passed through his mind. Finally he calmly spoke again.

"You can let go."

But she could not, "not if my own life had trembled in the balance". Her eyes filled with tears, her own blood rushed to her head and pounded in her ears, her lips went cold, but she could not make herself let go and condemn the boy. Finally "the pang of obeying him was spared me, and for the first and last time during the trials that surrounded me for four years, I fainted away".[28]

Phoebe Pember's story was typical of those who tried to care for the suffering and relieve their pain. Fisher's was the tale of hundreds of thousands who faced and met disease, wounds, and death manfully – and often cheerfully. Their numbers spoke for themselves. In the course of the war, 360,222 Union soldiers died, fully a quarter million of them from disease and infection of their wounds. Just over a quarter million Confederates perished in the conflict, three-quarters of them from sickness rather than from combat.

The fact is, when they went into battle, their likelihood of being wounded was high. When they were in camp, their odds of contracting some disease were even higher. The bullets that struck them hit with new and powerful impact. The organisms that attacked them were unknown and untreatable as yet. Wherever they went, Johnny Reb and Billy Yank stood in harm's way, and the treatments available to them afterwards were sometimes as dangerous as the enemies that sent them to the infirmaries.

For all their suffering, little in the way of medical advancement came as a result to temper the cost paid. More efficient hospital organization, and the advent of female nursing did evolve, as did some rudimentary understanding of the role of cleanliness in preventing disease. Evacuation of the wounded took a giant leap forward in speed and efficiency thanks to a reorganized ambulance corps in the North. But these were modest gains when measured against the price. The real medical lessons of this war would not be learned for decades, long after it was too late for the hundreds of thousands who perished in the "seething hell and black infernal background" of this conflict.

Below: The future could look very bleak to the soldier who lost his arms or his legs. Artificial limbs like these were in some use by then, offering to the disabled the command of a few simple tasks like eating.

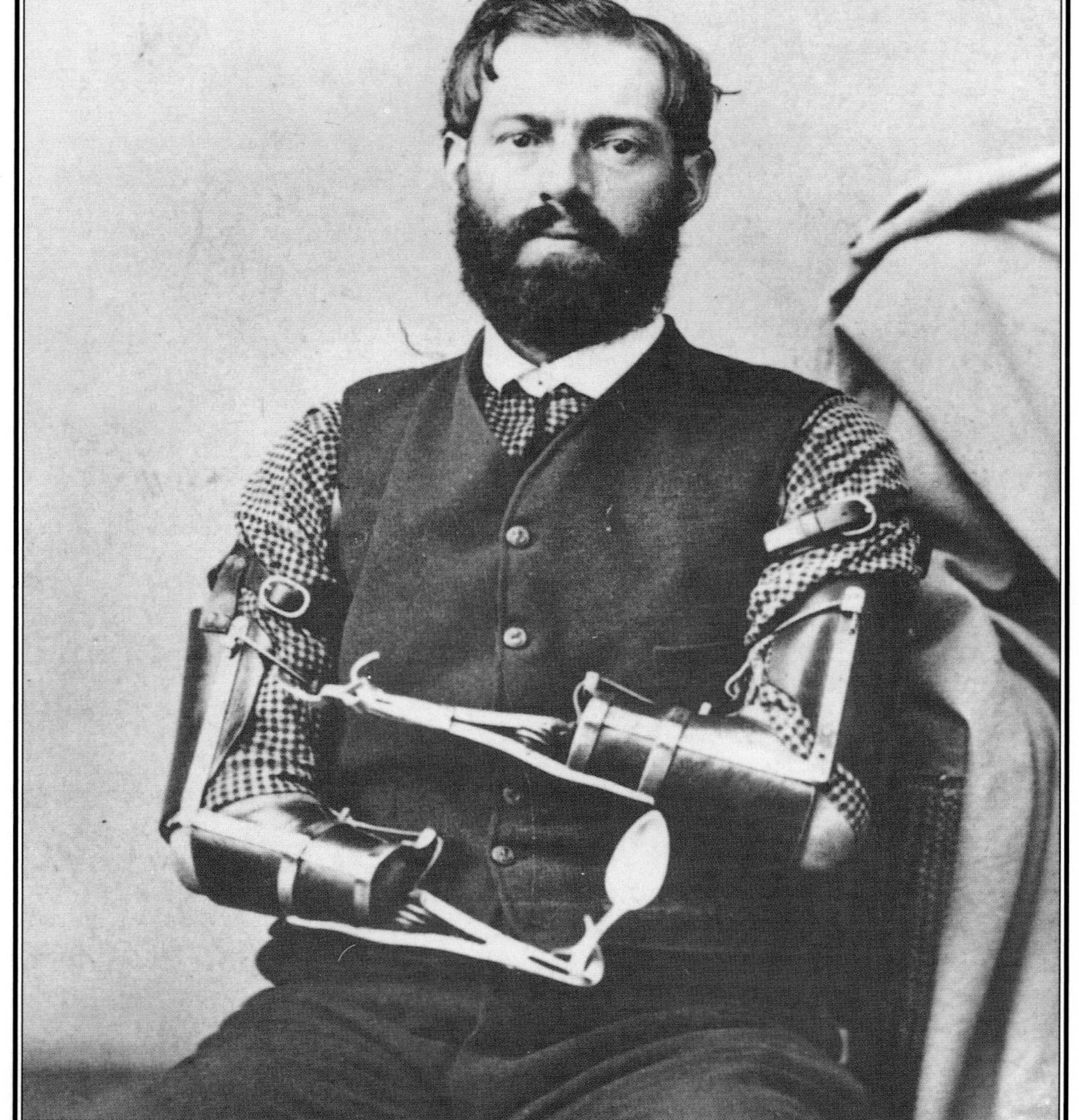

References

1 Walter Lowenfels, ed., *Walt Whitman's Civil War* (New York, 1961), pp.181-2.
2 Wiley, *Billy Yank*, p.23.
3 Wiley, *Johnny Reb*, p.245.
4 L.J. Wilson, *The Confederate Soldier* (Fayetteville, Ark., 1902), pp.19-20.
5 Wiley, *Johnny Reb*, p.248.
6 Wiley, *Billy Yank*, p.127.
7 Wiley, *Johnny Reb*, p.249.
8 Wiley, *Billy Yank*, p.133.
9 *Ibid.*, p.135.
10 *Ibid.*, p.136.
11 Paul J. Engle, ed., "A Letter from the Front", *New York History*, XXXIV (1953), pp.206-7.
12 Wiley, *Johnny Reb*, p.247.
13 Wiley, *Billy Yank*, p.240.
14 *Ibid.*
15 *Ibid.*, p.238.
16 L.W. Day, *Story of the One Hundred and First Ohio Infantry* (Cleveland, 1894), pp.77-8.
17 John O. Casler, *Four Years in The Stonewall Brigade* (Guthrie, Okla., 1893), p.78.
18 "Benjamin P. Pearson's Civil War Diary", *Annals of Iowa*, XV (1926), p.520.
19 Wiley, *Billy Yank*, p.139.
20 Wiley, *Johnny Reb*, p.267.
21 George H. Scott, "Vermont at Gettysburg", *Proceedings of the Vermont Historical Society*, I (1930), p.73.
22 Wiley, *Johnny Reb*, p.263.
23 William W. Blackford, *War Years With Jeb Stuart* (New York, 1870), pp.27-8.
24 George T. Stevens, *Three years in the Sixth Corps* (New York, 1870), pp.343-4.
25 *Ibid.*, pp.344-5.
26 Lowenfels, *Whitman*, p.293.
27 Phoebe Y. Pember, *A Southern Woman's Story* (Jackson, Tenn., 1959), pp.45, 146.
28 *Ibid.*, pp.66-8.

CHAPTER ELEVEN

On The March

In October 1864, with Atlanta lost, Hood pulled his beaten army away from Sherman and moved against the Federals' extended supply line. That done, and in the hope of drawing Sherman away from his base in Atlanta, Hood moved north. Initially the plan worked, but in order completely to achieve his objective, Hood decided to launch an invasion of Tennessee, hoping to regain possession of the eastern half of the state, recruit soldiers for his army, obtain supplies, and force Sherman to give up Atlanta.

Hood moved swiftly north, followed not by Sherman, but by Thomas and one corps of the Army of the Cumberland, and John M. Schofield and his Army of the Ohio. Unfortunately, Hood unwisely delayed his advance into Tennessee for three weeks, giving the Federals time to mass against him. Several weeks of maneuver followed as Hood marched toward Nashville in the heart of the state. Schofield withdrew before him, until he stopped at Franklin, and there on November 30 Hood attacked in the late afternoon in one of the bloodiest battles of the war. Six Confederate generals died, and by nightfall Schofield had to retire. But he had held Hood for a day while Thomas strengthened the defenses around Nashville, where Schofield soon joined him. On December 15-16 Hood attacked ferociously, and perhaps foolishly, virtually shattering his army in what would be the last major battle west of the Alleghenies.

Meanwhile, freed of the threat of Hood, Sherman left Atlanta to complete his severing of the Confederacy by marching across Georgia towards Savannah and the sea. In a progress virtually unimpeded, he took Savannah in December. Unlike the men of the Army of the Potomac, who spent the balance of 1864 in the tedium of the trenches around Petersburg, as they tramped on the march Sherman's men saw every day the sights of a world unknown to them.

SINCE THE overwhelming majority of young men who entered the ranks, North or South, were farmboys who had rarely if ever left their home counties, the trip to the war zone had about it the air of a grand tour. The men's eyes were opened to a host of scenes they had never dreamed of seeing. Even the manner of their travel was a "wonderment" to them for many had not even seen locomotives or steamboats, much less thought ever of riding them. When one Wisconsin lad made the trip from Madison to La Crosse by train, he had to confess that "it was a new experience for me". He sat awake the whole time. "I was afraid we were off the track every time we crossed a switch or came to a river."[1] Others going by boat felt similar experiences at the strange sounds and belching engines of the paddlewheelers. By the time they reached their destinations, most boys already agreed with the Ohioian who wrote home that "since I seen you last I hav seen the elephant". After a day and a night on a steamboat, and another hair-raising day on a train, he confessed that "we past through some of the damdes plases ever saw by mortel eyes". Some "god dames hills" he found to be as "dark as the low regeons of hell". When passing through a long tunnel, the train hit a heavy boulder on the track and "if the engen had not bin so hevy we would hav all went to hell . . . or some other seaport".[2] That was a lot of experience for a plowboy who had never been away from home.

Even before their trips, the boys could not help but be impressed by the send-off their towns gave them. Bands, cheering citizens, endlessly droning politicians, and bevies of handkerchief waving girls, bid them fulsome patriotic farewells. And once on the trains and boats, they were often met at succeeding towns by more of the same. "At the towns the girls swarmed on the

Daring Yankees take the view from Chattanooga's scenic Lookout Mountain, the most photographed spot of the war. Never had so many Americans turned tourist in their own land.

platforms to ask the boys for their pictures and to kiss the best looking ones", one Yankee remembered. A little French fellow got the most kisses, being held by his legs as he leaned out the train windows while other soldiers on the platforms lifted the ladies to his lips. "It was fun anyway", said a fellow soldier.[3]

Generally the young Yankees traveled farther, and saw a lot more of the country than did their foes-to-be, especially those boys from Ohio or Illinois who went to the front in Virginia early in the war. Chicago, Pittsburgh, Philadelphia, Baltimore, and Washington, were all sights for which farm life had not prepared them. In Philadelphia they were entertained at the Cooper's Shop, a volunteer hostelry that fed over 87,000 soldiers in its first year of operation. Pittsburgh became famous for the hot coffee that met the troop trains. All of the cities were overpowering in their sheer size and bustle. For many it was too much. A boy from rural New York complained that "Since I left Ninevah everything has been new, but I must say deliver me from citty life".[4]

Oddly enough, the nation's capital, the seat of the war and the burgeoning Union armies, disappointed many, though almost every soldier who came there could not help giving himself up to a bit of touring. Here were the great public buildings, the Capitol and the executive mansion. Here were the unfinished Washington Monument, the Navy Yard with its powerful warships. Here were tens of thousands of young men gathered to march against the Rebellion. And here a common soldier could even catch a glimpse of President Abraham Lincoln as he walked the Capital's streets or reviewed the new regiments. "We strolled from one end of the city to the other", wrote a Boston lad. Entering the Capitol, he wandered through its picture gallery, then climbed the steps to the dome and "had a fine view of Washington and the neighborhood, but I was struck with the mean appearance of the city of Washington with the exception of the Government Buildings". After all he had seen somewhat smugly he concluded that "there is not a building in the whole city which can be called a good one in comparison with the Stores and dwelling houses of Boston".[5]

Above: The experience of going off to war was an eye-opening one for young Yankees like these boys lined up somewhere in Mississippi. The South was a completely new world to them, hostile, yet exciting.

Below: These Rebs encamped near Pensacola, Florida, in April 1861, were seeing new parts of the world for the first time. There were boys from Mississippi who had never seen an ocean before, or a palmetto.

The men this self-important brahmin was about to fight felt much the same in their way, and saw the same "elephant" for the most part. Given the South's limited transportation facilities, Confederates more often rode to the seat of war in boxcars, into which they irreverently knocked holes in order to provide ventilation, as well as a means of viewing the passing countryside. Civilians watching as the trains rolled by, thought the boxcars, with soldiers' heads sticking out of their holes, looked like poultry wagons loaded with chickens.

For the Southern boys, the great wonders were the Mississippi River and its cities like Memphis and New Orleans, or Atlanta, Charleston, and of course Richmond. The distances traveled were just as great as for Billy Yank, though more often than not the journey took much longer thanks to the inadequate rail and river transportation available. It took one Texas company a full month to get from San Augustine to Richmond. Rebels, too, met with enthusiastic crowds that cheered them on and showered them with gifts, pies and goodies, and not a few kisses. Like their foe to the north, they would also find that as the war ground onward, the enthusiasm grew less and less, and in time many civilians would meet their passing only with scowls, regarding the soldiers now as competitors for the limited resources of the hard-pressed Confederacy.

But in 1861 all was fresh and gay. "I have Saw a rite Smart of the world Sence I left home", a North Carolinian from Buncombe County wrote to his father in the first days of the war, "But I have not Saw any place like Buncomb and henderson yet".[6] Confederates, too, could be just a bit chauvinistic about the merits of their home towns compared with those of the outside world. Yet most were awed by what they saw, even urging their brothers and friends back home to enlist so that they, too, might see and experience this great new world opening before them. This business of going to war and seeing the world – or the 'elephant' – was an experience of a lifetime not to be missed.

The basics of that experience were largely the same for Yank and Reb, differing chiefly in details and, of course, from the fact that through almost all of the war, Federals were invaders and Confederates were operating in their homeland. Yet the fact that Rebels operated in friendly territory did not remove the hardships or the dangers from their march to join their armies, or those armies' march to battle. Whoever it was that marched across the land, Union or Confederate, the Southern roads were just as bad, the mud just as thick, the swamps just as miserable. The only real difference came in rail travel, and that only later in the war when the Federals had appropriated and largely improved the quality of old lines, thus unleashing the irony that Yankee trains moved more reliably in the Confederacy than Southern cars did.

Indeed, rail travel was an adventure for everyone right up to the end of the war, and produced an unending string of memories of accidents and mishaps. When a division of Confederates was bound by rail from Jackson, Mississippi, to Meridian in September 1862, one car jumped the worn track. Convinced that the whole train was about to derail itself, Colonel Thomas Hunt, commander of the 9th Kentucky Infantry, though himself still recovering from a wound, leapt from his car to the ground. His staff officers, "not questioning rank", followed his lead, as did a considerable number of enlisted men. Shortly the train stopped to reposition the derailed car, and men still aboard the cars looked back to see their comrades strewn along several hundred yards of roadbed, lying down, sitting up dazed, feeling their heads and bones for breaks and scratches, and most of them laughing.[7]

The same command had to retrace its route the next summer, and not without similar mishap. As their train left Montgomery, Alabama, bystanders wondered that "all seemed in the highest spirits, cheering and yelling like demons". What the bystanders did not know was that the reason

'Bummer', Army of the Tennessee, USA

For all the differences between the Billy Yanks of the Eastern Theater and those of the West, no soldier was so distinctive to his army and region as the lean, hardened, ever resourceful, 'bummer' of the Army of the Tennessee. His uniform may have been the same as that of his eastern counterparts, but it showed in the hundreds more miles he marched, the greater variations of climate and weather he endured, and the increased uncertainties of re-supply available to this highly mobile army. Chief among these differences was the battered wide-brimmed hat he wore, as opposed to the ubiquitous kepi worn in the Army of the Potomac, and the fact that he traveled light, his kit reduced to the essentials; anything else he needed he could get from the land, a method of soldiering he became an expert at. From Tennessee to North Carolina men such as this would take it upon themselves to destroy the heart of the Confederacy.

for all the cheering was that, on the train to Montgomery just the day before, two whole regiments had almost disappeared. While steaming down a steep seven-mile grade from Wartrace, Tennessee, their train had run out of control, careering downward even faster, barely holding on to the track on the turns. One man of the 9th Kentucky calculated that they covered the seven miles in just over four minutes. "We thought every moment the car would be dashed to pieces against the rocks or be pitched off some of the cliffs and be ground into dust", wrote one Reb. He actually looked overhead on the wild ride, occasionally catching glimpses of the moon as it appeared through breaks in the overhead crags, and thought seriously about saying goodbye to it. Worse yet, some of his comrades, as many soldiers tended to do, had actually started the ride perched on top of the cars, and now they were holding on for their very lives. The last car on the train actually disintegrated, showering the track with timber and iron. When it flew apart, one Kentuckian on top of it suddenly found himself catapulted through space, flying over a telegraph wire and into a bramble bush. "Receiving no other injury than being 'powerfully' scratched", he thankfully joined the others from his car as they bivouacked beside the track to await the arrival of the next train. Miraculously, no one was fatally injured.[8]

Difficult as rail travel was between campaigns, it could be even more exasperating when on the way to battle, especially for the Confederates. Even at the outset of the war, Rebel trains frequently covered no more than a few miles an hour, with frequent stops for broken track, derailed cars, or broken-down engines. When in July 1861, men of General Joseph E. Johnston's small Army of the Shenandoah were moving from that valley eastward to join with another Rebel army immediately before the First Battle of Bull Run, only one single train was available to handle the entire command, a brigade at a time. As a result, to prevent breakdown to the vital engine, its engineer pushed it at no more than

Confederate Muskets and Rifles

A muzzle-loader gave you one shot at the enemy. If it failed then it was down to knives and bayonets.

1 Palmetto Armory, Model 1842 smoothbore musket with bayonet fixed in place and with ramrod in the stowed position.
2 D-guard side knife complete with protective scabbard
3 Dickson, Nelson and Company muzzle-loading rifle with ramrod in stowed position
4 Davis and Bozeman muzzle-loading rifle with ramrod in stowed position
5 D-guard side knife complete with protective scabbard
6 Tin drum canteen
7 Later design of Fayetteville muzzle-loading rifle with ramrod in stowed position
8 Unidentified muzzle-loading rifle with ramrod in stowed position
9 Waist belt complete with oval brass CS plate affixed
10 Mendenhall, Jones and Gardner muzzle-loading rifle with ramrod in stowed position and, shoulder strap
11 British Lancaster saber bayonet for Mendenhall, Jones and Gardner rifle
12 Scabbard for *11*

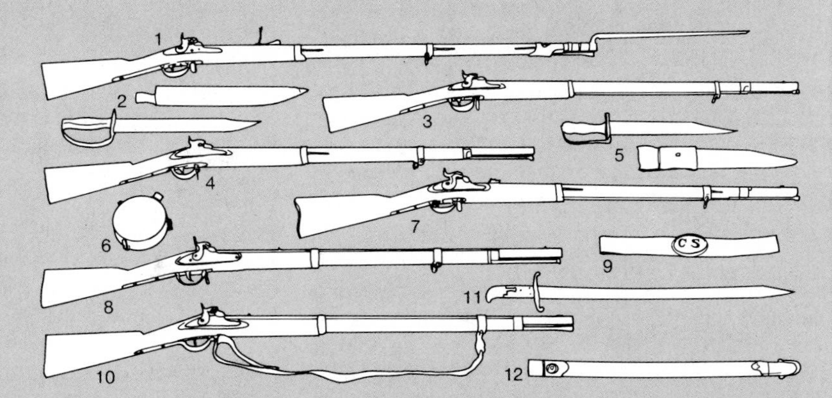

Artifacts courtesy of: Virginia Historical Society, Richmond, Va

four miles an hour. "We slowly jolted the entire day", wrote one Virginian, covering only thirty miles in eight hours. The next brigade took all night to convey, and the subsequent brigades moved faster. When the train stopped from time to time, the men invariably jumped out of their cars and started combing the the roadside for wild blackberries, often requiring their officers to spend half an hour or more getting them back on the train. As for the last of Johnston's army, when it boarded the by now overworked equipment, the poor old engine could take no more. Soon after departing it simply stopped. Some thought it had suffered a collision, but no one seemed ever to know what it had supposedly hit. Frustrated beyond reason by a delay that they feared would prevent them from reaching the battlefield in time, the men and officers decided that the train's conductor was a traitor who had intentionally slowed their progress. A military trial was immediately convened beside the tracks. Charging the hapless trainman with bribery and treason, it convicted him, and turned him over to a firing squad who promptly shot him.[9]

Steamboat travel could be just as hair-raising, and a lot of fun as well, especially for Rebs and Yanks who came from the western states in the Mississippi Valley, many of whom went to war with some experience of boats. In September of 1862 one Confederate brigade in Mobile, Alabama, boarded two old steamers, the *Waverly* and the *R.B. Taney*, for the trip to Montgomery. The *Waverly* was an old cotton boat, while the *Taney* turned out to be a much more finely appointed passenger or "packet" ship. Almost as soon as they embarked, the men on board the vessels began to shout jibes at each other, each ridiculing the other's boat, until taunts led to challenges. Inevitably, a steamboat race began.

The *Waverly* began the contest at a disadvantage, for her steam pressure was down, and the *Taney* handily passed her by, the men aboard the lead vessel cheering and shouting, their band playing, and even the *Taney's* steam calliope shrieking in victory. But most of the men in the regiment aboard the *Waverly* were old steamboatmen, and there was nothing that could raise their blood more than being beaten, especially by a fancy boat. They literally took control of the *Waverly*. Privates stripped to the waist and lined up in the boiler room, taking turns at furiously stoking the firebox with anything that would burn. Within a few minutes they had the old *Waverly* picking up steam, and speed, and driving over the waves "like a thing of life". Rapidly she caught up with the *Taney*. A mood of intense excitement took over on both vessels, so much so that no one even noticed when Sergeant Bartholomew Sullivan of the 4th Kentucky fell overboard from the *Taney* and was never seen again. All eyes were on the steam gauges and the vessels' bows. Finally, in an attempt to cut off the advancing *Waverly*, the *Taney* actually turned itself sideways in the narrow river to block passage, but the intrepid old cotton boat dashed past her just the same.[10]

Sometimes when traveling over the swampier Southern riverways, soldiers passed the time on their voyages by shooting local wildfowl, and even alligators, from the rails of their boats. Many other youthful soldiers spent the idle hours of travel with a good bottle. "Whiskey was freely used", a New York private wrote after a steamboat trip in 1863. "I 'piled in' down in the hole with a man half tight, while those that were

Above: The CSS *General Bragg*, like many other Rebel gunboats had once been a river steamer, and just the sort of vessel in which wary young soldiers of the Confederacy would have traveled to the war zone.

Below: As they traveled the war's highways, many young men like this Confederate took the opportunity of passing through a town to visit the local photographer, for patriotic – if amateurish – portraits.

wholly so made merry until a late hour."[11] Being drunk aboard ship accounted for many a man simply falling overboard, and may well explain for poor Sergeant Sullivan's disappearance from the *Taney*. Indeed, one Connecticut sergeant told of a night aboard ship when a private "was taken with the tremens and of all the Horride noises and actions I ever saw".[12] It took five men to subdue the delirious inebriate.

Some stiff drink may have been necessary to see a lot of young men through their travels, either by train or steamboat. With rare exceptions, the cars they rode were little more than boxcars with a few backless benches set on the flooring. These were cold in winter, stifling hot in summer, provided a bone-shatteringly rough ride, and were too tightly packed to allow for reclining, even assuming a man could get to sleep. No wonder that the men poured off of them at every opportunity, and at a journey's end it was not unusual to see whole regiments lay down on the station platform and drop into slumber. At the same time, while vessels like the *Taney* made river travel far more luxurious, there were all too many ships like the *Waverly*, many of them converted ferryboats, cotton transports, even livestock ships. One Maine Yankee boarded a boat for the trip south and found "men packed in a nasty hold so close that they could scarcely lie down", and many of them so drunk that they kept the rest awake. "We were huddled together more like a lot of pigs than human beings", a New Yorker said of his voyage. He had to sleep on the deck, and found his rations so nearly spoiled that he and others could hardly force them down. "The water was very dirty", he lamented, "yet we were glad to get enough of it".[13]

It could be even worse, especially for the Federals who had to travel on the ocean to reach Federal beachheads in South Carolina, Florida, or the Gulf coast. One Maine man recorded a nightmarish voyage to Ship Island, off the mouth of the Mississippi. "We have at least 300 men on board more than the ship can decently accommodate", he wrote, and "in the morning the air & filth between decks is enough to sicken a dog". The first day out he counted 300 men seasick, and "quite a number crazy drunk".[14] In a voyage lasting twenty-nine days, men could not sleep for the stifling heat in the overcrowded holds, they did not have room enough to prepare their rations properly, their water ran so low that they had to ration it, and men began to die of seasickness. Burials at sea became frequent ceremonies. "A sad sight this evening", wrote another Billy Yank; "a poor old father burying his son at sea". In time the illness hit almost everyone. "Sick myself", a soldier wrote in his diary while on the way to Ship Island. "O dear, sick enough; sea-sick and sick of the sea." The lice attacked the men in their sleep, the air was unbreathable day or night, and worse yet, many encountered storms and even hurricanes. "The squall struck us with terrible force", a Yankee wrote on March 4, 1862. "No one could walk or stand without holding on with both hands." When finally they reached their des-

Below: Traveling on the railroad could be more hazardous than steamboating, especially when track was likely torn up by raiders. Gangs like this one were constantly out repairing damaged rails.

Right: However he moved to the front, land, rail, or sea, most soldiers finally came down to the time-honored "shanks" mare'; and they had to be in good shape to deal with the roads and fields of rural America.

tination, "we rent the air with cheers".[15] After a similar experience en route to South Carolina, a Pennsylvania boy marveled at the scene of men sick all about him, "and ye gods what a time". Many men prayed, others swore, and at least a few simply gave up and "wanted to be throd [*sic*] overboard".[16]

However they reached the main armies, by rail or boat, eventually every soldier North and South had to make his way to the war by the one means common to them all. At the beginning of the war enthusiastic Yankees sang of John Brown's body moldering in the grave while his soul"goes marching on", and they sang it as they themselves marched. If any calculation of the total number of man-miles marched in the Civil War were possible, the figure would climb well into the hundreds of millions. While a number of regiments, most notably those assigned to post and permanent garrison duty, rarely moved at all during the war, others literally walked out several pairs of shoes. This was especially the case with the units operating west of the Alleghenies in the vastness of Kentucky, Tennessee, the Deep South, and the Trans-Mississippi. In the course of a single year some of these regiments might cover in excess of 1,000 miles on their feet. In the eleven months from the commencement of the Atlanta Campaign in May 1864, until the conclusion of the famed March to the Sea, the overall ground covered by General William T. Sherman's armies measured a straight-line distance of over 700 miles. Add to that the almost constant flanking movements and side-trips for intermediate objectives, and the total must exceed well over 1,000 miles. And the Confederates he opposed were marching with him every step of the way, and farther.

From the beginning of the war to the last, marching was a tiresome, often exhausting, exercise. At the outset, few were really ready for it, and their trial was made the worse by the fact that the first major campaign, culminating in the First Battle of Bull Run, took place in July, in northern Virginia, in stifling heat and humidity.

Confederate Pistols and Revolvers

In an era of enormous technical inventiveness, Southern manufacturers played their part, both by developing new pistol designs and ingeniously copying those of their foes. Only production limitations and the scarcity of materials restricted them. The results of their labors varied enormously, from flintlocks and crude percussion weapons to the latest types of revolver.

1 Virginia Manufactory 1st Model pistol alteration
2 Virginia Manufactory 2nd Model flintlock pistol
3 Ramrod for *2*
4 Revolver holster
5 Palmetto Model 1842 pistol with integral ramrod unstowed
6 J. and F. Garret pistol with integral ramrod stowed
7 J.H. Dance & Brothers Navy revolver
8 J.H. Dance & Brothers Army revolver
9 Le Mat First Model revolver
10 Le Mat Second Model revolver
11 Columbus Fire Arms Mfg. C. revolver
12 T.W. Cofer revolver
13 Tucker, Sherrard and Co. revolver
14 Griswold and Gunnison early model revolver
15 Clark, Sherrard and Co. revolver
16 Le Mat holster

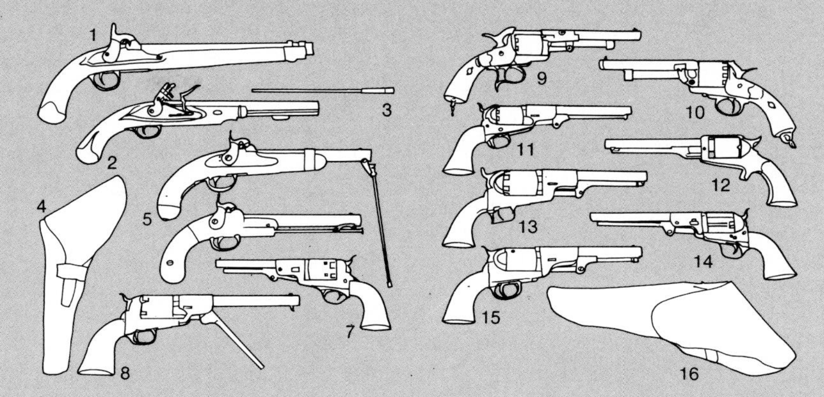

Artifacts courtesy of: Virginia Historical Society, Richmond, Va

It all started for the Federals like storybook soldiering. Leaving their encampments near Washington, they made an easy day of it initially, and though tired that night after covering only a few miles, still they relished their first night spent sleeping in the field. "Beneath the clear sky, studded with the sentinel stars, that paced their ceaseless round", wrote one Yankee, "we slept the sleep of soldiers".[17] But the next day it wasn't so easy, and by the next they were tired, dirty, sore-footed and insubordinate. With remarkable alacrity the hot, dusty road took the glamour out of war. Sunstroke, a constant companion in the summer months, claimed its first victims here, and scores of men on both sides would actually die of it during the war, exacerbated as it was by thirst and exhaustion. Nor was the occasional rainstorm necessarily a relief, for the dirt roads of the South were quickly turned into mires that sucked the boots and shoes from the soldiers' feet and soaked their heavy woolen or cotton uniforms. Even lightning could be an enemy, as eleven men of the 22nd Virginia found out in May 1864 when a bolt struck them on the road.

Perhaps it was because the march held so much of tedium mixed with the constant presence of danger, that the men on both sides took every opportunity of momentary escape. Whenever their officers called a halt in the course of the day, the men broke ranks to pick berries, brew coffee, play cards, or run off for a little quick foraging. These were volunteer soldiers, men who would never completely accept military discipline, and try as they might, their officers could never entirely control them. This became evident early on the march to Bull Run, when Sherman, then a colonel and a brigade commander, had to ride constantly up and down the lines of his men shouting "You must close up, you must not chase the pigs and chickens". It did him little good. Sherman himself confronted one soldier carrying a joint of mutton over his shoulder. "Didn't you know the orders against foraging?" asked the Colonel. "Yes, but I was hungry", came the reply, "and it was rebel mutton, anyhow." Insubordinate men even shouted back at his officers to "tell Colonel Sherman we will get all the water, pigs and chickens we want".[18]

Right: Routines varied, but most officers marched their men for 50 minutes, then rested them for 10. Whenever a halt was called, the fires for coffee were lit, and the cards and pipes came out.

Above: When the time came to embark on the march to battle, excitement passed all along the lines, as these Federals crossed the pontoon bridge over the Rappahannock on their way to meet with Lee and his Rebels.

Below: The roads, especially in summer were hot, dusty, hard and unforgiving, like this one in Mississippi in 1863. A bridge to cross was a lucky find. More often the men had to wade, then march on soaking wet.

Above: As he passed through an unknown and alien land, Billy Yank, moreso than his foe, was a tourist as well as a soldier. Sites like Falls Church, where Washington had worshipped, attracted the curious.

When they weren't foraging, the soldiers of both sides were often looting, and it frequently did not matter from whom. On the march to Bull Run, the 1st Massachusetts passed through Vienna, Virginia, and swarmed over a grocery store like locusts. Nothing was left, not even the grindstones and whole barrels of molasses. Out in the western theater of the war it was much the same. Men of John Hunt Morgan's Kentucky Confederate cavalry stole whiskey at every opportunity, sometimes even "officially" confiscating it from stores that they passed. When headquarters prohibited men of the Kentucky "Orphan Brigade" from using farmers' fence rails for firewood, someone found a loophole in the order where it specified only "whole" rails. Obeying the order to the letter, the men soon broke every nearby rail into small pieces. They burned the pieces, but no "whole" rails.[19] Some outfits became specially famed for their depredations while on the march, and word of their coming could lead even friendly civilians to hide their chickens and their silver and generally keep a low profile.

Even less destructive foraging could create its confusions and its mishaps. Late in the war, as the 2nd Kentucky Infantry passed through South Carolina, an officer came across an old slave who had undoubtedly seen his little peanut crop savaged by Confederates from one state after another. The colonel was not interested in nuts, but was curious if any of the French immigrants to the state had happened to settle in this area. "Say, uncle", he shouted to the black man, "are there any Huguenots about here?"

"Well, I declare, where be you ones from?" asked the slave in return.

"From way up in old Kentucky."

"Well, I thought so", said the Negro. "Why, in Tennessee they call 'em peanuts, in Georgia they goes by the name of goobers, in Alabama they is penders, here in South Carolina we call 'em ground peas, now you fellows way off dar in Kentucky call 'em hugonuts. Well I do declare."[20]

In fact, even slaves were not free from the raiding of passing soldiers, North or South. One Confederate regiment had a Mohawk sachem named Konshattountzchette in its ranks, though the men called him Flying Cloud. A Yankee bullet had removed much of his upper jaw, leaving him looking "rather hideous", an aspect not softened by his flashing dark eyes and swarthy complexion. For some reason, the slaves in South Carolina found him particularly terrifying, and his white comrades in arms soon learned to use his appearance to the best purpose. When foraging for food, they would send him to a slave cabin where he would give several war whoops and then shout what he wanted. "Beans", he cried before one cabin. While the women and children fled in terror, the men quickly produced the food they had been hiding. "Here, here, boss", they said meekly, whereupon Flying Cloud usually relaxed his appearance and reassured them: "Me no hurt you . . . cook beans quick."[21]

For all the similarities between the experiences of Yank and Reb on the march, still with only a few exceptions, there was one very basic difference that predetermined much of their opinion of what they saw and experienced. The Confederate soldier spent the entire war within the borders of the Confederacy. In effect, he was in his homeland, and however much special affinity he might feel for his native state, still he felt in varying degrees some measure of devotion to the South at large. As the war progressed, and more and more signs of the exhaustion and distress the burden of war placed on the Confederate heartland became evident, the more sorrowful became the Rebel soldier's trek from campaign to campaign. Burned or abandoned farmhouses, fields grown over with weeds, factories laid waste, bridges burned, and cities either deserted or else crowded to overflowing with refugees, all confronted his eyes. It saddened his heart, yet generally hardened his resolve as well, for the cause of all this hardship was in simple soldier logic, the enemy.

It could be especially heart-rending for the Confederates from states like Missouri, Kentucky, Maryland, and Tennessee, for their native

Below: More sober sights along the march were the scenes of the war's destructive force; as here at Johnsonville, Tennessee, shortly after a Rebel raid. Such sights were heartrending for all to see.

soil lay, in whole or part, behind Yankee lines through much of the war. With not chance of visiting home on furlough, and often no news of friends and family coming across the lines, these soldiers felt an additional anxiety. Consequently they marched with a quicker, lighter step on those occasions when the campaign was destined to take them back into their native states.

In the fall of 1862, when an ill-fated Confederate offensive sought to retake Kentucky from the Federals, the Orphan Brigade was ordered up from Mississippi to join in the fight. Alas, one obstacle after another stood in their way. After seemingly surmounting every impediment possible, they finally started the last leg of their march that would take them home. "All marched with a bouyant step," wrote one; "our hearts beat high with hope". Finally they came in sight of the mountains around Cumberland Gap, the gateway to Kentucky, just twenty miles away. The next day they would re-enter the Bluegrass state at last. But their army in Kentucky had been defeated and was already in retreat, and the next morning, lined up on the road to start their last march, they got their orders to turn around instead and march once more away from their homeland. "The silence that prevailed in the ranks then was not the silence of restraint", wrote one of the Kentuckians; "it was the silence of stern manhood bowed down by bitter disappointment".[22] When finally they began to march, a spontaneous shout of frustration surged through the entire brigade, then they fell silent and marched on.

The Federals were not immune to moments of sadness and reflection on the march, either. Particularly in Virginia, where the armies moved back and forth over roughly the same ground for three years, the invading Yankees frequently had to pass places they had seen before on previous campaigns, and witness sad remembrances. Marching south in the Shenandoah valley in May 1864, one small Federal army saw all along the way the graves of men who had fallen there in earlier operations. There was, wrote one Billy

Confederate Telegraphy Equipment

At the outbreak of war, the Confederates became the first into the field with their own corps of signalers. They also became adept practitioners of telegraphy. Indeed, so handy did some Reb's become with the telegraph key that they were perhaps the first in peace or war to 'wire tap'. Some former railroad telegraphers riding with Rebel partisans learned how to throw a wire across telegraph transmission lines, cut one, and tap into the break with a portable key. The consequence was a breach of Federal security, and a couple of waggish Rebel soldiers sending false messages of their own just to confuse the enemy. The creation of secret communications ciphers were among the most esoteric enterprises of the war. Complex keys and ciphers were in use in both armies, leading to equally innovative efforts at innovative efforts at cipher breaking. Communications were vital in this continental war.

1 Telegraph relay used by the Army of Northern Virginia
2 and 3 Brass encoding and decoding discs
4 Rubber insulated telegraph wire
5 Pocket telegraph relay

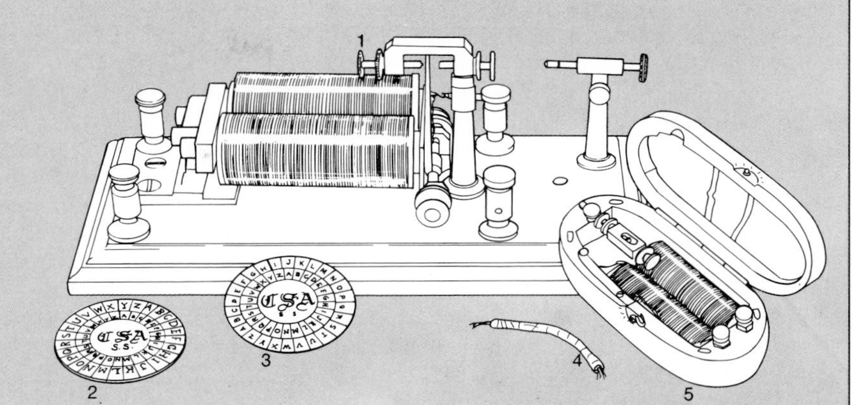

Artifacts courtesy of: The Museum of The Confederacy, Richmond, Va

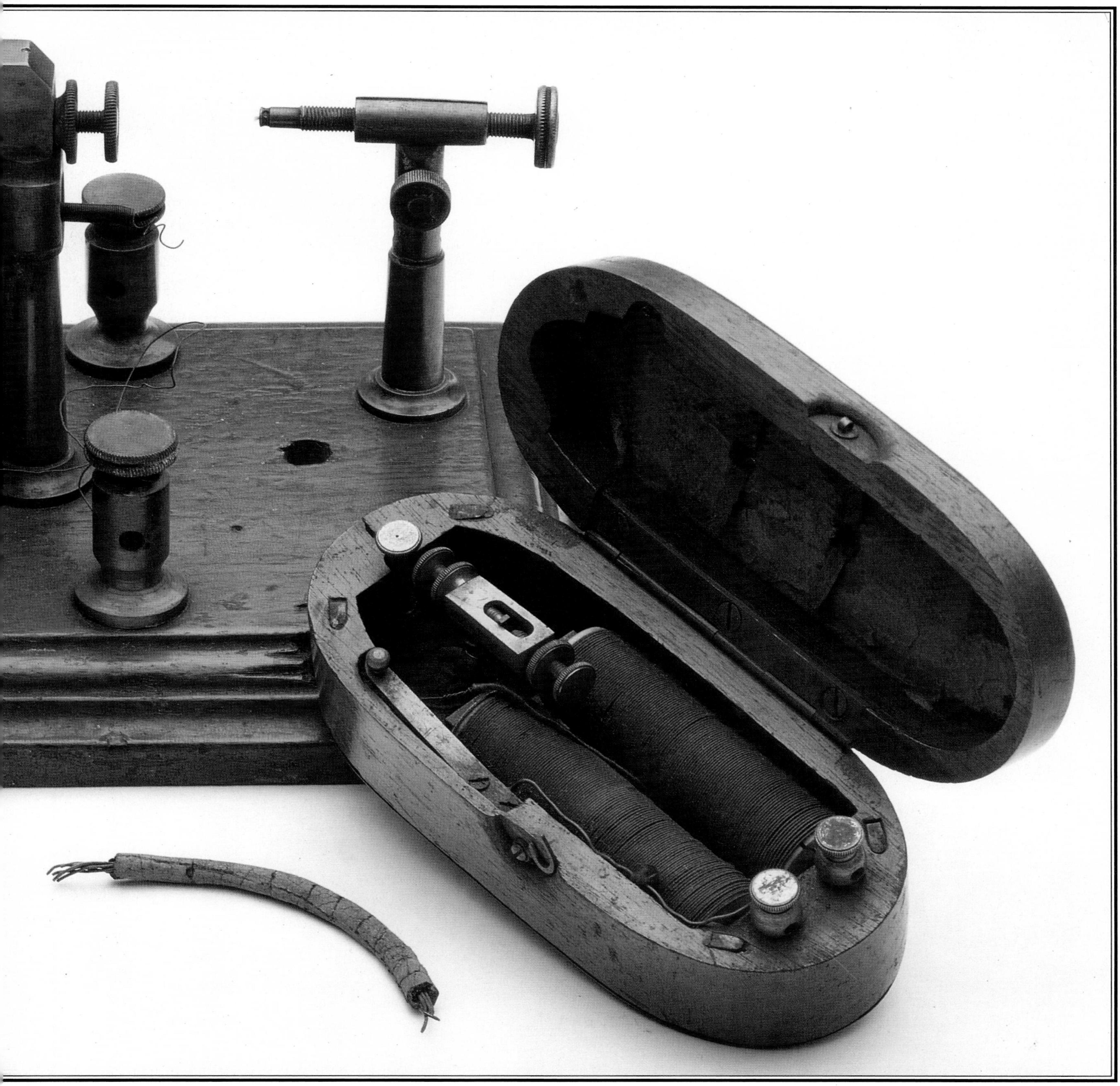

Yank, "perhaps not a mile of the whole route over which we passed along which there could not be seen a soldier's grave".[23] Passing by the old battlefield at Winchester, they saw the dead from the battle there in June 1863, hastily buried by the Confederate victors, barely covered by earth, and many with arms and legs protruding from the soil.

All the scenes of destruction were just as unnerving to the more reflective Yankees as they were to the Confederates, though others took a kind of perverse pride both in the visibly demonstrated might of the Union war machine, and in the punishment thus being dealt to the South for firing on Fort Sumter and starting the war.

Yet the sights of sadness were few compared to the curiosities that men from the North experienced in marching across the South. Of course, Virginia could be just as strange a place to a boy from Arkansas as to one from Maine, but at least Arkansas was essentially a part of the same culture, and to a degree even the same social order. For Yankees, however, men who had mostly only heard about the South from newspapers or the fiery oratory of petty politicians, the tramp across the fields of the Confederacy was the adventure of a lifetime. Nearly two million Northerners marched into the Confederacy during the war, virtually every one of them a "tourist".

With the smugness characteristic of his region, one soldier from Maine declared of Virginia that "in the hands of New England people this country might be converted into a garden". In the hands of its current inhabitants, however, most Federals agreed that it was a poor place at best. "The country is behind the times 100 years", said one Yank, echoed by yet another who declared that "everything is a hundred years behind the times". One wag explained to folks back home that "there is a good deal of this part of the world that the Lord has not finished yet". Of Louisiana he declared that the Almighty "meant the snakes & aligators to hold possession for a thousand or two years more before man [came] to occupy it".[24]

By and large the Yankees were not impressed with what they saw of the South. The relative poverty, the wide areas with little or no development, the limited literacy of the people, and all the signs of the hated institution of slavery, gave them a poor impression of the region. "I dont like this country nor the people that live here at all", wrote a Minnesotan, "and wouldn't live here if they would give me the best farm in the State and the prettiest Girl in the State for a Wife throwd in".

Few Northerners were prepared for the Southern heat. While remarking that the countryside in Virginia reminded him of New England, one Billy Yank went on to say that "the climate reminds me more of that infernal place down below that I have not seen but often heard of". Many complained that the air scorched their throats on its way to their lungs. Having to march and actively campaign in such a climate left thousands listless and in a near-constant state of exhaustion.[25]

Above: Evidence of the hard hand of war was everywhere. Scarcely a major Southern bridge escaped the torch, such as this one over the Potomac near Berlin, Maryland. The South would spend years rebuilding.

Below: Yanks particularly had to learn to adapt to life in the Southern climate, especially in the hot and humid summers. These Yankees in Tennessee have learned to take every chance to relax in the shade.

Wherever they marched, the soldiers were not much impressed with the inhabitants. The men they thought ignorant. "I dont believe the inhabitants even know the day of the week", wrote one Federal in Maryland. And the women they found generally to be crude and unattractive. "They are void of the roseate hue of health and beauty which so much adornes our Northern belles", declared one soldier. And the men found them too skinny by far. "They look more like polls than any thing else", one complained. "The women here generally are shaped like a lath, nasty, slab-sided, long haired specimens of humanity. I would as soon kiss a dried codfish as one of them".[26] The most ungallant description of all came from a Federal in Mississippi, who called the local girls "sharp-nosed, tobacco-chewing, snuff-rubbing, flax-headed, hatchet-faced, yellow-eyed, sallow-skinned, cotton-dressed, flat-breasted, bare-headed, long-waisted, hump-shouldered, stoop-necked, big-footed, straddle-toed, sharp-skinned, thin-lipped, pale-faced, lantern-jawed, silly-looking damsels".[27] Many Yanks

Private, Co. E, 23rd Virginia Infantry, CSA

Four years of heavy service characterized the 23rd Virginia Infantry, and by the end it showed on those fortunate few who could still answer the roll. Numbering perhaps 800 men when first mustered, the regiment had just 57 men and officers left to surrender with the Army of Northern Virginia at Appomattox. Along the way it had left its dead in the Shenandoah, at the Seven Days', at Cedar Mountain, Second Manassas, Chancellorville, Gettysburg, Cedar Creek, and more. They were typical of units that were raised in 1861. Formed chiefly from companies locally raised in Virginia and called such names as the "Brooklyn Grays" and "Louisa Grays", the regiment wore gray frock coats and trousers, with blue or black trim and distinctive yellow loops on their collars. Their leather belts and accoutrements were originally white, but hard service quickly soiled them. Some wore a 'B.G.' on their kepis for "Brooklyn Grays".

believed that the women of the South had loose morals. They drank in bar-rooms, swore "like troopers", and seemed to breed ceaselessly. Of course, Billy Yank mostly came into contact with the lower classes, the middle- and upper-class Southerners having fled before the armies, or else associating exclusively with the officers.

All the same, for all their grumbling, as they marched across the Confederacy the Federals also had to admit that there was much to like. "This country is so beautiful I wish I had been born here", one wrote of Virginia, and several areas like coastal Florida and middle Tennessee were thought exceptionally attractive. So were at least a few of the women, despite all that "slab-sided" and "lantern-jawed" hyperbole. One private in Kentucky declared that "I fell in love with Paducah while I was there, and I think I will settle there when the war is over. I never saw so many pretty women in my life".[28] Not a few such meetings led to marriages that lasted through the war and for years after.

Billy Yank's foe had far fewer opportunities to see new sights as he moved to the sound of the guns. Only once, in the Gettysburg Campaign in 1863, did a Confederate army actually penetrate well into undisputed Union territory, though in 1863 and 1864 cavalry and sizeable infantry raids also swept briefly across Ohio, Indiana, and Pennsylvania. States claimed by both sides – Maryland, Kentucky, and Missouri – also hosted a few major invasions, but the territory there was not all that unfamiliar to many Rebels, especially

Above: Both sides, despite the war, could stop for a moment to be moved or inspired by the beauty of the country they saw. Artist James Walker paints the Chattanooga valley from Lookout Mountain in 1864.

Below: Though often campaigning outside of home territory, men like these Federals on the street of Frederick, Maryland, could still relish seeing a new town – especially its ladies, saloons, and pie shops.

Left: No American, North or South, could be immune to the scenic splendor of a place like Point Lookout, on Tennessee's Lookout Mountain, and few who passed missed the chance to have a portrait taken.

Above: Most common of all sights seen in the wake of the marching armies, was the simple roadside grave, testimony to the life and death of a soldier who had gone before, never to return home.

those who enlisted from those states and who really looked on their invasion as a return home.

When in enemy country, as on the Gettysburg invasion, Confederate generals ordered their men not to forage or plunder, but of course to no avail. "I felt sorry for the farmers", wrote Robert Stiles, "some of whom actually concealed their horses in their dwelling houses, or, rather, attempted to conceal them, for we became veritable sleuth-hounds in running down a horse".[29] A few Confederates maintained that the farmers of Maryland and Pennsylvania freely gave their produce to the passing Rebels. "Many of them bade us help ourselves to poultry, milk, vegetables, fruit, honey, bread, whatever we wanted to eat", remembered John Caldwell of South Carolina.[30] Sometimes they paid in captured Northern greenbacks for their food, and more often with Confederate script which was, of course, worthless in the Union. But mostly they simply took what they needed.

That they did not threaten their unwilling hosts did not make the contributions any the less the fruit of intimidation. "Soldiers as hungry as were the Confederates could not be expected to refuse proffers of food", wrote one wag from a Texas brigade, "even when they suspected such proffers were made through unwarranted fear of ill-treatment". As a result, when one Texan came into camp near Chambersburg on the night of June 30, the eve of Gettysburg, he stared in wonder at what he saw. "Every square foot of an acre of ground not occupied by a sleeping or standing soldier, was covered with choice food for the hungry. Chickens, turkeys, ducks and geese squawked, gobbled, cackled and hissed in harmonious unison as deft and energetic hands seized them for slaughter, and scarcely waiting for them to die, sent their feathers flying in all directions; and scattered around in bewildering confusion and gratifying profusion appeared immense loaves of bread and chunks of corned beef, hams, and sides of bacon, cheeses, crocks of apple-butter, jelly, jam, pickles, and preserves, bowls of yellow butter, demijohns of buttermilk, and other eatables too numerous to mention".[31] Men slept with loaves of bread for pillows, their arms wrapped around hams as if they were wives.

The Confederate soldier never ate better during the war than he did in those few days of the invasion of Pennsylvania, and he enjoyed the sight of the plump and rosy-cheeked farm girls along the way, having much better things to say about them than his Yankee counterparts said of most Southern girls. Yet other than for those differences, men in blue and gray for the most part saw the same sights, heard the same sounds, smelled the same scents, as they moved across the landscape, marching to war. The ground of the battle-scarred continent was just as hard to sleep upon, for Yank or Reb alike, and for all of them the countryside through which they walked bore witness to the hardship and pain in the wake of warfare's passing, and admonished them of what lay ahead as they tramped toward the sound of the guns.

References

1 Wiley, *Billy Yank*, pp.36-7.
2 *Ibid.*, p.36.
3 *Ibid.*, p.37.
4 *Ibid.*
5 *Ibid.*
6 Wiley, *Johnny Reb*, p.26.
7 John S. Jackman Diary, September 23, 1862, Library of Congress.
8 *Ibid.*, May 25, 1863.
9 Davis, *Bull Run*, p.140.
10 Jackman Diary, September 27, 1862.
11 Wiley, *Billy Yank*, pp.31-2.
12 *Ibid.*, p.32.
13 *Ibid.*, p.33.
14 *Ibid.*
15 *Ibid.*, p.34.
16 *Ibid.*, p.33.
17 Davis, *Bull Run*, p.92.
18 *Ibid.*, p.96.
19 Davis, *Orphan Brigade*, p.188.
20 *Ibid.*, p.249.
21 *Ibid.*, p.247.
22 *Ibid.*, pp.135-6.
23 William C. Davis, *The Battle of New Market* (New York, 1975), p.34.
24 Wiley, *Billy Yank*, pp.96-7.
25 *Ibid.*, p.97.
26 *Ibid.*, p.100.
27 *Ibid.*, p.101.
28 *Ibid.*, pp.106-7.
29 Robert Stiles, *Four Years Under Marse Robert* (New York, 1903), p.199.
30 J.F.J. Caldwell, *The History of a Brigade of South Carolinians* (Philadelphia, 1886), p.133.
31 J.B. Polley, *Hood's Texas Brigade* (Dayton, Ohio, 1976), p.148.

CHAPTER TWELVE

The Face Of Battle

With the dawn of 1865, there was a sure sense in the North that the war was won. The Union was triumphant west of the Mississippi, Hood's army, once again under the command of Johnston, was so debilitated that it could not pose a serious threat to Sherman's conquest of the lower south, and Lee was still at bay in Petersburg and Richmond, with Grant ever decreasing the avenues of supply and escape. It was no longer a question of whether the Confederacy would fall, but only of when.

Having taken Savannah in December, Sherman began his march northward on February 1, his goal to disrupt the interior Confederacy, and move to join Grant for a massive final assault on Lee. Sherman met almost no serious opposition. In the forthcoming campaign, his troops forced the evacuation of Charleston on February 17, and four days later the Rebels began to leave Wilmington, North Carolina, their last major Atlantic port. The same day that Charleston fell, Columbia, capital of South Carolina, also fell and soon burst into flames. The only resistance came in small battles at Kinston on March 8-10, and at Averasborough, North Carolina, on March 16, both of which were relatively easy victories for the Federals. The last major battle of the campaign came at Bentonville on March 21, and once again the Confederates could not stop Sherman.

In Virginia, the contending armies did not wait for warm weather to strike at one another. In actions at Dabney's Mills south of the James River and in a raid in northern Virginia by Sheridan, more of Lee's tenuous supply lines were cut. Facing certain starvation, Lee struck back in a bold surprise attack at Fort Stedman on March 25, attempting to break the siege line and force Grant to contract his spreading tentacles. Despite great daring, the assault failed, though for the men involved they experienced yet again the terribly brutal sting of deadly battle.

IN THE summer of 1863, the 33rd Illinois had reached the sound of the guns, and lay behind its earthworks facing Vicksburg, Mississippi, waiting for the word to rise up, rush forward, and attack the Rebel lines. Minute after agonizing minute passed by, and still no order came. James Wilcox grew increasingly restive. "Oh how my heart palpitated!" he confessed to his diary. "It seemed to thump the ground (I lay on my face) as hard as the enemy's bullets. The sweat from off my face run in a stream from the tip ends of my whiskers." He had been a soldier for a long time now. He knew that he was supposed to remain quiet. But for eight minutes he had lain there, with enemy bullets and shells flying over his head, while he and his companions were not allowed to return fire. Twice the waiting proved to be too much for him. Unable to control his anxiety, he cried out, "*My God, why dont they order us to charge!*"[1]

For Wilcox, as for three million other Yanks and Rebs, all their experience as soldiers prepared them for this one moment. Enlistment and training, the drudgery of drill and camp routine, the risk of illness or wounds, the hazards of falling into enemy hands, the separation from home and loved ones – all of this they endured and suffered, so that now at last they might go into battle and acquit themselves well. It was the final measure of what success their armies had achieved in

This is how it ended for so many, death in a ditch or trench, swamp or field. Battle, the final test of the soldier, played no favorites in exacting its cost. A dead Reb at Petersburg, 1865.

turning raw men and boys into soldiers and fighting men. Of course, they never really became trained and professional *soldiers*, but when they set foot on the battlefield, these men behaved superbly. Though they freqeuntly ignored or subverted every lesson of discipline designed to prepare them for the fight, when the final test of arms came, they passed with honors. And when two armies close in battle, all else in warfare becomes incidental.

Whether facing its first battle or its fiftieth, an army took on a progressively more sober and serious aspect in the two or three days prior to a fight. Even before being told what was soming, the men in the ranks quickly learned how to read the signs. The first campaigns of the year came in the spring, when the roads were firm enough for marching and the temperatures at least minimally warm enough for the men to function. They received orders to tear down, burn, or simply abandon their winter quarters. Large stockpiles of supplies – crates of hardtack, barrels of salt pork, mountains of hay and fodder for the animals – grew throughout the army's encampments. The activities of couriers, inspections, arrival of new regiments, and the flood of camp rumors, all increased daily, and with increasing rapidity. Since the opposing armies tended to winter only a few miles from each other, the men knew that any movement could lead to battle. When the order came to prepare three or more days' rations in advance, it meant only one thing: the army was about to march – and when that happened, battle could be only a day or two away.

Above: For some outfits, if a chaplain were handy, a final prayer or even a service or mass might be said. While obviously posed, this scene though more formal would not differ too much from a pre-battle prayer.

Below: No time in a soldier's life was more uncertain than those final minutes before a battle. At first, like this regiment of Yanks, they would be halted behind the line to dress ranks and prepare themselves.

A combination of frightened introspection and nervous chatter and forced hilarity swept the marching columns as they moved toward certain confrontation with the enemy. Soon the distant sounds of sporadic firing gave evidence that scouts or perhaps a cavalry screen had encountered the advance outposts of the foe. It was not fighting – not yet – but rather the occasional shooting incidental to small and often isolated clashes as Yank and Reb felt each other out, seeking some clues as to numbers and positions. But when the main van of the armies were close enough to one another to hear those shots, veterans and amateurs alike knew that the next day men would begin to fight and die.

At the beginning of the war, when alike they were all new to battle, the men in blue and gray faced the coming fray with solemnity approaching reverence. The day before the first Battle of Bull Run, on July 20, 1861, one commander assembled the regiments of his division together in a field, ordered hats off and heads bowed, and prayed with them. "The God of battles was entreated for guidance, for shielding in battle, and for care of those so precious in our far-away homes."[2] Later that evening, while the generals and officers bent over their lamp-lit maps and made final plans to test the Almighty's attention to their prayers, the men in the camps lay on the ground, resting as much as they could. Rumor after rumor passed through the camps. They would move at 2 a.m., said one. Others gave exaggerated reports of the foe's strength, or even that the enemy had retired.

Few slept that night, north or south of Bull Run. "This is one of the most beautiful nights that the imagination can conceive", one Yankee wrote. Tens of thousands lay awake looking up into the heavens. "The sky is perfectly clear, the moon is full and bright, and the air as still as if it were not within a few hours to be disturbed by the roar of cannon and the shouts of contending men." Perhaps confused by the quiet that he encountered, one newspaperman passed through the Federal camps and thought them "a picture of enchantment". Five thousand blazing campfires sent a host of ghostly shadows across the Virginia fields and woods. In the distance, one regiment sang

the current version of "The Star-Spangled Banner". Another unit's band played romantic favorites, popular patriotic airs, and even a piece or two from an opera. "Everything here is quiet save the sounds of the music and the occasional shout of a soldier", wrote the newspaperman, "or the lowing of the cattle, whose dark forms spot the broad meadow in the rear". One Reb, on another campaign, awaiting his own baptism of fire, confessed that "often at the still hour of midnight I wish the next day will be the 'cross over,' and we will meet the 'grand army' on fair ground".[4]

However they passed that last night of innocence, most soldiers handled themselves well on the next morning, during the hours when most battles began. In fact, their pent-up anxiety and fears sometimes manifested themselves by an unaccountable rush to get into the fight. Often when the sporadic firing of pickets or cavalry skirmishers was first heard, the soldiers, without orders from their officers, spontaneously rushed from their bivouacks to their arms, lining up ready to march to the fight. Their officers usually told them to go back to their campsites and finish dressing, make their coffee and eat their rations, and not be in such an infernal hurry. When officers did give the order to form ranks and march, the men in the rear files often could not contain their anxiety and marched too quickly, causing congestion at the backs of regiments, and sometimes actually passing through the files in their front.

Finally, before every soldier's first battle there came a halt on the way to the action, as commanders reformed their ranks, dressed their lines, made certain that each infantryman stood about thirteen inches from the men on either side of him, and that the file closers on the flanks were in place to keep the lines straight and orderly in the last advance a hopeless task. This final halt could take an hour or more – sometimes two – and those were the longest, most agonizingly slow minutes the men had ever experienced. Their throats and mouths went dry. The muscles in their chest and abdomen tensed and contracted, making them feel as if heavy weights pressed down upon them. The untried soldier took short, difficult breaths. Even in cool weather he often felt sweat on his forehead and perspiration in his palms. All but the most indifferent felt some quaking in their hands, while others became drowsy and yawned, not from fatigue but rather from the sapping of energy by the enormous amounts of anxiety.

Private and Sergeant, 1st Texas Infantry

Men from the Confederacy's western regiments often wore very individualist dress, and even uniforms of whole regiments could vary considerably from the official regulations. The battle shirt, for instance, could sport oversize breast pockets, usually outlined against their plain or checked home-spun background. The 1st Texas was one of the better clothed western outfits, and at the beginning of the war sported gray frock coats and trousers, trimmed with blue, and gray kepis with stars and regimental numerals on the crown. Armed with Enfield rifles, the 1st Texas saw heavy service in the Army of Northern Virginia with John Bell Hood's Texas Brigade, from Seven Pines in May 1862 to the end at Appomattox. Consequently, clothing deteriorated with scant reissues, so that by the finish, uniforms as such had ceased to mean anything. The men simply redressed themselves with whatever they could find to hand.

All were frightened. "If you see anyone that says they want any afraid", wrote a Maine boy after his first fight, "you may know that it want me".[5] Ironically, for most Yanks and Rebs alike, fear of being killed or wounded did not rest uppermost in their minds. Rather, they feared that they would not "stand the gaff", as they said; that they would panic or turn coward at the last minute and disgrace themselves by running away. "I have a mortal dread of the battle field for I have never yet been nearer to one than to hear the cannon roar & have never seen a person die", one Yank wrote before his first battle. "I am afraid that the groans of the wounded & dying will make me shake, nevertheless I hope & trust that strength will be given me to stand up & do my duty."[6] Across the lines a similarly concerned Reb wrote home that "I may run but if I do I wish that some of our own men would shoot me down".[7]

As a result, when finally the green boys went into battle and fired their first shots and heard for the first time the whine of the enemy bullets as they whizzed past, there was a sense of tremendous relief. "With your first shot you become a new man", wrote a Confederate after his first engagement at Bull Run. "Personal safety is your least concern. Fear has no existence in your bosom. Hesitation gives way to an uncontrollable desire to rush into the thickest of the fight. The dead and dying around you, if they receive a passing thought, only serve to stimulate you to revenge. You become cool and deliberate, and watch the efect of bullets, the showers of bursting shells, the passage of cannon balls as they rake their murderous channels through your ranks . . . with a feeling so callous . . . that your soul seems dead to every sympathizing and selfish thought."[8] A Yankee echoed his sentiments. "After the first round the fear left me & I was as cool as ever I was in my life", he wrote. "I think I have been a great deal more excited in attempting to speak a piece in school or to make remarks in an evening meeting."[9] A Federal who fought at Shiloh in April 1862 confessed that "strange as it may seam to you, but the more men I saw kiled

Confederate Muskets and Rifles

Johnny Reb's weapons came from everywhere, from both state and private sources.

1 Morse smoothbore muzzle-loading musket complete with bayonet fixed in place and with ramrod stowed
2 State of Georgia smoothbore muzzle-loading alteration musket complete with bayonet and ramrod
3 Bayonet for *2*
4 J. P. Murray muzzle-loading rifle with ramrod in stowed position
5 Boyle, Gamble and MacFee bowie bayonet complete with protective scabbard
6 Cartridge box with embossed Georgia State seal plate as used by Confederate foot soldiers
7 C. Chapman muzzle-loading rifle
8 Muzzle ramrod associated with the C. Chapman rifle
9 Pulaski muzzle-loading rifle with ramrod in stowed position
10 W. J. McElroy knife complete with protective scabbard
11 H. C. Lamb muzzle-loading rifle with ramrod in stowed position
12 Late design of Read and Watson muzzle-loading rifle with ramrod in stowed position.

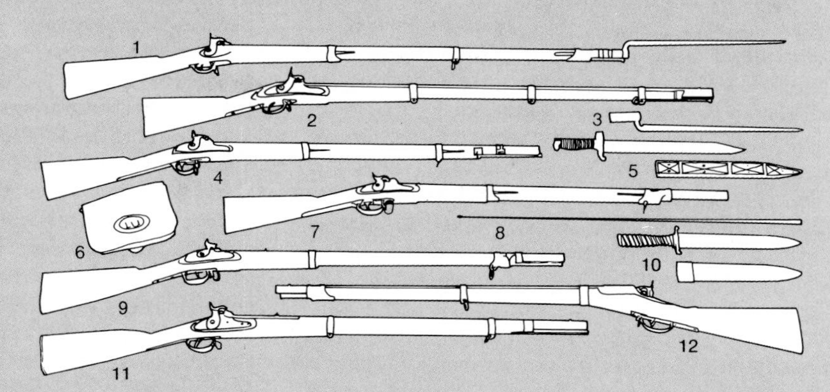

Artifacts courtesy of: Virginia Historical Society, Richmond, Va

the more reckless I became".[10] Men became disoriented, and at First Bull Run one Maryland Confederate outfit broke into halves. One dropped back, but the other, along with Private McHenry Howard, went onward, "and I with it", he wrote, "feeling as if in a dream, the whole thing was so sudden, unexpected and novel".[11]

The first-time experience could be the same, just as confusing, frightening, even humorous, whether the soldier met it as part of a great army, or with only a small group of companions. Youthful Private John H. Alexander was a new recruit to Company A of the 43rd Virginia Battalion of Cavalry, commanded by the famed Confederate raider John S. Mosby. Alexander's baptism of fire came in April 1864, during a raid on Yankee camps in Fairfax County, Virginia. In the darkness as they approached the enemy outposts, word came back along the line to be silent. "My heart jumped into my throat", Alexander recalled. "This began to look like business." He put his hand to his gun, only to be scolded by an old veteran, "Pshaw! we're just getting in hearing of 'em. Don't be scared." As they moved forward slowly, the sounds of the horses' hooves crushing leaves reminded him of a funeral march, "and there came solemn thoughts, and my partial enthusiasm died away".

Seeing some dark forms approaching, Alexander shouted "There they are", and drew his revolver, only to be told scornfully that it was only their own scouts. An impatient veteran asked sarcastically, "What the devil did you leave your mammy for?" Hopelessly jumpy now, Alexander shivered at every mournful call of the whippoorwill, and almost leaped out of his saddle when an owl hooted above him. Finally they dismounted, close to their prey, and advanced on foot. "Stalking one's fellow-kind is a grisly sort of business", he confessed. Then they were upon the sleeping Federals, Mosby shouted for a charge, and in they went. "There were shots and yells and running men and snorting horses and the odor of much brimstone, and – well, that's pretty much all that I know about the fight. Out

Captured Union Handguns used by Confederate Forces

When your supply of guns just gave out, the easiest thing was to take them from the enemy.

1 Model 1842 flintlock type of percussion pistol
2 Unidentified type of underhammer pistol
3 Colt Model 1860 design of fluted Army revolver
4 Smith and Wesson No. 2 Army revolver
5 Unopened tin of percussion caps for use with revolvers
6 Packet of six paper cartridges incorporating bullet and charge suitable for use with Colt Navy pistol
7 Colt Model 1851 Navy revolver
8 Opened tin of percussion caps
9 Pistol bullet mold device
10 Remington New Model Army revolver
11 Whitney Navy revolver
12 Massachusetts Arms Company Adams Patent Navy revolver
13 Colt Model 1849 Pocket revolver
14 Colt Model 1860 Army revolver
15 Colt Model 1849 Pocket revolver
16 Pistol tool associated with Colt Model 1860 Army revolver
17 Pistol flask containing gunpowder used to charge individual chambers

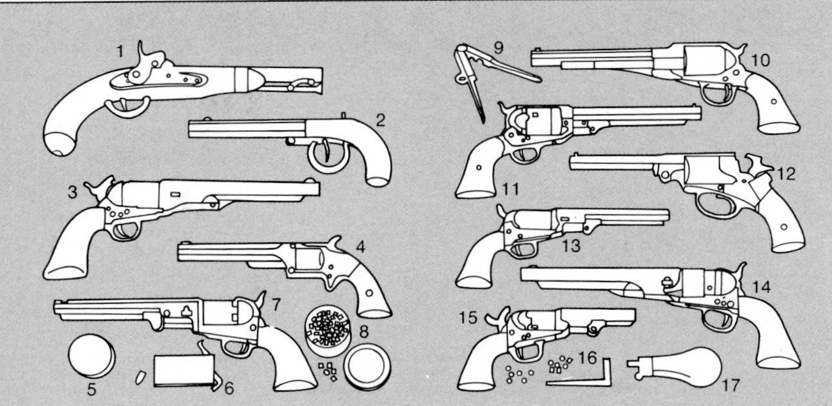

Artifacts courtesy of: The Museum of The Confederacy, Richmond, Va

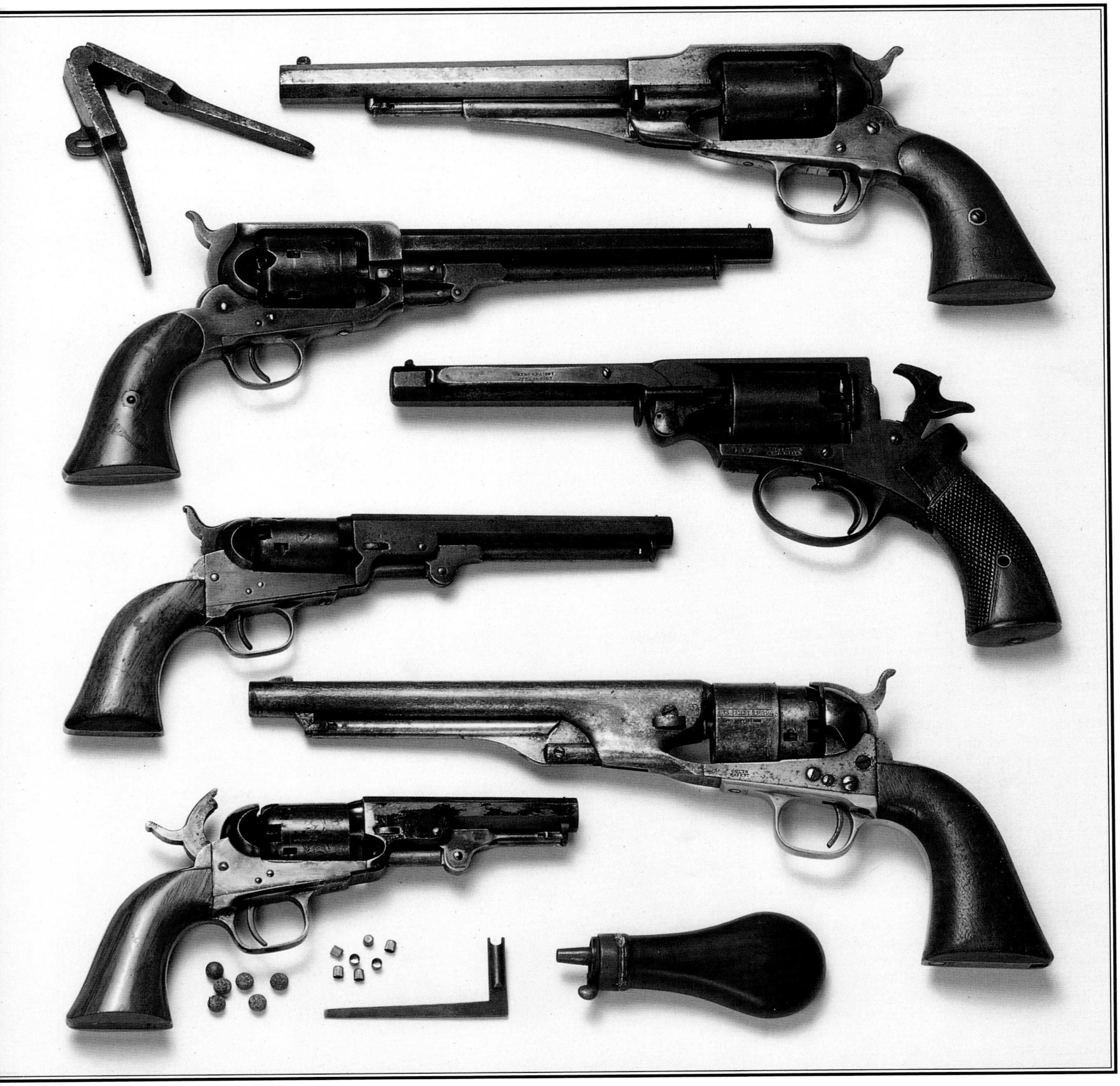

of a hazy uncertainty whether I was on my head or my heels, there comes to me the recollections that I started into the charge with the others; that I struck the limb of a tree and knocked my hat off; that I even stopped to pick it up (think of it!) and that as I started on a few straggling shots were winding up the affair." Realizing that the fight was done and he had not yet fired his revolver, he pointed it in the direction the Yankees had withdrawn and fired what proved to be the last shot of the "engagement". Later, taking stock of the affair, Mosby found that he had suffered no casualties except for one man who had briefly followed the retreating Yanks. After the fight was done, he said: "some d – d greenhorn behind him had let off his gun and shot him on the heel." A sheepish Alexander later recalled that "I did not say a word". So much for his first shot of the war.[12]

However they faced up to that first test in battle, once they were through it Johnny Reb and Billy Yank became "veterans", and generally thereafter they approached an impending fight rather differently. The fear and anxiety were still there, and certainly so was the danger. But they knew what to expect now, and except for some unusual circumstance, or the always unpredictable event when a veteran of a score of fights could suddenly lose his nerve, they knew how they were going to behave.

On the morning of a battle the non-commissioned officers roused the men out of their slumber at 2 or 3 a.m. with the "long roll" on the drums. There was much to be done. The soldiers dressed and assembled speedily for inspection, and then broke ranks to prepare rations. Ordinarily their officers ordered them to cook three days' worth, though to little purpose. Practical as always, Yank and Reb alike often cooked and ate it all right then, reasoning that what they ate they did not have to carry, and assuming that they would live off the land as they marched. Besides, it was better to march off to battle on a full stomach and risk hunger later, than to chance dying in battle with uneaten food still in their haversacks.

Meanwhile the ordnance officers issued ammunition. In both armies the standard prebattle issue amounted to sixty rounds of Minié cartridges and percussion caps. They put the caps in the leather cap-box on their belts, and forty of the rounds fitted into a cartridge box also on the belt. The remaining rounds went in their shirt or trouser pockets. This procedure out of the way, they were ready to march off to fight.

Above: Those whose courage was less steady might be unnerved by the sight of the destruction of war. Here at Henry Hill at Manassas, the ruins of Henry House told of the terrible force of artillery.

Below: Many looked to their colors to inspire them as they charged the enemy. Their flags, showing the bullet and shot holes of hard service, carried reminders of past victories to infuse the spirit.

Sometime before they went into action, and usually before they began their march, the assembled soldiers listened to their colonel exhort them to stirring deeds, or else heard a staff officer read aloud a written address from the brigade or army commander, all designed to arouse their martial ardor. Inevitably they heard references to the bravery they had shown in past fights, of the cowardice and barbarity of the foe, of those at home whose hearthsides the men were here to defend, and of the cause for which they would cheerfully lay down their lives if necessary. Often the speeches brimmed with the seemingly pompous posturing which men of that time took so very seriously. Before Shiloh, General Albert Sidney Johnston, commanding the Confederates, told his men that "The eyes and hopes of eight millions of people rest upon you".

> You are expected to show yourselves worthy of your race and lineage; worthy of the women of the South, whose noble devotion in this war has never been exceeded at any time. With such incentives to brave deeds and with the trust that God is with us, your general will lead you confidantly to the combat, assurred of success.[13]

Others could be less elevated. "Remember that

Above: Then they advanced over the torn and bloodied ground, like this terrain full of earthworks and defenses around Petersburg, Virginia in 1865, showing the hazards and impediments the soldiers had to face.

the enemy has no feeling of mercy or kindness toward you", General Thomas C. Hindman told his army prior to its December 1862 battle with Federals at Prairie Grove, Arkansas.

> His ranks are made up of Pin Indians, free negroes, Southern tories, Kansas jayhawkers and hired Dutch cutthroats. These bloody ruffians have invaded your country, stolen and destroyed your property, murdered your neighbors, outraged your women, driven your children from their homes and defiled the graves of your kindred.[14]

However they exhorted their men, once the rhetoric was done the officers of both sides usually gave the same instructions. Aim for enemy officers. Kill artillery horses. Wait until within range before firing, and then only on order. Aim at the knees. Stay quiet except in the charge. Leave the wounded where they fall. Do not break ranks to plunder. "If we whip the enemy", said Hindman, "all he has will be ours".[15]

A few of these pre-battle speeches proved positively depressing. The colonel of a midwestern regiment told his Billy Yanks that "The secessionists have ten thousand men and forty rifled cannon. They are strongly fortified. They have more men and more cannon than we have. They will cut us to pieces. Marching to attack such an enemy, so entrenched and so armed, is marching to a butcher shop rather than to a battle. There is bloody work ahead. Many of you boys will go out who will never come back again."[16] It was hardly a performance calculated to encourage the timid, and no doubt few in his regiment were saddened when the colonel shortly resigned.

Now and then some unexpected mirth lightened the tension during an officer's exhortation, and it was all too welcome, though usually at the expense of someone's dignity. At the Battle of Stones River, in Tennessee in December 1862, Colonel Granville Moody addressed his 12th Ohio before they launched into the fearful battle against the enemy. He had been a minister before the war, and now he led them in solemn prayer. "Now, boys, fight for your country and your God", he said, "and . . ." Just at that moment the first volley from the enemy came speeding past them. Forgetting all about the obligatory "amen" to close, he shouted ". . . and aim low!" Thereafter his men nicknamed him "Aim Low".[17]

This done, the regiments began their march to the fighting. At almost the same time, many of the men began lightening their personal loads, casting aside their blanket rolls, knapsacks, haversacks, even jackets and hats – anything that would possibly get in their way in the fight. Suddenly concerned about their mortality, and the possibility that they would see their maker by nightfall, many men also threw away decks of cards, dice, lurid novels and photographs, whiskey, and more. Though the veterans marched with a surer step, they were more quiet in the advance, in part because they did not feel the same nervousness which impelled so many first-

Below: If there was time just before going into the firing line, the men might rest awhile, even pull out their pipes and playing cards, or a last letter from home. It was a moment for quiet contemplation.

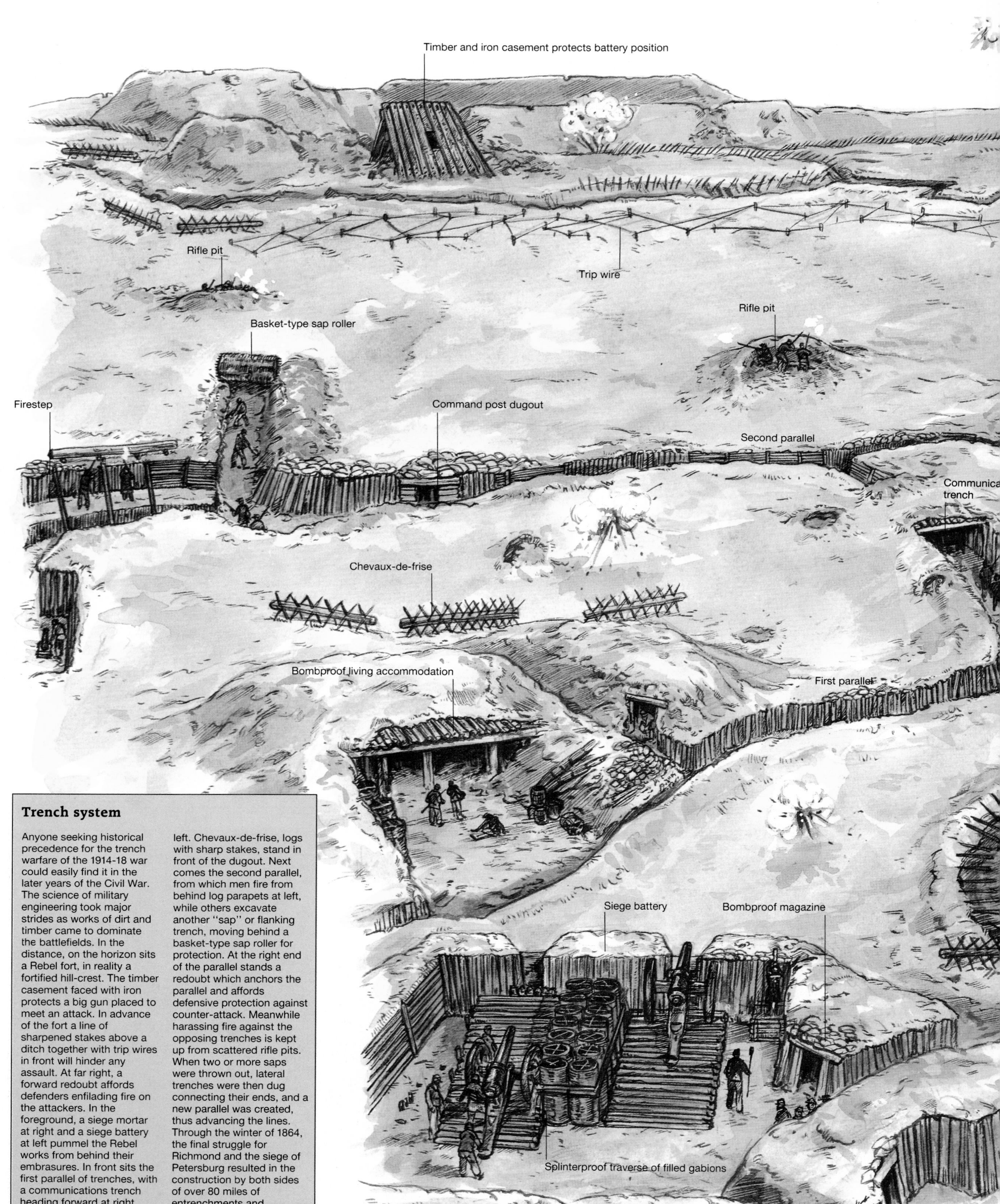

Trench system

Anyone seeking historical precedence for the trench warfare of the 1914-18 war could easily find it in the later years of the Civil War. The science of military engineering took major strides as works of dirt and timber came to dominate the battlefields. In the distance, on the horizon sits a Rebel fort, in reality a fortified hill-crest. The timber casement faced with iron protects a big gun placed to meet an attack. In advance of the fort a line of sharpened stakes above a ditch together with trip wires in front will hinder any assault. At far right, a forward redoubt affords defenders enfilading fire on the attackers. In the foreground, a siege mortar at right and a siege battery at left pummel the Rebel works from behind their embrasures. In front sits the first parallel of trenches, with a communications trench heading forward at right, and bombproof dugouts at left. Chevaux-de-frise, logs with sharp stakes, stand in front of the dugout. Next comes the second parallel, from which men fire from behind log parapets at left, while others excavate another "sap" or flanking trench, moving behind a basket-type sap roller for protection. At the right end of the parallel stands a redoubt which anchors the parallel and affords defensive protection against counter-attack. Meanwhile harassing fire against the opposing trenches is kept up from scattered rifle pits. When two or more saps were thrown out, lateral trenches were then dug connecting their ends, and a new parallel was created, thus advancing the lines. Through the winter of 1864, the final struggle for Richmond and the siege of Petersburg resulted in the construction by both sides of over 80 miles of entrenchments and redoubts such as these.

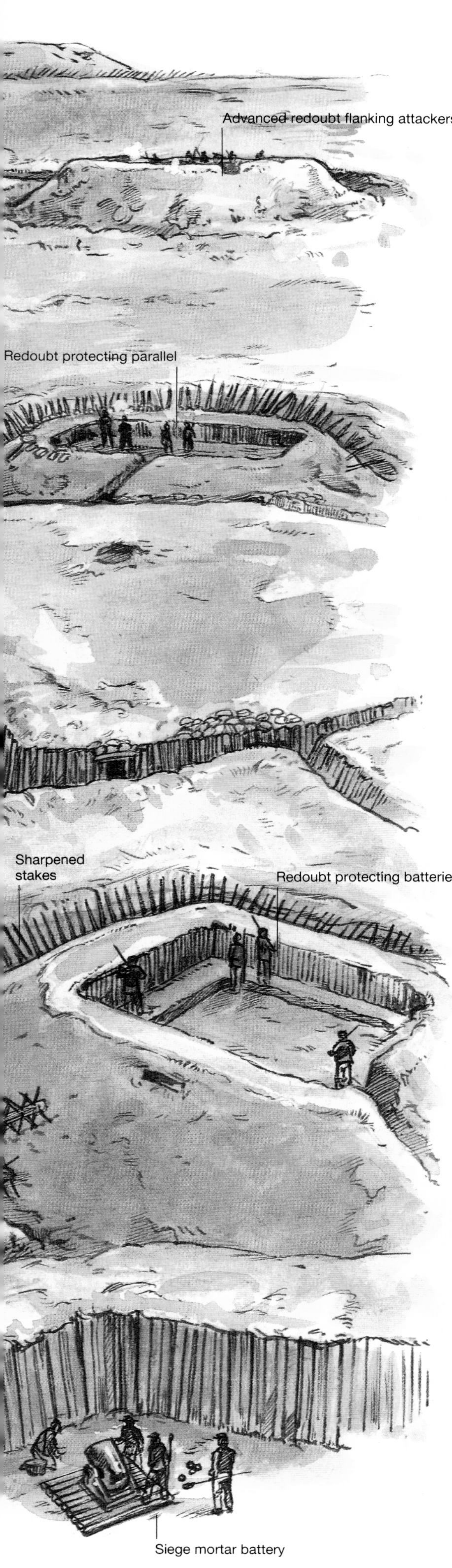

timers to chatter incessantly, but also because many believed in a certain law of averages. Every time a veteran survived one battle, so the logic went, it increased his chances of being hit in the next one. Noticing that one veteran regiment did not show the same alacrity to "see the elephant" as some new and untested units at Shiloh, one colonel explained that the old-timers "had seen the elephant several times, and did not care about seeing him again unless necessary".

In fact, before almost every battle of the war, many soldiers felt premonitions of their own death, wounding or capture. Most were proved wrong, but many were right, and thousands took precautions that they would be identified and taken care of after their deaths. They wrote their names and regiments and the addresses of their families on slips of paper, stuffing them into trouser pockets or pinning them on their shirts. Many made their messmates swear vows to search them out after the fight and, if slain, to see that their remains were returned to home and family. Hundreds of miles from home, in a strange country, Johnny Reb and Billy Yank did not want to lie for eternity among strangers in an unmarked grave. Thousands were not granted their last wish.

With the sounds of firing before them, the men moved steadily toward the fighting line. Soon they were confronted by signs of the carnage as wounded and dying men were carried to the rear by the stretcher-bearers and musicians. All too often, the veterans noted sardonically that it required two or three able-bodied soldiers to help to the rear a wounded comrade with nothing more than an injured hand or finger. Most of those they passed, whether shirkers or seriously wounded, cheered the fresh soldiers on, telling them to "give it" to the enemy. Frightened animals raced in panic away from the fighting and noise. Equally scared men who could not stand the fire rushed to the rear, sometimes disrupting the orderly formations of the advancing units they ran through. The scene was well calculated to unnerve even the most experienced and steadiest of veterans, and it could set to panic fresh troops awaiting their first taste of battle.

Finally they came to the staging area, either directly in a front line that was preparing for an attack or defense, or immediately behind it to serve as support. Civil War battles were not affairs of one continuous fight, but rather a series of localized actions between units in the immediate area. Rarely if ever was an entire army engaged in combat simultaneously. Men just arrived at the front watched or listened to the sound of battle from one of their flanks while waiting for their own assault to commence.

These were perhaps the most trying moments of all. The coolest of the men rested on their arms or on the ground, read a letter from home or smoked a pipe. The rest felt all the sensations that fear could induce. There was a tremendous feeling of solitude, of being alone amid thousands. Many silently repented their wicked ways, promising their god to reform if only he saw them through this fight – promises rarely kept. Some prayed, others sang, and many found all their senses heightened, taking in through eye, nose, and ear every aspect of the scene before them. These were the moments when, now under some fire from the enemy, the men felt a building tension and frustration, fear being gradually replaced by an anxiety to get moving, to fire back, to do *something, anything,* to put an end to the waiting. It was in this pre-battle silence, with all of these tremors running through the men, that the line finally grew silent as each man wrestled with his emotions and steeled his nerves. It was in such a deadly tense time of waiting that James Wilcox had been unable to stand it any longer, shouting, *"My God, why dont they order us to charge!"* And finally they did.

The orders were carried either by word of mouth or by bugles or drums. The colonels had their regiments fall in and sent them forward. Constantly they shouted at the men to maintain that thirteen-inch distance between each other,

Below: When they were just behind the battleline, in an attitude similar to these Federals resting in Virginia, Johnny and Billy faced a battle with their own fears. If they won it, they could emerge heroes.

to keep their line straight. They were not themselves allowed to fire, saving that for the final charge, but the enemy was certainly sending a hail of bullets and shells towards them. The men could hear the bumble-bee-like sound of the Minié bullets whizzing past, and now and then the thump of one hitting flesh and bone. Shells began to explode overhead and near their line, bringing more men down. And still the attackers' rifles remained silent. The tension mounted until it became intolerable. "Oh, dear!" one Yankee corporal cried; "when shall *we* fire?"[18] Finally, the order to fire came as an enormous relief.

There was little that was subtle about Civil War combat. One line advanced against another in its entrenched or hastily fortified position, usually atop some rise of ground. The advance itself was almost always across open ground. The soldiers charging could see their enemies in the distance, and their enemies had them in full view. The closer they got, the less the foe seemed like some propagandized abstraction, and more like just other Americans.

For all the slaughter they promoted, such unsophisticated tactics inevitably led to incredible heroism as well. "To mass troops against the fire of a covered line is simply to devote them to destruction", a Yankee general declared. "The greater the mass, the greater the loss – that is all."[19] Facing a fight like that, it took raw nerve to charge into the mouth of a cannon and a line of guns bristling with gleaming bayonets.

A day or so after the fight, as they wrote their letters home, the men in the ranks would often recollect that a great sense of calm came over them once the fight commenced, and that time passed away rapidly. "Time rolls off very fast in time of battle", one Rebel wrote in 1861, "when we had been in 3½ hours it appeared to me that it hadent been two".[20] In fact, the pace of activity during the fight was every bit as confused and exhausting as had been the hours leading up to it, only the men simply had no opportunity to reflect upon the chaos all around them. In the final rush to the enemy's line, many frequently broke away from their own ranks and rushed on too quickly, losing all track of where they were. They often exhausted themselves in their eagerness, and officers who ordered them to double-time in the assault – 165 steps per minute – sometimes wore out a regiment before it reached the foe. "We started in double quick from our entrenchments and went untill we were near broke down", a Reb of the 19th Virginia wrote of its charge at First Bull Run.[21]

Above: In rank upon endless rank they would march into the face of the firing. Here just part of the 2nd Rhode Island Infantry stands in formation. Multiplied by hundreds, this scene formed a battle line.

Below: When they attacked or defended, it was in open fields or woods, or amid the entrenchments and earthworks like these near Fort McGilvery and Fort Stedman, among the Petersburg fortifications.

The excitement was almost too much for some. "I with a number of others were sufferers from camp diarrhea, and up to that time we had found no cure", wrote William A. Fletcher of the 8th Texas Cavalry of his first action, "so, entering the battle, I had quite a great fear that something disgraceful might happen and it was somewhat uppermost in my mind; but to my surprise the excitement or something else had effected a cure."[22]

In the first flush of battle fever, very few men fired their rifles effectively. Often, especially

Above: When a soldier saw his comrades start to fall, as these men fell near the Dunker Church at Antietam, then courage and resolve stood their hardiest test. Only the steadiest would not be affected.

Below: And when it was all over, and the fight moved on to another field, those who had paid the price were often buried in shallow graves or else simply stripped and left, as grim testimony to what had been.

among fresh troops, the initial bullets were aimed more at the stars than the foe. "I recollect their first volley", one Reb wrote of a Virginia unit, "and how unfavorably it affected me. It was apparently made with the guns raised at an angle of forty-five degrees, and I was fully assured that their bullets would not hit the Yankees, unless they were nearer heaven than they were generally located by our people."[23]

A common problem among men of both sides came with their second shot. Amid the shouting and firing, most men were not conscious of the sound of their own rifle firing, nor of the kick against their shoulders when they did. Consequently, thousands improperly reloaded their weapons – forgetting to bite off the end of the paper cartridge before ramming it home, or else neglecting to place a percussion cap on the firing nipple – but when they pulled the trigger they did not notice that their gun had failed to discharge. Occasionally this oversight led to a situation in which the rifle could be more dangerous to friend than foe. After the three-day Battle of Gettysburg in July 1863, the victorious Federals retrieved 27,500 rifles from the battlelines, most if not all of them dropped by the wounded and killed. Nearly half of them were found to hold two unfired rounds in their barrels. Between three and ten loads crammed the breeches of another 6,000. And one rifle was filled almost to the muzzle with twenty-three cartidges.

Untold numbers of Yanks and Rebs lost their control and fired away wildly at anyone in sight, even their own men, a problem made the more prevalent early in the war thanks to the number of Union regiments clothed in gray and an equal number of Confederate outfits that wore blue. Only with experience did the soldiers learn to curb their nervous activity, none ever succeeding completely. Those in the advance either stood in the midst of the firing to reload, or else lay down on the ground, rolled over on their backs, and rammed their fresh cartridges home before rising once more and continuing the advance.

By this time the confusion was growing, the sense of detachment, of being alone amid chaos, increasing. Men and officers alike were swearing constantly, and in ways and with words they did not ordinarily use. Even chaplains or former ministers in the ranks were heard to utter most unclerical oaths. "The air was filled with a medley of sounds", a boy from Maine recalled, "shouts, cheers, commands, oaths, the sharp reports of rifles, the hissing shot, dull heavy thuds of clubbed muskets, the swish of swords and sabers, groans and prayers."[24]

Men began to act without thought of who or where they were. Some, despite all pre-battle resolutions and fears about cowardice, simply turned and ran. Most were sworn or spanked back into line by officers and file closers waving their swords. Others assumed a bloodlust they had never before experienced. "I acted like a madman", remembered one Pennsylvanian, "a kind of desperation seized me. I snatched a gun from the hands of a man who was shot through the head, as he staggered and fell. At other times I would have been horror-struck, and could not have moved, but then I jumped over dead men with as little feeling as I would over a log. The feeling that was uppermost in my mind was a desire to kill as many rebels as I could."[25]

After covering a good bit of ground, the officers generally felt it necessary to call a halt to the advance to reform their by-now thinned and disorganized ranks, prior to making the final push to the enemy's line or works. At this moment the fighting men were the most difficult to control. Their blood up, some simply could not be stopped from rushing headlong alone. Others, having stood the fire until this point, felt their courage ebb as they stood under fire, close enough now to see the face of the foe. "If I hadent seen the fix I was in, and run like blazes, I would have been a goner by this time", one Yank wrote in 1864, and thousands of others like him discovered at this penultimate moment in the attack that their feet seemed to have a will of their own.[26] "I limbered up for the rear as fast as legs cood carry", another Federal wrote after a battle, "and that was prety fast".[27]

With the men reformed, and as many of the shirkers and faint-hearted forced back into line as possible, the order for the final push went out. Forward they went, almost at a run, and now, thankfully, it all happened too fast for a man to think about where he was or what he was doing. Unable to take time to reload their guns, or too confused to remember to do so, some men simply picked up others from the fallen, or else grabbed their own rifles by the muzzles and used them as clubs as they reached the enemy line.

Hand-to-hand combat was not commonplace in the Civil War – despite the "evidence" of the stilted old Currier and Ives lithographs. By this point in the battle, nine times out of ten either the advancing lines were beaten back by massed fire before reaching the defending line, or else the defenders, seeing themselves outnumbered or else losing their own resolve, had pulled back. This is one of the reasons why there were so very few bayonet wounds in the war, for the men

Confederate Rifle-Muskets, Rifles and Accoutrements

1 Early type Richmond muzzle-loading rifle-musket with ramrod and shoulder strap
2 Raleigh Bayonet Factory socket bayonet complete with protective scabbard
3 Fayetteville muzzle-loading rifle, early type with ramrod
4 Fayetteville saber bayonet
5 CS embossed cap box
6 CS embossed cartridge box complete with carrying strap
7 Cartridge box, cap box and waist belt
8 Read and Watson muzzle-loading rifle, early type complete with ramrod
9 Cook and Brother muzzle-loading rifle complete with ramrod
10 CS embossed cap box
11 Georgia Armory saber bayonet housed in scabbard
12 CS embossed cartridge box
13 CS embossed tin drum water canteen with shoulder strap
14 Richmond muzzle-loading rifle-musket, late type
15 Waist belt with brass oval CS belt plate
16 Waist belt with brass frame buckle
17 Waist belt with brass rectangular CSA belt plate

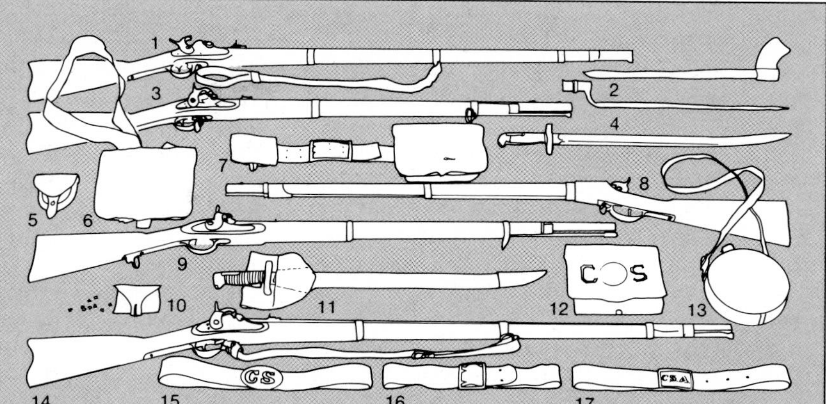

Artifacts courtesy of: Russ Pritchard Collection

simply did not get close enough to each other to use them. However, now and then, as in the bloody fighting at Gettysburg on July 3, 1863, at the height of the great Confederate assault, the opposing troops did come eye to eye and blow to blow. Never was the fighting more personal: not a battle, but hundreds of single combats. "Occasionally, when too sorely pressed, they would drop their rifles and clinch the enemy", wrote a Yankee from Maine, "until Federal and Confederate would roll upon the ground in the death struggle".[28]

In those last moments of the attack, and in the hand-to-hand fighting that might follow, the men on both sides filled the air with their own distinctive cries. The so-called "Rebel Yell" became world famous even before the war was done, though many would not agree in later years upon its exact nature or origin. First heard at Bull Run in July 1861, it appeared on nearly every other battlefield of the war, and most likely grew out of some pre-war sporting or hunting shout when the game was being pursued, or else from the so-called "hollering" used in the Southern Appalachian region where neighbors communicated with each other by a high-pitched yell from one hilltop to another. It varied from one theater of the war to another, and even took on a particularly savage air west of the Mississippi where Confederate Indian soldiers added their own war whoops to it. Wherever heard, it could demoralize a faint-hearted Federal. Indeed, in 1864, when General Jubal Early was told that a regiment could not attack the Yankees because there was no ammunition, he replied, "Damn it, holler them across".[29] And that is what they did. By contrast, the battle yell of Billy Yank was a much more disciplined "hurrah", and generally more in unison than the uncoordinated Rebel shouts. Deep-throated and lusty, still it sometimes adopted the more savage air of the Rebel cry as men became carried away in battle. On either side, ironically, these spontaneous yells grew not so much out of a desire to intimidate the foe, as to release pent-up tension for the yellers.

Union Longarms and Accoutrements

1 US Model 1816 smoothbore musket alteration with bayonet in place
2 Scabbard for above bayonet
3 Cap box and waist belt
4 US Model 1842 smoothbore musket
5 Socket bayonet for *4*
6 Cap box, waist belt and bayonet scabbard
7 US Model 1855 muzzle-loading rifle-musket
8 Socket bayonet for *6* and *7*
9 Rifle-musket cartridge box with shoulder belt
10 US Model 1861 muzzle-loading rifle-musket
11 Cap box
12 Socket bayonet and scabbard for *10*
13 British Pattern 1853 muzzle-loading type Enfield rifle-musket
14 Tompion, plug for top of barrel
15 Socket-type bayonet, scabbard and frog for use with *13*
16 Gun tools for use with rifle-muskets
17 Justice muzzle-loading rifle-musket
18 Ramrod for *17*
19 Non-commissioned officer's waist belt
20 Militia uniform waist belt with plate
21 .58 caliber paper cartridges

Artifacts courtesy of: The Civil War Library and Museum, Philadelphia, Pa: 1, 2, 4, 5, 7, 10, 13, 14, 16, 17, 18, 21; J. Craig Nannos Collection: 3, 6, 8, 9, 11, 12, 15, 19, 20

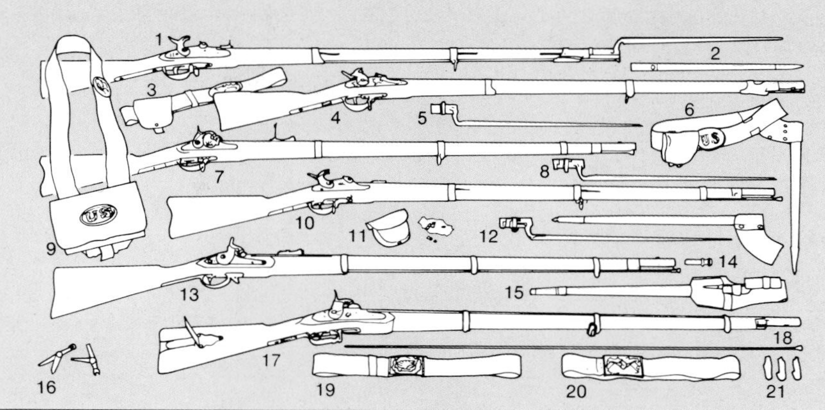

Private, 2nd New Hampshire Volunteer Infantry, US Army

For all its lauding as one of the world's first 'modern' wars, the Civil War saw in its early days a number of regiments that looked backward almost to the days of the Revolutionary War. One of these was the 2nd New Hampshire. To be sure, it gave first class service to the Federal cause, fighting from First Manassas through almost every major battle in the East, concluding with the occupation of Richmond in the last days of the war. Maybe they fought so long and well as amends for their outmoded garb. In 1861 they actually went to war wearing swallow-tail coats with red trim and facings, gray trousers, the usual black leather accoutrements, and an almost ludicrous "coal scuttle" cap. Their distinctive "NHSM" belt plate, standing for New Hampshire State Militia, was almost the only element of their attire that was orthodox and did not stand out as being slightly peculiar.

The shouting, the stabbing, the clubbing and firing, were quickly over. Few hand-to-hand combats lasted more than a few minutes before one side or the other – though most often the attacker – withdrew. Then there was the problem of keeping men from turning and simply running back to their own lines. No man wanted to be the last one killed in a failed assault, yet if some order were not maintained in a withdrawal, then the always-expected counter-assault could be disastrous. If such an attack did come, then all that Yank and Reb had just gone through was repeated, only with the roles reversed.

And thus the battle was fought. The more sophisticated matters of tactics, or seeking an exposed flank or a gap in the foe's line were all the province of the officers. The men in the ranks went where they were told and fought as they were ordered. If they won, the leaders got the credit, but win or lose, more often than not the blood on the soil came from the men in the ranks.

Inevitably there came lulls in the battle, and then – and only then – did the men realize the bone-crushing exhaustion they felt. The nervous tension before and during the fight was masked by the excitement of it all, but immediately after a fight was finished the men could find themselves so worn out that many fell asleep with the shot and shell still flying overhead. Now, too, the thirst and hunger set in, and with it often a post-battle depression, this last intense feeling especially heightened by what the soldier could see of his recent bloody work out on the battlefield. "When the fight was over & I saw what was done the tears came free", one soldier confessed later to his wife. "To think of civilized people killing one another like beasts. One would think that the supreme ruler would put a stop to it."[30]

Above: A dead Rebel marksman in the Devil's Den at Gettysburg has found the eternal rest that so many soldiers went to when they looked into the face of battle. Their war, at least, was done.

Above: When the battle was over, and for months thereafter, the soldiers of blue and gray had to live not only with the memories of what they had seen, but also the grisly reminders of the battlefields.

Men – the victors – walked over the field once the foe had withdrawn. Most plundered at least a little, picking up a better rifle, swapping boots or shoes with one less fortunate who would no longer need them. A few rifled pockets for money and valuables. But most observed some reverence for their fallen comrades and enemies, and most – no matter how many battles they saw – felt some shock and shame for the awful work. "The stiffened bodies lie, grasping in death, the arms they bravely bore, with glazed eyes, and features blackened by rapid decay", wrote a Georgian. "Here sits one against a tree in motionless stare. Another has his head leaning against a stump, his hands over his head. They have paid the last penalty. They have fought their last battle. The air is putrid with decaying bodies of men & horses. My God, My God, what a scourge is war."[31]

A scourge it certainly was, yet it produced from these men some incredible acts of heroism, examples of rising above themselves for their cause or their fellow soldiers. Despite its being the most dangerous post in the line, men would vie with one another to carry the regimental banners into the fight, and as soon as one color bearer fell, another rushed to take his place. In some regiments, as many as a dozen or more men would fall carrying the colors in a single battle. When an officer called for volunteers for a dangerous task, he seldom was wanting for men to do it. At the Second Battle of Bull Run, in 1862, several score Georgians went into the fight barefoot, even rushing headlong through briars and thorns, and leaving bloody footprints in their wake as they advanced to fight. So pronounced was the heroism of the men in blue and gray, that the Confederacy authorized a published Roll of Honor after every fight, to memorialize the names of the men who stood out for bravery. In the Union, Congress created the Medal of Honor, which would remain thereafter the nation's highest military award for valor.

Even in their death throes, the men could display magnificent courage and patriotism. "I can die contented", said an Iowa man after the Battle of Tupelo, Mississippi, in 1862. His abdomen was nearly ripped away by a Rebel shell, yet his only thought was for victory, and when told of the Union success he relaxed, expressed his happiness at the outcome, and died.[32]

"I see no reason to dread the future", wrote an Iowa soldier in January 1863, and both those who lived and those who faced their own death would have agreed with him. "If it is God's will that I find my grave", he wrote, "I hope to be ready". Hundreds of thousands faced that possibility with the same equanimity. 'Let it come when it may", he said, "I am determined to do my duty and come home honorably or never".[32] For all of them, whether they went home again or remained in the ground for which they fought, the men of North and South who looked into the face of battle and did not turn away, emerged from the fiery trial with honor unbounded.

References

1 Wiley, *Billy Yank*, p.70.
2 Davis, *Bull Run*, p.157.
3 *Ibid.*
4 Wiley, *Johnny Reb*, p.28.
5 Wiley and Milhollen, *They Who Fought Here*, p.252.
6 Wiley, *Billy Yank*, p.69.
7 Wiley, *Johnny Reb*, p.29.
8 *Ibid.*
9 Wiley and Milhollen, *They Who Fought Here*, p.252.
10 Wiley, *Billy Yank*, p.71.
11 McHenry Howard, *Recollections of a Maryland Confederate Soldier* (Baltimore, 1914), p.37.
12 John H. Alexander, *Mosby's Men* (New York, 1907), pp.46-50.
13 O.R., Series I, Vol. 10, Part 2, p.389.
14 *Ibid*, Vol. 22, Part I, p.83.
15 *Ibid.*
16 John Beatty, *Memoirs of a Volunteer* (New York, 1946), pp.25-6.
17 Wiley, *Billy Yank*, p.68.
18 *Ibid.*, p.71.
19 John M. Schofield, *Forty-six Years in the Army* (New York, 1897), p.146.
20 Wiley, *Johnny Reb*, p.30.
21 Joseph Higginbotham Diary, July 21, 1861, University of Virginia Library, Charlottesville.
22 Wiley, *Johnny Reb*, pp.31-2.
23 *Ibid.*, p.30.
24 Theodore Gerrish, *Army Life* (Portland, Me., 1882), p.177.
25 Oliver Norton, *Army Letters, 1861-1865* (Chicago, 1903), pp.106-9.
26 Wiley, *Billy Yank*, p.84.
27 *Ibid.*
28 Gerrish, *Army Life*, p.177.
29 Wiley, *Johnny Reb*, p.71.
30 *Ibid.*, p.33.
31 S. Joseph Lewis, Jr., ed., "Letters of William Fisher Plane, C.S.A.", *Collections of the Georgia Historical Society*, XLVIII (1964), p.223.
32 Joseph Sweney, "Nursed a Wounded Brother", *Annals of Iowa*, XXXI (1952), p.142.

CHAPTER THIRTEEN

VICTORY & DEFEAT

Spring in 1865 may have brought renewal to the land, but it brought death for the Confederacy. When on April 1 Union forces seized the important crossroads at Five Forks, Lee had no choice but to evacuate Petersburg and Richmond to avoid being completely cut off. The next day his men left the trenches, and the Confederate government packed and fled its capital. For Lee there remained a week of retreat, his last open field campaign, but it was one of flight. Action at Sayler's Creek on April 6 saw nearly one third of the Army of Northern Virginia captured. Two days later hard-riding Yankee cavalry had gotten across his escape route, threatening to crush him between themselves and Grant's infantry. Lee had no choice but to surrender.

The story was much the same in North Carolina. Held at bay by Sherman, Johnston and his dwindling army moved slowly toward the Virginia border, hoping to effect a junction with Lee. But Sherman was too strong for him. Seeing a continuation of hostilities to be fruitless, Johnston asked Sherman to cease actions pending surrender negotiations. After several days and severe argument between Sherman and Washington, Johnston also capitulated.

There would be other lesser surrenders to come, but now the nation's attention focused upon the two chases. On April 14, President Lincoln was assassinated at Ford's Theater in Washington, and a massive manhunt was launched for his assassin, John Wilkes Booth. And even more Yankees were searching for Jefferson Davis and his fleeing government. Finally Booth was cornered and killed on April 26, but Davis remained at large until May 10 before he was captured and imprisoned for more than a year.

With the war done, the question of what to do with former Confederates, of how to reconstruct the Union, and of what millions of Johnny Rebs and Billy Yanks would do with their lives, challenged the reunited but still bleeding nation.

THERE IS little that can be said that is good about any wars, except that inevitably they have to come to an end. Like all of the pestilences that afflict humankind, war cannot sustain itself indefinitely. And civil wars tend to consume themselves more rapidly than most others. The Civil War in America raged for 1,489 days, from the firing on Fort Sumter on April 12, 1861, to the last land engagement at Palmito Ranch, Texas, on May 12, 1865. During those forty-nine months of warfare, at least 10,455 shooting engagements of varying sizes took place, which meant that, on average, blue met gray somewhere on the continent seven times every day. Virginia was ravaged, one fifth of all engagements taking place in the Old Dominion. Not surprisingly, Tennessee ranked next, with almost 1,500 engagements within its troubled borders. Symbolic of the ferocity of the much-forgotten warfare west of the Mississippi, the state with the third greatest number of fights was Missouri. The conflict was truly continental in scope, with even California and the territory that would become New Mexico and Arizona totaling 163 engagements.[1]

Warfare on such a scale could not sustain itself forever. Indeed, as early as the summer of 1863, with the twin Union victories at Gettysburg and Vicksburg, leaving Lee with a shattered army and the Confederacy split in two by a Yankee-controlled Mississippi River, it was evident that only foreign intervention for the South, or a loss of will to win by the North, could prevent a Federal victory. Incredible resolve and sacrifice by Confederate soldiers and civilians prolonged the conflict perhaps as much as a full year longer than would have been thought possible.

Never before had the American continent seen such devastation. By 1865 and the war's end, Southern cities like Richmond looked more like the bombed out hulks of European cities after World War II.

When it came, it came almost all at once. On April 9, 1865, having forced Lee out of the defenses of Petersburg and Richmond and his tattered army out in the open, General Ulysses S. Grant speedily surrounded his old foe near Appomattox Court House, Virginia. Hopelessly outnumbered, and with nowhere to escape, Lee had to capitulate. The once-mighty Army of Northern Virginia would fight no more. A few days later, on April 26, near Durham Station, North Carolina, the other major Confederate force in the east, the Army of Tennessee, surrendered to William T. Sherman. A week and a day later, General Richard Taylor surrendered remaining Rebel troops in Mississippi, Alabama, and part of Louisiana, and on May 26 the Army of the Trans-Mississippi gave up as well. All organized resistance had finally ceased.

For the winners, victory was a heady feeling, indeed. "We are through with our work", exulted Thomas Osborn with Sherman's army.[2] When the news of Lee's surrender reached the camps of the Army of the Potomac, a few men cheered, and at least one black regiment fired its rifles in the air in celebration. Yet most men met the news with quiet, and a surprising measure of compassion for the feelings of their defeated foes. There were no scenes of wild cheering, of endless salutes and volleys. The victors were simply glad that they had won, and more pleased that at last it was all over. "Never shall I forget the feeling that passed over my soul just before retiring", cavalryman Roger Hannaford of the 2nd Ohio wrote of April 9; "the knowledge that *now* we could go to bed & *feel sure* of enjoying a full night's rest". For the first time in four years he knew that he would not be aroused by an alarm in the night. "The thought that I was certain, yes, certain of having a quiet night, the idea of security, was ineffable".[3]

Other Federals expressed surprise at the absence of exultant feelings when the first news of the surrenders reached them. "I remember how we sat there and pitied and sympathized with these courageous Southern men who had fought for four long and dreary years all so stubbornly, so bravely and so well", wrote a New Hampshire volunteer, "and now, whipped, beaten, completely used up, were fully at our mercy – it was pitiful, sad, hard, and seemed to us altogether too bad".[4] While many Yankees would retain hard feelings for their old foes for the rest of their days, the great majority seemed surprised at how quickly all hostility evaporated after the war officially finished. They had never wanted to fight their own kind. Now that it was done, they could not wait to put it all behind them.

It was not so easy across the lines. No Americans had ever been defeated in a war. Worse, Southerners had always entertained a substantial martial tradition. Now they were beaten. It was almost more than some could bear. "I would like to go out in the woods and die drunk and bury all my sorrows", one Kentucky Rebel cried after Johnston's surrender to Sherman. "This was the blackest day of our lives", declared another. "All was lost and there seemed to be no hope for the future".[5] When Lee's men learned that he had surrendered them to Grant, some became highly emotional. "Blow, Gabriel! Blow!" one North Carolinian shouted as he threw his rifle. "My God, let him blow, I am ready to die". Some could not accept defeat as final. "We will go home, make three more crops, and try them again", one soldier suggested to his commander. "My God, that I should have lived to see this day!" a South Carolinian with Lee exclaimed. "I hoped I should die before this day!" A cavalryman shook his fist heavenward and cried, "If General Lee has had to surrender his Army, there is not a just God in Heaven!"[6]

After the first shock, though, most of these men's feelings subsided to match those of the overwhelming number of their comrades. A North Carolinian observed of the army that "a feeling of collapse, mental and physical, succeeded for some hours" after the first news of their surrender. Neither men nor officers spoke much. "They sat, or lay on the ground in reflective mood, overcome by a flood of sad recollections". When they did speak, it was to comfort one another with reassurances that "they had discharged their duty, and therefore that they bore no share of the national disgrace".[7]

Of those who could not face defeat, a few hundred simply melted into the countryside rather than face the inevitable formal surrender ceremony. A handful even committed suicide. But for most, the extent of final resistance came when they buried their flags or tore them to shreds rather than give them up, and not a few preferred bashing their rifles to bits against a tree to handing them over. They were too tired and hungry and saddened to do anything more overt. In fact, their former foes now fed them, hundreds of Yankee supply wagons coming into the Confederate camps with hardtack and bacon and beef.

A relief at war's end, even if it did come in defeat, also played its part in calming the Southerners. Before long, with the guns silent and the formal surrender ceremonies being planned by the officers, the enlisted Union men began crossing the lines of their own accord, renewing old friendships, inquiring about relatives who had served on the other side, and simply sharing their comradeship and delicacies with men whom, though beaten, they admired and respected the

Above: Eventually the fighting had to come to an end, and when it did, it happened quickly. Here in the home of Wilmer McLean in Appomattox Court House, Lee and Grant met, not for battle, but for peace.

Below: Down near Durham Station, North Carolina, just 17 days after Lee's surrender, the South's other major army under Joseph E. Johnston capitulated to Sherman here in the little Bennett home.

more. A Pennyslvanian at Appomattox strolled into the depressed camps of the former foe after the surrender had been signed and found that "as soon as I got among these boys I felt and was treated as well as if I had been among our own boys, and a person would of thought we were of the same Army and had been Fighting under the Same Flag".[8]

According to the terms worked out by the generals in command, each of the surrendered Confederate armies had to endure some form of formal ceremony, not so much as a humiliation – though many felt it so – as simply an organized means of turning over weapons and equipment and signing formal paroles not to take up arms again against the United States government. All were conducted with an eye to the dignity and feelings of the beaten Confederates. When the Kentucky "Orphan Brigade" marched into Washington, Georgia, to surrender on May 4, they rode down the main street with flags flying.

Drummer, Co. F, 2nd Wisconsin Infantry, "Iron Brigade"

Hardly any other unit of the Civil War would achieve such lasting fame as the so-called "Iron Brigade" of Wisconsin and Indiana. Its three Wisconsin and one Indiana regiments fought with a ferocity, and suffered losses hardly equalled. Indeed, so heavy were its casualties that the unit only existed for two years. Formed largely of Irish and other immigrants, it endured 33% losses at 2nd Manassas in 1862, and nearly 60% in that whole campaign. Going into Gettysburg the following year it numbered almost 1,800; after the battle only 600 were left. The battle in Pennsylvania virtually destroyed the original brigade. Men of the 2nd Wisconsin, like their drummer, wore dark blue frock coats, and dark blue trousers, with the dark Hardee hat, their regimental number encircled by a brass bugle. "The Black Hat Brigade" they were called, a nickname proudly borne.

"Steadily they marched, the very horses seeming to vie with the riders in keeping up the military to the last", wrote John Jackman of the 9th Kentucky. "The Spring breezes gently waved the banners – banners that bore the marks of the contest, and that had the names of many fields written upon their folds – and the evening's sunlight, on the eve of fading from the hills, danced and quivered upon the long trusty Enfields, thus smiling pleasantly upon one of the last scenes of Southern pageantry".[9]

At Appomattox, the ceremony came on April 12. The Confederates were to march out of their camps and up the road leading to the small courthouse town. They would pass between ranks of Federal soldiers and officers until they reached the appointed spot, where they were to stack arms and lay down their furled colors. The Second Corps led the mournful procession, at its head the old Stonewall Brigade, formed and first led by the mighty Stonewall Jackson. As the first Confederates approached General Joshua Chamberlain of Maine, who was designated to formally receive the surrender, he ordered a bugler to sound a call for the Federal troops to move their rifles to "carry arms", a salute to the passing Rebels. The Confederate commander, General John B. Gordon, responded in kind, the proud old Second Corps springing to carry arms in response to the compliment of their former foes. Chamberlain was deeply moved. "On our part not a sound of trumpet more, nor roll of drum; not a cheer nor word nor whisper of vainglorying". Instead, he found "an awed silence rather, and breath-holding, as if it were the passing of the dead".[10] "It was a trying scene", wrote another Federal present. "And then, disarmed and colorless, they again broke into column and marched off, disappearing forever as soldiers of the Southern Confederacy". And for the past three days, here and there among the camps, regimental bands had already been heard playing "Auld Lang Syne".[11]

However the end came, and wherever, there was one question that had to be faced by every

Confederate and Union Art and Photographs

The Civil War era was a highly visual time, in part because people tended to be highly sentimental and romantic, and art and illustration very effectively conveyed these feelings, even to those who could not read. The widespread availability of the photograph in particular, caught the soldiers' fancy. Photography came of age as a mass medium just as the war began, and more than 2,000 photographers were in business by 1861. Probably more than one million soldier portraits were taken, most of them either ornately cased ambrotypes (tintypes), or else the less expensive paper prints on card stock called *cartes-de-visite*, because of their calling card dimensions. At the same time, many a soldier recorded the scenes of his daily life in naive crayon or watercolor art, cartoons, and occasionally full-scale paintings.

1 Wartime camp art. A pen and wash drawing
2 and 3 Cased images of loved ones
4 Example of a camp art. An oil painting on board
5, 6 and 7 Images of family and friends
8 Camp art
9 and 10 Cased images of loved ones, originating from the Union

Artifacts courtesy of: The Museum of the Confederacy, Richmond, Va

Above: When the end came, the victorious Union, so often defeated, so often forced to be patient in disaster, was jubilant. The Grand Review in May saw her proud armies march down Pennsylvania Avenue.

commander, Union and Confederate: How were all these men who had been soldiers for so long to be returned to civilian life? No one in the reunited nation had ever overseen disbanding armies of such proportions. Ironically, it proved to be a greater problem for the victors than for the vanquished.

At the time of the surrenders in April and May of 1865, the Union Army had at least 1,034,000 men in uniform, spread from the Atlantic to the Pacific, and from the Gulf of Mexico to the Ohio River and beyond. Worse, units from any one state might be found in several armies hundreds of miles apart. Sherman's army alone had men from seventeen different states scattered throughout its corps. Consequently, an army could not simply return to its region as a unit and disband there. Instead, each army corps had to be broken regiment by regiment, and the men sent home in that fashion.

An even greater challenge faced the Union War Department. For potential pension purposes, Washington needed to be sure that it had a service record of each man. Then there was the matter of calculating and delivering to each man his final soldier pay up to his date of discharge. Republican leaders in Washington, looking to their political future, wanted to be certain that each soldier returned home with money in his pocket and no complaints on his lips.

The plan finally arrived at succeeded admirably, no doubt because it approached a complex task with an uncomplicated solution. Simply stated, it reversed the means by which men had been brought into the army, employing the very same apparatus. Without altering individual army organization, the men were to be gathered at rendezvous points where muster and pay rolls would be created. Then the same rail and shipping lines which had brought them to the war in the first place would be used to return the individual regiments to their home states, generally to the cities where the regiments had originally mustered. There the men would be given their final discharges and their last pay issue. The scheme allowed for a staged discharge, starting with new recruits, hospital patients, and men whose enlistments were due to expire by May 31, 1865. Even before the last Confederate forces had surrendered, the first of the recall orders had gone out summoning men home.[12]

The armies that had defeated Lee and Johnston were to come to Washington; the army that subdued Taylor would go to New Orleans, Vicksburg, or Mobile; Federals in Tennessee rendezvoused in Nashville, and so on. Soon the trains and boats and roads of the South teemed with tens of thousands of blue-clad soldiers on their way home. They went with joy at first, then uncertainty over what lay ahead of them, a sense of insecurity at leaving a way of life which many had known for four years, and then again with happiness as the full realization of peace came over them. It was a joy that lightened their steps, so much so that Sherman's army covered the 156 miles to Richmond in just five and a half days, a rate of twenty-eight miles a day, much better than they usually made on active campaign.

The trip to the rendezvous points was usually orderly, the men being under strict orders not to steal or plunder. The war was over and all private property must be respected. To many, accustomed to foraging for years, it was too much to ask, but offenders when caught were treated very severely. More often, the men became sightseers, looking with wonder once more upon scenes of battle from earlier years. Also, they frequently befriended other returning soldiers they met along the road, Confederates with whom they shared rations and sometimes transportation.

Once at the rendezvous, the men encountered once more the age-old army game of "hurry up and wait". It took time to print all the needed forms, and more time for a small army of clerks to make out all the necessary rolls. Some volunteers, unable to contain themselves any longer, simply tried to skip all the formality and go home. As a result, that summer prisons in Washington and Richmond were full of men who could not wait and had to be brought back. To keep the men occupied, drills and reviews continued, none so impressive as the Grand Review in Washington, when on May 23 the Army of the Potomac passed in review down Pennsylvania Avenue, and the next day Sherman's veterans did the same. This done, on May 29 the first regiments from the two armies embarked at the Capital's railroad station for the journey home. It took forty days before the last of the two armies was on its way.

The entire transportation system of the North was pressed into service to get the men home, and it demonstrated what an impressive rail and river communications network America had, much of it stimulated originally by the needs of the war. Major cities like New York and Cincinnati were primary destinations, from which troops for individual states in the region were embarked. Once in their home states, the regiments were broken into companies and returned to their original mustering-in locations. Once there, as the companies assembled the men experienced touching scenes of reunion with old friends not seen for years. Brothers were reunited, families rejoined, and all amid the familiar scenes of boyhood.

The last day of service was bitter-sweet: parting from the friends made in the maelstrom of war, going off to home a civilian once more. The War Department purposely withheld final pay until this last day, and in all more than $270,000,000 was disbursed to the 800,000 soldiers mustered out by November 15, 1865. By February 1866 another 150,000 men were sent home, leaving the United States Army reduced to fewer than 80,000 men scattered among a number of garrisons in the South and far west.[13]

How different it was for their one-time foes. Once a Confederate soldier turned in his weapons and signed his parole, he was no one's responsibility. He had no government of his own any longer, and the government to which he had surrendered certainly felt no obligation to help him out. There would be no issue of pay, no provision of transportation home. Generous victors like Grant and Sherman did open their commissaries to the beaten Rebels, and men who claimed to own horses in Confederate batteries and cavalry outfits were allowed to keep the animals. But when or how a Confederate soldier returned home again was exclusively his own concern. In Johnston's army, men who lived west of the Mississippi were given water transportation to New Orleans or Galveston, but all the rest had to rely upon their feet to get them home. Within a few weeks, the roads of the South were crammed with former Confederates moving singly and in groups, walking and working their way home,

Above: In the last cruel days of the war the devastation of the once beautiful South became more and more widespread. In May 1865, a whole section of Mobile, Alabama was leveled by an arsenal explosion.

Below: For two days in May 1865, the lean and toughened Billy Yanks paraded down Washington's main street of power, showing to America and the world the armies that had preserved the Union and ended slavery.

passing through a land which had strained to the breaking point to support them during the war, and which was in no better condition to sustain them on this last march. A correspondent for the New York *Tribune* wrote with dismay of the scene he found "by seeing these poor homesick boys and exhausted men wandering about in threadbare uniforms, with scanty outfit of slender haversack and blanket roll hung over their shoulders, seeking the nearest route home; they have a care-worn and anxious look, a played-out manner."[14]

Their journey was made the worse by having to pass through a ravaged South whose every mile reinforced again and again the depth of their defeat. Reaching home could be even worse, as men found homesteads either destroyed by the armies, or else run down from neglect. Cities lay in ruins, whole forests were cut down, the transportation system – such as it had been – was destroyed. Ironically, those who were the poorest at the outset fared best, for the simple man's home and meager crop land rarely caught the eye of Federal raiders or Confederate renegades. For both high-born and low, there was little to come back to but a scramble to get in a crop, find a job if possible, and start rebuilding.

For some this was too much to face. Indeed, several thousand Confederates simply melted into the darkness the night before their surrender. At first they intended to band together and continue the war as guerrillas, but most soon abandoned that plan as clearly impractical. Others, too proud to concede defeat, headed toward the Rio Grande where they joined with a few generals who led their commands across the river into Mexico. Perhaps as many as 5,000 ex-Confederates crossed the border, offering their services to both sides involved in the civil war going on there, and settling down to start small colonies. Others went even farther, to Central and South America, to Europe and England and the Far East, to Canada, and a few even to the Orient. In all, about 10,000 Southerners took part in what became the largest expatriation movement in American history. Most eventually returned within a few years, disillusioned with their new homes, and longing for their old ones.

Because of the continued resistance in some backward areas, especially Texas and Missouri, Washington did not declare an official termination of the "insurrection" until August 20, 1866. Scores of small bands of ex-Confederates, mingled with renegade Federals, and men who had never worn any uniform, operated simply as outlaws. Many were hunted down, and more simply disbanded, some to make careers putting the "wild" in the so-called Wild West.

Confederate leaders like Lee counseled all who asked, to accept the verdict of the war, go home, and start building the South anew. From the first, too, these leaders tried to instill in the men who had followed them a strong sense of pride in what they had done, what they had stood and fought, and died, for. That their cause failed somehow only more ennobled their sacrifice, with the result that it was a rare Confederate indeed who held his head low in later years. Defeat did not mean dishonor, and with that soldier wit which even the hardest of circumstances could not dampen, some former Rebels even took to denying that they were in fact defeated at all. "We just wore ourselves out whipping the Yanks", they japed. For many, humor was all they had with which to face a hard future.

For all of the Johnny Rebs and Billy Yanks who went home after the end of the war, there lay ahead a new life unlike that known by their forefathers, and which would not have come about had it not been for the war. The conflict had made the United States a power on the world stage, and for the first time even simple farmboys became in some degree aware of the interrelationship of nations, since every one of them came to know that foreign intervention in their war was a theoretical possibility. They knew that just across their border France was adventuring in Mexico, and many regiments that might otherwise have gone to the Grand Review in Washington were instead rushed to the Mexican border to prepare to meet the Emperor Maximilian's French forces if need be.

More immediately apparent to the men who served was what they had seen and learned of their own country. Boys who ordinarily might never have set foot outside their home counties had seen more than "the elephant" or the "monkey show", as they called the war. They had seen America, some traveling thousands of miles, exploring cities undreamed of in their youth, and others literally saw the world aboard ships that called at every major foreign port. Moreover, these men had seen deeper within themselves than most men are called upon to delve, tested by trial and fire, and most were not found wanting. They were in a degree changed men, a generation who had paid with their blood and received in exchange a greater awareness, self-confidence, and assertion. For the next half-century, the course of the growing American nation, the conquest of the West by gun and rail and plow, and the beginnings of empire outside its borders, lay in the hands of this generation of battle-tested young men. And not just men who had worn the blue, either, for former Confederates as well took part. A host of them settled the new lands west of the Arkansas. Not a few donned the blue to serve in the United States Army out west. Some even fought in the war with Spain in 1898. They sat in Congress halls and legislatures, began industries

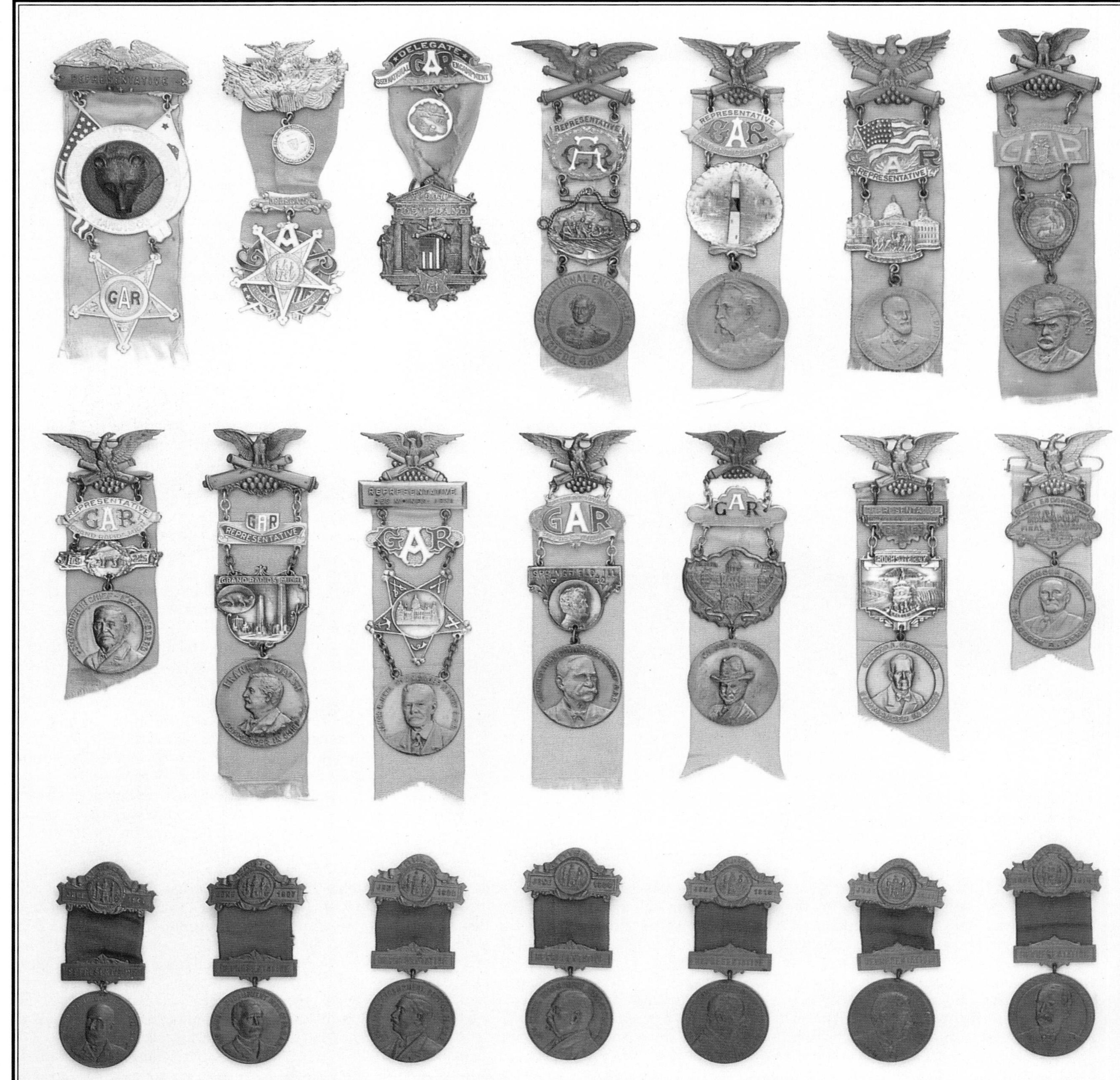

Veterans' Medals and Medals of Honor

For those who had fought in the greatest war of American history, special medals were struck.

1 A selection of Grand Army of the Republic National Encampment Badges as awarded to personnel who fought in the Union Army during the Civil War
2 A further selection of Grand Army of the Republic National Encampment Badges
3 Examples of National Encampment Badges awarded to members of the Union forces by the Grand Army of the Republic, Department of Pennsylvania
4 Selection of badges and insignia struck for and awarded by the Veteran Society to those personnel who had fought on the side of the Union during the Civil War
5 Badges struck for and awarded by Union units to commemorate formal post-war reunion gatherings
6 Army Medal of Honor, 1862 type, as awarded for conspicuous gallantry in battle. Complete with presentation case
7 Navy Medal of Honor, 1862 type, as awarded for conspicuous gallantry in battle. Complete with presentation case

Artifacts courtesy of: The Civil War Library and Museum, Philadelphia, Pa

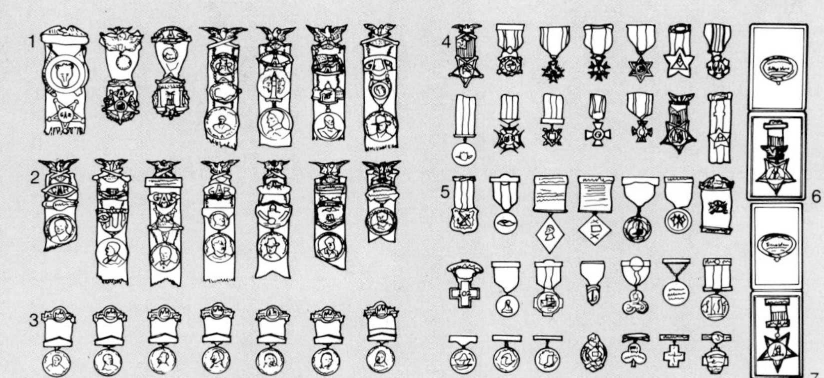

1st Cherokee Mounted Rifles, CSA

By far the Confederacy's most unusual soldiers were its Indian allies. At least 15 regiments and battalions were enlisted from the Cherokee, Choctaw, Osage, Creek, Chickasaw, and Seminoles of the South. Indifferent soldiers, unused to the discipline of the military and often enlisting for private reasons of their own which had nothing to do with the Confederate cause, they were troublesome soldiers but effective when they chose to fight. Best known amongst these units was the 1st Cherokee Mounted Rifles, which served the Confederate cause for almost four years to the day. Its colonel, Stand Watie, became the only Indian in the Confederacy to be promoted to rank of general. The uniforms of these Indian units were almost entirely ersatz, and were made up of whatever the trooper could pick up from the enemy, or scavenge from the indifferent Confederate commissary.

Above: The long-awaited final act for Johnny Reb and Billy Yank came at last. For Johnny it was his parole; for Billy, as with this Ohio regiment mustering out in 1865, it was one last ceremony of farewell.

and corporations, and in time came to stand side-by-side with their old foes – even in commemorating the war they had fought together.

In the end, for the common soldier, the old fraternal bonds of common blood and language made it impossible for the animosities of the war to last long. Indeed, many never felt real hatred of the enemy even as the conflict raged, as evidenced by the innumerable episodes of camaraderie and charity between the opposing sides. With the war done, only a few could preserve their anger. Men of both sides formed veterans organizations, both to gather for fraternal reasons, and to lobby for pensions. Washington granted increasingly attractive benefits to Union veterans, including land grants in the western territories for many, and the Grand Army of the Republic, as Union veterans styled their organization, became the most powerful political and social lobbying force of the era. Confederates, having no surviving government, could look only to their impoverished states for any sort of service pensions. A few were forthcoming from Virginia and other states, and in the end, ironically, Washington even began paying pensions to former Rebels and their widows. Where else in the world would a victorious government pay benefits to the men who had fought to disrupt it?

As the years went on, the aging veterans' ranks grew thinner and thinner. Still there were thousands of them able to attend the massive fiftieth anniversary reunion held in Gettysburg in 1913, and a few thousand still remained to come to Pennsylvania again in 1938 for a seventy-fifth anniversary. But from then on their numbers dwindled fast, and the last of them died in the 1950s, just as America prepared for the centennial of the war they had fought. All are gone now – but they are remembered for what they did. Rowdy, undisciplined, raucous, sentimental, anxious to share what they had as well as to steal from one another, incorrigible in camp and unconquerable in battle, they were Americans of their time.

To study and understand what it is that makes the Americal Civil War so distinctive among domestic conflicts, so gripping on the imagination not only of Americans, but also of the world, one must inevitably step down to the level of the common soldier and understand him. Indeed, the term is something of a misnomer, for Johhny Reb and Billy Yank were hardly "common". As a group they proved remarkable. "No encomium is too high, no honor too great for such a soldiery", declared Confederate General Braxton Bragg (a man roundly hated by most of the men to whom he paid tribute!). "In the absence of the instruction and discipline of old armies", he continued, "we have had in a great measure to trust to the individuality and self-reliance of the private soldier ". Unable to hope for the glory reserved for officers, and with no other reward to look to, "he has, in the contest, justly judged that the cause was his own, and gone into it with a determination to conquer or die". Leaders would receive the credit for winning or losing in the short term, he declared, but "history will yet award the main honor where it is due – to the private soldier".[15]

None could argue. For the hundreds of thousands of the dead, however they gave their lives, they would be recalled with honor, as General William B. Bate wrote of the dead after the Battle of Chickamauga: "While the 'River of Death' shall float its sluggish current to the beautiful Tennessee, and the night wind chant its solemn dirges over their soldier graves, their names, enshrined in the hearts of their countrymen, will be held in grateful remembrance."[16] For the millions who lived, the task before them with the coming of peace was almost as daunting as the trial through which they had passed, yet they faced it with the same simple bravery that they displayed on ten thousand battlefields of the war.

Late in April 1865, after Lee's surrender, Union Brigadier General Robert McAllister and a friend took a walk along a country road leading to Farmville, Virginia. Along the way they met a young Confederate resting beneath a tree. Barely nineteen, careworn, exhausted, malnourished, the Federals found him "very despondent". Yet he rose to talk with them and after a while joined them in their walk. In a few short minutes reserve grew into warmth, the boy forgot any animosity toward the former foe or pain at being defeated, and joined in free and lively discussion. Finally, when McAllister and his friend reached their camp, he found that the boy "seemed very reluctant to part with us". Yet part he must, for the Federals' road lay in one direction, and his, now solitary, path lay in another. Much lay ahead of them all.

"Well, sir, where are you going?" McAllister had asked him.

"Home, sir", the boy replied.

"Home."[17]

References

1 E.B. Long, *Day by Day*, pp.718-19.
2 Richard Harwell and Philip Racine, eds., *The Fiery Trail* (Knoxville, 1896), p.217.
3 Stephen Starr, *The Union Cavalry in the Civil War* (Baton Rouge, 1981), II, p.488.
4 Bruce Catton, *A Stillness at Appomattox* (New York, 1953), p.380.
5 Davis, *Orphan Brigade*, p.251.
6 Freeman, *Lees' Lieutenants*, III, p.740.
7 *Ibid.*, III, pp.740-1.
8 Catton, *Stillness*, p.380.
9 Undated clipping in Jackman Diary, Library of Congress.
10 Joshua Chamberlain, *The Passing of the Armies* (New York, 1915), pp.260-1.
11 Ida Tarbell, "Disbanding the Confederate Army", *Civil War Times Illustrated*, VI (January 1968), p.10.
12 Ida Tarbell, "How the Union Army was Disbanded", *Civil War Times Illustrated*, VI (December 1967), pp.4-5.
13 *Ibid.*
14 Tarbell, "Disbanding the Confederate Army", p.14.
15 Wiley and Milhollen, *They Who Fought Here*, p.268.
16 *Ibid.*
17 James I. Robertson, Jr., ed., *The Civil War Letters of General Robert McAllister* (New Brunswick, N.J., 1965), p.614.

APPENDIX

The specially commissioned color photographs of Civil War weapons, uniforms and personal belongings which have appeared throughout this book, represent perhaps the finest collection of contemporary artifacts brought together under one cover. As an additional source of information on each photograph's content and origin, Russ A. Pritchard, Director of The Civil War Library and Museum and technical advisor to the book has compiled this Appendix. Further information can also be obtained from the Bibliography and list of museums and societies on page 256.

Southern Banknotes pp.12-13, 14-15

Bank notes issued by railroads, insurance companies, counties, towns, parishes, corporations and merchants as well as state banks were quite common in the Southern states. These notes continued in circulation after the establishment of the Confederate States of America. With the formulation of a central government, the Confederacy resolved to issue currency affected by an Act of Congress on March 9, 1861. These first Confederate notes were issued at Montgomery, Alabama, the first capital. Subsequent issues occurred on March 16, 1861; August 19, 1861; December 24, 1861; April 17, 1862; April 18, 1862; September 23, 1862; March 23, 1863 and February 17, 1864. This brought the total currency in circulation, by some estimates to $2,250,000 by the war's end. With 72 major types of Confederate notes, many minor variations and a multitudinous variety of local and state notes, the possibilities for collectors of these little pieces of history is vast.

Union Banknotes and Coins pp.22-23, 24-25

The variety of United States and Northern State bank notes of the period rivals those of its Southern counterpart. The national Currency Act of 1863, was the instrument used to create a sound banking currency to replace generally insecure issues of local and state banks then in circulation. There was initial distrust of this new currency, however. In 1864, for example, $285 of paper currency could only purchase $100 of gold. The Federal Government also issued coinage, a luxury that the Confederacy throughout its brief existence, could never afford.

Union Zouave Uniforms and Equipment pp.34-35

Zouave uniforms originated among native North African troops recruited to serve in the French Army in the 1830s. Superb *esprit de corps* and elite status among these units, and their distinctive dress, did not pass unnoticed by foreign military observers. Elmer E. Ellsworth, a young amateur soldier is credited with the formation of the United States Zouave Cadets in Chicago in August 1859. His mentor was a former French surgeon and veteran of zouave service, Charles Q. Devilliers. The unit was so expert at military drill that in 1860 it traveled the east and mid-west demonstrating its skills and thus launched the zouave craze throughout the country. When war broke out the following year, a number of units both North and South rallied to the colors in zouave dress. Although many units continued in service, the popularity of the colorful apparel began to wane. Casualties among brightly clad troops and the basic impracticality of the uniform hastened its demise as the war progressed. Nevertheless, some units clung to their fancy uniforms throughout the conflict. The zouave was the epitome of the Victorian soldier made obsolete by improved military technology.

Confederate Unit Flags pp.36-37

Although the Confederate States of America had three National Flags and a battleflag authorized by law, flags extant today indicate usage of a great variety of patterns. Companies within regiments carried flags early in the war. Commanders of larger units adopted their own patterns, and military area commanders devised peculiar patterns for their areas. States also issued flags usually bearing some form of the state seal. Excellent collections exist today in most Southern state capitols, the premier collection, over 500 flags, being housed at The Museum of the Confederacy in Richmond.

Southern State and Confederate Buckles and Plates pp.40-41

During the decades before the war many states adopted distinctive accoutrement plates for wear by state militia. In most cases, these devices consisted of the state seal in various confugurations or the capital letters in the form of abbreviation of the state name. Out of expediency, many of these beautifully fabricated pre-war plates were pressed into service at the beginning of hostilities. Original production was limited and hard service caused many to be lost or destroyed. Today, all are scarce, most considered quite rare and all avidly collected.

The most prolific manufacturer was Emerson Gaylord of Chicopee, Massachusetts who is know to have produced the oval Maryland state seal plates for that state (fig 1). Similarity indicates that

The Civil War was immortalized by the work of many photographers. This image by Mathew Brady shows two of his assistants, posed in front of the equipment wagon with which he worked in the field.

he also made plates for Mississippi (fig 3), and Georgia in the immediate pre-war years. Some very few state plates were wartime Southern manufacture.

From the outset, Confederate forces were issued a bewildering array of distinctive central government accoutrement plates, usually oval or rectangular in shape, made of brass, bearing some variation of the letters CS or CSA. Issues were primarily to Confederate forces in western and deep south areas as indicated by excavated specimens but some were also issued in the Virginia theater of operations. These plates were fabricated in limited quantities and all are considered rare and very collectable.

The rectangular brass CSA plate illustrated (fig 13) is the most often seen of central government plates but there are many die variations of just this basic plate. Fig 16 has only been recovered in Virginia; fig 20, an only known specimen at this time, "was taken from a wounded Confederate officer in the streets of Sharpsburg, Maryland." Fig 21, fabricated of a brittle, pewter-like pot metal, is thought to have been made by Noble Brothers of Rome, Georgia. Fig 23, a large and heavy plate, has been recovered in Mississippi.

Due to extreme desirability, these plates have been expertly reproduced. While many are appropriately marked as replicas, some are not. Extreme care should be exercised by the purchaser when acquiring these plates.

Confederate Infantry Equipment pp.42-43

After some initial confusion, Confederate forces adopted gray as the color for uniforms. Pattern of clothing varied throughout the war and shades of gray spanned the spectrum into blacks and browns. Nevertheless, during most of the conflict the Confederate soldier was well armed and clothed. Confederate uniforms exist in most Southern state collections and the superb collection housed at The Museum of the Confederacy in Richmond boasts over one hundred items.

Union Infantry Equipment pp.44-45

The dress of Federal forces was more standardized than that of Confederates with the exception of zouave and some state units. As the war progressed, non-essential items were discarded and by 1863, the Federal infantryman was a well uniformed and equipped fighting man. Advances in weapons' technology caused changes in weapons issued, but the great majority of Federal foot soldiers carried muzzle loading longarms throughout the war. Excellent collections are housed at the Gettysburg National Military Park and Smithsonian Institution in Washington DC.

Imported Longarms pp.52-53

Arms and accoutrements were imported from England and Europe by both combatants. Approximately 500,000 Pattern 1853 Enfield Rifle-Muskets were purchased in England for Federal forces and some 400,000 acquired by agents of the Confederacy. Other models were imported in smaller quantities and saw limited use.

Confederate Small Arms Ammunition, Fuses and Bullet Molds pp.54-55

Surviving examples of Confederate small arms ammunition are extremely scarce, even though millions of rounds were manufactured. The Richmond Arsenal was the most productive, and fabricated a wide variety of ammunition. The Confederate ordnance facilities, however, were never able to master the manufacture of metallic cartridges, which hindered their war effort. The Virginia Historical Society in Richmond has a fine collection of this material.

Union Ammunition and Accoutrements pp.56-57

Federal ordnance facilities had the capability to produce metallic cartridges, a tremendous advantage when coupled with breechloading rifles and carbines. Yet Federals were still faced with the great variety of calibers of small arms ammunition ranging from .31 to .72, all of which were considered standard.

American and Imported Pistols used by Confederate Forces pp.60-61

Confederate forces utilized all weapons available, which accounts for the diverse types in service. Large numbers of revolvers were imported from England, particularly the Kerr and Adams, both of which saw extensive use. French pin-fire revolvers were also popular, but availability of ammunition was always a problem. Excellent collections of these weapons can be found at the Virginia Historical Society in Richmond, the West Point Museum at West Point, New York and the Gettysburg National Military Park.

Union Longarms and Equipment pp.62-63

Although the rifle-musket was the primary shoulder weapon of the Union soldier, substantial numbers of rifles, both muzzle and breechloading were issued to troops in the field. Of primary importance in firearms development were the magazine fed Spencer (fig 7) and Henry (fig 8). The Spencer was personally tested and recommended by President Lincoln. The Henry, probably the most advanced weapon used in the war, was the predecessor of the Winchester lever action weapons.

Confederate Cavalry Artifacts pp.70-71

At the beginning of the conflict, Confederate cavalry was superior to its Union counterpart, primarily due to the Rebels familiarity with weapons, horses and terrain. Much Southern equipment was captured Union material such as the Sharps carbine, Remington revolver and Model 1840 cavalry saber. As with the Union cavalry, the branch designation color, as shown on the piping of the shell jacket (fig 8) is yellow.

Union Cavalry Artifacts pp.72-73

Union cavalry had achieved the upper hand by mid-1863, with adequate leadership and far superior equipment. The Spencer carbine (fig 17) was the principal weapon for Union cavalry during the last two years of the war. With few exceptions, the usefulness of the saber was over, and repeating, rapid fire weapons dominated the battlefield.

Confederate and Imported Cavalry Carbines and Artillery Musketoons pp.76-77

Quite a few private contractors fabricated carbines and musketoons under contract to the Confederate Ordnance Department. J.P. Murray (Greenwood and Gray) produced substantial numbers (figs 2 and 7). Surviving specimens of Dickson, Nelson and Tarplay carbines (figs 1 and 14) are very rare. Most Confederate arms were either captured from the Union or imported.

Confederate Cavalry Carbines and Artillery Musketoons pp.78-79

The Richmond Arsenal produced the largest number of carbines (fig 13). Cook and Brother, the most prolific private contractor, fabricated substantial numbers of carbines and musketoons (fig 8 and 12), patterned after the English Pattern 1853 Enfield. All Confederate firearms show evidence of superior finish and hand fitting.

Union Cavalry Carbines pp.80-81

Almost all Union carbines were breechloading and fired special ammunition peculiar to each arm. Calibers varied from .36 to .69. While great advances in small arms were made during the war, problems created by lack of standardization created major problems. Most companies manufacturing these arms ceased to exist after the cessation of hostilities.

Union Edged Weapons used by Confederate Forces pp.84-85

Enormous quantities of Union material were captured in Federal arsenals in the Southern states at the beginning of the war. This was supplemented by other substantial captures in the major engagements in 1861 and 1862. Probably the most popular edged weapon of all among Rebel forces was the US Model 1860 cavalry saber, as shown by the many extant specimens in today's major collections.

Confederate and Union Edged Weapons pp.86-87

Confederate edged weapons, like their longarms and handguns, were usually inferior, hand-fabricated copies of existing Federal arms. Scarcity of materials and unskilled labor necessitated such expedients as the replacement of brass for iron. Federal weapons, with few exceptions, exhibit advanced manufacturing techniques and excellent quality.

Union and Confederate Handguns pp.90-91

The variety of handguns used by Federal forces is quite large. Most were government issue to which were added a number of private purchases. Different models of Colt and Remington are most prevalent. Confederate handguns were fabricated in limited quantities, the most common being the Griswold and Gunnison (fig 12) of which only about 3500 were produced. All Confederate handguns are considered rare.

Confederate Artillery Artifacts pp.98-99

Red piping and facings on uniforms of Confederate and Union uniforms indicated the artillery branch. As in other branches, much of the equipment used by Rebel artillery was captured, as indicated in this photograph by the Colt revolver (fig 12), and US Foot Artillery sword (fig 15).

Union Artillery Artifacts pp.100-101

Federal Artillery uniforms complied very closely to regulations. The branch color, red, is readily apparent. The short, shell jackets were worn by horse artillery, while the longer coats were used by foot artillery.

Artillery Pieces pp.104-105

The artillery pieces of both combatants were quite similar. The more popular types were the Ordnance rifle (fig 1), Parrott rifle and the smoothbore "Napoleon", (see pages 103-104), fabricated by both sides in various configurations. Confederate artillery also used many obsolete pieces updated by binding and rifling.

Field Artillery Projectiles
pp.108-109
As with small arms, there were great technological advances with artillery. Smoothbore pieces were becoming obsolete with the improvement in time and percussion fuses utilized by an array of rifled pieces of greatly increased range.

Confederate Naval Arms and Accoutrements
pp.118-119
The Confederate Navy used a combination of imported arms carried on ships constructed abroad and locally manufactured arms aboard craft constructed within the Confederacy. The Confederate Navy was small and outnumbered at best. Surviving relics are especially scarce.

Union Naval Arms and Accoutrements
pp.122-123
The Union Navy was well-equipped and expanded rapidly as the war progressed. Equipment and armament improved as iron ships replaced obsolete wooden vessels. The Civil War saw the birth of a steam navy and the beginning of two ocean fleets.

Confederate Camp Artifacts
pp.134-135
Much Confederate equipment was civilian material pressed into service, such as household or camp utensils. Field-expedient adaptations were common. The best equipment was usually captured from Union forces.

Union Camp Artifacts
pp.136-137
Blankets and rubber ground covers were standard Federal issue, as were metal canteens and tarred haversacks.

Confederate Correspondence
pp.140-141
The Confederate Postal Service was efficient and profitable. Stamps were available, but paper was difficult to obtain in the field. The standards of literacy in Confederate military correspondence varies considerably.

Confederate Books and Journals
pp.142-143
Diaries and Bibles were carried by a considerable number of Confederate military personnel. Diaries vary in content, though some are particularly accurate accounts of historical events. The large amount of Bibles to be found reflect the increasing importance of religion to military life as the war progressed.

Confederate Musicians' Equipment
pp.146-147
Both sides enjoyed basically the same music of pre-war origin, although some music was written as a result of the conflict. Most Southern instruments were of either pre-war manufacture or imported, although there was a major manufacture of drums in Richmond.

Union Musicians' Equipment
pp.148-149
In armies of both sides, bands existed at regimental level and above. Not only did they provide music on the march and entertainment in camp, but drums and bugles provided the combat communications system of commands and calls during battle.

Union Correspondence
pp.156-157
Correspondence from the Union side, was much the same as its Confederate counterpart, with the same complaints and praises, though the level of literacy was somewhat higher among Federal forces. Quality of paper was better, but the content was the same as any soldier's letter.

Confederate Personal Artifacts
pp.160-161
Camp amusements included games of chance, music, writing letters and reading. The Confederate soldier indulged in any activity he could dream up to break the tedium of camp life.

Confederate Prisoner of War Handicrafts
pp.164-165, 174-175
Confederate POW's had little to occupy their time, so many of them began to carve unique objects for loved ones at home, serviceable items for survivors and games with which to pass the time. A number were competent craftsmen and the surviving pieces provided wonderful examples of prison folk art.

Confederate Soldier Correspondence
pp.178-179
This group of letters written by Corporal John P. Wilson, Co I, 36th Virginian Infantry, expresses great love for his wife and children and his longing for them. The letters also touch on the basic concerns of the common foot soldier and his bond with home and family. Corporal Wilson did not survive the end of the war.

Confederate Medical Equipment
pp.190-191, 194-195
The Confederate Medical Department fought a hopeless battle against disease and infection. Commonplace childhood illnesses became fatal epidemics incapacitating whole regiments. Major medical breakthroughs were just around the corner, but twice as many soldiers in this war died of disease as were battlefield casualties. Amputation was the accepted procedure for wounds of the extremities. Body wounds were considered inoperable, and usually fatal given the high incidence of infection.

Confederate Muskets and Rifles
pp.202-203
The Confederate Ordnance Department encouraged private contractors to supply arms though most of their efforts at manufacture were unsuccessful. The output of those contractors who did succeed remained pitifully small, in some cases less than 1,000 pieces. many Confederate arms were worn out in service and others were destroyed at the end of the war. For these reasons, all specimens extant are considered rare.

Confederate Pistols and Revolvers
pp.206-207
In an effort to furnish arms to troops in the field, the Confederates utilized many obsolete arms of earlier manufacture. Most flintlocks were altered to the percussion system (fig 1), though in haste, some were not (fig 2). Some revolvers were fabricated in Texas (figs 7 and 8) and others were manufactured abroad (figs 9 and 10). All these weapons were produced in limited quantities.

Confederate Telegraphy Equipment
pp.210-211
The war years not only proved to be a great period of advance in the field of ordnance, but in other technologies as well. The military application of telegraphy was recognized very early on, and codes and ciphers developed to ensure secure communications of sensitive information. The formation of intelligence gathering agencies by both sides occurred parallel to this development. Scouts and spies also made use of this mode of communication throughout the war.

Confederate Muskets and Rifles
pp.220-221
Considering the almost total absence of manufacturing facilities in the South at the start of the war, it is a minor miracle that Southern industry was able to produce weapons at all. The diverse surviving examples are testimony to the efforts made in this direction. Not only did Confederate Ordnance supply newly made arms, but also a great many obsolete flintlocks altered to the percussion system (figs 2 and 11).

Captured Union Handguns used by Confederate Forces pp.222-223
As with Federal forces, the predominant sidearms in Confederate service were the Colt and Remington models. Either captured or secured before the war. Confederate forces imported more handguns than the Federal forces, primarily from England.

Confederate Rifle-Muskets, Rifles and Accoutrements pp.230-231
The Richmond Arsenal/Armory was the largest producer of longarms for the Confederacy (figs 1 and 14). Fayetteville Armory, North Carolina (fig 3), and Cook and Brother (fig 9), based in Athens, Georgia, the largest private arms manufacturer in the Confederacy, also produced comparatively large numbers of arms. Confederate accoutrements marked CS or CSA are particularly desirable today. The great bulk of Confederate accoutrements were umarked copies of existing Union materiel.

Union Longarms and Accoutrements
pp.232-233
By comparing Confederate arms to those used by Federal forces, it is quite obvious that almost all Confederate ordnance were direct copies with minor adaptations. Probably the three most heavily used arms of the war were the Model 1842 (fig 4), Model 1861 (fig 10) and the Pattern 1853 (fig 13), imported from England in large numbers.

Confederate and Union Art and Photographs
pp.240-241
Although photography was still in its infancy, soldiers carried images of loved ones to war with them. Sketches and artwork in ink and oils were also products of the soldiers' leisure time. There were accomplished artists in both armies.

Veterans' Medals and Medals of Honor
pp.244-245
At the start of the war, neither side had recognized awards for valor. To remedy this oversight, President Lincoln instituted the Medal of Honor (figs 6 and 7). Confederate efforts along these lines were unsuccessful due to wartime pressures. After the close of the conflict, veterans' organizations, even at regimental level, flourished in the North and were a major aspect of social life. Veterans in the impoverished South did not organize until the latter part of the 19th century.

INDEX

Page references for Army units are listed in **bold**; those for illustrations in *italics*

A

Abolition (of slavery) 11, 14, 24
Absterdam solid shot 108-9
Alabama, CSS 113, *114*, *116*, *117*, 122, 124, 169
Albemarle, CSS 114
Alexander, Gen E. P. 108
Alexander, Pte John H. *quoted* 222, 224, 235
Alexandria (La) 31, *158*
Ambulance *192*; corps *187*
Ammunition 224
artillery *104-5*, *110-1*
small arms *54-5*, *56-7*
Anderson, Maj Robert 170
Anderson, William 89
Andersonville (prison camp) 169, 173, 176, *176*, 180, 181, 183, *183*
Antietam (Sharpsburg), Battle of 34-5, 58, 95, *229*
Appomattox 68, 92, 111, 213, *238*, 240
Arkansas, CSS 114
Arlington 31
Armstrong rifle 108
Army of
the Cumberland 95, 199
Northern Virginia 7, 68-9, 75, 111, 213, 238
Tennessee 7, 58, 95, 151, 169, 238
the Ohio 199
the Potomac 7, 49, 58, 60, 62, 82-3, 113, 139, 145, 153, 155, 199, 201, 238, *242*
the Shenandoah 202
the Tennessee *201*
the Trans-Mississippi 238
Virginia 67, 80
Western Virginia 58
Art 240-1
Artifacts: *see* equipment; handicrafts
Artillery *20-1*, *94*, 95-111, *104-105*
equipment *98-9*, *100-1*
musketoons *76-7*, *78-9*
pieces *104-5*
projectiles *108-9*, *110*, *111*
Ashby, Turner 74-5, 80
Atlanta 153, 199, 206
Atlanta, CSS 126
Augusta Arsenal cartridge *54-5*
"Auld Lang Syne" 144, 240
Austrian weapons 52, 54
Averell, Gen William 82

B

Babbott, Pte Charles *quoted* 14
Badges, veterans' *244-5*
Baker, Enoch *quoted* 14
Bands 142, *145*, *146-7*, *148-9*
Banknotes *12-3*, *14-5*, *22-3*, *24-5*
Banks, Gen Nathaniel P. 153
Baron DeKalb, USS *124*
Baseball 151
Bate, Gen William B. *quoted* 247
Baton Rouge *89*
Battle *216*, 217-35
"Battle Hymn of the Republic" 145
Baxter's Zouaves *34-5*
Bayonets 47, *202-3*, *230-1*
Beaumont-Adams revolver 60-1
Beauregard, Gen Pierre *quoted* 17
Belgian weapons 52, *52-3*, 58
Belle Plain *170*
Benavides, Refugio 22
Bentonville, Battle of 217
Berdan, Hiram 64
Berdan's 1st United States Sharpshooters **64**, *65*
Big Bethel, Battle of 31, 33
Bilharz, Hall carbine *78-9*
Billings, John D. *quote* 132-3, 152
Black, Pte Edward 17
Blackburn's Ford *82*
"Black Hat Brigade" *239*
"Black Horse Cavalry" *69*, 70, 72
Blacks: *see* colored sailors; troops
Blakeslee cartridge *80-1*
Blockade, naval 124-5
Blunt, Maj Gen James G. *quoted* 24, 26
Books 140, *142-3*
Booth, John Wilkes 237
Bowie knife 50, 65, 123, *220-1*
Boyle, Gamble & MacFee bayonet *220-1*
Brady, Mathew *102*
Bragg, Gen Braxton 95, 97, 131, 247
Brandy Station, Battle of 83-4, *92*
Brannigan, Felix *quoted* 20
Breechloaders 60, 62
Brindle, Asa *quoted* 134
British weapons *52-3*
Britten shell *108-9*
Brother, Charles *quoted* 121
Brunswick rifle *52-3*
Buckles *40-1*
Bugle *34-5*, 145, *146-7*, *148-9*, 227
"calls" 44, 145
Bullet molds *54-5*, *56-7*, *60-1*
Bull Run (Manassas), 1st Battle of 20, 31-2, 38, 49, 69, 169, 170, 218-20, 222, *224*, 228
Bull Run (Manassas), 2nd Battle of 20, 67, 72, 82, 235, 239
"Bummer" *201*
Burnside, Gen Ambrose E. 95
Burnside carbine 64, *80-1*
Burton shell *108-9*
Butterfield, Brig Gen Daniel 145

C

Cairo (Ill) *39*, *124*
Caldwell, John F. J. *quoted* 215
Camp, Army 131-52
art *240-1*
artifacts *134-5*, *136-7*
Camp Butler *39*
Camp Douglas (prison) 176, *176*
Camp Morton *177*
Camp Sumter: *see* Andersonville
Candler, Capt Daniel 14
carbines, cavalry *76-7*, *78-9*, *80-1*
Carthage 31
Cartridges *54-5*, *56-7*, *58-9*
Casey, Brig Gen Silas 40, 47, 50, 52
"Cashier, Pte Albert": *see* Hodgers, Jennie
Castle Pinckney (prison) *20*, *168-9*
cavalry *27*, *47*, *66*, 67-93, *155*
Centralia Massacre (Missouri) 89
Chamberlain, Gen Joshua 240, 247
Chancellorsville, Battle of 113
Chaplain *218*
Chapman (C.) musketoon/rifle *78-9*, *220-1*
Charleston 9, 19, 46, 110-1, *120*, 127, 169, 217
Chattanooga 131, *198-9*, *214*
Cherokee Mounted Rifles, CSA *246*
Chickamauga, Battle of 243
Choctaw, USS 126
Cincinnati, USS *124*
City Point (cemetery) *18*
Clark, Sherrard revolver *206-7*
Clinch Rifles **138**
Clutter, Capt Valentine C. 111
Cobb, Howell *quoted* 28
Cofer (T.W.) revolver *206-7*
Coins *22-3*
Colored Infantry *26*, *28*, *133*
Colored sailors 115-6, 121
Colored troops 26, *26*, *28*
Colt Army pistol/revolver *42-3*, *56-7*, *60-1*, 82, *88*, *93*, *100-1*, *222-3*
(Army) revolving carbine/rifle *62-3*, 64-5, *65*
Navy pistol/revolver *58*, *65*, *69*, *98-9*, *222-3*
police revolver *90-1*
Columbia 217

Those who fought would never forget. Twenty years after the guns fell silent, veteran members of the Twenty-third Ohio meet together again. Beneath their battered banners they reminisce of days and comrades long gone.

Columbus revolver *206-7*
Commerce raiders 113, *114*, 125, 129
Commissary sergeant *144*
Confederate States of America 9
Confederate Treasury bill *14-5*
Connecticut Artillery *30-1*
Cook & Brother carbine/rifle *78-9*, *230-1*
Cooke, Chauncy *quoted* 14
Cooper, Lt Alonzo *quoted* 171
Correspondence 138, *138*, *146-7*, 156, *156-7*, *178-9*
Courts-martial *167*
Crime: *see* military law; punishment
Croft, Pte Samuel 16
Crump, Billy 154
CS cartridges (etc) *230-1*
CS plate 40-1
CS (A): *see also* Confederate States of America
Currier & Ives (lithographs) 230
Cutlasses *118-9*, *122-3*

D

Dahlgren boat howitzer rifle *104-5*, 128, *128*, *129*
Dance (J.H.) & Brothers revolver *206-7*
Daniel, John M. *quoted* *10-1*
"Davids" (Confederate torpedo boats) *128*
Davis, Jefferson 9, 18, 49, 72, 170, 237
Davis & Bozeman rifle *202-3*
Democratic Party 9
Desertions 164-5
Detroit *32*
D-guard knife *202-3*
Dickson, Nelson carbine/rifle *76-7*, *202-3*
"Dictator" mortar 106
Discharge 242
Disease 186, 188, 192
Dix, Gen John 172
"Dixie" 11
Dog tent 134
Drum 146-7, 148-9
"calls" 44-5, 224, 227
Durham Station *238*
Dyer shell *111*

E

Edged weapons, *84-5*, *86-7*, *93*, *98-9*, *100-1*, *202-3*, *230-1*
Edwards, Jay D. (*photos by*) 38
Eggleston, George G. *quoted* 46, 47
Eley percussion caps *80-1*
Elmira (prison) 174, *180*, 181
Emancipation Proclamation 26
Enfield carbine/musket rifle *52-3*, 54, *55*, 59, *76-7*, *219*, *232-3*, 240
English, Sgt Ed *quoted* 10, 17
Enlistment
Army 10-2, *16*, 17, 28, 34
Navy 120-1
Equipment *34-5*, *40-1*, *52-3*, *62-3*
artillery *98-9*, *100-1*, *134-5*
cavalry *90-1*, *92-3*
infantry *42-3*
medical *130-1*
personal *160-1*
see also uniforms
Ericsson, John 126
Ewell, Gen Richard 68

F

Farragut, Cde (later Adm) David G. 49, 67
Fayetteville 60
Fayetteville rifle *42-3*, *202-3*, *230-1*
Federal States: *see* Union
Field gun, 6-pdr *10-5*
Fife *146-7*, *148-9*
Finnegan, Gen Joseph 21
First engagement: *see* Fort Sumter 237
Five Forks, Battle of 92, 237
Flags *224*, 238
Confederate Army *36-7*, *146-7*
Confederate Navy *118-9*
Union Navy *122-3*
Fleetwood Hill: *see* Brandy Station, Battle of
CSS *Florida* 113, 118
Floyd, Gen John B. 148
Food 121, 154, 189-90
Forrest, Gen Nathan Bedford 86, 89, 92
Fort Delaware 176
Fort Donelson 49, 172
Fort Donelson, USS *121* (formerly CSS *Robert E. Lee)*
Fort Fisher 46
Fort Henry 49
Fort McRee 38
Fort Pillar 26
Fort Pulaski 110
Fort Putnam 106
Fort Stedman 217, *228*
Fort Sumter 9, 10, *18*, *19*, 110-1, *110*, 170, 237
Fort Wagner 27
Foster, Stephen 144
Franklin, Battle of 199
Frederick *214*
Fredericksburg, Battle of 58, 95, 145
Freeman, G. W. *34-5*
Fulton, Pte Edward *34-5*
Fuses
Confederate small arms *14-5*
Union artillery *100-1*

G

Gaines' Mill, Battle of 59
Gallager carbine *80-1*
Gardner, Alexander (*photo by)* gambling 154, *154*
Garret (J. & F.) pistol *20-7*
General Bragg, CSS *204*
Georgia State musket *220*
Gettysburg, Battle of *59*, 84, 105, 113, 214-5, 229, 232, *235*, 237-8; anniversary reunion 247
Gillmore, Gen Quincy A. 110
Gordon, Gen George B. 240
Grand Army of the Republic 247
National Encampment Badges *244-5*
Grand Review (1865) 242, *242*
Grant, Gen Ulysses S(impson) 49, 50, 54, 86, 92, 95, 113, 131, 153, 169, 185, 217, 237-8, 242
Greene rifle 62-3
Grierson, Col Benjamin 86, 89
Griswold & Gunnison *90-1*, *206-7*
Gun-howitzer
6-pdr 103
12-pdr *103*, 106
Guns: *see also* artillery; handguns, rifles; weapons
Gwyn & Campbell carbine *80-1*

H

Hagan, Sgt John *quoted* 16
Hale, Edward Everett 140
Hall rifle 58
Hampton, Gen Wade 89
Hampton Legion 33
Hampton Roads 126
Handguns *30-1*, 58, *58*, *60-1*, *70-1*, *75*, *90-1*, *122-3*, *206-7*, *222-3*
Handicrafts, prisoner of war *164-5*, *174-5*
Hannaford, Roger *quoted* 238
Hardee, Lt Gen William J. 39-40, 68
Hardee hat *44-5*, *100-1*, *107*, *239*
Hardee's Tactics 39-40
Harper's Ferry rifle *47*
Hawkins, Rush C. 33
Hawkins' Zouaves **33**
Hay, Charles C. 17
Head, Pte Truman *65*
headgear *34-5*
Henry Hill *224*
Henry repeating rifle *48*, 49, *56-7*, *58-9*, *62-3*, 65
Herald (Boston) *quoted* 11
"Highlanders" *20*, *21*
Hill, Gen Daniel Harvey *quoted* 138
Hindman, Gen Thomas C. *quoted* 138
Hodgers, Jennie ("Albert Cashier") 28, *29*
Hoffman, Col (later Brig Gen) William 172, *172*, 174, 181
Honey Springs, Battle of 26
Hood, Gen John Bell 185, 199, 219
Hooker, Gen Joseph 113
hospitals 184, 185-97
Hotchkiss shell *108-9*, *111*
Howe, Julia Ward 145
Hunchback, USS *128*
Hunter, Alvah, 114-5, 120-2, 129

I

Illinois Cavalry **88**
Illinois Infantry **49**, 217
Immigrants 19-21
Imported weapons 52, *52-3*, *76-79*
Indiana Infantry 239
Indians 21-2, 88-9, *246*
Infantry equipment *42-3*, *44-5*
Infantry Tactics (Casey) 40, 50-1, 52
Insignia: *see* buckles; medals; plates
Irish Brigade *20*, 21
"Iron Brigade" *239*
Ironclads 125-6, *126*, 128

J

Jackman, John *quoted* 246
Jackson, Gen Thomas J(onathan) ("Stonewall") 67, 75, 113, 240
Jackson, W. H. *quoted* 34
"John Brown's Body" 145, 206
Johnson's Island *173*
Johnston, Gen Albert Sidney 49, 68, 225
Johnston, Gen Joseph E. 49, 159, 185, 202, 217, 237-8
Jones, Pte Benjamin W. *quoted* 16, 29, 95, 97-8, 100, 103, 111
Jones, Jacob 28
Jones, Joseph 176
Joslyn carbine *80-1*
Journals *142-3*
Justice rifle-musket *232-3*

K

Kansas Colored Volunteers 26
Kearsarge, USS *116*
Keen, Walker carbine *78-9*
Kell, John *116*
Kelly, Henry *65*
Kelly's Ford 82
Kendal Green (hospital) *189*
Kenesaw Mountain 185
Kentucky Infantry 139, 146, 239
Kentucky State Guard *10*
Keokuk, USS 110
Kerr patent rifle *52-3*
revolver *60-1*
Keystone Zouaves *34-5*
Kirby Smith, Gen Edmund 88
Knoxville *47*
Konshattoutzchette 22, 209

L

Lamb (H.C.) rifle *220-1*
Lancaster bayonet *202*
Lance *68*, *72-3*
Lane, Walter P. 12, 14, 29
Last engagement: *see* Palmito Ranch
Lee, Robert E(dward) 58, 67-8, 92, 95, 113, 153, 169, 185, 217, 237-8, 243
Leech & Rigdon revolver 90-1
Le Mat revolver *206-7*
revolving carbine *76-7*, 78
Letter writing; *see* correspondence
Libby (prison) 171, *181*
Liberty Hall Volunteers 33
Life of Billy Yank, The (Wiley) 7, 29
Life of Johnny Reb, The (Wiley) 7, 29
Limber, horse-drawn *104-5*
Lincoln, Abraham 9, 24, 64, 68, 70, 72, 170, 172, 185, 200; assassination 237
Liquor 154-6
Loehr, Sgt Charles T. *quoted* 36
Longarms *52-3*, *62-3*, *232-3*
Lookout Mountain 131, *198-9*, *214*, *215*
Louisiana Infantry *166*
Louisiana Zouaves *28*
Louisville *10*
Lyman, Col Theodore 21, 29
Lynchburg Arsenal cartridges *54-5*
Lytle, A. D. (*photos by*) 89

M

McAllister, Brig Gen Robert 247
McCarthy, Carlton *quoted* 131
McClellan, Gen George B. 31, 49, 67-8, 75, 80, 95, 155
McClellan, H. B. 83, 93
McClellan saddle *71*, *72-3*, *87-8*
McElroy (W.J.) knife *220-1*
McDowell, Gen Irvin 70
McGowan, Brig Samuel 104
Macon Arsenal cartridges *54-5*
Maine Cavalry 83
Mallorie, Cpl Walter H. *34-5*
Manassas, Battles of: *see* Bull Run, Battles of
Manhattan revolver *90-1*
Man Without a Country (Hale) 140
Marching *205*, 206, 208, *208*, 218
March to the Sea 199, 206
Maryland Guard Zouaves **51**
Mason-Dixon Line 9, 10
Massachusetts Arms Co Adams revolver *222-3*
Massachusetts Volunteer Militia **97**
Maynard carbine *80-1*
Meade, Gen George G. 21, 113, 153, 169
Meagher, Brig Gen 21
Medals *244-5*
Medals of Honor
Army 28, 235, *244-5*
Navy *122-3*, *244-5*
Medical
equipment *190-1*, *194-5*
services 185-97
Mendota, USS *128*
Merrill carbine *54-5*, *80-1*
Merrimack, USS: *see Virginia*, CSS
Mexico 243-4
Miami, USS 129
Michigan Infantry 32
Military law 162-7
Minié bullet, 50-1, *54-5*, *58-9*, 224
Mississippi infantry **38**, **132**
Mississippi Rifle 46, 49, 58-9
Mobile 242, *243*
Money: *see* banknotes; coins
Monitor, USS 126, *126*
Montgomery 9
Moody, Col Granville 225
Morgan, Gen John Hunt 78, 84, 142, 180, 209

Morgantown *10*
Morse, George 62
Morse carbine/musket *78-9, 220-1*
Mortars *97, 106*
Morton, Oliver 11
Mosby, John Singleton 78, 80, 93, 222, 224
Mound City, USS *124*
Mullane shell *108-9*
Murfreesboro: *see* Stones River, Battle of
Murray (J.P.) carbine/rifle *76-7, 220-1*
Music 142, 144-5
equipment *146-7, 148-9*
Musketoons *76-7, 78-9*
Muskets *202-3, 220-1, 230-1, 232-3*

N

"Napoleon" gun-howitzer *103*, 106
Nashville 28, 199, 242
National Guard: *see* New York State Militia
Naval arms and accoutrements *118-9, 122-3*
Navy: *see also* sea, war at
Negroes: *see* colored sailors; colored troops
New Creek *20*
New Hampshire, USS *120, 125*
New Hampshire Volunteer Infantry **29, 234**
New Haven Arms Co 65
New Market 169
New Orleans *28*, 49, 96-7, 242
Newspapers 140
New York *8-9*
New York Cavalry **93**
New York Engineers 146
New York Infantry *17, 20*, **32, 33, 34-5**, 148
New York State Militia (National Guard) *11*, **32**, 33, **145**
Niagara, USS *115*
Norton, Pte Oliver W. *quoted* 38
Nursing 186, 196-7

O

Ocean Pond (Olustee), Battle of 21, 26
Oglethorpe Light Infantry 33
Ohio Cavalry **74, 83**
Ohio Heavy Artillery **47**
Ohio National Guard Light Artillery **179**
Ohio Volunteers **144**
Oldest soldiers 17-8, 33
Olustee: *see* Ocean Pond
Orange & Alexandria Railroad *83*
Ordnance rifles 106-7
Owen, Col Richard 177

P

Palmetto musket *202-3*
pistol *206-7*
Palmito Ranch 237
Parrott, Robert 106
Parrott rifle/shell *47, 98-9, 100-1, 102*, 106, *106, 108-9, 111*, 127
Passaic, USS 110, *127*
Paxon, Pte Thaddeus *34-5*
Pay
Army 14, 148, 242
Navy 121
Pember, Phoebe Y. *quoted* 197
Pennsylvania Cavalry **68**, 72-3, **155**
Pennsylvania Volunteer Infantry **34-5**
Pensacola *38, 97, 132, 200*
Perry carbine 62
Perryville, Battle of 95
Petersburg 46, 92, *102, 106*, 169, 185, 199, *217, 225, 228*, 237-8
Philadelphia *16, 186*, 200
Phoenix Iron Co., ordnance rifle muzzle No. 1 *104-5*
Photographs *240-1*
Pinfire revolver *60-1*
Pistols: *see* handguns
Pittsburgh 200
Plant revolver *90-1*
Plates *40-1*
Pleasanton, Gen Alfred 82-4
Point Lookout *163, 170*, 171, *215*
Polignac, Prince de 21
Pollard, E. 17
Pope, Gen John 67, 80, 82
Port Hudson 26, 113
Potomac, River *209*
Prairie Grove, Battle of 225
Price, Maj Gen Sterling 90
Prisoners of war 169-83
handicrafts *164-5, 174-5*
Prospect Hill *93*
Prostitution 158, *158*, 159
Provost Marshal *162*
Pryor, Col Roger A. 95, 97
Puffer, Pte Richard 26
Pulaski rifle *220-1*
Punishment, 162-3, *163*, 164-6

Q

Quantrill, William C. 89

R

Rader, Adam 153
Railroad transport *83*, 201-2, 204, *205*, 242
Army hospital car *193*
Raleigh bayonet *230-1*
"Rally Round the Flag" 145
Rappahannock, River *208*
Rattler, USS *124*
R. B. Taney, CSS 204
Read & Watson rifle *220-1, 230-1*
Read-Parrott shell *108-9*
"Rebel Yell" 232
Red River Campaign 153
Reed-Broun shell *108-9*
Remington/Remington Beals revolvers *70-1, 90-1, 222-3*
Republican Party 9
Revolvers: *see* handguns
Rhode Island Infantry **228**
Richmond (Va) 28, 31, 46, 49, 60, 67, 92, 106, 153, 158, 185, *189*, 196, 200, 217, 234, *236-7*, 237-8, 242
Richmond Arsenal cartridges *54-5*
Richmond howitzers 33, 97, 103
Rifle-muskets *230-1*
Rifles 50 *et seq*, 106-7, *202-3, 220-1, 230-1; see also* longarms
Rigden, Ansley revolver *90-1*
River gunboats 125-6, 204
Robert E. Lee, CSS: *see Fort Donelson*, USS
Rochester (NY) *10*
Rodman 10-inch cannon *106*
Rose, Col Thomas C. 181
Rosecrans, Gen William S. 95, 131
"Rush's Lancers" *68, 72-3, 155*
Russell, (Sir) William Howard *quoted* 11, 29, 52, 65

S

Sabers *84-5, 86-7, 93, 100-1*
Sabine Cross Roads, Battle of 153
Salisbury (prison camp) *182*
Saugus, USS *126*
Savannah 199, 217
Sawyer shell *111*
Sayler's Creek, Battle of 237
Scantlon, David 17
Schenkl shell *108-9, 111*
Schofield, Gen John M. 199, 235
Scott, Gen Winfield 39, 68, 70, 80
Sea, war at 112-39
Selma Arsenal primers 54-5
Semmes, Capt Raphael 114, *116*, 122, 124
Seven Days' Battles 67
Sharps, Christian 62
Sharpsburg: *see* Antietam, Battle of
Sharps carbine/rifle *62-3*, 64, *65*, 69, *69, 70-1, 78-9, 80-1, 83, 93*
Sharpshooters *64*
"Shebangs" *132*, 134, *138*
Shells: *see* artillery projectiles
Sheridan, Gen Philip H. 74, 89, 92-3, 217
Sherman, Gen William T(ecumseh) 38, 47, 74, 86, 131, 153, 169, 199, 208, 217, 237-8, 242
Shiloh, Battle of 49, 225
Sibley, Brig Gen Henry H. 132
Sibley tent 132, *132*, 133
Sigel, Maj Gen Franz 19, 20
Signals: *see* telegraphy equipment
6-pdr field gun *104-5*, 106
6-pdr gun-howitzer 103, 106
Slattery, Pte Jim *quoted* 9
Slavery, abolition of: *see* abolition
Sloan, Pte Jon Mather 17
Smith, Philip *quoted* 20
Smith & Wesson revolver *90-1, 222-3*
Smith carbine *80-1*
Songs 142, 144-5
Spencer, Christopher M. 64
Spencer carbine/rifle *62-3*, 64, *80-1*, 82, *82*, 88
Spiller & Burr revolver *90-1*
Springfield Rifle *33*, 54, 56, 58-9, *133*
Stanton, Henry B. *quoted* 11
Starr carbine *80-1*
revolver *90-1*
"Star-Spangled Banner" 12, 219
Stiles, Robert *quoted* 103, 111, 213
Stones River (Murfreesboro), Battle of 95, 225
Stuart, Gen James Ewell Brown (Jeb) 67-9, 70, 72, 75, 82-4, 89
Surry Light Artillery 95, 97
Sussex Light Dragoons *27*
Sutlers 154, *154*
Swords: *see* edged weapons; sabers; bowie knife
System of Cavalry Tactics 68

T

Tallahassee, CSS 113
Tallest soldiers 18
Tarpley, J. H. 62
"Tattoo" 145
Taylor, Gen Richard 238
Teaser, CSS *121*
Telegraphy equipment *210-1*
Tents 132, *132*, 133-6
Terry's Pattern carbine 76-7
Texas Infantry *219*
Thomas, Maj Gen George H. 131, 194; *quoted* 28
Thruston, Pte Henry C. 18-9
Townsend, George *quoted* 38
Training 31-47
Tranter revolver *60-1*
Trice, Capt John *quoted* 46
Tucker, Sherrard revolver *206-7*
12-pdr boat howitzer *104-5*
12-pdr gun-howitzer *103*, 106
Twiggs, Maj Gen David E. 170

U

Uhlinger revolver *90-1*
Uniforms
artillery *107*
infantry *34-5, 42-3, 44-5, 51, 64, 201, 213, 219, 234*
Navy *114, 125*
Union 7, 9
United States Artillery **107**
United States Cavalry **92**
United States Colored Infantry *28*, **133**
United States Sharpshooters **63**, *65*
United States Veteran Reserve Corps **171**

V

Van Buskirk, Capt David 18
Van Dorn, Col (later Gen) Earl C. 68, 170
Vedette (Confederate newspaper) 142
Veteran Reserve Corps (US) *171*
Veterans' medals *244-5*
Vicksburg 86, 95, 113, 217, 237, 242
Virginia, CSS (formerly USS *Merrimack*) 113-4, 125-6
Virginia Cavalry 36, **65, 69**, 70
Virginia Infantry 148, *212-3*
Virginia Manufactory pistol *206-7*
Von Borke, Heros *quoted* 75, 93

W

Wabash, USS 120
Walker, James (*painting*) 214
Washington (DC) 11, *30-1, 173, 188*, 200, 242, *242*, 243
Washington (Ga) 239
Washington Artillery of New Orleans 33, **96**, 97, 132
Washington Light Infantry **46**
Watie, Gen Stand 246
Waverly, CSS 204
Weapons *48*, 49-65
see also artillery; equipment; handguns; rifles
Webley revolver *60-1*
Wesson & Leavitt revolver *60-1*
West Point 39, 97
West Point Foundry 106
Westport, Battle of 90
Wheat, Maj Roberdeau 166
"Wheat's Tigers" **166**
Wheeler, Gen Joseph 68, 86
"When Johnny Comes Marching Home Again" 145
Whitman, Walt *quoted* 185
Whitney revolver *222-3*
Whitworth device/shell *108-9*
Whitworth rifle *52-3*, 59, 108, *108-9, 110*
Wickliffe, Col John C. 139
Wilcox, James *quoted* 217
Wiley, Bell I. 7, 29
Wilkie, Frank *quoted* 50
Williams solid bolt device *108-9*
Wilmington 217
Wilson, Maj Gen James 92-3
Wilson, Cpl John P. correspondence *178-9*
Wilson naval rifle *118-9*
Wilson's Creek, Battle of 31, 49
Winder, Brig Gen John H. 172-3, 181
Winslow, Capt John A. *116*
Wirz, Maj Henry 178, 181, 183
Wisconsin Infantry **239**
Women soldiers 28
Women's nursing corps 186, 196-7
Worsham, John *quoted* 139, 152

Y

Youngest soldiers 17

Z

Zouaves *10, 28, 33, 34-5*, 40, *51, 166*

Bibliography

Further reading to the Appendix subjects

Albaugh, William A. and Stewart, Richard D., *The Original Confederate Colt*
Albaugh, William A., Benet, Hugh Jr., Simmons, Edward N., *Confederate Handguns*
Albaugh, William A., *Confederate Arms*
Albaugh, William A., *Confederate Edged Weapons*
Albert, Alphaeus H., *Buttons of the Confederacy*
Albert, Alphaeus H., *Record of American Uniform and Historical Buttons*
Allen, Glenn C. and Piper, Wayne C., *The Battle Flags of the Confederacy*
Bailey, D. W., *British Military Longarms 1815-1865*
Belden, Bauman L., *War Medals of the Confederacy*
Brown, Rodney Hilton, *American Polearms 1526-1865*
Brown, Stuart E. Jr., *The Guns of Harpers Ferry*
Burns, Z. H., *Confederate Forts*
Caba, G. Craig, *United States Military Drums*
Cannon, Deveraux, D., Jr., *The Flags of the Confederacy*
Criswell, Grover C., *Confederate and Southern State Bonds*
Criswell, Grover C., *Confederate Currency*
Cromwell, Giles, *The Virginia Manufactory of Arms*
Crown, Francis J. Jr., *Confederate Postal History*
Daniel, Larry J. and Hunter, Riley W., *Confederate Cannon Foundries*
Davis, Rollin V. Jr., *U.S. Sword Bayonets, 1847-1865*
Davis, William C., *The Image of War*, Vols. 1-6
Dickey, Thomas S., and George, Peter C., *Field Artillery Projectiles of the American Civil War*
Dorsey, R. Stephen, *American Military Belts and Related Equipment*
Edwards, William B., *Civil War Guns*
Elting, John R. (ed.), *Military Uniforms in America*
Fuller, Claud E. and Stewart, Richard D., *Firearms of the Confederacy*
Fuller, Claud E., *Confederate Currency and Stamps*
Fuller, Claud E., *Springfield Shoulder Arms 1795-1865*
Fuller, Claud E., *The Whitney Firearms*
Garofalo, Robert and Elrod, Mark, *A Pictorial History of Civil War Era Musical Instruments and Bands*
Gary, William A., *Confederate Revolvers*
Gavin, William G., *Accoutrement Plates, North and South*
Gluckman, Arcadi, *United States Muskets, Rifles and Carbines*
Govt. Printing Office, *Uniform Regulations for the Army of the United States, 1861*
Hardin, Albert N. Jrs., *The American Bayonet, 1776-1964*
Hazlett, James C., Olmstead, Edwin and Parks, M. Hume, *Field Artillery Weapons of the Civil War*
Hill, Richard Taylor and Anthony, William Edward, *Confederate Longarms and Pistols*
Hopkins, Richard E., *Military Sharps Rifles and Carbines*
Howell, Edgar M., *United States Military Headgear, 1855-1902*
Huntingdon, R.T., *Hall's Breechloaders*
Jangen, Jerry L., *Bayonets*
Keim, Lon W., *Confederate General Service Accoutrement Plates*
Kerksis, Sydney C., *Field Artillery Projectiles of the Civil War, 1861-1865*
Kerksis, Sydney C., *Heavy Artillery Projectiles of the Civil War, 1861-1865*
Kerksis, Sydney C., *Plates and Buckles of the American Military 1795-1874*
Kickox, Ron G., *Collector's Guide to Ames U.S. Contract Military Edged Weapons, 1832-1906*
Laframboise, Leon W., *History of the Artillery, Cavalry and Infantry Branch of Service Insignia*
Lewis, Berkeley R., *Small Arms and Ammunition in the United States Service, 1776-1865*
Lewis, Emmanuel Raymond, *Seacoast Fortifications of the United States*
Lord, Francis A., *Civil War Collector's Encyclopedia*, Vols. 1, 2, 3 & 4
Madaus, H. Michael and Needham, Robert D., *Battleflags of the Confederate Army of Tennessee*
Madaus, H. Michael, *Rebel Flags Afloat*
Marcot, Roy, *Spencer Repeating Firearms*
McAfee, Michael J., *Zouaves . . . The First and The Bravest*
McKee, W. Reid and Mason, M. W., Jr., *Civil War Projectiles*
McKee, W. Reid and Mason, M. W. Jr., *Civil War Projectiles, Small Arms and Field Artillery*
Miller, Francis Trevelyan, (ed.), *The Photographic History of the Civil War*, 10 Vols.
Murphy, John M., *Confederate Carbines and Musketoons*
Peterson, Harold J., *The American Sword, 1775-1945*
Phillips, Stanley S., *Bullets Used in the Civil War, 1861-1865*
Phillips, Stanley S., *Civil War Corps Badges and Other Related Awards, Badges, Medals of the Period*
Phillips, Stanley S., *Excavated Artifacts from Battlefields and Camp Sites of the Civil War*
Pitman, John, *Breech-Loading Carbines of the United States Civil War Period*
Rankin, Robert H., *Small Arms of the Sea Service*
Reilly, Robert M., *United States Military Small Arms 1816-1865*
Riling, Ray (ed.), *Uniforms and Dress of the Army and Navy of the Confederate States*
Ripley, Warren, *Artillery and Ammunition of the Civil War*
Roads, C. H., *The British Soldier's Firearm 1850-1864*
Sellers, Frank M. and Smith, Samuel E., *American Percussion Revolvers*
Smith, Winston O., *The Sharps Rifle*
Stamatelos, James, *Notes on the Uniform and Equipments of the United States Cavalry, 1861-1865*
Steffen, Randy, *United States Military Saddles, 1812-1943*
Sylvia, Stephen W. and O'Donnell, Michael J., *Civil War Canteens*
Thomas, Dean S., *Cannons*
Thomas, Dean S., *Ready . . . Aim . . . Fire! Small Arms Ammunition in the Battle of Gettysburg*
Todd, Frederick P., American Military Equipage, 1851-1872, 4 Vols.
Wise, Arthur and Lord, Francis A., *Bands and Drummer Boys of the Civil War*
Wise, Arthur and Lord, Francis A., *Uniforms of the Civil War*

Locations of Major Civil War Collections

Atlanta Historical Society
3101 Andrews Drive, N.W.
Atlanta, Ga 30305

Augusta-Richmond County Museum
540 Telfair Street,
Augusta, Ga 30901

Chicago Historical Society
Clark Street at North Avenue, Chicago, Il 60614

Chickamauga-Chattanooga National Military Park
Fort Oglethorpe, Ga 30742

Civil War Library and Museum
1805 Pine Street,
Philadelphia, Pa 19103

Confederate Museum
Alexander Street,
Crawfordville, Ga 30631

Confederate Museum
929 Camp Street,
New Orleans, La 70130

Fredericksburg and Spotsylvania National Military Park
120 Chatham Lane,
Fredericksburg, Va 22405

Fort Ward Museum and Historic Site
4301 W. Braddock Road,
Alexandria, Va 22304

Gettysburg National Military Park
Gettysburg, Pa 17325

Grand Army of the Republic Memorial Hall Museum
State Capitol 419 N.
Madison, WI 53702

Milwaukee Public Museum
800 W. Wells Street,
Milwaukee, WI 53233

Smithsonian Institution
National Museum of American History, 900 Jefferson Drive, S.W.
Washington, DC 20560

South Carolina Confederate Relic Room and Museum
World War Memorial Building, 920 Sumter Street, Columbia, SC 29201

Springfield Armory National Historic Site
1 Armory Square,
Springfield, MA 01105

State Historical Museum of Wisconsin
30 North Carroll Street,
Madison, WI 53703

The Confederate Museum
188 Meeting Street,
Charleston, SC 29401

The Museum of the Confederacy
1201 E. Clay Street,
Richmond, Va 23219

Virginia Historical Society
428 North Boulevard,
Richmond, Va 23221

VMI Museum
Virginia Military Institute,
Jackson Memorial Hall,
Lexington, Va 24450

Warren Rifles Confederate Museum
95 Chester Street, Front Royal, Va 22630

West Point Museum
United States Military Academy, West Point, NY 10996

Picture Credits

The publisher wishes to thank the following organizations and individuals who have supplied photographs, credited here by page number and position. For reasons of space, some references are abbreviated as follows: **AFIP**, Armed Forces Institute of Pathology; **BA**, Burns Archive of Medical Photographs; **BHC**, Burton Historical Collection, Detroit Public Library; **CHS**, Chicago Historical Society; **HP**, Herb Peck; **IMP**, International Museum of Photography, Rochester, NY; **ISH**, Illinois State Historical Library; **KMH**, Kentucky History Museum, Frankfort, Ky; **LC**, Library of Congress; Department of Archives and Manuscripts, Louisiana State University, Baton Rouge, La; **MC**, Museum of the Confederacy, Richmond, Va; **MHS**, Missouri Historical Society; **MNHS**, Minnesota Historical Society; **MP**, War Library and Museum, MOLLUS-Pennsylvania, Pa; **NA**, National Archive, Washington DC; **NPG**, National Portrait Gallery, Smithsonian Institution; **NYH**, New York Historical Society; **RM**, Robert McDonald; **RP**, Ronn Palm; **SHS**, State Historical Society of Wisconsin; **SPA**, State Photographic Archives, Strozier Library, Florida State University; **UGL**, University of Georgia Libraries, Athens, Ga; **UR**, University of Rochester, Rochester, NY; **USA**, US Army; **USAMHI**, US Army Military History Institute; **USN**, US Navy; **VHS**, Vermont Historical Society; **VM**, Valentine Museum, Richmond, Va; **WMV**, War Memorial Museum of Virginia; **WVU**, W. Va University, Morgantown.

Positions: a, Above; b, Below; l, Left; r, Right; al, Above left; ar, Above right; bl, Below left; br, Below right; t, Top; bm, Bottom.

Endpaper map, MC; **1**, USAMHI; **2-3**, USAMHI; **4-5**, American Image Gallery; **6-7**, G. Rinhart Galleries Inc; **8-9**, USAMHI; **10**, (b) WVU, (t) KMH, (a) W. C. Davis Collection; **16**, (a) Lloyd Ostendorf Collection, (b) MC; **17**, (a) Richard E. Wood, (bl) USAMHI, (br) RM; **18**, (a) CHS, (b) USAMHI; **20**, (al) HP, (ar) USAMHI, (b) CHS; **26**, (a) USAMHI, (b) USA; **28** (a) USAMHI, (b) LC; **29**, (a) Spencer H. Watterson, (b) LC; **30-31**, LHC; **32**, (al) John A. Hess, (ar) BHC, (b) NA 111-B-3511; **38**, (a) MC, (b) USAMHI; **39**, (bl, a, br) NA; **47**, (ar) RM, (b) USAMHI, (al) Rev. Theo C. Walker; **48-49**, ISH; **50**, HB; **58**, RP; **59**, NA CN3633; **65**, (a) VHS, (b) RP; **66-67**, RM; **68**, (a) Dale S. Snair, (b) USAMHI; **74**, (al, ar) RM, (b) James C. Frasca; **75**, (a) MHS, (b) RP; **82**, (a) HB, (b) LC; **83**, (a) NA, (b) RP; **89**, (a, b) LSU; **92**, USAMHI; **93**, (a) LC, (b) RP; **94-95**, USA; **97**, (a) NA, (b) USAMHI; **102**, (a) NA, (b) LC; **103**, USA; **106**, (bl) USAMHI, (a) LC, (br) Southern Railway System; **110**, NA; **111**, CHS; **112-113**, NA; **115**, (a) USN, (b) WMV; **116**, (t) USAMHI, (bm) IMP; **120**, (a) USAMHI, (b) LC; **121**, (a) MHS, (b) USN; **124**, (a) USN, (b) NYH; **126**, (b) USN, (bm) NA; **127**, (b) USAMHI; **128**, (a, b) USN; **129**, (a, b) USN; **130-131**, USAMHI; **132**, (a) RP, (b) NA; **138**, (al) LC, (b) MP, (ar) Joe Canole; **139**, (a) USAMHI, (b) LC; **145**, (a) T. Scott Sanders Collection, (b) Gladstone Collection; **150**, (a, b) LC; **151**, (a) Leslie D. Jensen, (b) MNHS; **152-153**, Robert L. Kotchian; **154**, (a, b) USAMHI; **158**, (a) USAMHI, (b) NPG; **159** MC; **162**, USAMHI, **163**, (a) LC, (b) W. H. Over Museum; **167**, (a) USAMHI, (b) CHS; **168-169**, USAMHI; **170**, (a) NA, (b) USAMHI; **172**, (a, b) USAMHI; **173**, (a) Burton J. Austin, (b) USAMHI; **176**, (a) USAMHI, (b) David R. O'Reilly; **177**, (a) UGL, (b) USAMHI; **180**, (a) MC, (b) USAMHI; **181**, (b) CHS; **183**, (a, b) USAMHI; **184-185**, UR; **188**, NA; **189**, (a) LC, (b) NA, (b) VM; **192**, USAMHI; **193**, LC; **196**, (a, b) AFIP; **197**, BA; **198-199**, Richard F. Carlisle; **200**, (a) CHS, (b) SPA; **204**, (a) USAMHI, (b) Fred Slaton; **205**, (b) LC, (r) John A. Hess; **208**, (r) Rudolf K. Haerle, (a) LC, (b) CHS; **209**, (a) USAMHI, (b) LC; **212**, (a) LC, (b) USA; **214**, (a) CHS, (b) Benjamin B. Rosenstock; **215**, (l) Michael J. McAfee, (a) NA 111-B-3484; **218-217**, LC; **218**, (a) NA CN 4950, (b) SHS; **224**, (a) USA, (b) NA B-446; **225**, (a) MP, (b) USAMHI; **227**, NA; **228**, (a, b) USAMHI; **229**, (a) LC, (b) NA CN-286; **235**, (al) LC, (ar) USA; **236-237**, USAMHI; **238**, (a, b) LC; **242**, USAMHI; **243**, (a, b) USAMHI; **247**, LC; **248-249**, LC; **252-253**, USAMHI.

IOWA
NEBRASKA
MICHIGAN
LAKE MICHIGAN
ILLINOIS
INDIANA
OHIO
KANSAS
MISSOURI
KENTUCKY
TENNESSEE
ARKANSAS
INDIAN TER.
TEXAS
LOUISIANA
MISSISSIPPI
ALABAMA
GEORGIA
FLORIDA
NORTH CAROLINA
DES MOINES
Chicago
Springfield
Indianapolis
Cincinnati
St. Louis
Cairo
Louisville
Frankfort
Nashville
Memphis
Little Rock
Jackson
Vicksburg
Natchez
Baton Rouge
New Orleans
Mobile
Montgomery
Tallahassee
Milledgeville
Atlanta
Galveston
Lecompton
Tecumseh
Jefferson Cy.
GULF OF MEXICO
Delta of the Mississippi